P9-CFN-260

WINDOWS XP
HACKS™

Other Microsoft Windows resources from O'Reilly

Related titles
Windows XP Annoyances for Geeks

Windows XP in a Nutshell

Windows XP Unwired

Windows XP Personal Trainer

Windows XP Power Hound

Windows XP Pro: The Missing Manual

PC Hacks

PC Annoyances

Hacks Series Home
hacks.oreilly.com is a community site for developers and power users of all stripes. Readers learn from each other as they share their favorite tips and tools for Mac OS X, Linux, Google, Windows XP, and more.

Windows Books Resource Center
windows.oreilly.com is a complete catalog of O'Reilly's Windows and Office books, including sample chapters and code examples.

oreillynet.com is the essential portal for developers interested in open and emerging technologies, including new platforms, programming languages, and operating systems.

Conferences
O'Reilly brings diverse innovators together to nurture the ideas that spark revolutionary industries. We specialize in documenting the latest tools and systems, translating the innovator's knowledge into useful skills for those in the trenches. Visit *conferences.oreilly.com* for our upcoming events.

Safari Bookshelf (*safari.oreilly.com*) is the premier online reference library for programmers and IT professionals. Conduct searches across more than 1,000 books. Subscribers can zero in on answers to time-critical questions in a matter of seconds. Read the books on your Bookshelf from cover to cover or simply flip to the page you need. Try it today with a free trial.

SECOND EDITION

WINDOWS XP
HACKS™

Preston Gralla

O'REILLY®

Beijing · Cambridge · Farnham · Köln · Paris · Sebastopol · Taipei · Tokyo

Windows XP Hacks™, Second Edition

by Preston Gralla

Copyright © 2005, 2003 O'Reilly Media, Inc. All rights reserved.
Printed in the United States of America.

Published by O'Reilly Media, Inc., 1005 Gravenstein Highway North, Sebastopol, CA 95472.

O'Reilly Media, Inc. books may be purchased for educational, business, or sales promotional use. Online editions are also available for most titles (*safari.oreilly.com*). For more information, contact our corporate/institutional sales department: (800) 998-9938 or *corporate@oreilly.com*.

Editor:	Brian Sawyer	**Production Editor:**	Emily Quill
Series Editor:	Rael Dornfest	**Cover Designer:**	Hanna Dyer
Executive Editor:	Dale Dougherty	**Interior Designer:**	David Futato

Printing History:

February 2005:	Second Edition.
August 2003:	First Edition.

Nutshell Handbook, the Nutshell Handbook logo, and the O'Reilly logo are registered trademarks of O'Reilly Media, Inc. The *Hacks* series designations, *Windows XP Hacks*, the image of an antique fan, and related trade dress are trademarks of O'Reilly Media, Inc. All other trademarks are property of their respective owners.

Many of the designations used by manufacturers and sellers to distinguish their products are claimed as trademarks. Where those designations appear in this book, and O'Reilly Media, Inc. was aware of a trademark claim, the designations have been printed in caps or initial caps.

While every precaution has been taken in the preparation of this book, the publisher and author assume no responsibility for errors or omissions, or for damages resulting from the use of the information contained herein.

Small print: The technologies discussed in this publication, the limitations on these technologies that technology and content owners seek to impose, and the laws actually limiting the use of these technologies are constantly changing. Thus, some of the hacks described in this publication may not work, may cause unintended harm to systems on which they are used, or may not be consistent with applicable user agreements. Your use of these hacks is at your own risk, and O'Reilly Media, Inc. disclaims responsibility for any damage or expense resulting from their use. In any event, you should take care that your use of these hacks does not violate any applicable laws, including copyright laws.

 This book uses RepKover™, a durable and flexible lay-flat binding.

ISBN: 0-596-00918-6
[C] [UV]

Contents

Credits

About the Author

Preston Gralla is the author of more than 30 books about computers and the Internet, which have been translated into 15 languages, including *Internet Annoyances* and *Windows XP Power Hound*. He has been writing about technology since the dawn of the PC age, and has been an editor and columnist for many national newspapers, magazines, and web sites. He was the founding editor of *PC Week*; a founding editor, then editor, then editorial director of *PC/Computing*; and executive editor for ZDNet/CNet. Preston has written about technology for numerous magazines and newspapers, including *PC Magazine*, *Computerworld*, *CIO Magazine*, *Computer Shopper*, the *Los Angeles Times*, *USA Today*, the *Dallas Morning News* (where he was a technology columnist), and many others. He has been a columnist for ZDNet/CNet and is currently a columnist for TechTarget.com. His commentaries about technology have been featured on National Public Radio's "All Things Considered," and he has won the award for the Best Feature in a Computer Publication from the Computer Press Association. Under his editorship, *PC/Computing* was a finalist for General Excellence from the National Magazine Awards. Preston is also the editor of O'Reilly's WindowsDevCenter.com site. He lives in Cambridge, Mass., with his wife and two children—although his daughter has recently fled the nest for college. Between writing books, articles, and columns, he swims, plays tennis, goes to the opera, and contemplates the ram's skull hanging on the wall of his office.

Contributors

The following people contributed their hacks, writing, and inspiration to this book:

- Eric Cloninger was one of the original contributors to the Palm OS, working on tools for software developers. After 15 years in the Real World, Eric decided that living in a small town in Oklahoma wasn't so bad after all. When he's not writing software, Eric enjoys spending time with his family, tinkering with his John Deere tractor, and watching tornadoes roll across the plains. While he doesn't miss the traffic in the Big City, he does occasionally yearn for a spicy tuna roll.

- Rael Dornfest is CTO of O'Reilly Media, focusing on emerging technologies just this side of viability and some beyond the pale. He assesses, experiments, programs, fiddles, fidgets, and writes for O'Reilly in various capacities. Rael is Series Editor of the O'Reilly Hacks series (*http://hacks. oreilly.com*) and has edited, contributed to, and coauthored various O'Reilly books, including *Mac OS X Panther Hacks*, *Mac OS X Hacks*, *Google Hacks*, *Google: The Missing Manual*, *Essential Blogging*, and *Peer to Peer: Harnessing the Power of Disruptive Technologies*. He is also Program Chair for the O'Reilly Emerging Technology Conference. In his copious free time, Rael develops bits and bobs of freeware, particularly the Blosxom weblog application (*http://www.blosxom.com*), is Editor in Chief of MobileWhack (*http://www.mobilewhack.com*), and (more often than not) maintains his Raelity Bytes weblog (*http://www.raelity.org*).

- Jim Foley, a.k.a. The Elder Geek (*http://www.theeldergeek.com*), owns and operates a small consulting and web design firm in Cambridge, N.Y., that specializes in the integration of Windows XP technology into home and business environments. He is also the creator and owner of The Elder Geek on Windows XP, a web site that strives to provide relevant information related to Windows XP, including a notification service and Windows XP forum to keep readers informed of the latest XP tips, troubleshooting, and update developments.

- Nancy Kotary is a former O'Reilly editor. She spends her time working from her home in eastern Massachusetts, watching herself metamorphose into a soccer mom, and trying not to buy a minivan.

- Thomas Künneth is a senior professional at the German authorities, specializing in database systems and application development. He has a master's degree from Friedrich Alexander University Erlangen-Nuremberg in computational linguistics and the German language. Thomas started writing computer programs in the early 1980s. For a long time he was programming in C, and he has been writing Java programs since 2000. You can find out more about Thomas at *http://www. moniundthomaskuenneth.de*.

- Wei-Meng Lee is an experienced author and developer specializing in .NET technologies. He was awarded the Microsoft .NET Most Valuable Professional (MVP) award in 2003. Besides .NET development, Wei-Meng maintains a keen interest in wireless technologies and has coauthored many books and articles on mobile applications development and XML technologies. He is the author of *Windows XP Unwired* (O'Reilly).

- Kyle Rankin is a system administrator who enjoys troubleshooting, problem solving, and system recovery. He is the current president of the North Bay Linux Users' Group and the author of *Knoppix Hacks*.

- C. K. Sample, III maintains the weblog "3650 and a 12-inch" (*http://3650anda12inch.blogspot.com*), which discusses the use of a 12-inch PowerBook G4 and a Nokia 3650. He is a doctoral candidate in English at Fordham University, focusing on twentieth-century American and British literature, as well as twentieth-century world literature, biblical studies, and critical theory. C. K. (Clinton Kennedy; no relation) works in Fordham's Department of Instructional Technology and Academic Computing as the lab coordinator for Marymount College and the Fordham Graduate Center in Tarrytown, N.Y. His first "computer" was an Atari 400, and his first Mac was a PowerBook 5300CS. Originally from Jackson, Miss., C. K. currently lives in Bronxville, N.Y., with his fiancée, Kristin Landgrebe, and his pet Eclectus parrot, Misha, who is two years old.

- Margaret Levine Young has coauthored many books, including *The Internet for Dummies*, *Windows XP: The Complete Reference*, *UNIX for Dummies*, *Internet: The Complete Reference*, and *Poor Richard's Building Online Community*. She has a bachelor's degree in computer science from Yale and lives in Vermont.

Acknowledgments

Any book is a cooperative venture, and this one was more so than many. Thanks to editor Brian Sawyer, who, in the midst of the birth of his first child, managed somehow to help birth this book as well; I only hope it didn't cost him as many sleepless nights as did his newborn son. Thanks also to the book's first editor Nancy Kotary. Thanks to Rael Dornfest for his laserlike focus on making sure that every hack was exceedingly useful and moved well beyond the obvious. Laurie Petrycki and Dale Dougherty offered valuable advice and feedback in the early stages of writing. Many thanks to Tim O'Reilly, who entrusted me with this project, albeit in a very different form than when it was first conceived, and who gave very targeted advice and pointers in the important early phases of writing.

Thanks also to my copyeditor, Audrey Doyle, and to the production team at O'Reilly: Emily Quill, Robert Romano, Jessamyn Read, Jamie Peppard, Claire Cloutier, Reg Aubry, Katherine Pinard, Peter Ryan, Keith Fahlgren, and Lydia Onofrei. And, many, many thanks go to diligent technical reviewer extraordinaire Eric Cloninger, who spent many hours watching reruns of *The Sopranos* on TiVo and reading way into the early morning hours.

As always, thanks to my family. Lydia put up with my usual diet of late-night deadlines, and Mia let me get my work done when we were on her grand audition tour for college ballet programs. As for Gabe, his advice and recommendations on which hacks to cover was an enormous help. Gabe also wrote the Firefox search engine that provided the core of "Build Your Own Firefox Search Engine" **[Hack #44]**, and provided valuable insight into how to write the hack.

Preface

Windows XP marks the biggest change to the Windows OS since the advent of Windows 95. It combines the stability of the NT/2000 operating system with the user-friendliness and hardware support of the consumer Windows line—and it does so literally because those two operating systems have been combined for the first time in XP. Although there are two versions of XP—Home Edition and Professional Edition—the differences between them are relatively minor and have to do primarily with security and administrator tools. Under the hood, they're the same OS.

XP marks several other changes as well. DOS is no longer a part of the underlying OS, although it's still available as a command prompt. Multimedia and graphics have been built into the operating system more directly than before and are no longer treated as an afterthought. And cosmetically, XP has been given a makeover, in both the way it looks (rounded windows and almost cartoonish at times) and the way it works.

All this is good news for would-be operating-system hackers. Because of the operating system's greater stability, those who work under the hood of XP can concentrate on actually getting work done and making the OS more effective, rather than trying to fix its shortcomings. Because of the richer interface and greater support for graphics and multimedia, you can more easily change the way the operating system works and looks. And because the OS offers a variety of tools for recovering from errors, you can hack to your heart's content without worrying that you'll damage the OS beyond recognition.

This collection is based on the hands-on, real-world experience of those who in many cases have been using PCs well before any version of Windows even existed. They have wrestled with each new version of Windows as it was released, and found ways to take advantage of every nook and cranny of the operating system. When XP came out, they applied that hard-earned knowledge to it as well, and came up with ways to take advantage of the myriad new features of the operating system.

The results are 120 hacks that are useful, frequently entertaining, and will save you countless hours at the keyboard. Whether you want to speed up your PC, customize XP's interface, hack your wired and wireless network, get more out of the Web, make better use of email, use the Registry to bend the operating system to your will, or use XP for countless other useful tasks, you'll find what you're looking for here. And each hack doesn't just show you *how* to do something; it also teaches *why* it works. Each hack is a starting point, rather than an ending point, so that you can apply the knowledge you've gained to create new hacks of your own. Try it out—who knows, in the next edition of this book, you might get a hack of your own published.

This second edition has been significantly updated from the first edition of the book. It takes into account all the changes made by Service Pack 2 (SP2), and adds a good deal of new material, such as using the open source browser Firefox, the Google Desktop, Microsoft's own MSN Desktop Search, and Gmail. It's also beefed up its coverage of wireless technologies and Internet security, including killing spyware.

How to Use This Book

You can read this book from cover to cover if you like, but each hack stands on its own, so feel free to browse and jump to the different sections that interest you most. If there's a prerequisite you need to know about, a cross-reference will guide you to the right hack. If you're not familiar with the Registry yet, or you want a refresher, you might want to spend some time in Chapter 9 to get a good grounding.

How This Book Is Organized

This book is not a mere tips-and-tricks compendium that tells you where to click, where to drag, and what commands to type. It takes advantage of XP's flexibility and new features, recognizes that there are specific tasks you want to accomplish with the operating system, and offers you bite-size pieces of functionality that you can put to use in a few minutes. It also shows how you can expand on their usefulness yourself. To give you this kind of help, the book is organized into 13 chapters.

Chapter 1, *Startup and Shutdown*

With XP, startup and shutdown can mean much more than turning on your PC or selecting Shut Down from the Start menu. With hacks in this chapter, you can change the picture that appears on the startup

screen, speed up the sometimes endless startup and shutdown processes, hack the Registry to control many different aspects of startup
and shutdown, customize multiboot options, and much more.

Chapter 2, *The User Interface*

XP lets you change the way it looks and works more than any other version of Windows, and this chapter shows how to do it. Want a speedy,
stripped-down version of the OS? It's in here. Want to build your own
themes and find thousands more online? It's in here as well. So are
hacks for controlling the Control Panel, Start menu, and taskbar; creating transparent windows; and building your own cursors and icons. It
also shows you how to make your PC look and work like a Mac, and
how to give Linux a try without having to actually install any software.
The hacks don't stop there, so interface hackers might want to head
here first.

Chapter 3, *Windows Explorer*

Windows Explorer provides a basic window into XP and lets you manage files and folders, among other tasks. When hacked, it does much
more as well. This chapter shows how to customize folder icons and
balloon tips, improve the context menu, find files fast by mastering the
indexing service's query language, get more disk space by using NTFS
compression, keep your PC secure with encryption, and more.

Chapter 4, *The Web*

You probably spend a significant portion of your computing life on the
Web, so why not make the most of it? Want to find information fast,
straight from your browser, without having to head off to sites like Google? This chapter teaches you how to do it. You can also kill pop ups,
stop spyware, surf anonymously without a trace, and speed up file
downloads. If you host your own web site, you'll find out secrets of
using the built-in Internet Information Services (IIS) web server. The
chapter also shows you how to hack the free browser Firefox, which
some people consider the best browser on the planet. In addition, it
teaches you how to surf the Internet ad-free and shows you how you
can literally Google your desktop by using Google technology to search
through your email and files. There are many more hacks here as well.

Chapter 5, *Networking*

XP was built for networking, and this chapter shows you how to take full
advantage of it. Tweak your DNS settings for faster Internet access, make
your home network run better, use command-line tools for trouble-free
network operations, or get the most out of using the Voice over Internet
Protocol (VoIP) for making inexpensive phone calls. This chapter helps
you get the most out of XP's powerful, built-in ability to connect.

Chapter 6, *Email*

Email is both the greatest productivity-booster and the greatest time-waster known to humankind. This chapter ensures that you'll stop wasting time and get more out of email. Slam spam, open blocked file attachments in Outlook and Outlook Express, get better email software, and retrieve web-based email using a normal email client. And you'll learn many ways to get more out of Google's email service, Gmail. There's all that and more here.

Chapter 7, *Wireless*

It's an unwired world, and XP is at the center of it. XP was built with wireless in mind, includes built-in wireless discovery of networks, and because of that, makes it easy to set up home and corporate wireless networks, as well as connect to hotspots when people travel with their laptops or PDAs. So, in this chapter, you'll find out about wireless hacking—everything from war driving to finding wireless networks, protecting your home wireless network, using wireless encryption, solving hotspot woes, and more.

Chapter 8, *Security*

From the moment you turn on your PC and connect to the Internet or a network, you're in danger. Snoopers and intruders can try to get into your system; crackers might try to install Trojans to take control of your computer or turn it into a *zombie* and use it to launch attacks against other PCs or web sites. The hacks in this chapter, though, will show you how you can use the Internet and networks, and still be safe. You'll learn how to hide files and folders using encryption, how to test your PC's vulnerabilities, how to use firewalls to harden your PC against attacks, how to punch holes through firewalls, and more.

Chapter 9, *The Registry*

If you're going to hack XP, you'll need to use the Registry. It's that simple. This chapter goes beyond merely teaching you how to use the Registry and how it's organized (although it covers that in detail). It also shows you how to hack the Registry itself—for example, by offering hacks on how to use *.reg* files to edit the Registry safely, and how to track and restore Registry changes.

Chapter 10, *Applications*

XP comes with a basic suite of built-in utilities, with the emphasis on *basic*. But you can hack these basic utilities so that they're much more useful powerhouses. Store multiple clips on the Clipboard, extend your real estate with virtual desktops, build a better backup strategy, take better screenshots, or use a universal instant messenger. In addition to utilities, an operating system needs applications to do much of its work.

So, this chapter shows you how to hack them as well. Have older Windows applications that have a hard time running under XP? This chapter shows you how to make sure they run. You can also use command-line shortcuts to customize how each application runs, open and create Microsoft documents without Microsoft Office, and more.

Chapter 11, *Graphics and Multimedia*

In XP, Windows gets serious about multimedia and graphics for the first time. In this chapter, you'll see how to get the most out of them, with hacks for saving streaming audio to your PC, making videos with Movie Maker, sharing music without the spyware, and converting images easily. Music lovers will find several ways to hack iTunes and how to take advantage of the new music format Ogg Vorbis.

Chapter 12, *System Performance*

No matter how fast your PC is, it's not fast enough. This chapter shows you ways to hack XP to juice up its performance. Get the most out of your RAM, use the Performance Console to speed up system performance, and use a variety of Registry hacks to make XP run. For those who have upgraded to SP2, or are considering it, you'll also see how to combat SP2 upgrade woes.

Chapter 13, *Hardware*

By itself, an operating system can't do a thing; it needs hardware to run on. In this chapter, you'll see how to use XP to hack your hardware. Remap your keyboard, set up a direct cable connection between PCs for a quick-and-dirty network, uncover "hidden hardware" with the Device Manager, and get better resolution on your laptop and your LCD screen. And yes, there are more hacks here as well.

Conventions Used in This Book

This book uses the following typographical conventions:

Italic

Used to indicate new terms, URLs, filenames, file extensions, directories, and folders.

`Constant width`

Used to show code examples, verbatim searches and commands, the contents of files, and the output from commands.

`Constant width bold`

Used in examples and tables to show commands or other text that should be typed literally.

Constant width italic
> Used in examples, tables, and commands to show text that should be replaced with user-supplied values.

Color
> Used to indicate a cross reference within the text.

Pay special attention to notes set apart from the text with the following icons:

> This icon indicates a tip, suggestion, or general note. It contains useful supplementary information or an observation about the topic at hand.

> This icon indicates a warning or note of caution.

The thermometer icons, found next to each hack, indicate the relative complexity of the hack:

 beginner   moderate   expert

Using Code Examples

This book is here to help you get your job done. In general, you may use the code in this book in your programs and documentation. You do not need to contact us for permission unless you're reproducing a significant portion of the code. For example, writing a program that uses several chunks of code from this book does not require permission. Selling or distributing a CD-ROM of examples from O'Reilly books *does* require permission. Answering a question by citing this book and quoting example code does not require permission. Incorporating a significant amount of example code from this book into your product's documentation *does* require permission.

We appreciate, but do not require, attribution. An attribution usually includes the title, author, publisher, and ISBN. For example: "*Windows XP Hacks,* Second Edition, by Preston Gralla. Copyright 2005 O'Reilly Media, Inc., 0-596-00918-6."

If you feel your use of code examples falls outside fair use or the permission given above, feel free to contact us at *permissions@oreilly.com.*

Safari Enabled

 When you see a Safari® enabled icon on the cover of your favorite technology book, that means the book is available online through the O'Reilly Network Safari Bookshelf.

Safari offers a solution that's better than e-Books. It's a virtual library that lets you easily search thousands of top tech books, cut and paste code samples, download chapters, and find quick answers when you need the most accurate, current information. Try it free at *http://safari.oreilly.com*.

How to Contact Us

We have tested and verified the information in this book to the best of our ability, but you might find that features have changed (or even that we have made mistakes!). Please let us know about any errors you find, as well as your suggestions for future editions (we take these seriously), by writing to:

O'Reilly Media, Inc.
1005 Gravenstein Highway North
Sebastopol, CA 95472
(800) 998-9938 (in the U.S. or Canada)
(707) 829-0515 (international/local)
(707) 829-0104 (fax)

You can also send us messages electronically. To be put on the mailing list or request a catalog, send email to:

info@oreilly.com

To ask technical questions or comment on the book, send email to:

bookquestions@oreilly.com

The web site for *Windows XP Hacks*, Second Edition lists examples, errata, and plans for future editions. You can access this page at:

http://www.oreilly.com/catalog/winxphks2

For more information about this book and others, see the O'Reilly web site:

http://www.oreilly.com

Got a Hack?

To explore Hacks books online or to contribute a hack for future titles, visit:

http://hacks.oreilly.com

Startup and Shutdown

Hacks 1–7

Possibly the most overlooked part of XP is the way people start up and shut down their systems. How much do *you* think about startup and shutdown? Probably not much. Press a button to start your PC, click a few buttons to shut it down, and that's it.

In fact, there's a lot you can do to get more productive—and to have a little customization fun—when using startup and shutdown. You can create boot menus and choose from customized startup options; you can create your own boot screen; you can perform automated tasks every time you shut down your PC; and you can stop unnecessary programs and services from starting so that you increase the speed of your PC. In this chapter, you'll learn all that, plus other ways to master and customize system startup and shutdown.

 Customize Multiboot Startup Options

#1 Edit or create a startup menu that lets you choose which operating system to boot into in multiboot systems, or create a menu that lets you choose different startup options for your single operating system if you have only XP installed.

If you've installed another operating system (in addition to XP) on your system, your PC starts up with a multiboot menu, which allows you to choose the operating system you want to run. The menu stays live for 30 seconds, and a screen countdown tells you how long you have to make a choice from the menu. After the 30 seconds elapse, it boots into your default operating system, which is generally the last operating system you installed.

You can customize that multiboot menu and how your PC starts by editing the *boot.ini* file, a hidden system file, to control a variety of startup options, including how long to display the menu, which operating system should be the default, whether to use the XP splash screen when XP starts, and similar features. And as you'll see later in this hack, you can also use the file to create a startup menu that will allow you to choose from different versions of your operating system—for example, one that you'll use for tracking down startup problems, and another for starting in Safe Mode.

The *boot.ini* file is a plain-text file found in your root *C:* folder. You might not be able to see it because it's a system file, and if you can see it, you might not be able to edit it because it's a read-only file. To make it visible, launch Windows Explorer, choose View → Tools → Folder Options → View, and select the Show Hidden Files and Folders radio button. To make it a file you can edit, right-click it in Windows Explorer, choose Properties, uncheck the Read-Only box, and click OK.

Editing Files

To edit the file, open it with a text editor such as Notepad. Following is a typical *boot.ini* file for a PC that has two operating systems installed on it—Windows XP Home Edition and Windows 2000 Professional:

```
[boot loader]
timeout=30
default=multi(0)disk(0)rdisk(0)partition(1)\WINDOWS
[operating systems]
multi(0)disk(0)rdisk(0)partition(1)\WINDOWS="Microsoft Windows XP Home
Edition" /fastdetect
multi(0)disk(0)rdisk(0)partition(2)\WINNT="Windows 2000 Professional" /
fastdetect
```

As you can see, there are two sections in the file: [bootloader] and [operating systems]. To customize your menu and startup options, edit the entries in each section. Before editing *boot.ini*, make a copy of it and save it under a different name (such as *boot.ini.old*) so that you can revert to it if you cause problems when you edit the file.

Following are details about how to edit the entries in each section:

[boot loader]
    This section controls how the boot process works; it specifies the default operating system and how long a user has to make a selection from a boot menu, if a boot menu has been enabled. The timeout value specifies, in seconds, how long to display the menu and wait for a selection before loading the default operating system. If you want a delay of 15 seconds, for example, enter 15 for the value. Use a value of 0 if you want the default operating system to boot immediately. If you want the menu to be displayed indefinitely and stay on-screen until a selection is made, use a value of -1. The default value specifies which entry in the

[operating system] section is the default operating system. (The default value is used even if there is only one operating system in the [operating system] section.) To change the default operating system, edit the setting, in our example, to default=multi(0)disk(0)rdisk(0)partition(2)\ WINNT.

So, in our example, if you change the menu settings so that the screen appears for 10 seconds before loading the default operating system, and the default operating system is Windows 2000 Professional, the section reads:

```
[boot loader]
timeout=10
default=multi(0)disk(0)rdisk(0)partition(2)\WINNT
```

[operating system]

This section specifies which operating systems are present on the computer, and detailed options for each one. XP uses the Advanced RISC Computing (ARC) path to specify the location of the boot partition. In our example, the ARC path is:

```
multi(0)disk(0)rdisk(0)partition(1)\WINDOWS
```

The first parameter, which identifies the disk controller, should be 0. The second parameter, the disk parameter, should also be 0. The rdisk parameter specifies the disk number on the controller that has the boot partition. The numbers start at 0. So, if you have three hard disks installed and the second hard disk has the boot partition, the setting is rdisk(1). The partition parameter identifies the partition number of the boot partition. Partitions start with the number 1. The final section, which in our example is \WINDOWS, specifies the path to the folder where the operating system is installed.

To the right of the ARC path in the example is ="Microsoft Windows XP Home Edition" /fastdetect. The words within quotes are what will appear on the boot menu next to the entry. To customize the text on the menu you can change these words to whatever you wish—for example, "My Favorite Operating System." The /fastdetect switch disables the detection of serial and parallel devices, which allows for faster booting. The detection of these devices isn't normally required in XP because the functions are performed by Plug and Play drivers, so as a general rule it's a good idea to use the /fastdetect switch. The /fastdetect switch is only one of many switches that you can use in the *boot.ini* file to customize how the operating system loads. Table 1-1 lists others you can use.

Table 1-1. Switches for boot.ini

Switch	What it does
/BASEVIDEO	Starts XP using the standard VGA driver. It's most useful if you can't boot normally because of a video driver problem.
/BOOTLOG	Logs information about the boot process to the *ntbtlogl.txt* file in the *C:\Windows* folder.
/CRASHDEBUG	Loads the debugger at boot, but the debugger remains inactive unless a crash occurs.
/DEBUG	Loads the debugger at boot and runs it.
/F*DETECT	Disables the detection of serial and parallel devices.
MAXMEM:n	Specifies the maximum amount of RAM that XP can use.
/NOGUIBOOT	Does not allow the XP splash screen to load during boot.
/NODEBUG	Stops the debugger from loading.
/SAFEBOOT:switch	Forces XP to boot into the safe mode specified by the switch parameter, which can be minimal, network, or minimal(alternate shell). In minimal safe mode, only the minimum set of drivers necessary to start XP are loaded. In network safe mode, networking drivers are loaded in addition to the minimum set of drivers. In minimal(alternate shell) the minimum set of drivers are loaded and XP boots into the command prompt.
/SOS	Displays the name of each driver as it loads and gives descriptions of what is occurring during the boot process. It also offers other information, including the XP build number, the service pack number, the number of processors on the system, and the amount of installed memory.

When you've finished editing the *boot.ini* file, save it. The next time you start your computer, its settings will go into effect.

In our example, if we want the menu to appear for 45 seconds, the default operating system to be Windows 2000, and the XP splash screen to be turned off when we choose to load XP, the *boot.ini* file should look like this:

```
[boot loader]
timeout=45
default=multi(0)disk(0)rdisk(0)partition(2)\WINNT
[operating systems]
multi(0)disk(0)rdisk(0)partition(1)\WINDOWS="Microsoft Windows XP Home
Edition" /fastdetect /noguiboot
multi(0)disk(0)rdisk(0)partition(2)\WINNT="Windows 2000 Professional" /
fastdetect
```

Create a Startup Menu Even If You Have Only One Operating System

Even if you have only one operating system, you can create a boot menu that will let you choose to load your operating system with different parameters. For example, for menu choices, you might have your normal operating system; a mode that lets you trace any startup problems; and Safe Mode. To give yourself the option of operating systems with different parameters, create separate entries for each new operating system choice. For example, for the version of the operating system that traces potential startup problems, you could create this entry:

```
multi(0)disk(0)rdisk(0)partition(1)\WINDOWS="Trace Problems XP Home Edition"
/fastdetect /bootlog /sos
```

This entry creates a startup log and displays information about the drivers and other operating system information as it loads.

For the version of the operating system that loads in Safe Mode but that still allows networking, you could create this entry:

```
multi(0)disk(0)rdisk(0)partition(1)\WINDOWS="Safe Start XP Home Edition" /
fastdetect /safeboot:network
```

The *boot.ini* file would look like this, assuming that you want the menu to display for 30 seconds and you want normal XP startup to be the default:

```
[boot loader]
timeout=30
default=multi(0)disk(0)rdisk(0)partition(1)\WINDOWS
[operating systems]
multi(0)disk(0)rdisk(0)partition(1)\WINDOWS="Microsoft Windows XP Home
Edition" /fastdetect
multi(0)disk(0)rdisk(0)partition(1)\WINDOWS="Trace Problems XP Home Edition"
/fastdetect /bootlog /sos
multi(0)disk(0)rdisk(0)partition(1)\WINDOWS="Safe Start XP Home Edition" /
fastdetect /safeboot:network
```

If you're leery of using a text editor to edit *boot.ini* directly, you can use the System Configuration Utility **[Hack #4]** instead. Type msconfig at a command prompt or in the Run box and click the BOOT.INI tab, shown in Figure 1-1. You'll be able to add several switches (but not as many as you can if you edit the *boot.ini* file yourself using a text editor).

See Also

- "Create Multiple Startup Profiles with Advanced Startup Manager"
  [Hack #5]

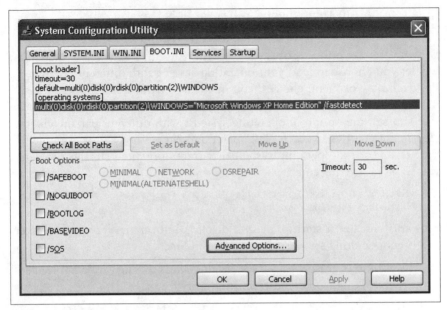

Figure 1-1. The System Configuration Utility

HACK #2 Change the Picture That Appears on the XP Startup Screen

You're not stuck with XP's default splash logo on the startup screen; use any picture or logo of your choosing.

One of the nice things about XP is how malleable it is. Don't like the way it looks? No problem; change it. Take my splash screen, please!

> The techniques in this hack work only with versions of XP *before* SP2. If you have SP2, they won't work, and they could harm your system. If you have SP2 and want to change your boot screen, your best bet is to use downloadable software, such as Style XP from Tgtsoft at *http://www.tgtsoft.com/ download.php*.

Many people, myself included, would prefer to see a more interesting splash screen (also called the *startup screen*) than the default gives you on startup. You can change your splash screen to any of hundreds that have been created, or make one of your own—for example, with your picture or company logo on it.

To choose from already created splash screens, go to *http://www.themexp. org* and click Boot Screens. You'll find more than 1,000 of them, organized by categories such as Sports, TV/Movies, and so on. I live in wintry but civilized New England, and during the winter I like to imagine myself in a far wilder place, so I use a picture of wolves in the wilds of Alaska for my splash screen. You can see it pictured in Figure 1-2. Nice way to greet the new day, don't you think?

Figure 1-2. My startup screen, which lets me imagine myself in the wilds of Alaska

Once you've found the image you want to use as your splash screen, download it. It will be downloaded as a *.zip* file. I create a general folder for all my boot screen files, called *C:\Bootscreens*, and then for each boot screen I download I create a new folder—in this instance, *C:\Bootscreens\Wild*.

It's possible that something will go wrong with your new boot screen, so before making the change, create a system restore point by choosing Control Panel → Performance and Maintenance → System Restore and following the instructions. If something goes wrong, you can revert to that restore point.

Unzip the contents of the *.zip* file into the folder. There will be one or more files, including *ReadMe* files. The boot screen itself, however, will be named *ntoskrnl.exe*. If you have XP Service Pack 1 installed, you might have to use a different file, named *ntoskrnlSP1.exe*, which might also be in the down-loaded *.zip* file. Check the documentation of the file you download to make sure. If you're not sure if you have Service Pack 1 installed, it's easy to find out. Right-click My Computer and choose Properties → General. Your version of the operating system will be displayed. If you have Service Pack 1, it will say so on that screen.

The *ntoskrnl.exe* file is an executable file that contains the XP boot screen. During the boot process, XP executes this file, found in *C:\Windows\ System32*, which in turn displays the boot screen graphic. So, to change your boot screen, replace your existing *ntoskrnl.exe* file with the one you just downloaded. But wait: there's more.

> Never download and use a boot screen that is packaged inside a *.exe* file rather than a *.zip* file, and that you install by running an installation program. Always use *.zip* files and install the boot screens manually, instead of using an installation program. Many boot screen installation programs that change your boot screen contain spyware that they install on your PC without telling you, so stay away from them. For details about how to detect and kill spyware, see "Kill Spyware and Web Bugs" **[Hack #34]**.

You might think that all you have to do is copy the new *ntoskrnl.exe* over the existing one and then restart your computer for the changes to take effect. That's not quite the case, though. First you have to get around a feature of Windows XP that protects system files from being overwritten. Windows File Protection automatically replaces certain files with the original XP version of the file if they've been replaced, and *ntoskrnl.exe* is one of those files. However, if you make the change in Safe Mode, Windows File Protection won't kick in and you can safely copy the file.

> Windows File Protection protects many other files, not just *ntoskrnl.exe*. Also included are *.dll*, *.exe*, *.fon*, *.ocx*, *.sys*, *.tff*, and, depending on your system, other file types such as *.ax*, *.cpl*, *.cpx*, *.dll*, *.exe*, *.inf*, *.rsp*, and *.tlb*.

Reboot your PC and press F8 immediately to get into Safe Mode. Now go to the *C:\Windows\System32* folder and find the *ntoskrnl.exe* file. Copy it to another folder or rename it as a backup so that you can revert to it when you no longer want to use your new boot screen, or if something goes wrong when you install the new screen. Now copy the new *ntoskrnl.exe* file into *C:\ Windows\System32*. (If you have to use the *ntoskrnlSP1.exe* file, rename it to *ntoskrnl.exe* first, and then copy it over.)

Reboot your computer again but don't go into Safe Mode this time. Now your new splash screen will appear every time you start your PC. To revert to your old splash screen, repeat the steps, copying your original *ntoskrnl.exe* file over your new one.

Choose from Multiple Splash Screens on Startup

Depending on my mood, I might not want to be greeted by huskies every morning. There are times when I want to be greeted by the normal startup screen, and other times when I want to see Andy Warhol's famous painting of Marilyn Monroe, or Al Pacino from the movie *Scarface*, which are all available from *http://www.themexp.org*. So, I've made a startup menu that lets me choose which graphic should be my startup screen.

To create a startup menu, first download all the screens you want to use. Then rename the *ntoskrnl.exe* or *ntoskrnlSP1.exe* of each so that the filename describes the screen—for example, *ntospacino.exe*, *ntosmonroe.exe*, and *ntosspongebob.exe*. Copy them into *C:\Windows\System32*. Don't touch the existing *ntoskrnl.exe* file there; you'll keep that as one of your options. Because you're not changing that file, you don't have to boot into Safe Mode to make any of these changes.

Following the instructions in "Customize Multiboot Startup Options" [Hack #1], create a multiboot screen by editing your *boot.ini* file. In the [operating systems] section of the *boot.ini* file, create a new entry for each screen from which you want to choose. Copy the existing primary XP entry and append /kernel=newbootscreenfilename.exe to the end of it, where *newbootscreenfilename.exe* is the filename of the boot screen you want to use for that entry. Also edit the description so that it describes the boot screen. For example, if the primary entry is:

```
multi(0)disk(0)rdisk(0)partition(1)\WINDOWS="Microsoft Windows XP Home
Edition" /fastdetect
```

you would create this entry for the SpongeBob startup screen:

```
multi(0)disk(0)rdisk(0)partition(1)\WINDOWS="SpongeBob Startup Screen" /
fastdetect /kernel=ntosspongebob.exe
```

Create as many entries as you want in the [boot loader] section. My *boot.ini* file looks like this:

```
[operating systems]
multi(0)disk(0)rdisk(0)partition(1)\WINDOWS="Microsoft Windows XP Home
Edition" /fastdetect
multi(0)disk(0)rdisk(0)partition(1)\WINDOWS="SpongeBob Startup Screen" /
fastdetect /kernel=ntosspongebob.exe
multi(0)disk(0)rdisk(0)partition(1)\WINDOWS="Pacino Startup Screen" /
fastdetect /kernel=ntospacino.exe
```

```
multi(0)disk(0)rdisk(0)partition(1)\WINDOWS="Marilyn Monroe Startup Screen"
/fastdetect /kernel=ntosmonroe.exe
```

Whenever you start up XP now, you'll be able to choose from your normal startup screen or any of the others you've put on the menu. If you have a laptop, for example, you might set up a menu that lets you choose a businesslike startup screen at work and a more entertaining one at home.

Build a Startup Screen from Any Graphic

So far, this hack has shown you how to use a startup screen that someone else built. But you're not limited to that; you can turn any graphic into a startup screen using BootXP (downloadable from *http://www.bootxp.net*). It's shareware and free to try, but it costs $7.95 if you decide to keep using it.

The program will convert graphics from many different formats to a boot screen graphic, then use it as your boot screen, or build a boot menu for you so that you can choose from multiple boot screens. That way, you don't have to edit the *boot.ini* file yourself.

It's a surprisingly simple program to use. Select a graphic that you want to use as a boot screen, and then click a button to convert it to the 640×480-pixel, 16-color bitmap startup screen standard. Preview the graphic, and if it's what you want, tell the program to set it as your boot screen. The program provides a variety of options, including choosing a different progress bar that alerts you that XP is loading, restoring your original startup screen, or randomizing your boot screen so that it randomly selects one you've created each time you boot. You can also use the program to download already created startup screens from *http://www.bootxp.net*.

See Also

- "Create Your Own XP Themes and Find Thousands Online" [Hack #17]

Speed Up Boot and Shutdown Times
#3
Shorten the time it takes for your desktop to appear when you turn on your PC, and make XP shut down faster as well.

No matter how fast your PC boots, it's not fast enough. Here are several hacks to get you right to your desktop as quickly as possible after startup.

Perform a Boot Defragment

There's a simple way to speed up XP startup: make your system do a boot defragment, which will put all the boot files next to one another on your hard disk. When boot files are in close proximity to one another, your system will start faster.

On most systems, boot defragment should be enabled by default, but it might not be on yours, or it might have been changed inadvertently. To make sure that boot defragment is enabled on your system, run the Registry Editor [Hack #83] and go to:

```
HKEY_LOCAL_MACHINE\SOFTWARE\Microsoft\Dfrg\BootOptimizeFunction
```

Edit the Enable string value to Y if it is not already set to Y. Exit the Registry and reboot. The next time you reboot, you'll do a boot defragment.

I've found many web sites recommending a way of speeding up boot times that might in fact slow down the amount of time it takes to boot up and will probably slow down launching applications as well. The tip recommends going to your *C:\WINDOWS\Prefetch* directory and emptying it every week. Windows uses this directory to speed up launching applications. It analyzes the files you use during startup and the applications you launch, and it creates an index to where those files and applications are located on your hard disk. By using this index, XP can launch files and applications faster. So, by emptying the directory, you are most likely slowing down launching applications. In my tests, I've also found that after emptying the directory, it takes my PC a few seconds *longer* to get to my desktop after bootup.

Hack Your BIOS for Faster Startups

When you turn on your PC, it goes through a set of startup procedures in its BIOS before it gets to starting XP. So, if you speed up those initial startup procedures, you'll make your system start faster.

You can speed up your startup procedures by changing the BIOS with the built-in setup utility. How you run this utility varies from PC to PC, but you typically get to it by pressing the Delete, F1, or F10 keys during startup. You'll come to a menu with a variety of choices. Here are the choices to make for faster system startups:

Quick Power On Self Test (POST)
> When you choose this option, your system runs an abbreviated POST rather than the normal, lengthy one.

Boot Up Floppy Seek
> Disable this option. When it's enabled, your system spends a few extra seconds looking for your floppy drive—a relatively pointless procedure, especially considering how infrequently you use your floppy drive.

Boot Delay

Some systems let you delay booting after you turn on your PC so that your hard drive gets a chance to start spinning before bootup. Most likely, you don't need to have this boot delay, so turn it off. If you run into problems, however, you can turn it back on.

Fine-Tune Your Registry for Faster Startups

Over time, your Registry can become bloated with unused entries, slowing down your system startup because your system loads them every time you start up your PC. Get a Registry clean-up tool to delete unneeded Registry entries and speed up startup times. Registry First Aid, shown in Figure 1-3, is an excellent Registry clean-up tool. It combs your Registry for outdated and useless entries and then lets you choose which entries to delete and which to keep. It also creates a full Registry backup so that you can restore the Registry if you run into a problem.

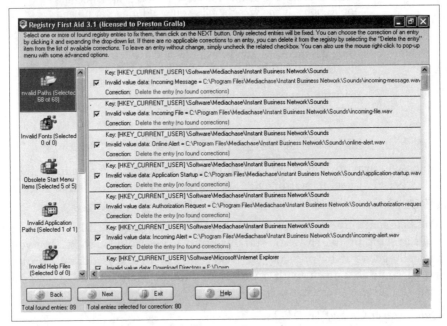

Figure 1-3. Cleaning the Registry with Registry First Aid

Registry First Aid is shareware and free to try, but it costs $21 if you decide to keep using it. Download it from *http://www.rosecitysoftware.com/ Reg1Aid/index.html.*

After you clean out your Registry, you might want to try compacting it to get rid of unused space. The Registry Compactor, available from *http://www. rosecitysoftware.com/RegistryCompactor/index.html*, will do the trick. Compacting your Registry reduces its size and decreases loading time. It's shareware and free to try, but it costs $19.95 if you decide to keep it.

Speed Up Shutdown Times

It's not only startup times that you'd like to speed up; you can also make sure that your system shuts down faster. If shutting down XP takes what seems to be an inordinate amount of time, here are a couple of steps you can take to speed up the shutdown process:

Don't have XP clear your paging file at shutdown. For security reasons, you can have XP clear your paging file (*pagefile.sys*) of its contents whenever you shut down. Your paging file is used to store temporary files and data, but when your system shuts down, information stays in the file. Some people prefer to have the paging file cleared at shutdown because sensitive information, such as unencrypted passwords, sometimes ends up in the file. However, clearing the paging file can slow shutdown times significantly, so if extreme security isn't a high priority, you might not want to clear it. To shut down XP without clearing your paging file, run the Registry Editor and go to:

```
HKEY_LOCAL_MACHINE\SYSTEM\CurrentControlSet\Control\Session Manager\Memory
Management
```

Change the value of `ClearPageFileAtShutdown` to 0. Close the Registry and restart your computer. Whenever you turn off XP from now on, the paging file won't be cleared, and you should be able to shut down more quickly.

Turn off unnecessary services. Services take time to shut down, so the fewer you run, the faster you can shut down. For information on how to shut them down, see "Halt Startup Programs and Services" [Hack #4].

HACK #4 Halt Startup Programs and Services

Increase your PC's performance and speed up startup times by shutting off applications and services that you don't need.

One of the best ways to speed up your PC without having to spend money for extra RAM is to stop unnecessary programs and services from running whenever you start your PC. When too many programs and services run automatically every time you start up your system, startup itself takes a long time, and too many programs and services running simultaneously can bog down your CPU and hog your memory.

Some programs, such as antivirus software, should run automatically at startup and always run on your computer. But many other programs, such as instant messenger software, serve no purpose by being run at startup. And while you need a variety of background services running on your PC for XP to function, there are many unnecessary services that run on startup. For example, on many systems, the Wireless Zero Configuration Service runs to automatically configure a WiFi (802.11) network card, even though no such card is present in the system.

Eliminating Programs That Run at Startup

Stopping programs from running at startup is a particularly daunting task because there is no single place you can go to stop them all. Some run because they're put in the *Startup* folder, others because they're part of logon scripts, still others because of Registry settings, and so on. But with a little bit of perseverance, you should be able to stop them from running.

Cleaning out the Startup folder. Start by cleaning out your *Startup* folder. Find it in *C:\Documents and Settings\<User Name>\Start Menu\Programs\Startup*, where *<User Name>* is your Windows logon name. Delete the shortcuts of any programs you don't want to run on startup. As with any shortcuts, when you delete them, you're deleting only the shortcut, not the program itself. (You can also clear out the startup items by going to Start → Programs → Startup and right-clicking items you want to remove.) Next, clean out your *Scheduled Tasks* folder. Go to *C:\WINDOWS\Tasks*, and delete the shortcuts of any programs that you don't want to run automatically on a schedule.

> You can bypass all the programs in your *Startup* folder on an as-needed basis. To stop XP from loading any programs in the *Startup* folder, hold down the Shift key during boot-up. No programs in the *Startup* folder will run, but the items will still remain there so that they will start up as they would normally the next time you boot.

Using the System Configuration Utility. Taking the previous steps will stop the obvious programs from running at startup, but it won't kill them all. The best tool for disabling hidden programs that run on startup is the Startup tab in the System Configuration Utility, shown in Figure 1-4. To run it, type `msconfig` at a command prompt or in the Run box and press Enter. (If that doesn't work, first do a search for *msconfig.exe*, and then when you find the file, double-click it.)

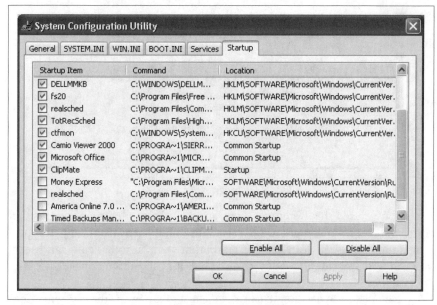

Figure 1-4. The Startup tab of the System Configuration Utility

To stop a program from running at startup, go to the Startup tab in this utility and uncheck the box next to the program. It can sometimes be difficult to understand what programs are listed on the Startup tab. Some, such as America Online, are clearly labeled. But often, you'll see a phrase or collection of letters, such as *fs20*. That's the name of the running file—in this case, *fs20.exe*, which is Free Surfer mk II, an excellent free pop-up killer. As you can see from the picture, I've chosen to let this useful tool run on startup.

To get more information about a listing, expand the width of the Command column near the top of the Startup tab. Expand it enough and you'll see the startup command that the program issues, including its location, such as *C:\ Program Files\Free Surfer\fs20.exe*. The directory location should be another hint to help you know the name of the program.

When stopping programs from running at startup, it's best to stop them one at a time rather than in groups. You want to make sure that you're not causing any system problems by stopping them. So, stop one and restart your PC. If it runs fine, stop another and restart. Continue doing this until you've cleared all the programs you don't want to run automatically.

Each time you uncheck a box and restart your PC, you'll get a warning, shown in Figure 1-5, stating that you've used the System Configuration Utility to disable a program from starting automatically. If you don't want to see that warning, disable it by checking the box in the dialog box itself.

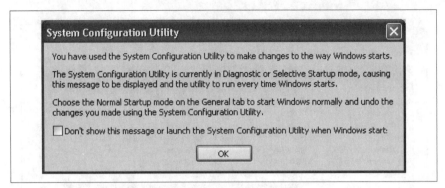

Figure 1-5. Check the box to disable the program warning

After you've used the System Configuration Utility to identify programs that run on startup, you might want to try disabling them from with the programs themselves. So, run each program that starts automatically, and see if you can find a setting that allows you to halt it from running on startup.

Using the Registry to halt programs running on startup. Even the System Configuration Utility won't necessarily let you identify and kill all programs that run on startup. You might also need to hack the Registry to disable them. To do so, run the Registry Editor [Hack #83] and go to HKEY_CURRENT_USER\ Software\Microsoft\Windows\CurrentVersion\Run. The right pane will contain a list of some of the programs that automatically run at startup. The Data field tells you the path and name of the executable so that you can determine what each program is. Right-click any program you don't want to run, and choose Delete. That will kill any programs that run specific to your logon. To kill programs that run for every user of the system, go to HKEY_ LOCAL_MACHINE\SOFTWARE\Microsoft\Windows\CurrentVersion\Run and follow the same instructions for deleting other programs you don't want to run at startup.

Disabling Services That Run at Startup

Constantly running in the background of XP are *services*—processes that help the operating system run, or that provide support to applications. Many of these services launch automatically at startup. While you need many of them, there are also many that aren't required and that can slow down your system when they run in the background.

You can disable services at startup by using the System Configuration Utility, similar to the way you halt programs from running at startup, except that you use the Services tab instead of the Startup tab. But the System Configuration Utility doesn't necessarily list every service that launches on startup. A bigger problem is that disabling services is more of a shot in the dark than disabling programs. When you disable a program, you can get a sense of what the program does. But when you disable a service through the System Configuration Utility, there's often no way to know what it does.

A better way of disabling services at startup is via the Services Computer Management Console, shown in Figure 1-6. Run it by typing `services.msc` at the command prompt. The Services Computer Management Console includes a description of all services so that you can know ahead of time whether a particular service is one you want to turn off. It also lets you pause the service so that you can test out your machine with the service off to see whether it's needed.

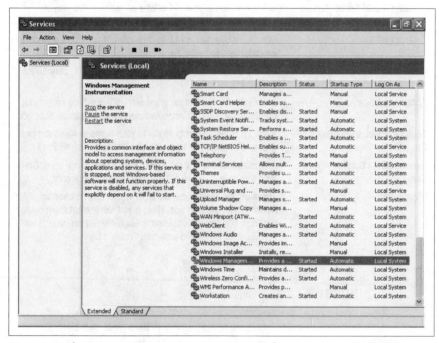

Figure 1-6. The Services Computer Management Console

After you run the console, click the Extended tab. This view will show you a description of each service in the left pane when you highlight the service. The Startup Type column shows you which services launch on startup—any services with "Automatic" in that column. Click that column to sort together all the services that automatically launch on startup. Then highlight each service and read the descriptions.

When you find a service you want to disable, right-click it and choose Properties. In the Properties dialog box that appears, choose Manual from the

"Startup type" drop-down list. The service won't start automatically from now on, but you can start it manually via the console. If you want the service disabled so that it can't be run, choose Disabled. To test the effects of turning off the service, turn off any services you don't want to run by clicking "Stop the service" in the left pane, or by right-clicking the service and choosing Stop.

Table 1-2 lists some common services you might want to halt from running at startup.

Table 1-2. Services you might want to turn off

Service	What it does
Portable Media Serial Number	Retrieves the serial number of a portable music player attached to your PC.
Task Scheduler	Schedules unattended tasks to be run. If you don't schedule any unattended tasks, turn it off.
Uninterruptible Power Supply	Manages an Uninterruptible Power Supply (UPS) connected to your PC.
Automatic Updates	Automatically checks for Windows updates. (You can check manually by going to *http://windowsupdate.microsoft.com*.)
Telnet (service available on XP Pro only)	Allows a remote user to log in to your computer and run programs. (This will not be found on all versions of XP Pro.)
Wireless Zero Configuration Service	Automatically configures a WiFi (802.11) network card. Disable this only if you're not using a WiFi network card.
Messenger	Turns off the Messenger service, which can be used to deliver spam via pop ups. (This is not the instant messaging program Windows Messenger.) For more details, see "Stop Pop Ups with SP2 —and Without It" [Hack #33].

HACK #5   Create Multiple Startup Profiles with Advanced Startup Manager

If you need to start different programs on startup, depending on what you need to do on your PC, create different startup profiles with this startup utility.

With the hacks covered in this chapter, you can customize how XP starts up. But there's one thing these hacks won't be able to do for you—create different startup profiles. For that, you need downloadable software.

Let's say, for example, you have a laptop that you sometimes run attached to a keyboard, monitor, and an always-on Internet connection, and other times you travel with it, so it is not connected to the Internet. When you use it when you travel, you use it primarily in airplanes, airports, and other places where you typically aren't connected to the Internet. You also run a piece of monitoring software that will send a signal to a call center if your laptop is stolen. You don't need to run that software when you're not on the road.

Ideally, you would have one set of programs that run automatically at home and another set of programs that run when you're on the road. At home, you might want instant messenger software and file sharing software to load at startup; on the road, you don't want that software to load automatically, but you do want your monitoring software to load.

Advanced StartUp Manager—a piece of shareware from Ray's Lab (*http://www.rayslab.com*), shown in Figure 1-7—lets you create multiple startup profiles so that you can have separate profiles for your laptop at home and the road—or for any other purpose. It's free to try, but it costs $19.95 if you decide to keep it.

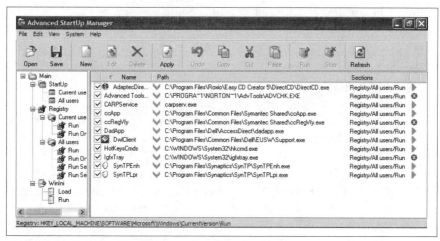

Figure 1-7. Creating multiple startup profiles with Advanced StartUp Manager

In addition to creating a profile for traveling and one for home, you might want to create other profiles. For example, when you want to play games, you'll want to start your system with a minimal number of services and programs running in the background, so you'll create a profile that disables a variety of services, such as the Indexing service, the Task Scheduler, and the Themes service that lets you apply themes to your PC. If you frequently need to troubleshoot your network, you'll want to create a network-troubleshooting profile that automatically starts networking analysis software, such as Qcheck [Hack #67].

To create a profile, add all the programs you want to run on startup by having them start from the *Startup* folder, the Registry, or the *Win.ini* file.

Where you want them to start from is up to you. To add a program, just highlight where you want it to run from, choose File → Add Program, and choose the program's executable file. You can add switches, if you want, in the Flags field of the screen you use to add the program. You can also choose whether the program should run for just one specific user or for all users of the machine. To delete a program from the profile, right-click it and choose Delete.

When you have built a profile with all the programs you want to run at startup, save it by choosing File → Backup Configuration as, and then choosing a name for the profile. Create as many profiles as you want. To load a profile, choose File → Open Backup, and choose the profile you want to load. After you've loaded a profile, the next time you start your computer it will load with that startup software. Be aware that this means you can't choose a profile when you boot your system. You have to run Advanced StartUp Manager before you exit XP, choose the profile you want to run next time you start XP, and then exit.

See Also

- OSL2000 (*http://www.osloader.com*) lets you boot from up to 100 separate operating systems (including multiple copies of XP or other versions of Windows), lets you boot from a second hard disk, and offers a variety of other features, such as an automatic boot timer. It's shareware and free to try, but it costs $25 if you decide to continue using it.

- For software to customize shutdowns, try ShutDown NOW! (*http://www.dworld.de/winsoft.htm*). It gives you just about every option you can imagine for shutdown. You can specify applications to launch or documents to load automatically before shutdown, schedule shutdowns, perform actions such as ejecting and loading CDs on shutdown, empty directories on shutdown, and the list goes on. It's shareware and free to try, but if you keep using it you're expected to pay $19.50.

- For a free shutdown manager, try Switch Off (*http://yasoft.km.ru/eng/switchoff*), a simple shutdown utility that runs in your system tray. It lets you schedule shutdowns and perform other tasks on shutdown, such as locking your workstation, and it also lets you do any of them quickly from the system tray. It's not nearly as powerful as ShutDown NOW!, but it's free.

Miscellaneous Startup and Shutdown Hacks

Here's a grab bag of ways to customize the way you start up and shut down your system.

You can control the way you start up and shut down your PC in many small ways. This grab bag of four hacks shows you the best of them.

Create One-Click Shutdown and Reboot Shortcuts

Turning off or rebooting XP involves a several-step process: click the Start menu, choose Shut Down, and then select Shut Down or Restart. If you want, however, you can exit or reboot much more quickly, by creating a shortcut that enables one-click shutdowns. You can also use the shortcut to customize the shutdown or reboot—for example, by displaying a specific message or automatically shutting down any programs that are running.

First, create a shortcut on your desktop by right-clicking the desktop, choosing New, and then choosing Shortcut. The Create Shortcut Wizard appears. In the box asking for the location of the shortcut, type shutdown. After you create the shortcut, double-clicking it will shut down your PC.

But you can do much more with a shutdown shortcut than merely shut down your PC. You can add any combination of several switches to do extra duty, like this:

```
shutdown -r -t 01 -c "Rebooting your PC"
```

Double-clicking that shortcut will reboot your PC after a one-second delay and display the message "Rebooting your PC." The shutdown command includes a variety of switches you can use to customize it. Table 1-3 lists all of them and describes their use.

Table 1-3. Switches you can use with shutdown

Switch	What it does
-s	Shuts down the PC.
-l	Logs off the current user.
-t *nn*	Indicates the duration of delay, in seconds, before performing the action.
-c "*messagetext*"	Displays a message in the System Shutdown window. A maximum of 127 characters can be used. The message must be enclosed in quotation marks.
-f	Forces any running applications to shut down.
-r	Reboots the PC.

I use this technique to create two shutdown shortcuts on my desktop—one for turning off my PC, and one for rebooting. Here are the ones I use:

```
shutdown -s -t 03 -c "See you later!"
shutdown -r -t 03 -c "You can't get rid of me that quickly!"
```

Automatically Turn On Num Lock, Scroll Lock, and Caps Lock

When you start your PC, Num Lock, Scroll Lock, and Caps Lock don't automatically toggle on. You can automatically turn each of them on or off whenever your PC starts, for all accounts on the PC. As a practical matter, most people probably want to have only Num Lock automatically turned on, but this Registry hack allows you to force any combination of keys on or off. Run the Registry Editor [Hack #83] and go to HKEY_USERS\.Default\Control Panel\Keyboard. Find the String value InitialKeyboardIndicators. By default, it is set to 0, which means that Num Lock, Scroll Lock, and Caps Lock are all turned off. Set it to any of the following values, depending on the combination of keys you want turned on or off:

0   Turns off Num Lock, Caps Lock, and Scroll Lock

1   Turns on Caps Lock

2   Turns on Num Lock

3   Turns on Caps Lock and Num Lock

4   Turns on Scroll Lock

5   Turns on Caps Lock and Scroll Lock

6   Turns on Num Lock and Scroll Lock

7   Turns on Caps Lock, Num Lock, and Scroll Lock

Exit the Registry. When you restart, the new setting will take effect.

Stop Error Messages from Displaying on Startup

If you constantly see an error message that you can't get rid of—for example, from a piece of software that didn't uninstall properly and continues to give errors on startup—you can disable it from displaying on startup. Run the Registry Editor and go to HKEY_LOCAL MACHINE\SYSTEM\CurrentControlSet\Control\Windows. (This key holds a variety of Windows system settings, such as the location of your system directory.) Create a new DWORD called NoPopupsOnBoot and give it a value of 1. Exit the Registry and reboot for the setting to take effect. To disable it, either delete the DWORD value or give it a value of 0.

Give More Time for Processes to Close at Shutdown

When you shut down Windows, XP gives each process, service, or application 20 seconds to close before the operating system turns off the computer. If the process, service, or application doesn't shut down within 20 seconds, a dialog box appears, prompting you to either wait 20 more seconds, immediately end the process, service, or application, or cancel shutdown.

If this dialog box appears frequently, you might be running an application, service, or process that often takes more than 20 seconds to close. To solve the problem, you can increase the amount of time that XP waits to display the dialog box so that the dialog box will no longer appear. To do so, run the Registry Editor and go to `HKEY_CURRENT_USER\Control Panel\Desktop`. Look for the `String` value `WaitToKillAppTimeout`. Edit the value by entering the amount of time you want XP to wait before displaying the dialog box, in milliseconds. The default is 20000, or 20 seconds. If you want XP to wait 25 seconds, enter the value 25000. Exit the Registry and reboot.

HACK #7 Control User Logins by Hacking the Registry

Make better use of the XP login screen.

If your system contains more than one user account, or if you've set up XP to require logins, you'll have to log in to XP before you can begin to use it. But you needn't stay with the default XP login rules; you can use a single Registry key to customize how you log in. For example, you can display custom text before login, and you can remind anyone with an account on the PC to change their password a certain number of days prior to the password's expiration.

To control logon options, run the Registry Editor [Hack #83] and go to the `HKEY_LOCAL_MACHINE\SOFTWARE\Microsoft\Windows NT\CurrentVersion Winlogon` subkey, which contains a variety of logon settings (as well as some settings not having to do directly with logons). Following are the most important values you can edit to customize logons.

`DontDisplayLastUserName`
> This setting lets you control how the system logon dialog box is used. If this `String` value is present and set to 1, all users will have to enter both their username and password to log on. If the value is 0, the name of the last user to log on will be displayed in the system logon dialog box.

`DefaultUserName`
> This `String` value contains the name of the last user who logged on. It will be displayed only if the `DontDisplayLastUserName` value is not present or is set to 0.

LegalNoticeCaption

This String value, used in concert with the LegalNoticeText value, displays a dialog box prior to logon that contains any text you want to display. (The text doesn't have to be a legal notice, but this value is often used for that purpose.) The box has a title and text. The LegalNoticeCaption value will be the dialog box's title.

LegalNoticeText

This String value, used in concert with LegalNoticeCaption, contains the text that you want to be displayed inside a dialog box displayed prior to logon.

PasswordExpiryWarning

This DWORD value lets you display a warning message to users a certain number of days before their passwords are set to expire. It lets you determine how many days ahead of time the warning should be issued. To edit the value, click the decimal button and enter the number of days.

ShutdownWithoutLogon

This String value enables or disables a button on the XP logon dialog box that lets the system shut down. A value of 1 enables the button (so that it is shown); a value of 0 disables the button (so that it is not shown).

Shell

This String value really doesn't have to do with logons, but it's one you should know about. It determines the shell—the user interface—that will be used by XP. The default is Explorer.exe, but it can be another shell as well—for example, the Program Manager from older Windows versions. Type in the name of the program; for example, Progman.exe for the Program Manager, or Taskman.exe for the Task Manager.

AutoRestartShell

This DWORD value doesn't have to do with logons either, but it's another good one to know. It sets whether to automatically restart the Windows shell if the shell crashes. A value of 1 automatically restarts the shell. A value of 0 tells XP not to restart the shell, forcing you to log off and then back on again to restart it.

Now that your system's startup and shutdown are under control, let's move on to the user interface.

CHAPTER TWO

The User Interface
Hacks 8–20

The Windows XP makeover was the biggest change Microsoft made to the Windows interface since it moved from Windows 3.1 to Windows 95. Rounded-edge windows, large, cartoonlike icons, and a completely redesigned Control Panel are just a few of the most obvious changes. It's not merely the way XP *looks* that has been changed, but how it *works* as well. It is based on a more stable kernel and finally gets rid of its DOS-based heritage.

But let's face it: XP's interface isn't perfect. As shipped, its cartoonish user-friendliness might help newbies, but it can frustrate power users. XP's graphical user interface (GUI) need not be one-size-fits-all, though. Under the hood, you can make countless changes to the way it looks and functions. In this chapter, you'll learn how to hack your way to a better GUI—one that reflects your own preferences, not the market-driven designs of Microsoft engineers. You'll even learn how to make your PC work like a Mac and run Linux, without actually having to install either operating system.

HACK #8 Customize the GUI with Tweak UI

Want to bend XP's interface to your will without getting your hands into the Registry or having to excavate through menus three levels deep? Then get this supremely useful freebie from Microsoft and create your own customized version of XP.

There are countless ways to customize XP's interface, including Registry hacks and menus and options hidden four layers deep. But if you're the kind of person who lives in the express lane, juices up on double espressos, and wants to hack away at the interface fast, you need Tweak UI.

Download Tweak UI for free from Microsoft at *http://www. microsoft.com/windowsxp/pro/downloads/powertoys.asp.* It's part of a suite of free, unsupported utilities from Microsoft called XP PowerToys, but it's far and away the best one.

Tweak UI lets you tweak not only the interface, as the title suggests, but also many other system settings, such as how Internet Explorer's search works, whether to automate your logon upon system startup, and whether to enable CD autoplay so that the CD immediately starts up whenever you pop it into your drive. In this hack, you'll learn how to use it and apply that knowledge to create a speedy, stripped-down version of XP. Figure 2-1 shows Tweak UI in action, customizing the display of thumbnail pictures in Windows Explorer.

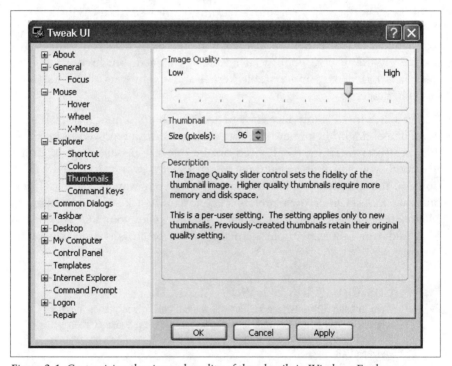

Figure 2-1. Customizing the size and quality of thumbnails in Windows Explorer

I don't have room to show you all the ways you can hack the user interface with Tweak UI, but here are some of the highlights:

- The General section lets you control XP's animated effects, fades, and shadowing. Also worthwhile in that section is "Show Windows version on desktop." Check the option and it displays, in the lower-right portion of your screen, your exact version of XP—for example, "Windows XP Home Edition Build 2600.xpsp1.020828-1920 (Service Pack 1)," as shown in Figure 2-2. I find it useful for knowing whether I need to add XP Service Packs, or for providing the information to tech support if I have an operating system problem that needs to be solved. You'll have to log off or restart your PC before it will display your version.

Windows XP Home Edition
Build 2600.xpsp1.020828-1920 (Service Pack 1)

Figure 2-2. Displaying your exact version and build of XP on your desktop

> You can also force the operating system to display your exact version and build of XP on your desktop by using a Registry hack. Run the Registry Editor **[Hack #83]**. Go to HKEY_CURRENT_ USER\Control Panel\Desktop, and find the DWORD value PaintDesktopVersion. Change the value to 1. Exit the Registry and reboot. To remove the version and build number, change the value back to 0. In beta versions of XP, the value was turned on by default, but when the product shipped, it was turned off.

- In Tweak UI you also can hide desktop icons that apparently can't be deleted from the desktop, such as the Internet Explorer, Microsoft Outlook, My Computer, My Documents, My Network Places, and Recycle Bin icons. To do this, go to the Desktop section and uncheck the boxes next to the icons you want to vanish. You won't have to log off for the changes to take effect. (You can force the Registry to do the same thing **[Hack #13]**.)

- In the Explorer section, customize the taskbar and desktop by enabling or disabling balloon tips and determining which programs will be allowed to show up on the Frequently Used Programs List, among other customizations.

- Customize how Windows Explorer looks and functions by controlling the quality of image thumbnails; changing the way shortcuts look; determining whether to include Help, Recent Documents, and Logoff on the Start menu; and many similar options.

There's a lot more as well; to find it all, download it and try it all out.

Create a Speedy, Stripped-Down Interface with Tweak UI

While it might be fun to use Tweak UI to fiddle with the UI, its real power becomes apparent when you use it to create your own customized XP interfaces. For example, you might be the type who is concerned about only one thing when you use your PC: pure functionality. You want to get your work done fast, and you don't want to be bothered by the extra frou-frous that XP throws in your way and that slow down your system. Here's how to create a speedy, stripped-down interface using Tweak UI:

Turn off animations, fades, and similar features. Animations and fades are pretty, but they require system resources and slow down your system. You can turn off a wide variety of these animations and fades from the General section of Tweak UI. Uncheck the boxes next to all of them, such as "Enable menu animation," "Enable menu selection fading," "Enable tooltip animation," and the many others listed there.

Speed up right-click menu displays, hovers, and other mouse actions. If you want menus to appear with absolutely no delay when you right-click an object or icon, go to the Mouse section and move the Menu speed slider all the way to the left. Test how fast the menus will display by right-clicking the test icon. From this section, you can also increase your mouse sensitivity so that it responds more quickly to your clicks and drags. In the Mouse Sensitivity section, decrease the numbers next to Double-Click and Drag, and see the results by double-clicking the test icon.

The Mouse section also lets you change the mouse's sensitivity to "hovering"—for example, displaying a tool tip when you hover your mouse over an icon. To speed up the hover display, highlight Hover underneath the Mouse section, then decrease the numbers next to "Hover sensitivity" and "Hover time." Test out your settings using the test icon.

Decrease the image quality of thumbnails in Windows Explorer. Windows Explorer uses up RAM when it displays thumbnails, which can slow down your system because the RAM could instead be used for your applications or the operating system itself. Use Tweak UI to give thumbnails the minimum amount of RAM only. Go to the Explorer → Thumbnails section and in the Image Quality area, move the slider all the way to the left, to the lowest setting for image quality. Decrease the thumbnail size, in pixels.

You can also completely turn off thumbnails so that they aren't displayed in Windows Explorer. From Windows Explorer, choose View → Details, or choose View → List.

Delete unnecessary desktop icons.   Desktop icons take up RAM and clutter your interface, so you want as few of them as possible on your desktop if you want a stripped-down version of XP. You can delete most desktop icons, but some of them such as Outlook and Internet Explorer apparently can't be deleted. However, Tweak UI lets you delete them. Go to the Desktop section and uncheck the boxes next to the icons that you want off the desktop. (You can force the Registry to do the same thing [Hack #13].)

Hide Control Panel applets.   The Control Panel is filled with applets that you will rarely, if ever, use, and they clutter up the interface, making it more difficult to find the applets you do want to use. To hide applets, go to the Control Panel section and uncheck the boxes next to the applets that you want to hide. (You can force the Registry to do the same thing [Hack #9]. That hack also shows you how you can run the applets, even after you've removed their icons.)

Clean up the right-click New menu.   When you right-click the desktop and choose New, you can automatically create a new document by choosing from a submenu. That submenu can offer many choices of which document types to create, depending on the applications you have installed on your PC and how those applications handle their installation process. In many instances, those choices can be little more than clutter because you might rarely need to create new documents of certain types. Strip down that submenu to the essentials so that it has only those document types that you frequently create. Choose Templates, and uncheck the boxes next to the document types you rarely create. For example, most people rarely use the Briefcase [Hack #29], but that is one of your choices, so remove that unless you regularly move files using it. (To add power to the right-click context menu in Explorer, see "A Power User's Hidden Weapon: Improve the Context Menu" [Hack #28].)

Enable autologon.   If you're the primary person who uses your PC, you can enable autologon so that you're logged on automatically when the system starts. Choose Autologon from the Logon section, check the box next to "Log on automatically at system startup," and make sure your username, domain, and password are correct.

Control the Control Panel

Whether you're a fan of the new Control Panel or not, there's a lot you can do to make it more palatable—like hiding applets you never use, recategorizing the ones you do use, and displaying all applets in a simple-to-use cascading menu.

When I first started using XP, one of the things that annoyed me most was its new Control Panel. Yes, the big new icons for running applets are certainly pretty, but the Control Panel's several-layer organization forces you to click far too many times to get to the applet you want. And its clutter of applets that I rarely, if ever, use makes it even more difficult and confusing.

My first reaction was to click the Switch to Classic View button to do away with the new design, but the Classic View has its problems as well: its long, alphabetized list of thumbnails is just as difficult to navigate as the new Control Panel.

The solution? Start by cleaning up the Control Panel, hiding applets that you rarely, if ever, use. Note that when you hide the applets, you can still use them; you just won't see their icons in the Control Panel.

In this hack, you'll not only find out ways you can control the Control Panel, but you'll also see how you can apply that knowledge to create different customized Control Panels.

Hide Unused Applets with the Registry

To hide unused applets using the Registry, run the Registry Editor [Hack #83] and go to HKEY_LOCAL_MACHINE\SOFTWARE\Microsoft\Windows\CurrentVersion\ Control Panel\don't load.

The key, as its name implies, determines which Control Panel applet icons are not loaded into the Control Panel. You'll still be able to run those applets from the command line after you hide them (as explained later in this hack); you just won't be able to see their icons in the Control Panel.

To hide an applet, create a new String value whose name is the filename of the applet you want to hide. For example, to hide the Mouse Control dialog box, the String value would be *main.cpl*. See Table 2-1 for a list of Control Panel applets and their filenames.

Table 2-1. Control Panel applets and their filenames

Applet	Filename
System Properties	*sysdm.cpl*
Display Properties	*desk.cpl*

Table 2-1. *Control Panel applets and their filenames (continued)*

Applet	Filename
Network Connections	*ncpa.cpl*
Accessibility Options	*access.cpl*
Add or Remove Programs	*appwiz.cpl*
Add Hardware Wizard	*hdwwiz.cpl*
Internet Properties	*Inetcpl.cpl*
Region and Language Options	*intl.cpl*
Game Controllers	*joy.cpl*
Mouse Properties	*main.cpl*
Sound and Audio Devices	*mmsys.cpl*
User Accounts	*nusrmgr.cpl*
ODBC Data Source Administrator	*odbccp32.cpl*
Power Options Properties	*Powercfg.cpl*
Phone and Modem Options	*telephon.cpl*
Time and Date Properties	*timedate.cpl*
Speech Properties	*sapi.cpl*

Create separate String values for each applet you want to hide, then exit the Registry. The applets will vanish from the Control Panel. To make a hidden applet appear again, delete its string value from this same registry key.

Hide Unused Applets with XP Pro's Group Policy Editor

If you have XP Professional, you don't need to get your hands dirty with the Registry to hide unused applets; instead, you can use XP Professional's exceedingly useful Group Policy Editor to accomplish the same task. The Group Policy Editor is primarily used for setting network and multiuser policies and rights, but it can also be used to customize the way XP looks and works. (For example, to use it to hack away at the Start menu and taskbar, see "Hack the Start Menu and Taskbar" [Hack #10].) Run the Group Policy Editor by typing gpedit.msc at the Run prompt or command line.

Once you've run it, go to User Configuration\Administrative Templates\ Control Panel, the section that handles the Control Panel. As you can see when you get there, you can do a lot more than hide the Control Panel's unused applets in this section of the Group Policy Editor; you can also control many other aspects of how the Control Panel looks and functions.

Now right-click "Show only specified Control Panel applets," and choose Properties. You'll see the screen pictured in Figure 2-3.

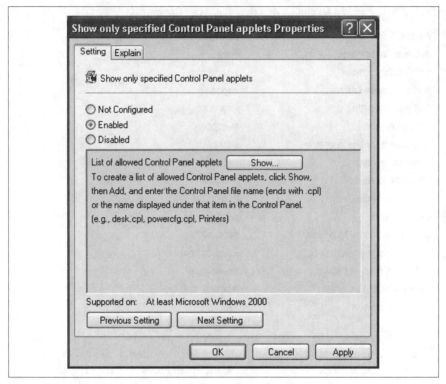

Figure 2-3. Disabling Control Panel applets in the Group Policy Editor

Get ready for a bit of counterintuitive selecting. To disable Control Panel applets, you must choose the Enabled radio button because you're enabling the feature to show only certain Control Panel applets. Strange, but true.

When you do this, you'll hide *all* applets in the Control Panel, which is a bit draconian. If you don't want to see any applets at all for some odd reason, you're done; just click OK. But you'll most likely want to show some applets, so to add them, click the Show button. The Show Contents screen appears. Click Add, and you're ready to list all the Control Panel applets that you want to appear. For each item that you want to appear, type in its Control Panel filename, which you can find in Table 2-1. For example, if you want the Date and Time dialog box to appear, type in timedate.cpl.

You can also use Tweak UI **[Hack #8]** to hide Control Panel applets.

When you've listed all the Control Panel applets that you want to appear, click OK and exit the Group Policy Editor. Only the applets you've chosen to display will now appear in the Control Panel.

This technique is most useful when you're hiding most of the applets in the Control Panel and you want to display only a few. There's another way to use the Group Policy Editor to hide applets, and it's better suited for when you want to hide only a few applets. In User Configuration\Administrative Templates\Control Panel, double-click "Hide specified Control Panel applets" and choose Enabled. After you click Enabled, choose Show → Add and type in the Control Panel filename (which you can find in Table 2-1) for each applet you want to hide. Click OK in each dialog box that appears. When you exit the Group Policy Editor, the specified applets will no longer appear in the Control Panel.

To customize other aspects of how the Control Panel works, follow the same instructions as outlined previously—right-clicking the item you want to change, choosing Properties, and then picking your options.

How to Run Hidden Applets

Hiding applets cleans up the Control Panel, but leaves you with another problem—what if you need to run an applet whose icon you've hidden? This is simple to do. At the Run box or command line, type in the name of the applet you want to run—such as Inetcpl.cpl for the Internet Properties applets—and press Enter. See Table 2-1 for a list of filenames.

Recategorize Control Panel Applets

Hiding applets goes only partway toward cleaning up the Control Panel. You can also recategorize applets and put them in any category you want. For example, by default, the Mouse Properties applet can be found in the Printers and Other Hardware category, but if you prefer that it instead be found in Accessibility Options, you can move it there.

To put an applet into any category you want, you need two pieces of information: the filename of the applet (for example, *main.cpl* for the Mouse Properties dialog box), and the Registry value for each Control Panel category (for example, 0x00000007 (7) for Accessibility Options). For filenames of each applet, see Table 2-1. For the Registry value for each Control Panel category, see Table 2-2. With these two pieces of information in hand, you can recategorize any or all Control Panel applets.

Table 2-2. Control Panel categories and their Registry value data

Control panel category	Value data
Accessibility Options	0x00000007 (7)
Add or Remove Programs	0x00000008 (8)
Appearance and Themes	0x00000001 (1)
Date, Time, Language, and Regional Options	0x00000006 (6)
Network and Internet Connections	0x00000003 (3)
Other Control Panel Options	0x00000000 (0)
Performance and Maintenance	0x00000005 (5)
Printers and Other Hardware	0x00000002 (2)
Sounds, Speech, and Audio Devices	0x00000004 (4)
User Accounts	0x00000009 (9)
No category	0xffffffff

To recategorize a Control Panel applet, run the Registry Editor [Hack #83] and go to HKEY_LOCAL_MACHINE\SOFTWARE\Microsoft\Windows\CurrentVersion\Control Panel\Extended Properties\{305CA226-D286-468e-B848-2B2E8E697B74}2. The key {305CA226-D286-468e-B848-2B2E8E697B74}2 is the container that holds all Control Panel categories. (Remember that it's safest to back up your Registry first [Hack #86].)

Now find the Registry key of the applet you want to recategorize. The filename of the applet will appear on the end of the key; for example, %SystemRoot%\system32\main.cpl is the Mouse Properties dialog box. Turn to trusty Table 2-1 for a list of other filenames for Control Panel applets.

Change the key's DWORD value to the value of the Control Panel category into which you want the applet to appear, as detailed in Table 2-2. For example, if you want the applet to appear in the Performance and Maintenance category, give it a value of 5. The value will then be displayed in the Registry as 0x00000005(5).

When you're done, exit the Registry. The applet will now appear in the new category.

Display Control Panel Applets in a Cascading Menu

If you're a "just the facts, ma'am" type, you'll want to bypass the Control Panel altogether. Rather than clicking effete icons, you can instead force XP to display Control Panel applets in a cascading menu when you choose Control Panel from the Start button, as shown in Figure 2-4.

To force the Control Panel to display as a cascading menu, right-click the taskbar and choose Properties → Start Menu. Click the Customize button

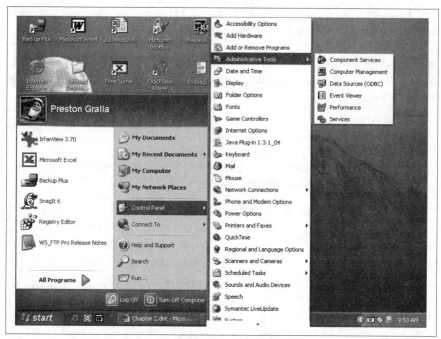

Figure 2-4. Turning the Control Panel into a cascading menu for quick access to applets

and choose the Advanced tab. In the Control Panel heading, choose "Display as a menu." Click OK twice.

Build Customized Control Panels

Armed with all this Control Panel hackery, you can build customized Control Panels. For example, you can build a Control Panel for computer newbies, which hides the more technical applets and categories. Hide the applets in the Network and Internet Connections category, the Performance and Maintenance category, and the Sounds, Speech, and Audio Devices category—that way, newbies can't get into trouble by making changes that will affect the system in unexpected ways.

For system administrators, group all system-type applets into a single category, such as Network and Internet Connections. You'd probably want to keep all the existing applets there, but also add the Administrative Tools, Scheduled Tasks, and System applets to it, as well as the Printers and Faxes applet. (If the administrator has to handle other hardware, such as scanners, add the Scanners and Cameras applet as well.)

For those who like to hack their systems and want instant, stripped-down access to customization tools, take all the applets that are now in Network and Internet Connections, and all those in Performance and Maintenance, and group them into the Appearance and Themes category. Then force the Control Panel to display as a cascading menu, and all of the hackery-type applets will be available instantly because the Appearance and Themes category is at the top of the cascading menu and all the relevant applets will be available directly from it.

Hack the Start Menu and Taskbar

XP Professional's Group Policy Editor gives you instant access to changing more than three dozen interface settings. Here's how to use it to create your own personalized Start menu and taskbar.

XP Professional's Group Policy Editor does more than just customize the Control Panel [Hack #9]; it gives you control over many aspects of XP's interface as well—in particular, the Start menu and taskbar. In fact, it gives you quick access to more than three dozen separate settings for them.

Run the Group Policy Editor by typing gpedit.msc at the Run prompt or command line. Go to User Configuration\Administrative Templates\Start Menu and Taskbar. As you can see in Figure 2-5, the right pane displays all the settings you can change. If you click the Extended tab at the bottom of the screen, you'll be shown a description of the setting that you've highlighted, along with an explanation of each option. Settings you can customize include showing the My Pictures icon, the Run menu, and the My Music icon on the Start menu; locking the taskbar so that it can't be customized; and many others. To change a setting [Hack #9], double-click it and choose the options from the menu it displays.

There's not room in this hack to go into detail about each setting you can change, so I'll tell you about some of my favorites. I've never been a big fan of My Documents, My Pictures, and My Music. In fact, I never use those folders, so there's no point having them on the Start menu. The settings in the Group Policy Editor let you get rid of them.

If you share your PC with other people, the Group Policy Editor is a great way to make sure no one can change the Start menu and taskbar except you. So, when you have the Start menu and taskbar working the way you want, they'll stay that way until you want to change them. Enable "Prevent changes to Taskbar and Start Menu settings," and no one will be able to change their settings except you. Select "Remove drag-and-drop context menus on the Start Menu," and no one except you will be able to remove or reorder items on the Start menu. You can even stop anyone else from shutting down Windows by selecting "Remove and prevent access to the Shut

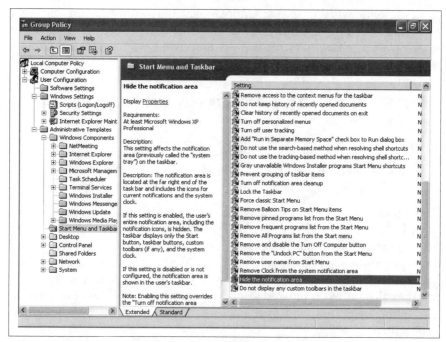

Figure 2-5. Customizing the Start menu and taskbar in the Group Policy Editor

Down command." (Of course, they can still shut down your PC the old-fashioned way: using the power switch.)

Among the many entries here are a lot of pointless ones, by the way. You can remove the Log Off entry on the Start menu, for example, which certainly isn't high on my list of must-haves. But who knows, you might want to do that, or make any of the many other changes the Group Policy Editor allows. Go in there yourself and muck around; you'll find plenty to change.

Hack the Taskbar with Tweak UI

You can use Tweak UI [Hack #8] to hack the taskbar to a limited degree. Go to its Taskbar section, and you can disable or enable balloon tips, and enable or disable warnings when you're low on disk space. Underneath the Taskbar section, you'll find a Grouping subsection that controls how taskbar "grouping" works. When you run too many programs with too many files open, all of them can't fit individually on the taskbar. So, XP groups files from the same application with each other. For example, if you have four Word files open, it shows only a single icon for Word on the taskbar, with the number 4 inside it. Click the icon, and a list of all four files pops up. You can then choose which to open. Tweak UI lets you control how that grouping works;

you can decide whether to first group applications with the most windows, or instead first group applications that you use the least. You can also choose to group all applications with two or more windows open, three or more windows open, and so on.

Clean Up the Most Frequently Used Programs List
#11

Make this infrequently used tool useful. Ban programs from the Most Frequently Used Programs List, change the number of programs on the list, or do away with it altogether to make more room for the Pinned Programs List.

Windows keeps track of programs you use frequently and puts them on the Most Frequently Used Programs List, which appears on the new Windows XP–style Start menu (not the Classic-style Start menu) between the Pinned Items List at the top and the All Programs link at the bottom. The Most Frequently Used Programs List is a quick way to access programs you use often. But the rules for when programs appear on that list and disappear from the list are murky at best, and there appears to be no logic to what programs appear there.

There is some hidden logic, however. XP bans a variety of programs from the list. If any of the following words or phrases is included in the program's shortcut name, the program will be excluded from the list: Documentation, Help, Install, More Info, Readme, Read me, Read First, Setup, Support, and What's New.

Additionally, the following executables are excluded from the list: *Setup.exe*, *Install.exe*, *Isuninst.exe*, *Unwise.exe*, *Unwise32.exe*, *St5unst.exe*, *Rundll32.exe*, *Explorer.exe*, *Icwconn1.exe*, *Inoculan.exe*, *Mobsync.exe*, *Navwnt.exe*, *Realmon.exe*, and *Sndvol32.exe*.

Banning Programs from the List

You might want to ban other programs from the list, not just those that XP bans by default. Just because you use a program a time or two doesn't mean you want it on the Start menu's Most Frequently Used Programs List. You can ban programs from the list using a Registry hack.

Run the Registry Editor [Hack #83] and go to HKEY_CLASSES_ROOT\Applications. Underneath this key, you'll find a series of subkeys, each representing an application. The primary purpose of these subkeys, as you'll see later in this hack, is to determine whether the program appears on the Open With dialog box that appears whenever you try to open an unknown file type. But you can also add a value to any of the subkeys which will ban programs from appearing on the Most Frequently Used Programs List.

Look for a subkey that is the executable name of the application you want to ban from the list—for example, visio.exe for the Visio business illustration program. Once you find the application's subkey, create a new String value for that subkey, named NoStartPage. Leave the value blank. Exit the Registry. You might have to reboot for the setting to take effect and the program to be banned from the list.

Another use for HKEY_CLASSES_ROOT\Applications. While you're rooting around in HKEY_CLASSES_ROOT\Applications, you might want to hack the Open With dialog box (shown in Figure 2-6) that appears whenever you try to open an unknown file type. Each application's subkey in HKEY_CLASSES_ROOT\Applications controls whether that particular application will show up on the dialog box.

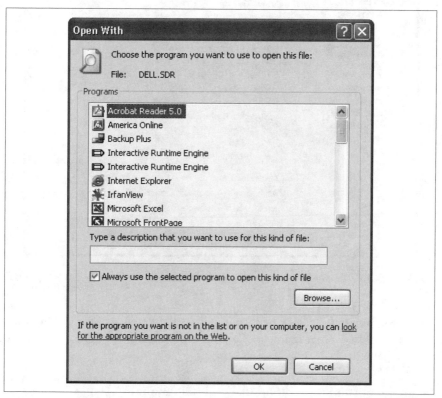

Figure 2-6. Hacking the Open With dialog box

If you want to ban a particular program from the Open With dialog box, look for the application's subkey underneath `HKEY_CLASSES_ROOT\ Applications`, add a `String` value named `NoOpenWith`, and leave the value blank.

Ban programs from the Most Frequently Used Programs List with Tweak UI. If you don't want to muck around in the Registry, you can ban programs from the Most Frequently Used Programs List using Tweak UI [Hack #8]. Run Tweak UI, and choose Taskbar → XP Start Menu. You'll see the screen shown in Figure 2-7, with a list of programs and checks next to most or all of them.

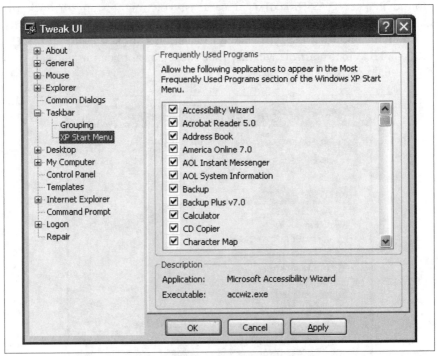

Figure 2-7. Using Tweak UI to ban programs from the Most Frequently Used Programs List

Each program with a check next to it will be allowed to appear on the Most Frequently Used Programs List. To stop a program from appearing on the list, uncheck the box and click OK.

Change the Number of Programs That Appear on the List

By default, the Most Frequently Used Programs List has room for six programs, but you can change that default and have more or fewer programs appear. Right-click the Start button and choose Properties → Customize → General. The Customize Start Menu dialog box, shown in Figure 2-8, appears. To customize the number of programs to include on the list, edit the "Number of programs on Start menu" box. You can choose any number between 0 and 30. Be aware, though, that depending on your screen resolution and whether you're using large or small icons, the entire list might not appear if you choose a large number. No matter how high your resolution is, for example, don't expect there to be room for 30 programs.

Figure 2-8. Customizing the number of programs on the Most Frequently Used Programs List

Make Room for the Pinned Programs List

The Pinned Programs List, just above the Most Frequently Used Programs List on the XP-style Start menu, gives you instant access to any program you want. You, rather than the operating system, decide what programs go there. To add a program to it, drag the program's icon or filename to the Start menu, and when the menu pops up, drag it to the spot on the list where you want it to appear.

This list makes a lot more sense than the Most Frequently Used Programs List: after all, you know better than XP what programs you want within easy reach. So, do what I do: kill the Most Frequently Used Programs List as a way to make more room for the Pinned Programs List. When you kill the Most Frequently Used Programs List, there will be a big blank space between the Pinned Programs List and the All Programs button. Drag programs to fill that space; the shortcuts will stay there until you delete them.

You can kill the Most Frequently Used Programs List with a Registry hack. Run the Registry Editor [Hack #83] and go to HKEY_CURRENT_USER\Software\ Microsoft\Windows\CurrentVersion\Policies\Explorer. Create a new DWORD called NoStartMenuMFUprogramsList and give it a value of 1. You'll have to reboot or log off and back on for the setting to take effect. When it does, the nice big blank space will be left for you to fill with pinned programs.

HACK #12   Rename and Change "Unchangeable" Desktop Icons and System Objects

To create the perfect XP interface, you want to be able to give every desktop icon and system object the name and icon of your choice. Here's how to do it—even to objects that appear to be unchangeable.

Interface hackers (myself included) are a details-oriented bunch. We want to be able to control every part of the interface so that it reflects our personality. That means being able to choose our own icons for desktop items and system objects, give new names to system objects, and create our own balloon tips—for example, adding a balloon tip to the Recycle Bin saying "Take out the trash!"

But it's not as simple as you might think. Microsoft has a way of protecting its own. For example, it won't let you change the text and balloon tips associated with a variety of system objects, such as the Recycle Bin, Outlook, Internet Explorer, My Computer, and My Network Places.

You can normally change both the name and the balloon text (text that appears when you hover your mouse over the icon) of all the icons on your desktop, but you can't change these. Normally, to change the name and balloon text of an icon, first you right-click the icon and choose Properties. To change the name of the icon, you choose the General tab and, in the box at the top, type in the name that you want to appear beneath the icon.

Then, to change the balloon text, you click the Shortcut tab and in the Comment box type in the text that you want to appear. When you're ready to make the change, click OK. The icon name and balloon text should now be changed.

But when you try to do this for system objects such as Outlook, Internet Explorer, My Computer, and Network Neighborhood, it won't work. The proper options don't appear when you right-click them and choose Properties.

There are ways, however, to change them in any way you want so that you can create your own personalized XP interface.

The Registry to the Rescue

The Registry is your best tool for personalizing XP. It will let you change both the text and balloon tip associated with system objects. First, you need to know the object's class ID (CLSID), which uniquely identifies each system object. Table 2-3 lists the CLSIDs for common desktop objects.

Table 2-3. CLSIDs for desktop objects

Desktop object	CLSID
My Computer	{20D04FE0-3AEA-1069-A2D8-08002B30309D}
Recycle Bin	{645FF040-5081-101B-9F08-00AA002F954E}
Microsoft Outlook	{00020D75-0000-0000-C000-000000000046}
Internet Explorer	{FBF23B42-E3F0-101B-8488-00AA003E56F8}
The Internet	{3DC7A020-0ACD-11CF-A9BB-00AA004AE837}
My Network Places	{208D2C60-3AEA-1069-A2D7-08002B30309D}
Briefcase	{85BBD920-42A0-1069-A2E4-08002B30309D}
Dial-Up Networking	{992CFFA0-F557-101A-88EC-00DD010CCC48}

Armed with the proper CLSID, it's easy to change the name and balloon text of system objects. First, use Table 2-3 to find the CLSID for the object whose name or balloon text you want to change. Then run the Registry Editor [Hack #83], go to HKEY_CLASSES_ROOT\CLSID, a key that lets you change characteristics of system objects, and highlight the CLSID whose name or balloon text you want to change. For example, to change My Computer, highlight the subkey HKEY_CLASSES_ROOT\CLSID\{20D04FE0-3AEA-1069-A2D8-08002B30309D}. Keep in mind that HKEY_CLASSES_ROOT\CLSID has many CLSIDs listed under it, so it might take you a while to find the proper subkey.

Once you find the right subkey, if you want to edit the name of the object, open the Default value and type in the text that you want to appear underneath the object. If you want to edit the balloon text for the object, open the InfoTip value and type in the text that you want to appear as balloon text. Once you're done, exit the Registry and reboot.

You might also be able to force the changes to take effect without reboot-ing. After you exit the Registry, go to your desktop and press F5 to refresh the screen. The new names and balloon tips might appear now.

Change the Desktop Icons of System Objects

You can hack objects besides names and balloons with this method. You can also change the desktop icons of system objects that appear to have unchangeable icons.

First, using Table 2-3, find the CLSID for the object whose icon you want to change. Then run the Registry Editor, go to HKEY_CLASSES_ROOT\CLSID, and look for the CLSID subkey from Table 2-3 for the object whose icon you want to change. Open the subkey and then the DefaultIcon subkey under that. For example, to change the icon for My Computer, open the subkey HKEY_CLASSES_ROOT\CLSID\{20D04FE0-3AEA-1069-A2D8-08002B30309D}\DefaultIcon. Change the Default value to the path of the icon that you want displayed. Exit the Registry. You might have to reboot for the new settings to take effect.

> Some people aren't able to change their icons using this method. Instead of editing HKEY_CLASSES_ROOT\CLSID, they have to edit HKEY_CURRENT_USER\Software\Microsoft\Windows\CurrentVersion\Explorer\CLSID\, and that does the trick.

HACK #13   Remove "Nonremovable" Desktop Icons

To create your own customized XP interface, you need to be able to remove certain desktop icons. A Registry hack lets you remove any you want, including those apparently protected by XP.

Creating the perfect, customized XP interface doesn't mean just changing icons; it also means removing them. For example, many power users look down their noses at America Online, and yet, on many systems, that icon can't be removed easily.

America Online isn't the only icon protected in this way; many others are as well. Which desktop icons are protected on your system will depend on your exact version of XP (for example, SP-1) and the manufacturer of your PC. The Recycle Bin is protected on all versions, but the America Online icon is protected on some systems, and not on others.

To customize XP to your liking, you'll want to be able to delete these pro-tected icons. To do so, you'll need a Registry hack. Run the Registry Editor [Hack #83] and go to HKEY_LOCAL_MACHINE\SOFTWARE\Microsoft\Windows\

CurrentVersion\Explorer\Desktop\NameSpace. Here's where you'll find various special desktop icons. They're not listed by name, but instead by CLSID—for example, {645FF040-5081-101B-9F08-00AA002F954E} for the Recycle Bin. Table 2-3 [Hack #12] lists CLSIDs of common desktop objects, so use it to find the CLSID of the icon you want to delete.

To remove an icon from the desktop, simply delete the key of the icon—for example, {645FF040-5081-101B-9F08-00AA002F954E} for the Recycle Bin. Then exit the Registry, go to your desktop, and press F5 to refresh the screen. The Recycle Bin icon should now be gone.

> On some systems, the icons might not be deleted immediately. Instead, after making the Registry change, you might have to right-click the icon and choose Delete.

Some CLSIDs in HKEY_LOCAL_MACHINE\SOFTWARE\Microsoft\Windows\ CurrentVersion\Explorer\Desktop\NameSpace can be deleted from the desktop without having to go through this procedure, but when you try to delete them they might give you a special warning message. For example, when you try to delete Microsoft Outlook from the desktop, you get the warning message "The Outlook Desktop icon provides special functionality and we recommend that you do not remove it." If you like, you can edit that message to display whatever you want. In the CLSID's subkey—for example, {00020D75-0000-0000-C000-000000000046} for Microsoft Outlook—you'll find the value Removal Message. Edit this value to whatever text you want, and your warning message will appear whenever someone tries to delete the icon.

Keep in mind that when you remove desktop icons you're removing only icons, not the underlying feature or program. So, the Recycle Bin still works even if you remove its icon. To open the Recycle Bin, go to C:\RECYCLER and open the folder inside it. To restore an item that's been deleted, right-click it and choose Properties → Restore. Delete items as you would any other item.

> Some manufacturers make America Online a nonremovable desktop icon. If that's the case with your PC and you want to remove it, delete the CLSID {955B7B84-5308-419c-8ED8-0B9CA3C56985}. America Online will still work, but its icon will no longer be on the desktop.

Hack Your Way Through the Interface

#14   Use Registry hacks to make a grab bag of great interface changes.

Hidden in the mazes of the Registry are countless ways to hack XP's interface. Following are some of my favorites.

Hide All Icons in the Notification Area

The system tray, also called the notification area, is the small area on the far-right side of the taskbar, in which utilities and programs that run in the background, such as antivirus software, show their icons.

I don't find it a particularly intelligent use of screen real estate, so I prefer not to see the icons there. To hide them, run the Registry Editor [Hack #83] and go to HKEY_CURRENT_USER/Software/Microsoft/Windows/CurrentVersion/ Policies/Explorer. Among other things, this key controls the display of objects throughout XP. Create a new DWORD called NoTrayItemsDisplay. Assign it a value of 1. (A value of 0 will keep the icons displayed.) Exit the Registry and reboot.

While you're at the HKEY_CURRENT_USER/Software/Microsoft/Windows/ CurrentVersion/Policies/Explorer key, you can also delete the My Recent Documents icon on the Start menu. Create a new DWORD called NoRecentDocsMenu. Assign it a value of 1. (A value of 0 will keep the icon displayed.) Exit the Registry and reboot.

Hide Only Certain Icons in the Notification Area

You might want to display some icons in the notification area but hide others. If so, you can hide icons on a case-by-case basis. You'll do it by delving through menus, though, not by hacking the Registry. Right-click the taskbar and choose Properties → Taskbar. The Taskbar and Start Menu Properties dialog box appears. This dialog box, as the name implies, lets you control how the taskbar and Start menu look and function.

In the Notification area of the dialog box, check the box next to "Hide inactive icons," then click Customize. The Customize Notifications dialog box appears.

Click the program's listing in the Behavior column, and choose from the drop-down menu to hide the icon when the program is inactive, to always hide it, or to never hide it (see Figure 2-9). Click OK twice. Your changes will take effect immediately.

Figure 2-9. Hiding inactive icons

Add Specific Folders to the Open Dialog Box

When you use certain Windows applications (such as Notepad) to open a file, on the left side of the Open dialog box are a group of icons and folders (such as My Documents, My Recent Documents, Desktop, My Computer, and My Network) to which you can navigate to open files.

Good idea, bad implementation. Do you really keep documents in My Computer? Unlikely, at best. It would be much more helpful if you could list only those folders that you use, and if you could choose to put *any* folder there, not just ones XP decides you need.

In fact, you can do it with a Registry hack. It'll let you put just the folders of your choosing on the left side of the Open dialog box. Note that when you do this, it will affect XP applications such as Notepad and Paint that use the Open and Save common dialog boxes. However, it won't affect Microsoft Office applications and other applications that don't use the common dialog boxes.

Run the Registry Editor and go to `HKEY_CURRENT_USER\Software\Microsoft\Windows\CurrentVersion\Policies\comdlg32`. This is the key that determines how common dialog boxes are handled. You're going to create a subkey that will create a customized location for the folders, and then give that subkey a series of values, each of which will define a folder location.

 This works with XP Home Edition only, not XP Professional.

To start, create a new subkey underneath HKEY_CURRENT_USER\Software\ Microsoft\Windows\CurrentVersion\Policies\comdlg32 called Placesbar, and create a String value for it named Place0. Give Place0 a value of the topmost folder that you want to appear on the Open dialog box, for example, C:\Projects.

Next, create another String value for Placesbar called Place1. Give it a value of the second folder that you want to appear on the Open dialog box. You can put up to five icons on the Open dialog box, so create new String values up to Place4 and give them values as outlined in the previous steps. When you're done, exit the Registry. You won't have to reboot for the changes to take effect. Figure 2-10 shows an example of an Open dialog box customized in this way.

If you do not want any folders to appear in common Open dialog boxes, you can do that as well. In HKEY_CURRENT_USER\Software\Microsoft\Windows\ CurrentVersion\Policies\comdlg32 create a new DWORD value called NoPlacesBar and give it a value of 1. Exit the Registry. If you want the folders back, either delete NoPlacesBar or give it a value of 0.

Turn Off System Beeps

To me, system beeps that my PC makes when it encounters certain system errors are like balloon tips—gnatlike annoyances that I can do without. So, I turn them off using a Registry hack. Run the Registry Editor [Hack #84] , go to HKEY_CURRENT_USER\Control Panel\Sound, and find the Beep and ExtendedSounds String values. Set each value to No. Exit the Registry and reboot. The beeps will no longer sound.

Use Your Own Graphic for Your User Account

This one isn't a Registry hack, but I couldn't resist putting it in here since it's one of the more useful ways to customize the interface. The Windows XP graphic for your user account on the Start menu might not be to your taste, and your choice of other graphics to display there isn't particularly inspiring, either. After all, not everyone wants to be pictured as a rubber ducky, a snowflake, or a pair of horses.

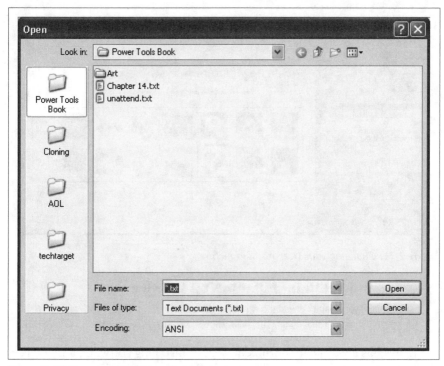

Figure 2-10. A customized Open dialog box

But you're not limited to XP-supplied pictures for your user account; you can use any picture in *.gif*, *.jpg*, *.png*, or *.bmp* format. In this hack, I'll show you how to use your own picture.

To change your User Account picture to any one that you want, from the Control Panel choose User Accounts, then pick the account you want to change and choose Change my picture → Browse for more pictures. Navigate to the picture you want to use and click OK. Figure 2-11 shows the screen you'll use to change your picture; it also shows the customized User Account picture I use during the winter holiday season.

If you have a digital camera or scanner attached to your PC, a button will show up on the screen shown in Figure 2-11 that lets you take a picture with the camera, or scan a picture with the scanner, and then immediately use that picture for your user account.

For those interested in saving keystrokes, there's a quicker way to get to the screen letting you customize your picture. From the Windows XP–style Start menu, click your picture, and the screen appears.

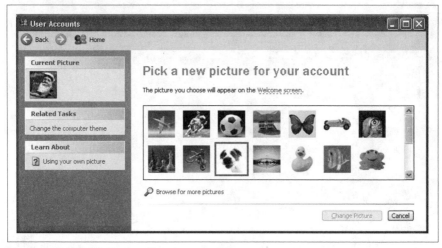

Figure 2-11. Changing your User Account picture

Remove "Uninstallable" XP Utilities

Think you can't uninstall Windows Messenger, WordPad, and similar components? Think again. This hack shows you how.

Windows has always had a problem with uninstalling software, and it's particularly poor at uninstalling its own utilities, such as WordPad or Windows Messenger. Uninstalling these utilities can free up hard-disk space if your hard disk is starting to fill up. And if you never use Windows Messenger, you most likely will want to uninstall it because the program frequently launches itself automatically even after you've shut it down repeatedly, kind of like Dracula returning from the dead. It won't bother you any longer if you uninstall it.

To remove XP utilities and components, you normally choose Control Panel → Add or Remove Programs → Add/Remove Windows Components to get to the Windows Components Wizard, shown in Figure 2-12. To uninstall a utility or component, just follow the wizard's instructions.

Ah, but there's a catch. A number of Windows utilities and components—notably Windows Messenger and WordPad—don't show up in the Windows Components Wizard so there's no apparent way to uninstall them. But you can, in fact, remove these components. XP has a Setup Information file that controls what appears in the Windows Components Wizard. If you edit this file, you can force these components to appear in the wizard, and then you can remove them as you would any others.

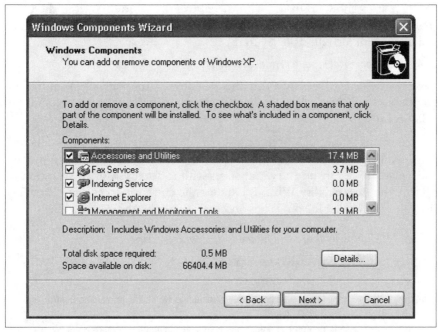

Figure 2-12. The Windows Components Wizard

To start, use Notepad or another text editor to open the Setup Information file, *sysoc.inf*, which is generally found in the *C:\WINDOWS\INF* folder. For safety's sake, make a backup of the file before editing it, so you can revert to it if you need to. You should also set up a system restore point before making the changes. To set up a system restore point, choose Control Panel → Performance and Maintenance → System Restore and follow the instructions.

 C:\WINDOWS\INF is a hidden folder, so if you want to view its contents, you will have to enable hidden folders by going into Windows Explorer and choosing Tools → Folder Options → View → Show Hidden Files and Folders.

When you open the file, look for the line describing the program you want to uninstall. Lines in the file have the format:

```
program=program.dll,OcEntry,program.inf,,numeral
```

Programs that are uninstallable have the word hide (or HIDE) embedded in the string. When this word is included in the string, the program won't show up in the Windows Components Wizard. The Pinball game entry, which doesn't show up in the wizard, looks like this:

```
Pinball=ocgen.dll,OcEntry,pinball.inf,HIDE,7
```

To force it to show up in the wizard, remove the word HIDE from the entry that refers to the component you want to remove. For example, if you want to remove Pinball, edit its entry to this:

```
Pinball=ocgen.dll,OcEntry,pinball.inf,,7
```

Save the *sysoc.inf* file, then run the Windows Components Wizard. The component will now show up in the wizard. Remove it as you would any other component.

Keep in mind that not all of the entries in *sysoc.inf* are as easy to understand as Pinball and WordPad. For example, if you want to remove Windows Messenger, look for the entry that starts with the text msmsgs. If you want to remove the Accessibility Wizard, look for the entry for AccessOpt. Table 2-4 lists the "uninstallable" programs and their entries in the *sysoc.inf* file.

Table 2-4. "Uninstallable" programs and their sysoc.inf entries

Entry	What entry refers to
AccessOpt	Accessibility Wizard
MultiM	Multimedia components, including Media Player, Volume Control, and Sound Recorder
CommApps	Communications components, including Chat, Hyperterminal, and Phone Dialer
AutoUpdate	Windows Automatic Update
TerminalServer	Terminal Server
dtc	Distributed Transaction Coordinator
dom	COM+
WBEM	Windows Management Instrumentation
Pinball	Pinball game
MSWordPad	WordPad
msmsgs	Windows Messenger

You might run into a few gotchas when trying to remove "uninstallable" components. On some systems, you simply won't be able to remove Windows Messenger because Windows Messenger won't show up on the Windows Components Wizard even after you edit the *sysoc.inf* file. And some components, such as Terminal Server, will show up in the wizard if you edit the *sysoc.inf* file, but the wizard still won't let you uninstall them.

Hide Components You Don't Want to Be Uninstalled

You can use this same technique in reverse to hide components you don't want to be uninstalled accidentally. Simply put the word HIDE in the proper place in the entry that you don't want to show up in the Windows Components Wizard. For example, if you want to hide the uninstall entry for the fax utility, edit its entry by changing:

```
Fax=fxsocm.dll,FaxOcmSetupProc,fxsocm.inf,,7
```

to:

```
Fax=fxsocm.dll,FaxOcmSetupProc,fxsocm.inf,HIDE,7
```

HACK #16 Make Your PC Work Like a Mac

Feeling jealous about some of the Mac's nifty features? Envy it no more. Use these tools to make your PC look and work more like a Mac.

Have you ever wished you could turn your PC into a Mac? You're not alone. A lot of Windows users have eyed its slick user interface and handy features with envy. But you no longer need to envy the Mac because in this hack, I'll show you how to make your Windows PC look and work more like a Mac.

Let's start with changing the visual appearance of XP to get a Mac-like experience. It involves three steps. First we'll change the boot screen. Then we'll replace the default logon screen. Finally we'll make Windows and its icons more Mac-like.

Get a Mac-Like Boot Screen

When you start your machine, you'll see a vendor-specific welcome screen, which provides access to BIOS settings. Depending on your setup, after that you might see a menu that lets you boot from one of multiple operating systems [Hack #1]. But if you run only one instance of Windows XP, you will be greeted immediately by the Windows splash screen. To get an almost complete Mac experience, we are going to replace the default Windows logo with something more Panther-like (at the time of this writing, Panther is the name of the latest version of Mac OS X, Version 10.3). To do this, we use BootSkin by Stardock (*http://www.stardock.com/products/bootskin*), which is free for noncommercial use.

After downloading and installing the program we need to obtain a Mac-like boot skin. A particularly nice one is called G5, available at *http://www3. wincustomize.com/skins.asp?library=32&SkinID=740*. Once you have downloaded it, you need to import it into BootSkin. From BootSkin, choose File → Import from file. After you import it, it will show up in BootSkin, as shown in Figure 2-13.

To get an idea how your boot screen will look, you can choose G5 from the list and click the Preview button. Clicking Apply saves your settings and

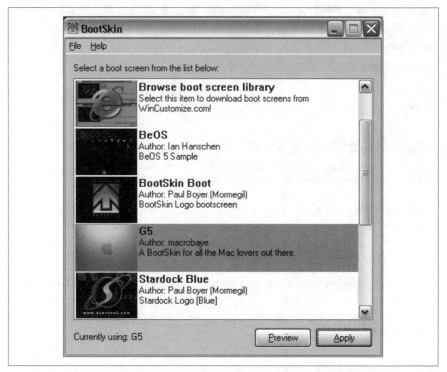

Figure 2-13. The BootSkin main window with the G5 boot skin imported

presents the G5 splash screen upon your next boot. Modifying existing boot
screens is easy. Once you have imported a skin, you can find it in the skins
directory, which defaults to *C:\Program Files\Stardock\WinCustomize\
BootSkin\skins*. Documentation is available through the BootSkin Help
menu.

> For more ways to change your boot screen, see "Change the
> Picture That Appears on the XP Startup Screen" **[Hack #2]**.

Changing the Logon Screen

The next step in transforming your PC into a Mac is to replace the default
Logon screen with a more Panther-like version. Use the free program Logon-
Studio by Stardock (*http://www.stardock.com/products/logonstudio*). Download the main program as well as a logon screen called Mac OS X Panther
(*http://www.wincustomize.com/skins.asp?library=26&SkinID=1476*).

After you install LogonStudio, unzip *Mac_OSX_Panther_LogonXP.logonxp.
zip* into a directory named *Mac_OSX_Panther_LogonXP.logonxp*. Now,

move the newly created folder into the installation directory of LogonStudio, which has the default of *C:\Program Files\WinCustomize\LogonStudio*.

Now, when you run LogonStudio, the Mac OS X Panther screen will appear in the list of available logons, as shown in Figure 2-14.

Figure 2-14. LogonStudio's main screen

Select it and click Apply. To see how the new logon screen looks (as shown in Figure 2-15), you can press Windows-L.

Changing the Appearance of Windows and Menus

The next step is to change Windows' overall visual appearance so that it's more Mac-like. Use WindowBlinds from Stardock (*http://www.stardock. com/products/windowblinds*).

 For an in-depth look at how to use WindowBlinds, see "Give XP a Makeover with WindowBlinds" **[Hack #18]**.

It's shareware; the registration fee is $20, although you can use a free version that has nag screens and some features disabled. Download the program and a visual style called Brushed Panther (*http://www.wincustomize.*

Figure 2-15. The Panther-like logon screen

com/skins.asp?library=1&SkinID=3476). After launching WindowBlinds, choose "Install skin from disk" to load the skin, as shown in Figure 2-16.

Change the desktop wallpaper to one that closely resembles Apple's blue one. If you've installed LogonStudio, go to *C:\Program Files\WinCustomize\ LogonStudio\Mac_OSX_Panther_LogonXP.logonxp* and find *Bitmap_100*. Use that file as your wallpaper by right-clicking the Windows desktop, choosing Properties → Desktop, and clicking the Browse button. Navigate to the file *Bitmap_100*, choose it, click Open, and then OK.

Give Your PC Mac-Like Features

At this point, we have a PC that looks very much like Mac OS X, from its boot screen to its logon screen, and to its entire look and feel. But we've changed only the way Windows *looks*. Now we're going to give it Mac-like features as well.

Konfabulator. A popular Mac tool called Konfabulator displays so-called *widgets*, which are mini-applications that fulfill a particular task, such as displaying the state of your notebook's battery, the current CPU usage, or the weather forecast for your town. Widgets are not applications written in

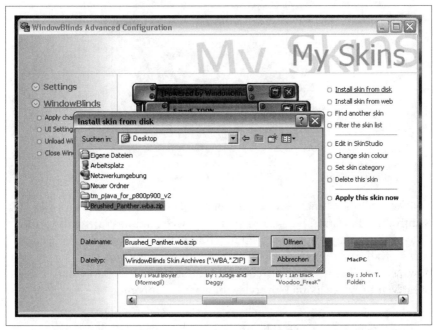

Figure 2-16. Installing the Brushed Panther visual style

ordinary programming languages like C++ or Java; rather, they are written in JavaScript and can therefore be developed easily. So, not surprisingly, there are a huge number of available widgets. In the upcoming Tiger release of Mac OS X (early 2005), Apple is expected to include a new feature called Dashboard, which closely resembles Konfabulator. For a long time Konfabulator has been a Mac OS–only application. Fortunately, though, a new version works for Windows (*http://www.konfabulator.com*). The program is shareware; you can try it for free, but if you decide to keep it, the registration fee is $25.

Konfabulator neatly integrates itself into Windows. You can access its functions by clicking an icon in the notification area to install a new widget. Once you have selected the widget in the file dialog box, you will immediately see it on-screen. Moving the mouse over a widget and pressing the right-mouse button produces a menu which you can use to close a widget or to modify its settings, as shown in Figure 2-17.

Some settings are widget-specific but others apply to all widgets. One nice feature is called Konspose, which hides all widgets that are in Konspose mode until a certain key is pressed. Just like on the Mac, the default key for this is F8.

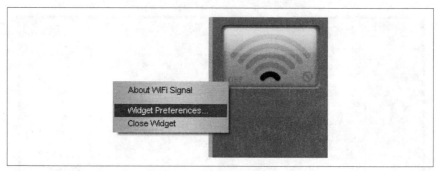

Figure 2-17. The Konfabulator WiFi widget with its menu

Switching between windows and applications. The Panther release of Mac OS X introduced an intuitive way to switch between applications and windows called Exposé. If you press the F9 function key you get neatly arranged previews of all open windows. F10 does a similar thing but shows only windows belonging to the current application. This is particularly useful because it provides a quick overview of what is happening on-screen.

Entbloess 2 by Nipaco Enterprises (*http://www.entbloess.com*) brings Exposé-like features to XP. The program is shareware; it's free to try, but the registration fee is $7.99 if you continue to use it. Figure 2-18 shows the program in action.

The Dock. Another eye-catching feature of Mac OS X is called the Dock. Dock-like functionality has been present in several operating systems, and even the Windows taskbar can be considered some sort of Dock. The basic idea is to have some drop zone where you drag files and programs you need frequently. Accessing them is as simple as clicking the corresponding icon, which remains visible all the time. Additionally, the Dock shows all currently running programs. If you minimize an application window, program output takes place in the Dock.

What makes the Mac OS X version so outstanding is its visual appearance, with lots of nice animations. Several programs for Windows deliver a Mac-like Dock experience. One of them is called ObjectDock (*http://www. stardock.com/products/objectdock*), yet another application by Stardock. The program is free to use. One you have installed the main application, make sure to download the Panther X Future (*http://www.wincustomize.com/skins. asp?library=29&SkinID=2924*) and Striped Mac (*http://www.wincustomize. com/skins.asp?library=29&SkinID=78*) extension packs. You need to unzip these in folders that match the name of the archive without the *.zip* extension.

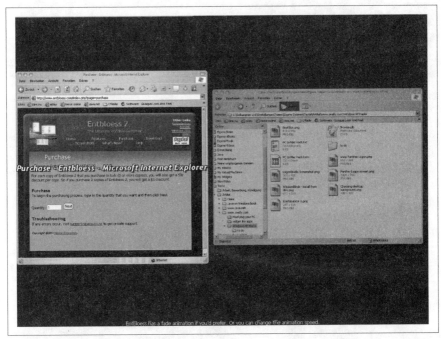

Figure 2-18. Entbloess in Exposé mode

Put the *MacOSX* folder in the installation directory of ObjectDock, which by default is *C:\Program Files\Stardock\ObjectDock*. The Striped Mac folder must reside in the *Backgrounds* directory.

> If you decide to uninstall the various pieces of software used in this hack, make sure that you first reset XP to its original appearance before uninstalling. If you don't, XP might still look Mac-like, even though you've uninstalled the underlying software.

To get a nice Mac-like background, open the configuration dialog of Object-Dock and choose Striped Mac, as shown in Figure 2-19.

To change the icons of applications, launch the desired program, right-click its icon in ObjectDock (Figure 2-20), and open the Properties dialog box.

Now you have a PC with a Mac OS X–like Dock.

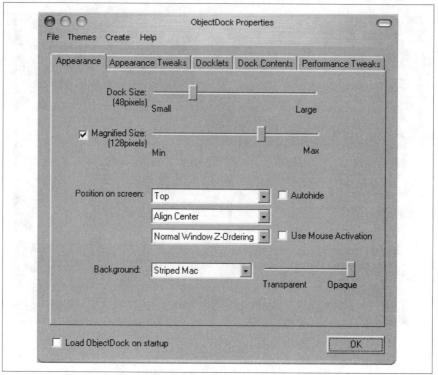

Figure 2-19. The configuration dialog box of ObjectDock

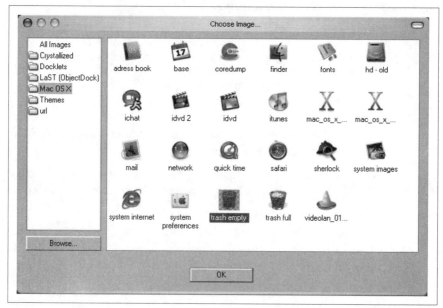

Figure 2-20. Choosing an icon from the Mac OS X package

The Results

That's it; you're done. You've put considerable effort into transforming your PC into a Mac. Figure 2-21 shows what the final results look like.

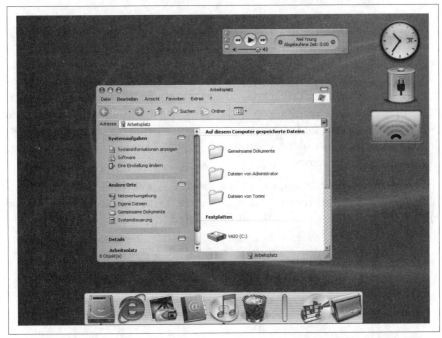

Figure 2-21. My Sony notebook running Windows XP Pro, but looking much like Mac OS X Panther

See Also

- "Customize Multiboot Startup Options" [Hack #1]
- "Change the Picture That Appears on the XP Startup Screen" [Hack #2]
- "Customize the GUI with Tweak UI" [Hack #8]
- "Create Your Own XP Themes and Find Thousands Online" [Hack #17]
- "Give XP a Makeover with WindowBlinds" [Hack #18]

—*Thomas Künneth*

Create Your Own XP Themes and Find
Thousands Online

HACK
#17

Customize the way XP looks and sounds, and dress it up with themes from the best sites on the Internet.

Themes control just about every part of the way XP looks and sounds, including its background wallpaper, colors, icons, cursors, sounds, fonts, and screen saver, as well as the visual style of its windows and buttons. By default, your computer uses the basic Windows XP theme, which some people refer to as *Luna* because it was called that during XP's development. You can apply countless themes to XP, though it ships with only two: the basic Windows XP theme and the Windows Classic theme—a more stolid-looking theme, based on older versions of Windows, which uses rectangular windows and solid colors.

To change between themes, right-click the desktop and choose Properties → Themes. Choose the theme you want to use from the drop-down list, as shown in Figure 2-22. Click OK, and the theme will be applied.

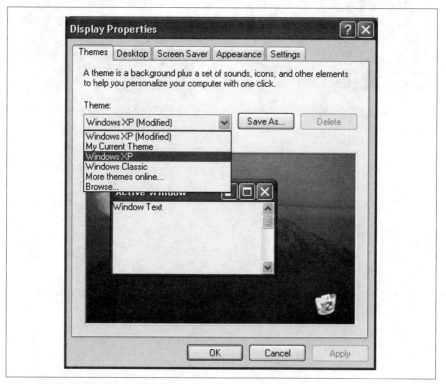

Figure 2-22. Applying a new theme

Note that if you choose "More themes online..." from the drop-down list, you won't actually be able to get more themes online, so choosing that option is a bit of a bait-and-switch. When you choose it, you'll be sent to a web page suggesting that you buy Microsoft Plus! for Windows XP. There's no need to buy it if you're looking to use more themes, though. Instead, you can make your own and get thousands more online from non-Microsoft sites.

Roll Your Own Themes

If you're like me (and most other people), you won't be happy with the basic themes that come with XP. What good is an operating system, after all, if you can't bend it, twist it, and make it your own?

There's no single, central place you can go to make themes in XP. Instead, you'll have to customize each part of XP individually and then roll it all up into a single theme. Once your system is using all the elements of your theme, save the theme with the following instructions.

Start off by right-clicking the desktop, choosing Properties, and then customizing your desktop using the following tabs:

Desktop
> Lets you customize the desktop background and color, as well as which system icons should appear on your desktop.

Screen Saver
> Lets you choose a screen saver and control its functions and features. It also adjusts power controls for your monitor.

Appearance
> Lets you customize the colors, style, and font size for windows, toolbars, and buttons. It also controls effects, such as whether to use fade effects, whether to show shadows under menus, how to smooth the edges of screen fonts, and similar effects.

Settings
> Lets you choose your screen resolution, color quality, and advanced features such as the screen refresh rate.

Next, customize your mouse pointers by typing `main.cpl` in the Start → Run box and pressing Enter. The Mouse Properties dialog box will appear, allowing you to choose a preset pointer scheme or to select individual pointers you want as part of your theme.

To choose system sounds for your theme, type `mmsys.cpl` from the Run box and press Enter. The Sounds and Audio Devices Properties dialog box will appear. Click the Sounds tab and choose a preset sound scheme or select individual sounds for different system and program events.

When you're finished customizing, go back to the Themes tab of the Display Properties dialog box, choose Save As, and save the theme to either *My Documents* or *C:\Windows\Resources\Themes*. Now you can use the theme as you can any other.

Get XP Themes Online

This has been a rather roundabout way of creating your own themes. And face it, few of us (including myself) are visual artists or sound artists. So, even better than rolling your own themes is going online and choosing from thousands you can download for free from many Internet sites. Some people make themes and post them as a hobby, many companies create themes as a way to market products, and movies and TV shows frequently create themes as a way to get free publicity.

Or course, many online themes might violate copyright laws; people create themes using characters, sounds, and people from popular entertainment and then post them online for others to use. The entertainment companies' lawyers will tell you the themes are illegal; on the other hand, others say the themes fall under the fair use provisions of the copyright laws. Who's right? I don't know, and at this point, I'm not even sure the courts do. As to which themes you can download and use, let your conscience be your guide.

A few popular theme sites are *http://www.themeworld.com* and *http://www. topthemes.com*, and the themes section of the download site *http://www. tucows.com*. In addition, many general software download sites include theme sections. Movie studios are good places to find themes, as are web sites created for movies.

> Some theme sites use a lot of pop-up ads. To get rid of them, see "Stop Pop Ups with SP2—and Without It" [Hack #33]. And you should always run anti-spyware software [Hack #34] when downloading and installing themes to make sure you don't get infected.

Depending on the theme you download, you might have to install it differently, so check with the site from which you download, or check within the download itself. As a general rule, though, to use a theme that you download, install it into the *C:\Windows\Resources\Themes* folder. Typically, a file with the extension *.theme* will be installed into that directory, and all the associated art, sound, icon, wallpaper, and cursor files will be installed into a subfolder of *C:\Windows\Resources\Themes*. Once you've installed the new theme, choose it as outlined previously in this hack.

These are a few of my favorite themes. My hard disk is too full of themes to list them all, but I'll give you some of my current and all-time favorites that I found online. I favor several Wallace and Gromit themes from the *http://www.topthemes.com* site. (If you haven't come across them before, Wallace and Gromit are hilariously understated claymation animations from the Oscar-winning animator Nick Park.)

I must say, though, that being an opera fan, my favorite theme of all time is the one I found on *http://www.themeworld.com*, based on Verdi's opera *Don Carlo*. There's nothing like starting up your computer in the morning and being greeted by the sweeping sounds of one of the most dramatic operas of all time. I can almost see the Grand Inquisitor making his way onstage, preparing to burn an idolater or two at the stake. Figure 2-23 shows the wallpaper from the theme, which was chosen to match the mood of the opera. Other elements include the Startup sound taken from the orchestral prelude of the opera's last act, the Shutdown sound from the last seconds of the opera, and many other sounds and icons.

Figure 2-23. The wallpaper from the Don Carlo theme, based on the Verdi opera

See Also

- Style XP, shareware from TFT Soft LLC at *http://www.tgtsoft.com*, manages your themes, lets you automatically rotate them on a schedule, and lets you easily customize them, among other things.

Give XP a Makeover with WindowBlinds

Control freaks, rejoice. With the powerful WindowBlinds utility, you no longer need to suffer with plain, common GUI elements such as the standard toolbars and scrollbars. You can modify and skin Windows to your heart's content.

In the years immediately following World War II, Bill Levitt realized that GIs needed homes. He planned and built a community outside New York City that he called Levittown. There were two models of homes in Levittown and there was very little distinction between them. Levittown was the first "cookie cutter" community and remains the epitome of that term.

The Windows XP user interface is a *cookie cutter* experience. Frequently, users don't bother to replace the Bliss (green field and blue sky) background, and it's even rarer for someone to change the Windows XP standard menu or colors. Fortunately, you don't have to settle for the same desktop as the guy in the next office. One way you can customize your Windows XP experience is to use themes **[Hack #17]**. An even better way is to use a software package called WindowBlinds to *skin* (customize many aspects together) the user interface.

WindowBlinds is created by a company called Stardock and can be downloaded from its web site at *http://www.stardock.com*. It is sold by itself (for $19.95) or as part of a larger package called Object Desktop (for $49.95). A free trial also is available from the Stardock web site.

 If you use a P2P client to download software, be warned that there is a common virus that spreads itself by pretending to be an installer for WindowBlinds. Make sure you've got the real thing. The virus is passed around through P2P apps. The smartest thing to do and the best way to avoid the virus is to pay for this software!

After you install WindowBlinds, you will not notice any immediate changes. Activate the software by selecting Control Panel → Display Properties and then clicking the Appearance tab.

WindowBlinds makes several changes to the Appearance settings, as shown in Figure 2-24. The Add button allows you to search for and add skins to the

"Windows and buttons" pop up and the Delete button removes skins from the pop up. The small icon button to the right of the "Windows and buttons" drop-down box leads you to the SkinStudio web site (discussed a little later in this hack).

Figure 2-24. Displaying settings with WindowBlinds installed

Choose a skin from the "Windows and buttons" drop-down list. If a skin has more than one "subdesign," you can choose those from this dialog box as well. A subdesign of a skin might be the same thing in different colors; a skin might look good in brown, green, and blue, so the author could include all three subdesigns in the package.

WindowBlinds includes a number of skins when the software is installed. One of the more interesting skins is called Colony. The Colony skin shows some of the abilities of WindowBlinds. Choose Colony from the pop up and click the Apply button. Notice the textured areas around the window borders, the customized menu bars, and the smooth buttons on the taskbar. These are things that make WindowBlinds more useful than Windows XP themes and manually changing each aspect of the interface yourself.

Click the button labeled WindowBlinds when you have a skin selected to display the WindowBlinds Advanced Configuration screen (shown in Figure 2-25). From this screen, you can modify almost any part of the user interface that WindowBlinds modifies.

Figure 2-25. WindowBlinds Advanced Configuration screen

By clicking Basic Settings, you can allow the skin to change the standard window buttons, the taskbar and toolbar buttons, as well as menu borders, progress bar controls, and the status bar—or any subset of these options (perhaps you want your own window buttons, for example). You can also allow the skin to change the background and have custom sounds. If, for some reason, you don't want to allow the skin to override any part of the user interface, you can change it from this screen. When you are satisfied with the changes you have made, click "Apply changes" on the left of the screen.

Some skins look nice on the desktop but might not look so hot when viewed in another program. For example, some skins do not handle fonts correctly, which might interfere with word processing. WindowBlinds includes the ability to change its behavior for individual programs by clicking the Per Application item on the left side of the screen. From this screen, you can add programs to the list and modify their behavior individually.

Downloading Skins from the Internet

The most popular programs today allow users to customize Windows. Around this notion, users have created independent web sites to share their ideas and their creations. One such web site is WinCustomize, at *http://www.wincustomize.com.*

The WinCustomize web site is free. If you find a skin you like, you need only click the Download link to download it to your computer. However, if you want to access some of the advanced features, you must register with the web site. There is no cost to register, but there are different levels of access, depending on your level of participation or willingness to pay. There is an advantage to registering with the web site; you are given better search tools, which is useful considering that more than 2,000 custom skins are available for download!

WinCustomize is associated with Stardock, maker of WindowBlinds and Object Desktop, and therefore it has the most skins for its software. If you aren't finding what you want, you might look at some of these other web sites:

- *http://www.lotsofskins.com*
- *http://www.skinbase.org*
- *http://www.deskmod.com*
- *http://www.deviantart.com*

Each site sports different features, but they all provide skins for various programs. The DeviantArt web site is unique in that it is more interested in digital art as an art form instead of simply pushing skins out the door. Some of the artwork on the site might not be suitable for everyone, but if you are interested in the digital medium, this is a good site to investigate.

Creating Your Own WindowBlinds Skins

If you can't find a skin that suits your tastes, you can create your own skin for WindowBlinds. Not only can you create a skin from scratch, but also you can modify existing skins as you wish using SkinStudio. You can download SkinStudio from the Stardock web site for free, but you are reminded that you should register the software.

Creating a skin from scratch is not a simple project. As with most facets of our lives, practice in the art of making skins makes perfect. You can modify many elements of the Windows user interface, and you will need good tools and advanced skills to make your own skin look correct. Instead of jumping into this at the deep end, let's learn from those who have perfected the art, by modifying an existing skin.

One of my favorite WindowBlinds skins is called Liquid2, which emulates the Macintosh OS X user interface (I'm a closet Mac user). One of the aspects of Liquid2 that I do not like is that the Start button has the word "Liquid" on it. I prefer something a little more familiar, like the word "Start."

I used Photoshop to create the images in Figure 2-26. The Start button template consists of five separate subimages in the same file, each subimage being 57×23 pixels. The first subimage is the normal image, the next is when the button is pressed, followed by the disabled image, the focused image, and the default image. Once I am happy with the button, I need to save it somewhere I can access it. Since it is going to be part of the Liquid skin, I save the file as *C:\Program Files\Stardock\Object Desktop\ WindowBlinds\Liquid2\StartButtonNew.bmp*.

Figure 2-26. The replacement Start button with five subimages

Now that we have a suitable image, it's time to use SkinStudio to modify the skin. Bring up the skin browser (File → Edit). The skin browser looks different from the standard file browser. Click the box next to WindowBlinds Skins, locate the skin named Liquid2, and click the Edit button.

Figure 2-27 shows the Edit window for the Liquid2 skin. The box in the top left is for exploring the many different elements in the user interface. The box in the top middle is for previewing the skin. The box in the top right is for modifying individual attributes of the user interface. The box in the lower left gives you help and allows you to zoom in on portions of the screen. In the lower right is another editor for individual attributes.

To replace the Start button, click the box next to desktop in the Explorer box, then click Taskbar, and finally, the Start button, as shown in Figure 2-27. In the lower right, click the pop up next to the words "Adjusted Image." Inside the list should be our new Start button named *startbuttonnew.bmp*. After you choose the new button, click the XP Taskbar button in the Preview area.

Once you are happy with the modified skin, click the Save button on the toolbar (the third button from the left). Saving a skin does not make it active. To make the skin active, click the Apply button on the toolbar (the seventh button from the left). The new Start button should now show up on the taskbar. If you click the button, the darker-colored image should appear as long as the mouse button is pressed.

SkinStudio is a very complicated program with many settings that you can modify. The official documentation is rather limited, but you can find an

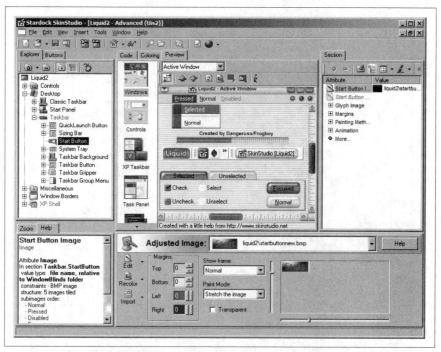

Figure 2-27. The SkinStudio editor

excellent tutorial that covers SkinStudio at *http://www.aleksyandr.com/ tutorial.htm*.

—Eric Cloninger

Make Your Own Cursors and Icons

#19

Don't settle for the icons and cursors that Microsoft built for you. Roll your own with downloadable software.

If you're not happy with the cursors and icons that XP ships with, don't despair. You can easily make your own with Microangelo, from *http://www. microangelo.us*. It's shareware and free to try, but if you continue using it, you're supposed to pay $54.95. You can create animated icons or regular icons—in both the standard 32-pixel and large 48-pixel sizes—and a variety of cursors as well. Use paint-type tools and build your icons and cursors on a grid, as shown in Figure 2-28. A preview is available, so you can see the effects of what you do as you work.

What I find most useful about the program is that you can import existing cursors, icons, or other graphics, edit them, and then save the edited versions. I'm no great artist, so I find editing existing graphics much easier than

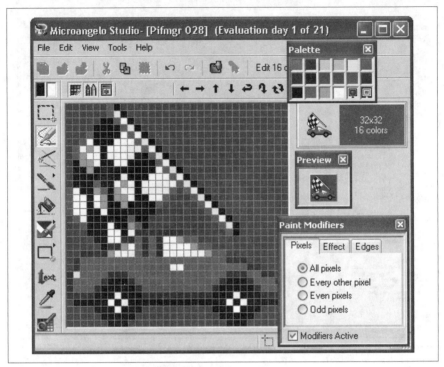

Figure 2-28. Creating an icon with Microangelo

creating ones from scratch. The fine art of pixel placement in tiny icon images can be trickier than expected.

For a big selection of cursors, get CursorXP Free from *http://www. windowblinds.net*, the same company that makes the interface-customizing program WindowBlinds [Hack #18]. CursorXP Free is free, as the name implies. Install it, and a new CursorXP tab is added to the Mouse Properties dialog box, shown in Figure 2-29.

The Mouse Properties dialog box lets you choose from a variety of new cursors that ship with the program. By clicking the Options/Configure button at the bottom of the dialog box you can also customize how each cursor works and looks. (The button toggles between Options and Configure, depending on whether you click the Configure button at the top of the dialog box.) You can also import cursors that you've created with Microangelo or another program.

If you want a more powerful version of the program that includes special effects—the ability to colorize cursors, add trail effects, and more—you can try CursorXP Plus from the same site. The Plus version costs $10 to register.

Figure 2-29. Customizing cursors with CursorXP Free

If you want to create cursors from scratch, your best bet is Axialis AX-Cursors (*http://www.axialis.com*). It's shareware and free to try, but it costs $14 if you decide to keep using it. In addition to providing drawing tools, it lets you convert any existing graphic into a cursor. It also lets you do a screen capture and convert what you've captured to a cursor, and it includes an exceptionally wide range of cursor-editing tools. To give you a sense of its power, I'll create a cursor from scratch and make it larger than normal. If you have a parent with poor eyesight, you can make custom cursors that he can easily see.

Since I'm not artistically inclined, I'm not going to use the program's drawing tools. Instead, I'm going to search the Internet for a graphic that I'll start with, then have AX-Cursors automatically turn it into a cursor. Then I'll resize it to be very large.

A rocket is a good shape for a cursor, so I search for a drawing of one by doing a Google image search by going to *http://www.google.com*, clicking Images, and then searching for the word "rocket." Rather than a photograph, I find a bold-looking drawing of a rocket with a limited number of colors; that will make the best cursor. Figure 2-30 shows the results of the search. I'm going to use the rocket in the lower-right portion of the screen as a starting point.

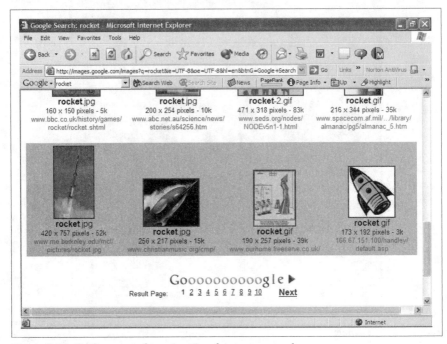

Figure 2-30. Finding a graphic using Google's image search

I save the graphic to my hard disk by clicking it to see the full-size graphic, then right-clicking the large image, choosing Save As, and saving it to my disk. AX-Cursors can import graphics in only a handful of formats: *.bmp*, *.jpg*, *.dib*, and *.rle*. In this case, I have a *.gif* file. So, before importing it, I convert it to a *.jpg* file **[Hack #99]**.

Now I run AX-Cursors. I want to create a large cursor, so first I set the cursor size by choosing Draw → New Image Format. I have the option of saving it as an icon of 32×32, 48×48, 64×64, or 72×72. I choose the largest size and the 256-color option.

Next I choose Draw → Import Bitmap, and choose the rocket image that I've just saved. The program lets me crop the image so that I can import just part of it, but in this instance I want the whole thing, so I don't crop it. I can also set the cursor's transparency. In this instance, because the cursor is going to be for someone with eyesight problems, I choose no transparency. After I'm done, the picture is converted into a cursor that I can edit, as shown in Figure 2-31. Notice that you're given tools to edit the cursor in the middle of the screen. On the right side of the screen, you can see a picture of the original graphic.

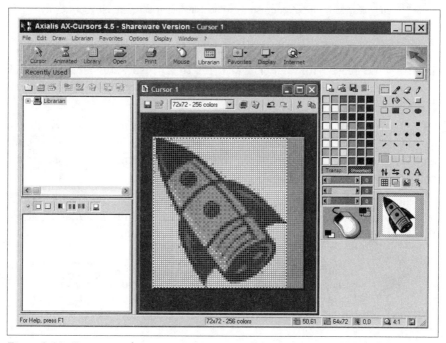

Figure 2-31. Converting the image into a cursor

The cursor looks good to me, so I save it by choosing File → Save. It's now ready to be used. So, I exit the program, choose Control Panel → Printers and Other Hardware → Mouse → Pointers → Browse, and choose the icon I've just created. It's done; you can see it in action in Figure 2-32.

Figure 2-32. The completed cursor in action

See Also

- For a collection of more than 7,000 free icons you can download and use, go to *http://www.iconarchive.com*. Also see *http://www.iconbazaar. com* for a collection of free icons.

- For a collection of free cursors to download and use, go to *http://www. 1freecursors.com*. Note that some cursor and icon sites use a lot of pop-up ads. To get rid of them, see "Stop Pop Ups with SP2—and Without It" [Hack #33].

Instant Linux

#20 Want to know what all the fuss is about when it comes to Linux? Here's an easy way to try it out and use it, without installing software on your PC; it runs straight from a CD.

The Linux operating system inspires intense devotion among its adherents. There's good reason for that: it's fast, it's free, it isn't subject to the same kinds of security woes that bedevil Windows computers, and it can be just plain fun.

Of course, it can be just plain maddening as well. And the thought of installing an entirely new operating system alongside XP, or reformatting your hard disk...let's just say that unless you really know you want to use Linux, you don't want to go there.

But there's a way to get instant Linux: use the free software called Knoppix. It runs straight from a CD, so you don't need to do any installation at all. Just boot your computer from your CD, and *voilà*: instant Linux.

> If you find that you want to know more about Knoppix, and perhaps even install it on a system, you should get a copy of *Knoppix Hacks* by Kyle Rankin (O'Reilly), from which this hack is excerpted.

Download Knoppix

The simplest way to get started with Knoppix is to download a CD image, burn it to a CD, and then boot from the CD. To obtain the latest version of Knoppix, download the CD image from one of Knoppix's mirrors or send away for a CD. If you have an unmetered broadband Internet connection and a CDR/RW drive, simply download the CD image; it's the best way to get Knoppix. A collection of mirrors listed at *http://www.knopper.net/ knoppix-mirrors/index-en.html* provides CD images in ISO form over HTTP, FTP, or rsync. If you use Bittorrent (a peer-to-peer file-sharing application designed for sharing large files), you can use the Knoppix torrent link on this page. When you click a mirror you are taken to a licensing agreement page. Have your lawyer read through the software license (your lawyer reviews all of your software licenses before you accept, right?), click Accept to proceed, and then choose a file from the list that is presented. In addition to the latest version of Knoppix, most mirrors host a few past CD images with their MD5sum (explained in a moment).

When trying to decide which CD to choose, it helps to understand the scheme Knoppix uses for naming CD images. Here is an example ISO filename:

```
KNOPPIX_V3.4-2004-05-17-EN.iso
```

Deciphering the filename isn't tricky and can be quite informative. In the aforementioned example, KNOPPIX is followed by the current version, in this case 3.4. Following the version is a date stamp, which indicates the CD image's release date; in our example, the CD was released on May 17, 2004. These date stamps indicate the incremental version. After the date stamp, there is a language code, in this case EN for English. Knoppix is a German project, and while the default language can be changed with cheat codes at boot time, the Knoppix project releases both German and English CDs to save English-speaking users from having to enter a language cheat code at every boot. English-speaking users want to get images with the EN language code, and German-speaking users want to get images with the DE language code. Everyone else can choose either of the images and use a language cheat code at boot time.

Select the latest version of Knoppix by clicking the filename. The 700MB file can take anywhere from a few hours to a day to download, depending on the speed of your broadband Internet connection and the current load of your mirror.

Once the image is downloaded, you might want to confirm that the full file has been downloaded correctly and is an exact copy of the original file. An *MD5sum* is a checksum created from a large stream of data using the MD5 algorithm and is often used to verify that large files downloaded correctly. Practically speaking, an MD5sum-generating program takes your Knoppix ISO file and creates a fingerprint that only that one file is capable of making. Changing even a single bit affects the MD5sum; therefore, if any errors occur during the download process, the generated sum is different from the one listed on the mirror. If both MD5sums match, the file you have is exactly like the file on the mirror.

A number of utilities are available for creating an MD5sum under Windows. One such tool can be found at *http://www.md5summer.org*. Once you install this program, run it and navigate to the Knoppix ISO you want to verify, and click OK. On your Linux machine you will probably find that the md5sum utility is already installed. You'll need to install it if it is not. Once md5sum is installed, make sure the *.md5* file from the mirror is in the same directory as the image, and then type:

```
greenfly@clover:~$ md5sum -cv KNOPPIX_V3.4-2004-05-17-EN.iso.md5
KNOPPIX_V3.4-2004-05-17-EN.iso OK
greenfly@clover:~$
```

If the MD5sums match, you are dropped back to a prompt; otherwise you receive the following error:

```
greenfly@clover:~$ md5sum -cv KNOPPIX_V3.4-2004-05-17-EN.iso.md5
KNOPPIX_V3.4-2004-05-17-EN.iso FAILED
md5sum: 1 of 1 file(s) failed MD5 check
greenfly@clover:~$
```

You can also generate an MD5sum from the command line by typing:

```
greenfly@clover:~$ md5sum KNOPPIX_V3.4-2004-05-17-EN.iso
7ee0382655abf194aa300a98100cacde  KNOPPIX_V3.4-2004-05-17-EN.iso
```

Compare the MD5sum you generate to the corresponding *.md5* file from the mirror. If both match, you have a complete ISO and are ready to create a CD.

You can burn the Knoppix ISO to a CD using your favorite CD burning software. It is important that you select Burn Image or an equivalent option on your CD burning software. Do not select the option to burn a data CD; you will end up with a CD containing a single ISO file, which will not boot.

> If you don't want to bother with downloading and burning a CD, you can receive a Knoppix CD through the mail from a number of third-party vendors. There is a list of vendors to choose from at *http://www.knopper.net/knoppix-vendors/index-en.html*. These vendors are unaffiliated with the Knoppix project itself and also offer other Linux distributions on CD. When ordering, make sure the version the vendor is offering is the latest version by comparing its release date with the latest release on one of the Knoppix mirrors. You can purchase a Knoppix CD for $5 plus shipping, which is a small price to pay if you want to avoid the hassle of downloading and burning a CD.

Boot Knoppix from a CD

For computers purchased in 2000 and after, booting Knoppix is as simple as putting the CD in the CD-ROM drive and restarting the computer. For some computers, however, booting Knoppix might require changing the boot order in the *BIOS*. The BIOS is the screen that appears when you first boot a machine, and it usually lists the amount of RAM and the hard drives it detects. Older systems that don't support booting from a CD require that you boot from a floppy.

If your computer supports booting from a CD-ROM, but won't boot the Knoppix CD by default, your problem is probably the system boot order setting in the BIOS. To change the boot order and save it, you must enter the BIOS setup, which you can do at boot time by pressing a special key. Some

BIOSes tell you at boot time the key to press to change BIOS settings; the common ones are Esc, F1, F2, F10, and Del.

Once in the BIOS, find the section that changes boot device order. On some BIOSes you change this setting by selecting a tab along the top labeled Boot, while on others the option might be named "Boot device order" or something similar. Once you have found this setting, move the CD-ROM device so that it is listed before any hard drives. If you can't find or change this option, or you need other information specific to your system, refer to the BIOS manual that should have come with your computer or motherboard. Once you have changed the boot device order, save your settings, which should reboot the computer, and after detecting the Knoppix CD, you should be placed at the Knoppix boot prompt.

Boot Knoppix from a Floppy

Some older computers do not support booting directly from a CD-ROM. For these computers, you must first create a boot floppy that enables the system to boot off of the Knoppix CD-ROM. Fortunately, Knoppix has made this process easy. The boot floppy process has changed between Knoppix 3.3 and 3.4. Knoppix 3.4 uses a new boot process that requires two floppy disks. To create these floppies, first boot Knoppix from a machine with a floppy drive that is capable of booting from a CD-ROM. Once the machine has booted, insert a blank floppy into the drive and click K Menu → KNOPPIX → Utilities → Create boot floppies for Knoppix. This script automates creating boot floppies with a progress bar and a prompt that lets you know when to insert the next disk.

Once the floppies have been created, put the first floppy in the floppy drive, leave the CD in its drive, and reboot. The floppy contains a boot loader and kernel image that your system can use to boot far enough along that the CD-ROM can then be loaded.

The Knoppix Boot Prompt

Once you have booted from either a CD or a floppy, you are presented with the Knoppix boot screen, as shown in Figure 2-33.

To boot directly into Knoppix, either press Enter or wait a few seconds, and Knoppix starts the boot process. At this boot prompt, you can enter special Knoppix cheat codes to control the boot process. Press F2 and F3 at this prompt to display some of the cheat codes.

As Knoppix boots, it displays colorful output while it detects your hardware. Once it has detected and set up your hardware, it automatically

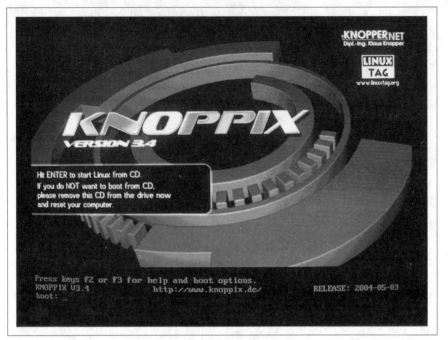

Figure 2-33. The Knoppix boot screen

launches into the desktop environment and finishes by opening a web browser showing Knoppix documentation. At this point, you can launch programs, browse the Web, and play games. When you log out of the desktop environment, Knoppix shuts down and ejects the CD for you. If you use a floppy to boot Knoppix, remember to eject it, or the next time you start your computer, it will try to boot into Knoppix again.

Explore the Desktop

Now you've booted from Knoppix. What's next? It's time to figure out what these windows, icons, and strange panels are for, and then to explore on your own.

After you boot, you should be looking at the default Knoppix desktop, as shown in Figure 2-34.

The desktop. Probably the first thing that grabs your attention is the Konqueror web browser window that opens when the K Desktop Environment (KDE) is started. KDE is one of the two most popular desktop environments for Linux (Gnome being the other). KDE's job is to manage your complete desktop environment. It draws your wallpaper, provides you with

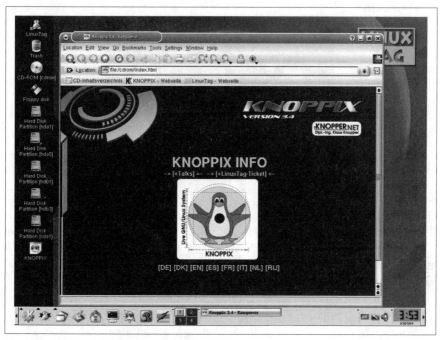

Figure 2-34. The default Knoppix desktop

access to your programs through the menus and icons on the desktop, and manages the windows that appear once you launch an application. Once KDE starts, the first thing you see is the Knoppix help page. This web page contains information and help for Knoppix in many different languages and includes links to sites to purchase Knoppix CDs as well as get additional information. The help is available offline, which makes it very useful even when your network connection isn't working.

The desktop itself contains shortcuts to the hard drives, CD-ROMs, and floppy drives on your system (Figure 2-35). Click any of the drive icons to automatically mount the drive as read-only and open up the mounted file-system in Konqueror. Under KDE, the default is to open a directory or launch a file with a single click, which might take some adjustment if you are used to double-clicking icons on the desktop. As Knoppix defaults to mounting these filesystems as read-only, you can view and open the files you see, but you can't edit, delete, or move any of the files on these filesystems. You can, however, copy the files to your desktop and edit them from there. To make these filesystems writable, right-click the drive icon and select Actions → Change read/write mode. The right-click menu also gives you options to unmount and, if the device is a CD-ROM, to eject the media.

Figure 2-35. Desktop icons

The K Menu. The KDE panel spans the entire bottom portion of your screen. On the left of the panel is the K Menu, represented by the K Gear icon. Click this icon to display the K Menu which contains most of the graphical applications and some of the command-line applications within Knoppix organized into categories like Editors, Games, Internet, and Settings (Figure 2-36). If you are new to KDE, Linux, or Knoppix, you will want to explore each category in this menu and get acquainted with how all the applications on the CD are organized.

At the top of the K Menu is a section reserved for recently used applications. As you run programs from within the K Menu, their icons will show up in this section to provide quick access if you want to run them again. Below this section is the Applications section with submenus for more items. After Utilities, instead of more application submenus, you will find icons that run specific KDE applications.

The K Menu is worth getting familiar with. Browse through the different categories and try out the huge library of programs Knoppix includes. Since everything runs from CD, you can't really harm anything with your experiments. Now that you are familiar with the K Menu, let's move on to the other parts of the Knoppix desktop.

The panel. The panel is the gray bar along the bottom of the screen containing the K Menu and other items. The panel is like an extensible Windows taskbar. It allows for applets to be embedded in it; the default Knoppix panel (Figure 2-34) has several of these. To the immediate right of the K Menu are two other menus. The first has a penguin icon and is a shortcut to the Knoppix submenu. The next menu lists all the applications open across all desktops. To lower all visible applications, click the next icon, which looks a bit like a desk with a pencil on it. Click the icon again to raise all

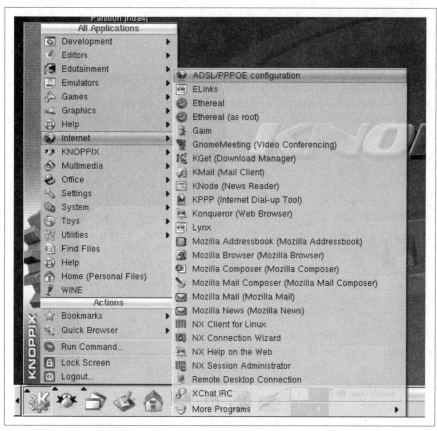

Figure 2-36. The K Menu

application windows. Next to those icons you will find many shortcut icons for applications in the K Menu. These are meant to provide quick access to applications you commonly run. Right-click any of these icons to display a context menu that gives you the option to move or delete the icons. Drag-and-drop icons from the K Menu to add them to the panel.

To the right of the application icons you will see a box with the numbers 1, 2, 3, and 4 in it. This is known as a desktop pager, and it allows you to quickly switch desktops by clicking the appropriate number, or, if you prefer, Ctrl-Tab cycles through your applications, and Ctrl-Shift-Tab cycles through the desktops. By default Knoppix has four virtual desktops that allow you to reduce clutter by grouping open programs onto different desktops. The pager highlights the active desktop so that you don't get lost.

Next to the pager is the task list, which shows all your open applications. Click the program name to raise and lower the program window. Right-click any of the windows in the task list to see a list of actions you can perform on that window such as closing, maximizing, and moving the window to a different desktop.

After the task list are a few useful applets grouped in the system tray. Many applications that run in the background will put an icon here to give you quick access to the program's options. First you see a flag to represent the KDE keyboard tool that lets you change which keyboard locale you are using on the desktop. Next you will see a screen display applet that is new to Knoppix 3.4. Click this applet to change screen resolution and monitor frequency on the fly. The speaker icon represents the KDE mixer applet, which lets you change your volume settings. If Knoppix was unable to configure your sound card, you will notice that the mixer applet has a red slash through it. Finally at the far right of the panel is a clock. Before you can adjust the date and time you will need to create a root password. To do so, open a terminal window and type:

```
knoppix@ttyp0[knoppix]$ sudo passwd
Enter new UNIX password:
Retype new UNIX password:
Passwd: password updated successfully
```

Experiment with the panel. Click and drag icons to move them around on the panel. Drag the applet handles to move them. Right-click icons and applets to see a list of options for the applet including removing it from the panel completely. Drag icons from the desktop or the K Menu and drop them on the panel to add them. To resize the panel, right-click it and choose your size from the Size menu.

See Also

- *Knoppix Hacks* by Kyle Rankin (O'Reilly)

—Kyle Rankin

CHAPTER THREE

Windows Explorer
Hacks 21–31

You use Windows Explorer every day, probably many times a day, without giving it much thought. You open it, view some files, delete others, drag a few around to different folders, and then you're back on your way.

But Explorer can make your life easier in many ways. For example, you can use it to hide files by encrypting them, give yourself more hard-disk space by compressing files, and easily find the files you want by using the indexing service and its query language. And there are ways to hack Explorer to make it much easier to use—for example, by customizing its right-click context menu. In this chapter, I'll show you how to do all that, and more.

HACK #21 Generate Folder and File Listings for Printing or Editing

Longtime PC users and former Mac users alike are often shocked when they realize there's no easy, built-in option to print a list of files in a folder. This hack creates a context-menu right-click option to create such a list, which you can then edit, copy, paste, and—most usefully—print.

How many times have you been browsing through directories in Windows Explorer and wished you could generate a text file or printout listing the files and folders? It seems like such a simple request that it's amazing the option isn't available. You don't believe me? Right-click a folder and see for yourself if there is an option to list or print the structure. There isn't, but there is a workaround that doesn't require any third-party software. Here's how to create a context menu item [Hack #28] that, when clicked, generates a printable (and editable) text-file listing of the selected directory.

To create the entry in the context menu it's necessary to first create a *batch file*. A batch file is a text file that contains a sequence of commands for a computer operating system and uses the *.bat* extension. The format for the *.bat* file is:

```
dir /a /-p /o:gen >filelisting.txt
```

The name of the *.txt* file can be whatever you like. In this example, I've used *filelisting.txt*, but it could just as easily be *filelist*, *listoffiles*, *namedfiles*, or even *Wally* if you enjoy the bizarre in your file-naming schemes. Once you've decided on the filename, create the file in Notepad, as shown in Figure 3-1.

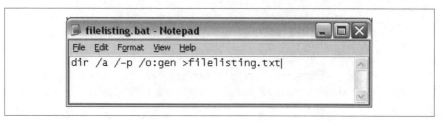

Figure 3-1. Creating a batch file in Notepad

Save the file in your *WINDOWS* folder, as shown in Figure 3-2, making sure to use the *.bat* extension and not the default *.txt* extension. It's important to set "Save as type" to All Files and "Encoding" to ANSI.

Now that we have the *.bat* file created, the next step is to make it functional and easily accessible by integrating it into the context menu that opens when a right-click is executed. Open Windows Explorer and choose Tools → Folder Options → File Types tab → Folder → Advanced → New to open the New Action box shown in Figure 3-3.

In the Action box, type the name that you want to appear in the context menu. Once again, you have wide latitude in choices; something like Create File Listing will probably be most useful, but you can name yours something more confusing if you like. Browse to the location of the *.bat* file you created, and select it in the box labeled "Application used to perform action." Click OK, and you'll see that Create File Listing (or whatever you chose as an action name) has been added as one of the Actions in the Edit File Type window, as shown in Figure 3-4. Do the standard Windows dance of clicking OK again to close all the open windows.

That's it! Congratulations. You've created a new item on the context menu that's ready to go to work. So, now that it's there, what can you do with it?

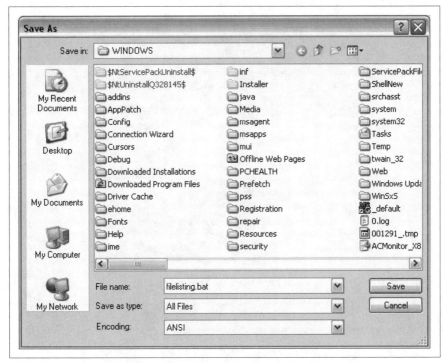

Figure 3-2. Saving filelisting.bat

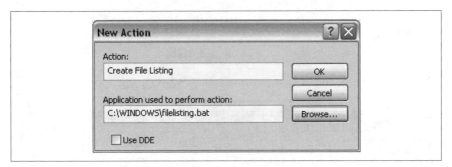

Figure 3-3. Creating a new action for the context menu

Open up Windows Explorer. Navigate to whatever folder you want to use as the basis for the file list, and right-click to open the context menu. Click the Create File Listing item (see Figure 3-5), and the list will be generated and displayed at the bottom of the open Notepad window as *filelisting.txt*. Figure 3-6 shows the file listing generated from the Sample Music folder shown in Figure 3-5. Since it is a text file, it can be fully edited, copied, pasted, printed, and so on, for any purpose.

Figure 3-4. The revised Edit File Type box with your new action

Figure 3-5. Your new context menu action: Create File Listing

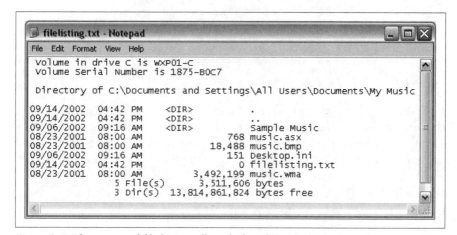

Figure 3-6. The generated file listing, all ready for editing and printing

If for any reason you want to remove the Create File Listing entry from the context menu, you must edit the Registry [Hack #83]. Navigate to HKEY_CLASSES_ROOT\Folder\shell\ Create_File_Listing and delete the Create_File_Listing key in the left pane. Close RegEdit and reboot to complete removal.

Alternative Method for Users of Outlook XP

If you happen to be a user of Outlook XP, another method is available for printing directory listings that requires no system modifications. Using the Outlook bar, you can generate a nicely formatted listing with a few mouse clicks:

1. Open Microsoft Outlook.
2. Choose View → Outlook Bar → Other Shortcuts.
3. The three default selections listed are My Computer, My Documents, and Favorites. Select one and navigate the tree until the directory is displayed in the right pane.
4. When the display matches what you'd like to print, click the printer icon on the Outlook toolbar.

—Jim Foley

HACK #22 Control Windows Explorer with Command-Line Shortcuts

Create customized Explorer views from the command line, and save your favorite views in desktop shortcuts.

I rarely open Windows Explorer in its default view. Instead, I generally want to open it at a specific location, with a specific set of viewing features—for example, with the Folders bar in the left side on or off.

I launch Windows Explorer from the command line, along with a set of switches for controlling how it opens. I also create desktop shortcuts out of these command-line launches so that my favorite views are always only a couple of clicks away.

For example, when I want to open Windows Explorer to the *C:\Power Tools Book\Hacks* subfolder only, with no folders above it, and using the Folders bar, I open the command prompt and issue this command:

```
explorer /e,/root,c:\Power Tools Book\Hacks
```

When I do that, the view pictured in Figure 3-7 appears.

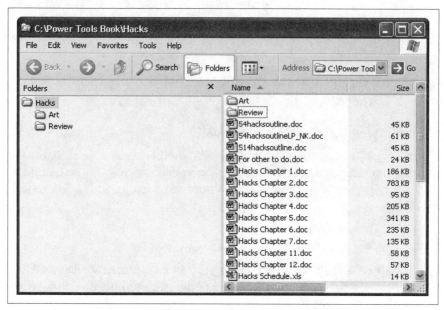

Figure 3-7. Opening Windows Explorer to a specific folder with a specific view

Compare that view with my default view that I get when I launch Windows Explorer the normal way (shown in Figure 3-8).

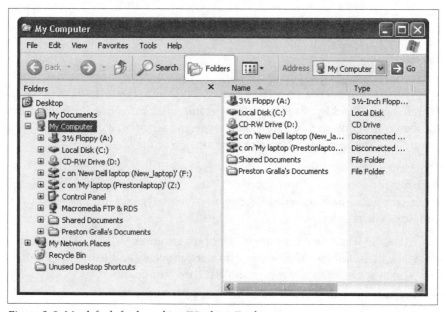

Figure 3-8. My default for launching Windows Explorer

Not only does the Explorer view in Figure 3-7 open to a specific subfolder, but it also shows no folders above it. In contrast, Figure 3-8 shows the entire structure of my hard disk and opens to *C:\.* I use the view in Figure 3-7 when I want to work exclusively on a specific subfolder and want to get to it quickly.

This is just one of the many uses for launching Windows Explorer from the command line with switches; no doubt you'll be able to find other uses for it. You'll be able to use it not only on the command line and with desktop shortcuts, but also if you run scripts and batch programs.

The syntax for running Explorer from the command line with switches is:

```
explorer [/n] [/e] [,root,object] [[,/select],subobject]
```

You don't have to use switches; you can type `explorer` by itself, though doing that launches your default Explorer view.

Here is an explanation of how to use the switches and syntax:

/n

Opens Windows Explorer without displaying the Folders bar, the tree structure of the hard drive. Instead, it launches the view shown in Figure 3-9.

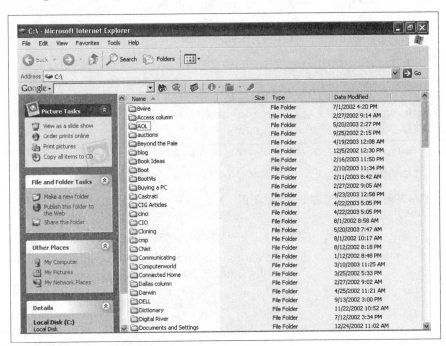

Figure 3-9. The view of Explorer using the /n switch

/e

   Opens Windows Explorer displaying the Folders bar.

/root,*object*

   Opens Windows Explorer to a specific object, such as a folder, without displaying the folders above it, as shown in Figure 3-7. You can also use Globally Unique Identifiers with this switch, as explained later in this hack.

[[/select],*subobject*]

   Opens Windows Explorer to a specific file or folder that is then highlighted or expanded. You can use the subobject switch only without the /select parameter. When you include the /select parameter, the branches are not expanded, the folder is highlighted, and the subobject is highlighted in the right pane.

Create Desktop Shortcuts for Explorer

Typing command-line shortcuts can quickly give you a case of carpal tunnel syndrome, so a better idea is to run them as desktop shortcuts. Right-click the desktop, choose New → Shortcut, and in the location box type the Explorer command-line syntax you want to use. Click Next and give the shortcut a descriptive name—for example, "Hacks folder"—and click OK.

Using Globally Unique Identifiers with Command-Line Switches

You might want to open Explorer to certain system folders—for example, to My Network Places. To do so, run explorer from the command line and follow it with a space, two colons, and the Globally Unique Identifiers (GUIDs) that identify specific system folders, like this:

```
explorer  ::{208D2C60-3AEA-1069-A2D7-08002B30309D}
```

That command opens Windows Explorer to My Network Places.

If you're using switches, similarly put a space and two colons in front of the GUID, like this:

```
explorer /e, ::{208D2C60-3AEA-1069-A2D7-08002B30309D}
```

You can use GUIDs in desktop shortcuts, batch files, and scripts, as well as at the command line. Table 3-1 lists the GUIDs for various system folders.

Table 3-1. GUIDs for system folders

Folder name	GUID
My Computer	{20D04FE0-3AEA-1069-A2D8-08002B30309D}
My Network Places	{208D2C60-3AEA-1069-A2D7-08002B30309D}
Network Connections	{7007ACC7-3202-11D1-AAD2-00805FC1270E}
Printers and Faxes	{2227A280-3AEA-1069-A2DE-08002B30309D}
Recycle Bin	{645FF040-5081-101B-9F08-00AA002F954E}
Scheduled Tasks	{D6277990-4C6A-11CF-8D87-00AA0060F5BF}

HACK #23 Empower Windows Explorer with PowerDesk Pro

Supplanted by this most powerful utility, Windows Explorer will no longer draw curses or contribute to increased Macintosh sales.

I'm guessing that you have a Leatherman multitool. No hacker worth his weight in solder would leave home without it. In fact, I'll go further and guess that you have at least two. You probably have a large one that you keep in your glove box and a small one that you carry with you at all times, even to weddings (just in case). If I'm correct—or if you're wondering where to buy such a useful tool—you will love PowerDesk Pro.

PowerDesk Pro is the multitool of utilities. This beast is no mere Swiss Army Knife. There's no unnecessary toothpick, leather punch, or nail file here; it's a pair of vise grips with four screwdrivers, a strong blade, wire cutters, pliers, an Allen wrench, a corkscrew, and a bottle opener. It's the software those guys on *Junkyard Wars* would use if they put down their cutting torches and picked up a computer.

OK, maybe I'm being melodramatic, but PowerDesk Pro really is a useful utility for your computer. PowerDesk Pro combines much of the functionality of Windows Explorer, the old Windows File Manager, WinZip, and a host of other programs. If you find yourself with more than one program open for manipulating files, you probably need PowerDesk Pro. While many of the features of PowerDesk Pro are available in Windows XP, PowerDesk Pro puts them all in one convenient location. PowerDesk Pro also runs on older versions of Windows, which might not have the advanced file-handling features Windows XP has.

PowerDesk Pro is available from VCOM at *http://www.v-com.com/product/ PowerDesk_Pro_Home.html*. PowerDesk Pro sells on the VCOM web site for $49.95. You can also download an evaluation version that has fewer features.

When you install PowerDesk Pro on your computer, the installer will ask you if you want to associate zip and other archive files with PowerDesk Pro. If you already use a zip file manager, such as WinZip, you might not want to allow PowerDesk Pro to handle these types by default. After installing PowerDesk Pro, you should not need to restart your computer.

While PowerDesk Pro is a separate application, it is integrated into Windows Explorer, so you have access to many of its features even when you aren't running it. In Windows Explorer, if you right-click with the mouse you will see a submenu called PowerDesk, where you have access to many of PowerDesk Pro's functions.

When you start PowerDesk Pro you will be faced with a window that looks similar to the one shown in Figure 3-10. As you click around PowerDesk Pro, most of the things you see should look familiar. Those that aren't so familiar are grouped well, so they are easy to find and understand.

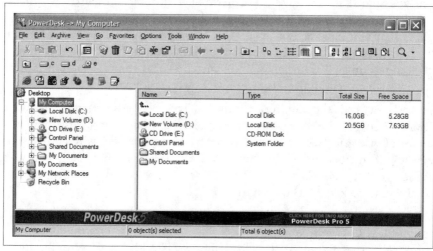

Figure 3-10. The PowerDesk Pro main window

Each toolbar that shows up in PowerDesk Pro is configurable. Use the Options → Customize Toolbar menu item to modify the toolbars as you wish. The bottom toolbar in Figure 3-10 is called the Launchbar and is similar to the Quick Launch area of the Windows XP taskbar. You add programs by dragging icons onto the Launchbar and dropping them.

When you restart PowerDesk Pro, you are placed back at the location you were when you left. I find this to be such a simple, yet useful, feature. If you create a shortcut to PowerDesk Pro, you can force it to open at a specific location by putting the name of the directory after the program name in the Target field of the shortcut properties.

PowerDesk Pro has so many features that we could spend an entire chapter of this book describing them, and even then we'd miss some things. So, I'm going to give a brief summary of the coolest features and leave the rest as an exercise for the reader:

- Most Windows Explorer features are available from the File and Tools menus. You can open, delete, and rename files. You can map network drives, format disks, and empty the trash.

- PowerDesk Pro provides Move To and Copy To icons on the main toolbar, context menu, and File menu for moving and copying files to a specific location. You can re-create this functionality [Hack #26] in Windows Explorer without using PowerDesk Pro.

- The File Finder feature provides many options for finding files on your computer. You can have PowerDesk Pro search for Microsoft Word documents beginning with the word *Hack*, modified in the last three days, and containing the word *wireless*.

- PowerDesk Pro has the ability to find and rename a group of files according to parameters that you define. For example, let's say you have a bunch of digital photographs from your trip to Belize. The digital camera doesn't know you went to Belize, and neither does Windows XP. Using PowerDesk Pro, select the files you want to rename and choose File → Rename. PowerDesk Pro shows a list of the files to be renamed and gives you a place to rename the files to something like *Belize 2003 Vacation.JPG*. The first file will be named *Belize 2003 Vacation.JPG*, the second file will be named *Belize 2003 Vacation (1).JPG*, and so on. PowerDesk Pro also has a more powerful group-rename feature that uses wildcards and pattern matching to find files and choose their new names.

- PowerDesk Pro provides a built-in FTP client for transferring files from a remote file server (much like WinFTP). The connection to the remote server appears as if it were just another folder on your computer. PowerDesk Pro FTP can even resume interrupted downloads.

- You can convert image files between the numerous available formats with File → Convert Picture Format.

- Security-conscious users will appreciate the Destroy File feature. This feature not only deletes a file from the filesystem, but also wipes the disk drive where the file existed. Needless to say, using this feature will also prevent *you* from recovering the file, so don't test it out on your favorite photo from the Belize vacation.

- If you are truly security-conscious, do not use the Encrypt/Decrypt feature of PowerDesk Pro. Details on the algorithm they use are not available. In the security world, it's common practice to describe how your cryptography works and rely on the strength of the key to protect the data. PowerDesk does allow you to choose 56-bit Data Encryption Standard (DES) encryption for your data, but 56-bit encryption is the bare minimum these days. Do you want to trust your financial data to the bare minimum? I didn't think so.

- PowerDesk Pro manages zip file archives as well as files that are stored using the older UUENCODE format.

- For copying files between two locations, use the Dual Pane view. This view displays two independent file browsers side by side, so you can easily copy files from one to the other without worrying about other windows getting in your way.

- If you find yourself managing the same set of files on two different disks, the Compare Folders feature is a great timesaver. Select the folder you want to compare, and let PowerDesk Pro find the other folder and compare the contents.

- I run a network at home, and some of our computers do not run Windows XP. PowerDesk Pro provides a level playing field between the different versions of Windows so that I can always be assured that I have the tools I need on every computer I use.

There is so much more to PowerDesk Pro than what I've outlined here. If the things you've read here interest you, download the evaluation version and try it for yourself.

—*Eric Cloninger*

Better File Rename
#24   Rename multiple files quickly and easily.

I hate to admit it, but sometimes I'm impatient. Why should I waste my time doing the same thing over and over again? If you've ever had to rename more than one file at a time, you know how foolish it is to have to click, pause, click again, type the new name, hit Enter, and then *repeat for each file*, just to rename them—especially if there's some sort of pattern to what you're doing. Unix expatriates will find this procedure especially annoying after using powerful wildcards and other Unix pattern-matching syntax. Better File Rename (well worth the $19.95 shareware registration fee from *http://www.publicspace.net/windows/BetterFileRename/*) does all you might imagine a file-renaming utility would do, and more. It's conveniently accessed via the context menu, a right-click away from any group of selected files.

Figure 3-11 displays some of the options for renaming files based on pattern or placement in the filename (beginning or end of filename). For each pattern or placement option, you get a powerful set of variables and settings to choose from so that you can rename files in all sorts of ways, quickly and easily.

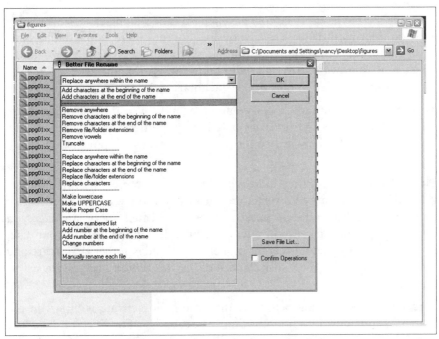

Figure 3-11. Better File Rename options

One of the ways to use this utility is to append a prefix to a list of files that belong to the same project but begin with entirely different filenames (such as a list of figures for a book). It's also especially useful for digital-camera owners who don't like the numerical or other automatically generated names for their files. While you might remember that a bunch of pictures with random numbers for filenames are pictures of your daughter, appending her name to each filename in one step with Better File Rename is easier than trying to remember such details or doing the painfully slow click-and-rename dance for each one. You can also change a whole list of filenames from upper- to lowercase, and vice versa. The pattern-replacement and automatic successive-numbering options are especially useful. Impatient control freaks, rejoice!

—Nancy Kotary

Find Files Faster by Mastering the Indexing Service's Query Language

Got a hard disk filled with many files, and no easy way to find what you want quickly? Use the Indexing Service and its query language to get what you want—fast.

Packrats like me (and my editor) have a hard time finding exactly what they want on their hard disks. I have thousands of files there, some dating back close to 10 years, which I dutifully copy to a new system every time I upgrade my hardware. After all, who knows when I might need to find the list of books I planned to take out of the library in 1996?

XP's Search Companion is too slow and the kinds of searches it can perform are fairly limited. It can't find files based on properties such as when the file was last printed or the word count of a file, or using a sophisticated search language.

The Indexing Service, first used with Microsoft Internet Information Services (IIS), is a far more powerful tool. It can perform searches hundreds of times faster and includes an exceedingly sophisticated query language you can use for performing searches. It works by indexing the files on your disk, and then, when you do a search, it queries that index rather than searching through your entire hard disk. The indexes the service creates are called *catalogs*.

By default, the Indexing Service is turned off. To activate it, first run the Search Companion by choosing Start → Search[→ For Files or Folders]. From the Search Companion, choose Change Preferences → With Indexing Service. If the With Indexing Service option isn't available, and instead you see Without Indexing Service, it means the Indexing Service is already turned on.

When you activate the Indexing Service, it won't be available immediately. First it has to build an index, which can take a substantial amount of time, depending on the number of files on your hard disk and your processor speed. It's best to start the Indexing Service and leave your computer on overnight so that it can complete indexing.

To turn off the Indexing Service from the Search Companion, choose Change Preferences → Without Indexing Service. When you do that, you'll use the normal Search Companion. The index will remain intact; when you do a search, you just won't search through it. You can always turn the index back on when you want.

Using the Indexing Service's Query Language

The Indexing Service's query language is a sophisticated language, letting you search on file properties—such as the author of documents or the number of bytes in a document—using Boolean operators and other search criteria.

The language uses tags to define search criteria. For example, to search for the phrase "That dog won't hunt," the query would be:

```
{phrase} That dog won't hunt {/phrase}
```

You can search for text in the query language using either phrase or freetext. A phrase search searches for the exact words in the exact order, like this:

```
{phrase} old dog barks backwards {/phrase}
```

The search results will include only files whose text includes that exact phrase.

A freetext expression search looks for any words in the phrase and returns files that have any one of the words in the phrase. It works like the Boolean OR operator. So, the query:

```
{freetext} old dog barks backwards {/freetext}
```

returns many more searches than the phrase query, since it returns results that contain any of the words in the phrase.

Searching Using Properties

The Indexing Service's query language's power is contained in the way it can search not just for text, but also for document properties. The syntax for searching using properties in a query is:

```
{prop name=property name} query {/prop}
```

where *property name* is the name of the property, such as those listed in Table 3-2, and *query* is the text you're searching for. For example, to search for all documents last edited by Preston Gralla, you would enter:

```
{prop name=DocLastAuthor} Preston Gralla {/prop}
```

Queries can use *and ? wildcard characters, as well as Unix-style regular expression queries (for more on regular expressions, see *Mastering Regular Expressions* from O'Reilly). To use these wildcards, you must use the {regex} tag, like this:

```
{prop name=filename} {regex} *.xl? {/regex} {/prop}
```

The Indexing Service indexes not just the text of each document, but also all the summary information associated with each document. (To see summary information for any document, right-click the document and choose

Properties → Summary.) In addition to searching for properties in the summary, you can also search for the properties found in Table 3-2, which lists the most important properties you can use to search.

Table 3-2. Important properties for searching via the Indexing Service

Property	Description
Access	The last time the document was accessed.
All	All available properties. Works with text queries, but not numeric queries.
AllocSize	The total disk space allocated to the document.
Contents	The contents of the document.
Created	The time the document was created.
Directory	The full directory path in which the document is contained.
DocAppName	The name of the application in which the document was created.
DocAuthor	The author of the document.
DocByteCount	The number of bytes in the document.
DocCategory	The type of document.
DocCharCount	The number of characters in the document.
DocComments	Comments made about the document.
DocCompany	The name of the company for which the document was written.
DocCreatedTime	The time spent editing the document.
DocHiddenCount	The number of hidden slides in a PowerPoint document.
DocKeyWords	The keywords in the document.
DocLastAuthor	The name of the person who last edited the document.
DocLastPrinted	The time the document was most recently printed.
DocLineCount	The number of lines contained in the document.
DocLastSavedTm	The time the document was last saved.
DocManager	The name of the manager of the document's author.
DocNoteCount	The number of pages with notes in a PowerPoint document.
DocPageCount	The number of pages in the document.
DocParaCount	The number of paragraphs in the document.
DocPartTitles	The names of document parts, such as spreadsheet names in an Excel document or slide titles in a PowerPoint slide show.
DocRevNumber	The current version number of the document.
DocSlideCount	The number of slides in a PowerPoint document.
DocTemplate	The name of the document's template.
DocTitle	The title of the document.
DocWordCount	The number of words in the document.
FileName	The filename of the document.
Path	The path to the document, including the document filename.

Table 3-2. Important properties for searching via the Indexing Service (continued)

Property	Description
ShortFileName	The 8.3-format name of the document.
Size	The size of the document, in bytes.
Write	The date and time the document was last modified.

Searching Using Operators and Expressions

The query language also lets you use a variety of operators and expressions for both text and numbers:

EQUALS *and* CONTAINS *operators*

When you're creating a query using text, you can use the EQUALS and CONTAINS operators to narrow your search. Use the EQUALS operator when you want the exact words matched in the exact order, like this:

```
{prop name=DocTitle} EQUALS First Draft of Final Novel {/prop}
```

This query finds all documents with the title "First Draft of Final Novel." The query won't find a document with the title "Final Draft of First Novel" or "First Draft of Novel." The EQUALS operator works like the phrase expression.

Use the CONTAINS operator when you want to find any of the words in the document, in the same way you would use the freetext expression.

Relational operators

Use the following relational operators when you're searching using numbers:

=   Equal to

!=   Not equal to

<   Less than

<= Less than or equal to

>   Greater than

>= Greater than or equal to

Date and time expressions

You can use the following formats when searching using dates and times:

```
yyyy/mm/dd hh:mm:ss
yyyy-mmmm-dd hh:mm:ss
```

You can also use date and time expressions in combination with relational operators—for example, to look for files that were created within the last two days:

```
{prop name=Created}  >-2d  {/prop}
```

Table 3-3 lists the date and time abbreviations you can use.

Table 3-3. Date and time expressions that work with relational operators

Abbreviation	Meaning	Abbreviation	Meaning
Y	Year	D	Day
Q	Quarter	H	Hour
M	Month	N	Minute
W	Week	S	Second

Boolean operators

The query language also uses the Boolean operators detailed in Table 3-4.

Table 3-4. Boolean operators used by the Indexing Service's query language

Boolean operator	Long form	Short form
AND	&	AND
OR	|	OR
Unary NOT	!	NOT
Binary NOT	&!	AND NOT

Use the unary NOT when you're searching using numbers rather than text. For example, to search for all documents that do not have seven PowerPoint slides, use the query:

```
{prop name=DocSlideCount} NOT = 7 {/prop}
```

Use the binary NOT to narrow a search, by combining two properties in a query. For example, to search for all documents with an author of "Preston Gralla" that are not titled "Chapter 10," use this query (on one line):

```
{prop name=DocAuthor} Preston Gralla  {/prop} NOT
{prop name=DocTitle} Chapter 10  {/prop}
```

Alternative verb forms

You can use the double-asterisk wildcard (**) to search for alternative forms of verbs in a document. For example, the query:

```
{prop name=Contents} run** {/prop}
```

returns all documents with the word "ran" or the word "run."

Ranking the Order of Search Results

If you're doing a search likely to return many results, you'll want the most-relevant searches to appear at the top of the results, and the least relevant to appear at the bottom. You can determine the relative importance of each term in your search and have the results weighted by that importance by using the weight tag. Note that it does not get a closing tag:

```
{weight value=n} query
```

The value parameter ranges between 0.000 and 1.000.

If you are searching for the three terms "fire," "ice," and "slush," and you want to weight "fire" most heavily, "ice" second-most heavily, and "slush" least heavily, you can use this syntax (on a single line) in your query:

```
{weight value=1.000}fire AND {weight value=.500}ice AND {weight value=.
250}slush
```

Editing the Indexing Service's "Noise" Filter

You can force the Indexing Service to ignore more words when you search, or you can have it ignore fewer words, simply by editing a text file. In a text file called *noise.eng*, usually found in *C:\Windows\System32*, you can find the list of words the Indexing Service ignores. (The extension *.eng* is for English. You can find noise filters from other languages as well—for example, *noise.deu* for German, *noise.fra* for French, and so on.)

The *noise.eng* file contains common articles, prepositions, pronouns, conjunctions, various forms of common verbs, and similar words. Open it in Notepad or another text editor, add words you want it to ignore, and delete words you don't want it to ignore. Then save the file, and the Indexing Service will follow your new rules.

HACK
#26

Force Windows Explorer into True Usefulness
Here's a grab bag of ways to make better use of Explorer.

There are plenty of small ways you can hack Explorer to make your computing life more productive—for example, by hacking the right-click shortcut menu. Try out these hacks and see.

Add Shortcut Menu Items to Specific File Types

When you right-click a file in Explorer, you get a shortcut menu that includes a list of programs with which you can open the file. But the programs you want to open those files might not always be on the shortcut menu. It's easy to add new programs to that list. Let's say you want to add a shortcut menu item that allows *.gif* files to be opened with the freeware graphics viewer IrfanView [Hack #99]. From Windows Explorer, choose Tools → Folder Options → File Types. In the Registered File Types list, select the file type for which you want to add a new shortcut menu item. In our example, we'll choose a

GIF file. After this hack, any time you click a file of this type, you'll get a new choice to open the file with.

Once you've chosen your file type, choose Advanced → New. You'll see the New Action dialog box shown in Figure 3-12.

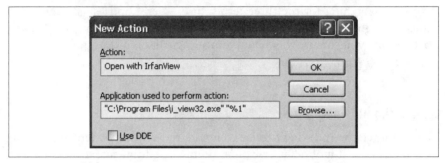

Figure 3-12. Adding a new program to the shortcut menu

In the New Action box, type the text you want to appear on the shortcut menu—for example, Open with IrfanView. In the "Application used to perform action" box, enter the executable program you want to open the file with, including the full path. Surround it by quotation marks. Then leave a space and type %1. The %1 is a placeholder; it will be used as a substitute for the name of the file on which you right-click. In our instance, the entire string looks like this:

```
"C:\Program Files\i_view32.exe" "%1"
```

Click OK. The change will take place immediately, and the new command will appear on the shortcut menu for the specified file type.

Add Global Shortcut Menu Items to All File Types

The previous section of this hack showed how to add shortcut menu items on a file-type-by-file-type basis. In other words, it will be available only on the shortcut menu for the one specific file type you specify. But you can also add that shortcut menu item to every type of file by using a Registry hack. This is useful when you have a program that can open a wide variety of file types, and you don't want to have to add a shortcut menu item for every one of those file types. I use the IrfanView graphics viewer for many different types of graphics, so I want it to show up on all those types. Although it will also show up on file types I won't use it with, such as Word files, it's still worth putting it on the menu globally because of all the time I save by not having to add shortcut menu items over and over again for each file type.

Run the Registry Editor [Hack #83] and go to HKEY_CLASSES_ROOT*. Create a new subkey called Shell if it doesn't yet exist. The Shell subkey can control parts of the user interface. Create a new subkey under Shell and name it what your new command will be—for example, OpenWithIrfanView. For the default value of the new subkey, type in the text you want to appear on the shortcut menu—for example, Open with IrfanView. Create a new subkey named Command under the subkey you just created. This subkey will contain the command string you want to be executed to open the file. For the default value of the Command subkey, enter the command string you want to be executed when the shortcut menu item is chosen—for example:

```
"C:\Program Files\i_view32.exe" "%1"
```

Exit the Registry. The new shortcut menu item should be available immediately, though you might need to reboot for it to take effect.

Edit File Association Actions

You can use Windows Explorer to change how XP handles file types; for example, you can choose the default action when the file type is double-clicked, choose the application associated with the file type, choose the icon for the file type, and choose whether the extension should be displayed or hidden in Windows Explorer. To perform most of these actions, choose Tools → Folder Options → File Types, choose the file type for which you want to customize an action, and then click Advanced. You'll see the screen shown in Figure 3-13.

From the Edit File Type dialog box, you can change the icon, edit the action to be taken on the file, and choose whether to display the file type in Windows Explorer. The dialog box is fairly self-explanatory. For example, click Change Icon to change the icon; to edit any action, highlight it and click Edit. If you want to change the application associated with the file, choose Tools → Folder Options → File Types, choose the file type whose association you want to change, click Change, and then choose the application you want to be associated with the file type in the same way as shown in Figure 3-12.

Remove Context Menu Items from Explorer

Explorer's menus can get messy at times. But you can use a Registry hack to clean it up a bit by removing two items from the Tools menu: Map Network Drive and Disconnect Network Drive. Run the Registry Editor and go to:

```
HKEY_CURRENT_USER\Software\Microsoft\Windows\CurrentVersion\Policies\
Explorer
```

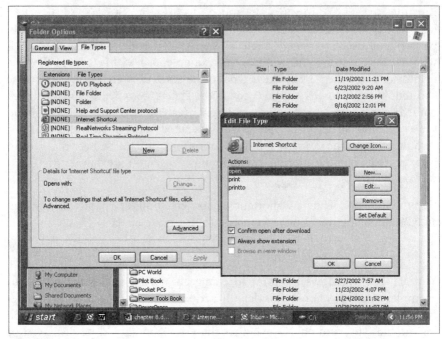

Figure 3-13. Editing file associations and their actions

Create the `DWORD` entry `NoNetConnectDisconnect`. Give it a value of 1. Exit the Registry. You might have to reboot for the setting to take effect and the items to disappear from the menu. To place the items back on the Explorer menu, edit the value to 0, or delete the entry.

Organize the All Programs Menu with Explorer

If you're using the default Windows XP Start Menu view and you're not happy with the way your All Programs menu is organized, you can use Windows Explorer to modify it. The All Programs menu is nothing more than a collection of shortcuts found in two folders: the *C:\Documents and Settings\ <Your Account>\Start Menu* folder (where <Your Account> is your account name), and the *C:\Documents and Settings\All Users\Start Menu* folder. Items you want to appear at the very top of the All Programs menu should be put in one of the *\Start Menu* folders (depending upon whether you want the item to appear on only *your* All Programs menu, or on the All Programs menu of all users). Items you want to appear on the lower part of the All Programs menu should be put into the *\Start Menu\Programs* folder, again, depending on whether you want the item to appear on only *your* All Programs menu, or on the All Programs menu of all users.

Customize Folder Icons and Balloon Text

Make it easier to recognize specific folders and remember their contents by
giving them their own pictures and identifying text.

All folders are not created equal; some are more important than others.
Folders I use for writing books and articles or for storing digital music, for
example, are more vital to me than folders that hold tax records from eight
years ago.

So, I like to give myself visual clues when browsing my computer about
what each folder holds and how important it is to me. I have so many folders on my hard disk that I can't always immediately recall the purposes of
some of them, so for some I also create balloon text that describes the purpose of the folder when I hover my mouse cursor over the folder.

To force a folder to display a specific icon and to have it display balloon text
when you hover your mouse cursor over it, create a *Desktop.ini* file in that
folder. That file contains instructions on which icon to use and balloon text
to display.

> If you don't want to display customized balloon text, you
> can display an icon for any folder without having to create a
> *Desktop.ini* file yourself. Right-click the folder you want to
> customize, choose Properties → Customize → Change icon,
> and browse to the icon you want to use. When you do that,
> you'll automatically create a *Desktop.ini* file that will display
> the proper icon.

Before creating the file, choose the icon you want to use for the folder. Icons
end in a *.ico* extension. You can also use *.bmp* bitmap files as icons. Make
sure to note the name of the icon or bitmap, including its full path. If you
want, create your own icon [Hack #19].

Not all icons are in *.ico* files, however. Many are part of entire icon libraries
in *.dll* files. For example, you'll find hundreds of icons in the *shell32.dll* file
found in the *C:\WINDOWS\System32* folder. Each icon in a *.dll* file is
assigned an index number, starting with 0. To use icons in *.dll* files, you'll
need to know the index number for the specific icon. You won't be able to
find out the index number by examining the file manually; instead, you'll
need third-party software. Resource Tuner (*http://www.heaventools.com*) lets
you examine the resources of any file and, among other things, will let you
browse through the file's icons and show you their index numbers. It's
shareware and free to try, but it costs $34.95 if you keep using it.

Figure 3-14 shows Resource Tuner looking inside *Shell32.dll* and listing the index number for an icon.

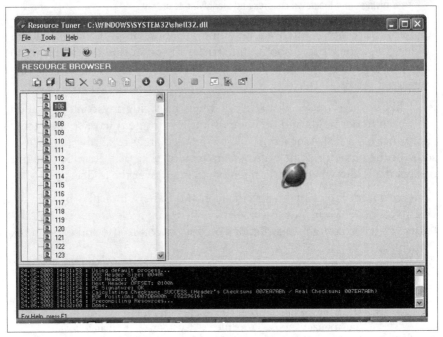

Figure 3-14. Using Resource Tuner to find the index number of an icon

For my *Music* folder, I'm going to use a *.bmp* file of cover art of the mezzo-soprano Cecilia Bartoli.

Now it's time to create the *Desktop.ini* file. Using a text editor like Notepad, create it in the folder you want to customize. I'm going to customize my *C:\Music* folder, so that's where I create it. Here's what my file looks like:

```
[.ShellClassInfo]
IconFile=C:\MusicPics\Bartoli.bmp
IconIndex=0
InfoTip=The Best of Puccini, Donizetti, Verdi, and the Rest
```

The heading, [.ShellClassInfo], is required, so make sure to put that at the top of the file. The IconFile= entry should point to the file you want to use as an icon—and again, it can be a *.ico* file, a *.bmp* file, or an icon found in an icon collection, such as in a *.dll* file. Make sure to include the file's full path. The IconIndex= entry should point to the index number of the icon if the file is in an icon collection. If it's not in an icon collection, use the number 0. The InfoTip= entry should point to the text you want displayed as balloon text.

After you create the *Desktop.ini* file, you need to define the folder you want to customize as a system folder for it to be able to display the icon and balloon text. At the command prompt, issue the command `attrib +s` *foldername*, where *foldername* is the name of the folder you're customizing.

Now you're done; the icon and balloon text should display. Figure 3-15 shows what mine looks like.

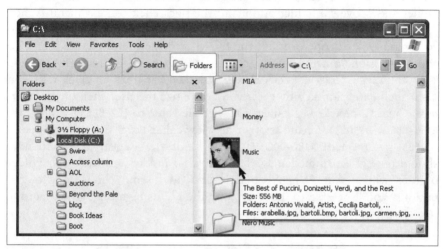

Figure 3-15. My Music folder with an icon and balloon text

A Power User's Hidden Weapon: Improve the Context Menu

The context menu is an often-underused tool. But with these four additions and edits to the menu, it'll turn into a powerhouse that you'll use every day.

Windows Explorer's right-click context menu is one of the most basic of all XP tools; it provides many shortcuts for whenever you want to take action on a file or a folder. But the right-click menu is missing several basic options, such as choosing a specific folder to which you want to move or copy the file you've highlighted, instead of just cutting or copying the file. And when you install new applications, they have a nasty habit of adding their own options that you'll rarely use in the right-click menu.

The end result: a right-click context menu cluttered with options and lacking several basic useful ones. But you can extend the power of the menu with these four hacks.

Add Copy To Folder and Move To Folder Context Menu Options

I spend a lot of time copying and moving files between folders. More often than not, when I click a file in Explorer, I want to copy or move it to another folder. That means I spend a good deal of time dragging files around or copying and pasting them.

But with a Registry hack, you can save yourself time: you can add Copy To Folder and Move To Folder options to the right-click context menu. When you choose one of the options from the menu, you browse to any place on your hard disk to copy or move the file to, and then send the file there. To add the option, run the Registry Editor [Hack #83] and go to HKEY_CLASSES_ ROOT\AllFilesystemObjects\shellex\ContextMenuHandlers. shellex tells you it's a shell extension key that lets you customize the user shell or the interface. Create a new key called Copy To. Set the value to {C2FBB630-2971-11d1- A18C-00C04FD75D13}. Create another new key called Move To. Set the value to {C2FBB631-2971-11d1-A18C-00C04FD75D13}. Exit the Registry. The changes should take effect immediately. The Copy To Folder and Move To Folder options will appear. When you right-click a file and choose one of the options, you'll be able to move or copy the file using a dialog box like the one shown in Figure 3-16.

Figure 3-16. Specifying a destination using the Copy To Folder option

Add and Remove Destinations for the Send To Option

The right-click context menu does have one useful option, Send To, which allows you to send the file to any one of a list of programs or locations—for example, to a drive, program, or folder.

It would be nice to edit that list, adding new locations and programs and taking away existing ones that you never use. How locations and programs show up on the menu appears to be somewhat of a mystery, but, in fact, it's easy to hack. Go to *C:\Documents and Settings\<User Name>\SendTo*, where *<User Name>* is your username. The folder will be filled with shortcuts to all the locations you find on your Send To context menu. To remove an item from the Send To menu, delete the shortcut from the folder. To add an item to the menu, add a shortcut to the folder by highlighting the folder, choosing File → New → Shortcut, and following the instructions for creating a shortcut. The new setting will take effect immediately; you don't have to exit Windows Explorer for it to go into effect.

Open the Command Prompt from the Right-Click Menu

I began computing in the days of DOS, and I still can't give up the command prompt. When it comes to doing down-and-dirty tasks like mass deleting or renaming of files, nothing beats it. I find myself frequently switching back and forth between Windows Explorer and the command prompt.

Often, when using Windows Explorer, I want to open the command prompt at the folder that's my current location. That takes too many steps: opening a command prompt and then navigating to my current folder. However, there's a quicker way: you can add an option to the right-click context menu that will open a command prompt at your current folder. For example, if you were to right-click the *C:\My Stuff* folder, you could then choose to open a command prompt at *C:\My Stuff*.

To add the option, run the Registry Editor **[Hack #83]**, then go to HKEY_LOCAL_ MACHINE/Software/Classes/Folder/Shell. Create a new key called Command Prompt. For the default value, enter whatever text you want to appear when you right-click a folder—for example, Open Command Prompt. Create a new key beneath the Command Prompt key called Command. Set the default value to Cmd.exe /k pushd %L. That value will launch *Cmd.exe*, which is the XP command prompt. The /k switch puts the prompt into interactive mode. That is, it lets you issue commands from the command prompt; the command prompt isn't being used to issue only a single command and then exit. The pushd command stores the name of the current directory, and %L uses that name to start the command prompt at it. Exit the Registry. The new menu option will show up immediately. Note that it won't appear when you right-click a file; it shows up only when you right-click a folder.

> While many of us like fussing around with the Registry rather than doing things the easy way, there's also a way to add this option to your right-click context menu without editing the Registry. Download and install a free copy of Microsoft's Open Command Window Here PowerToy from *http://www.microsoft.com/windowsxp/pro/downloads/powertoys.asp*. Many other PowerToys are on that page as well, and we cover them in other places in the book.

Clean Up the Open With Option

When you right-click a file, one of the menu options is Open With, which provides a list of programs for you to open the file with. This list changes according to the type of file you're clicking. Depending on the file type, the list can get long because programs frequently add themselves to this list when you install them. Making things worse, there are times when the listed programs aren't applicable. For example, do you really want to open a *.bmp* bitmap graphics file with Microsoft Word? I think not.

You can clean up the Open With list by using a Registry hack. Run the Registry Editor and go to HKEY_CURRENT_USER\Software\Microsoft\Windows\CurrentVersion\Explorer\FileExts. Look for the file extension whose Open With list you want to edit and find its OpenWithList subkey—HKEY_CURRENT_USER\Software\Microsoft\Windows\CurrentVersion\Explorer\FileExts\.bmp\OpenWithList, for example. The subkey will have an alphabetical list of String values. Open each value and examine the value data. It will be the name of one of the programs on the Open With list (Winword.exe, for example). Delete any entry you don't want to appear. Don't delete the value data; delete the String value listing. In other words, if the value data for the a String value is Winword.exe, delete the entire string rather than just the value data. Exit the Registry.

HACK #29 Take Your Work on the Go with Offline Files and the Briefcase

Here are two ways road warriors can more easily take files with them when they leave home or the office, and then synchronize files back to their desktop PCs when they return.

If you use a laptop on a corporate LAN, you might sometimes store files on the network and forget to bring them home or with you on the road. This frequently happens to people who, like me, are absent-minded on occasion (or more than on occasion—after all, I once left my car keys in the refrigerator).

If you have XP Professional, you can use its Offline Files feature to automatically synchronize folders from the LAN to your notebook so that whenever you leave the office the latest version of your files will be available. To enable the use of offline files, choose My Computer → Tools → Folder Options → Offline Files tab, and select the checkbox next to Enable Offline Files (see Figure 3-17).

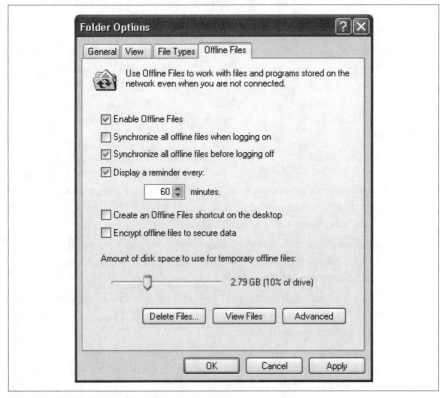

Figure 3-17. Enabling offline files

You won't be able to use Offline Files if you have enabled Fast User Switching. To turn off Fast User Switching, choose Control Panel → User Accounts → "Change the way users log on or off," uncheck the box next to Use Fast User Switching, and click Apply Options.

As you can see, this tab contains a number of options for using offline files. Here's what you need to know about each to take best advantage of offline file synchronization:

Synchronize all offline files before logging off. Make sure to choose this option. When you do, the most recent copies of files will automatically be copied to your laptop. If you don't choose this option, you'll get only a partial synchronization, which means you won't have the latest version of all your files. Also, keep in mind that you have to log off or turn off your PC for this option to work. If you only physically disconnect your PC from the network, the files won't be copied.

Synchronize all offline files when logging on. If you choose this option, as soon as you connect back to the network, your files will be synchronized from your laptop back to the LAN. That means you won't be able to use them locally, and you'll have to use them on the LAN. If you don't choose this option, you'll be able to continue using your files locally and can then manually synchronize any folders you want to the LAN.

Display a reminder every... If you've disconnected from the network, this option will automatically flash a balloon message at you, telling you at an interval of your choosing that you've been disconnected. More than anything, this is an annoying option and is useful only if you frequently disconnect from your LAN accidentally.

Create an Offline Files shortcut on the desktop. If you choose this option, XP creates a desktop shortcut to the *Offline Files* folder it creates when you enable the use of offline files.

Encrypt offline files to secure data. If you're concerned about the security of your files, choose this option. As the name implies, it will encrypt your offline files.

Amount of disk space to use for temporary offline files. When you use offline files, Windows caches files from the LAN onto your hard disk temporarily. This option lets you determine the exact amount of disk space to allocate to those temporary offline files.

After you've set up your laptop to use Offline Files, you have to choose the specific folders on the server that you want to make available to you offline. Open Windows Explorer, right-click the network folder, and choose Make Available Offline. If there are subfolders in the folder, you'll be asked whether you want to make those subfolders available as well.

After you do this, when you log off the network, the server copies to your laptop all the folders you've marked. They'll be available to you in the same way as any other folders are, via your applications, via Windows Explorer, in My Computer, or in My Network Places. Work with them on your laptop, and then, when you next connect to the network, they'll be synchronized to the network folders, depending on the options you've chosen.

On-Demand and Scheduled Synchronizations

If you'd like, instead of synchronizing when you log off the network, you can synchronize manually on demand, or you can set up a schedule for automated synchronization. To synchronize on demand manually, in Windows Explorer choose Tools → Synchronize. From the dialog box that appears, select the items in the Logon/Logoff tab that you want to synchronize, and click Synchronize. To set up times to synchronize, use the On Idle and Scheduled tabs.

Use the Briefcase for Mobile File Transfers

Offline Files works only if you have XP Professional and if you have a LAN to which both your laptop and desktop connect. But if you need to synchronize files between two computers not on a network—even if you don't have XP Professional—there is still a way to synchronize files between computers: use the Briefcase. It's not as easy to use as Offline Files, but it still does the trick. It synchronizes files between your two machines by using removable media such as a CD, zip drive, or flash drive/USB Keychain device.

> Using floppy disks is not recommended, unless you have very few files or very tiny files that you need to transfer and have no other way of transferring them, such as email attachments.

To use the Briefcase to transfer files from a laptop to a desktop computer, first format the media you're going to use if it needs to be formatted. With the removable media in the drive, open Windows Explorer, click the media's disk folder, and choose File → New → Briefcase. If you're going to be using more than one Briefcase at a time, rename the Briefcase with a descriptive name. The Briefcase is a folder, like any other folder on your computer. Open it, and then click Finish to close the dialog box that appears.

Copy into the Briefcase the files you're going to want to transfer to your laptop and keep synchronized between the two computers. You can copy files from different folders. If you're going to add files to the Briefcase over time, or if you expect the files in the Briefcase to grow, make sure to leave enough extra room on the disk. Eject the media from your desktop. (If you get an error message when trying to eject a CD, close Windows Explorer and then eject it.) Place the media in your laptop, and move or copy the Briefcase folder to the laptop's hard disk. Remember to move or copy the entire folder, not the individual files in the folder. Work on the files as you would normally. Add or delete files as well. When it's time to transfer the files back to your PC, copy the Briefcase from your laptop to the removable media, and put the removable media in your desktop. Open the Briefcase folder.

To synchronize all the files back to your desktop, choose Briefcase → Update All and, from the Update Briefcase dialog box (shown in Figure 3-18), click Update. To synchronize individual files, select them, choose Briefcase → Update Selection, and click Update.

Figure 3-18. Synchronizing all the files in a Briefcase back to a desktop PC

A Closer Look at the Briefcase

It's a good idea to examine the files in your Briefcase before you synchronize so that you know the status of each. As you can see in Figure 3-19, you'll see whether each file has been updated and therefore needs to be updated on your current machine, or whether it was unchanged. The Briefcase folder also shows you the file's original location on the computer, as well as other details such as file size.

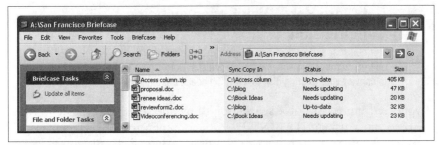

Figure 3-19. The Briefcase folder

Right-click any file in the Briefcase, and choose Properties → Update Status; you'll get updated information about each file. You can also perform the following tasks:

Update
> This button updates the file. Only this file, and no others, will update.

Split from Original
> This button breaks the link between the Briefcase file and the file on the hard disk. You won't be able to do automatic updates. The file on the hard disk will be listed as an Orphan in the status field in the Explorer view. You can still copy the file, even though the automatic link no longer works.

Find Original
> This button opens the folder on your computer that holds the original file.

See Also

- Backer (*http://www.cordes-dev.com/english/overview.html*) is a combination backup/synchronization program that lets you synchronize your laptop data with a desktop PC or server. It also lets you synchronize with a server while you're traveling, transfer files between PCs, and archive old versions of files. It's shareware and free to download, but if you decide to keep using it you're supposed to pay $24.

Get More Hard-Disk Space by Using NTFS Compression

The quickest and easiest way to give your system more room is to use XP's built-in compression scheme for NTFS disks. Here's how to use it—and how to convert your existing disk to NTFS if it doesn't already use it.

If you need more hard-disk space, don't buy another hard disk right away. First, consider using NTFS (NT File System) compression, which can give significantly more hard-disk space by compressing all the files on your PC. NTFS's on-the-fly compression capabilities can shrink the size of individual files and folders, or entire drives. When you use it, the files or folders will be compressed when they're on your hard disk to save space, but they will be decompressed automatically when you use them, and then compressed again when stored on your hard disk. This means that, unlike with a compression program such as WinZip (*http://www.winzip.com*), you don't have to deal with decompressing as well as compressing files. You can also easily turn compression on and off.

Note that NTFS compression isn't available with a FAT32 filesystem, so if you have a FAT32 system you'll first have to convert to NTFS, as explained later in this hack. If you're not sure which filesystem your volume uses, right-click your volume in Explorer, choose Properties → General, and look for the information next to File System.

How much disk space can you save by using NTFS compression? That depends largely on the kinds of files you have on your system. Bit-mapped graphics files are very compressible, so you'll save quite a bit of hard-disk space if you have many of them. Document files, such as Word files, are also reasonably compressible, while certain kinds of files, such as PDF (Adobe Acrobat) files, are barely compressible at all.

If you use NTFS compression on a file, the file can't be encrypted using XP's encrypting capabilities, so be careful not to compress any files that you want to encrypt.

In tests on my own PC, I found that bit-mapped *.tif* graphics files were compressed by more than 80 percent—a folder full of them shrunk from 295MB to 57MB. Word files shrunk by 66 percent—a folder full of them shrunk from 131KB to 44KB. PDF files, by way of contrast, hardly compressed at all: a group of them shrunk by just more than 6 percent, from 5.59MB to 5.27MB.

When you use compression, you might notice a slight drop in system performance. There might be a slight lag when opening or closing files, depending on the speed of your system, because the files have to be decompressed for you to open them and compressed when you save them. With newer systems, though, you probably won't notice a lag. On my now-aging 1.8GHz desktop, for example, I don't see a difference between working with files that have been compressed and working with files that haven't been compressed.

You can use NTFS compression on individual files, folders, and entire disks. To use NTFS compression on a file or folder, right-click the file or folder in Windows Explorer and choose Properties → General → Advanced. You'll see the screen shown in Figure 3-20.

Figure 3-20. Enabling compression on files and folders to save hard-disk space

Check the box next to "Compress contents to save disk space," click OK, and click OK again when the Properties dialog box appears.

If you want to compress an entire drive, right-click it in Windows Explorer and choose Properties → General → "Compress drive to save disk space." You'll be asked for confirmation, and then every folder and file on the drive will be compressed, one after another. Depending on the size of the drive, the procedure can take several hours. You can continue to use XP while the compression takes place. During that time, however, you might be prompted to close a file you're working on so that XP can compress it.

By default, XP visually differentiates between compressed files and decompressed files; compressed files are shown in blue. If for some reason your compressed files aren't blue, and you want them to be, from Windows Explorer choose Tools → Folder Options → View, scroll down, and select the checkbox next to "Show encrypted or compressed NTFS files in color."

Don't compress system files or *.log* files (files that contain logging information). If you do, your system can take a severe performance hit because these files are in frequent background use and compressing and decompressing them constantly takes up CPU power. If these files are in folders that are compressed, you can decompress just those individual files by unchecking the "Compress contents to save disk space" box next to them. You can also decompress the folder in which they are located in the same way.

How Compressing Folders Affects Underlying Files

When you compress files in a folder, they are all, obviously, compressed. But things can get confusing when you mix compressed folders and decompressed folders on a hard disk, or when you have compressed files in decompressed folders and vice versa. What happens, for example, when you move a decompressed file into a compressed folder, or move a compressed file from a compressed folder into a decompressed folder? The possibilities can set your head spinning. Here are the rules that apply when you're mixing compressed and decompressed files and folders:

- Files copied into a compressed folder are automatically compressed.
- New files created in a compressed folder are automatically compressed.
- Files moved into a compressed folder from a separate NTFS volume are automatically compressed.
- Files moved into a compressed folder from the same NTFS volume retain their compression settings. So, if the file was compressed, it will remain compressed. If the file was not compressed, it will not be compressed.
- If you move a file from a compressed folder to a decompressed folder in the same NTFS volume, the file will remain compressed.
- If you move a file from a compressed folder to a decompressed folder on a different NTFS volume, the file will no longer be compressed.
- Files copied or moved from a compressed folder on an NTFS volume to a FAT32 volume are decompressed.
- Files attached to emails are decompressed.

Checking How Much Disk Space NTFS Compression Saves

When you compress a file or folder, it doesn't appear that you're actually saving any disk space; when you view a file listing in Windows Explorer, the size of the compressed files will remain the same as they were before compression. In fact, though, the files have been compressed and space has been saved. Explorer reports on only the decompressed file size, not the compressed file size. To see the compressed size of a file or folder, right-click it in Windows Explorer and choose Properties → General. You'll see two listings of the file size, one titled "Size" and the other titled "Size on disk." The "Size on disk" listing reports on the compressed size of the file, while the "Size" listing reports on the decompressed size, as shown in Figure 3-21.

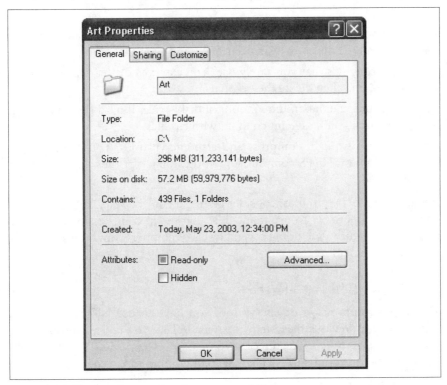

Figure 3-21. Viewing the true size of a compressed file

When to Use Zip Files and When to Use NTFS Compression

Another way to gain extra space on your hard disk is to use XP's built-in zip capabilities. Zip is an industry standard for file compression, and it compresses files much more effectively than NTFS does. In tests, I found that zip compression shrunk graphics files twice as effectively as NTFS compression—the resulting zip files were half the size of the NTFS-compressed files.

But that doesn't mean you should use zip compression all the time; there are times when using NTFS compression is a better bet. When files are zipped, for example, you can't open them in their application by double-clicking them. First you have to open the zip archive, and then double-click the file.

As a general rule, zipped files are not as convenient to use and handle as NTFS-compressed files. The exception is that zip lets you archive a group of files into a single folder, which you can then send to others via email or on disk.

What does this mean? On a day-to-day basis, NTFS compression is a better bet for files you frequently use. However, there are a number of reasons to use zip files instead:

- When you need to send a large file or files to someone via email. You can zip all the files into a single archive, and send that along.

- For storing files that you rarely use. You can create zip archives to store the files, and then delete the originals.

- For gaining the maximum amount of disk space. If hard-disk space is at a premium, you'll save much more with zip files.

- When you want to compress and also encrypt files. You can't encrypt files that have NTFS compression; you can encrypt files that have been zipped.

If you decide to use zip files, consider getting a copy of WinZip (*http://www.winzip.com*). It's easier to use than XP's built-in zip compression and offers many more features, including several levels of compression, built-in links to email, and much more.

Convert Your Hard Disk to NTFS

To use XP compression or encryption, you have to use NTFS. But if you instead have a previous filesystem, such as FAT32, you're not left out—you can convert it to NTFS. To convert a volume to NTFS, use XP's convert utility. To convert a volume to NTFS, at a command prompt, type:

```
convert d: /fs:ntfs
```

where d: is the volume you want to convert.

You can also use a number of parameters along with the utility:

/v   This runs the utility in verbose mode, which provides information about the volume being converted.

/nosecurity
    This sets the security privileges on the converted disk so that its files and folders can be used by anyone.

/x   Use this parameter if you're on a network and want to make sure another user cannot disrupt the conversion process by trying to access the drive while you're converting it. This parameter dismounts the drive from the network.

Hacking the Hack

If you convert to NTFS, here's a Registry hack for increasing its performance. Whenever you view a directory on an NTFS volume, the filesystem updates the date and timestamp to show the last time the directory was accessed. If you have a very large NTFS volume, this continual updating process can slow system performance. To disable automatic updating, run the Registry Editor [Hack #83] and go to HKEY_LOCAL_MACHINE\SYSTEM\CurrentContolSet\Control\ Filesystem. Look for NtfsDisableLastAccessUpdate. If it's not present, create it as a DWORD. Set the value to 1.

HACK #31 Put a Command-Line Prompt on Your Desktop

Command-line junkies always want the command prompt within easy reach. Here's how to put a command prompt directly on your desktop, so it's there whenever you need it.

If you use the command line regularly—for example, to launch Windows Explorer with shortcuts [Hack #22]—you'd like the command line within easy reach. In fact, you'd like it right on your desktop. XP has no built-in way to do that for you.

But there's a great free program called MCL (*http://www.mlin.net/MCL. shtml*) that runs as a small command line you can put anywhere on your desktop, as shown in Figure 3-22.

Figure 3-22. Putting the command line right on your desktop with MCL

Use it as you would use the normal command line, including any normal switches that you use to launch programs.

But MCL does more than just let you enter commands. It includes a number of other goodies that the XP command prompt doesn't, including these:

- It keeps a history of your last 100 commands, so you can easily reenter or edit any commands you've already typed.
- It includes an AutoComplete function that finishes your commands for you.

- It lets you launch URLs directly from the command line. If you type a URL, your default browser will open to that URL.
- It can be minimized to the System Notification area.
- It can be launched with a hotkey. The default is Ctrl-Alt-M.

The program has a few eccentricities you'll have to keep in mind when using it. When executing a DOS command, you have to use the % prefix. For example, to copy a file from *C:\Favorite Files* to *C:\Summer*, you'd use this command:

```
%copy C:\Favorite Files\Gabecamp.doc C:\Summer\Gabecamp.doc
```

To open to a specific directory in Windows Explorer, precede the command with a $. So, to open to *C:\Program Files*, you'd issue the command $C:\ Program Files.

Command-line fans will also want to get a copy of 4NT (*http://www.jpsoft. com*). Run it instead of the normal command prompt and get countless new features, such as a command-line editor for modifying and re-executing previous commands; the ability to copy, delete, and rename groups of files and directories with a single command; a built-in file viewer; the ability to select or include files by a variety of criteria, including date, time, and size; the ability to append descriptions (up to 511 characters) to files; and an exceedingly powerful batch language. It's shareware and free to try, but if you continue to use it, you're expected to pay $69.95.

See Also

- The free Command Prompt Explorer Bar (*http://www.codeproject.com/ csharp/CommandBar.asp*) lets you open a command-line toolbar from directly within Windows Explorer. It combines the command line with Windows Explorer navigation, so not only can you use the command line, but also you can navigate through your PC using Explorer.
- Cygwin is a free command shell plus a set of applications that make your Windows XP installation perform more like a Linux environment. If you know what a *bash prompt* is and you lament the lack of one on Windows, download the Cygwin installer at *http://www.cygwin.com*. Cygwin installs differently than most applications. You download a small application that manages the rest of the installation process. You must have an active Internet connection when you run the installer so that it can find the correct *packages* on Cygwin mirror servers located all over the globe.

CHAPTER FOUR

The Web
Hacks 32–48

All of us live on the Web these days, and the demarcation between the operating system and the Web has gotten fuzzier with each iteration of Windows. XP has even more web-based tools built into it than its predecessors.

In this chapter, you'll find hacks that make using the Web even better. You'll find hacks for protecting your privacy when you surf, killing pop-up ads and spyware, giving Internet Explorer a face-lift, hacking the great new free Firefox browser, searching the Internet, using the new Google Desktop and MSN Desktop Search, speeding up file downloads, and more.

HACK #32 Give Internet Explorer a Face-Lift

Don't like the way Internet Explorer looks? A better-looking browser is just a Registry edit away.

Everything about Internet Explorer screams, "Dull, dull, dull!" From its generic-looking logo to the plain background for its toolbars, you just better hope the content you're visiting is enough to keep you awake. But you don't need to be stuck with its plain-Jane looks; these Registry hacks will let you change it however you'd like.

Change the Internet Explorer Logo

Internet Explorer has both a static and an animated logo. The static logo displays when the browser is inactive, and the animated logo displays when the browser is locating a site, connecting, and actively downloading pages or images from the Web. Because you have the choice of displaying large or small icons on the Internet Explorer toolbar (to switch back and forth between the two, choose View → Toolbars → Customize → Icon Options → Large/Small icons), there are two sizes of both the static and animated logos.

Before you begin, you'll need to create new logos to replace the existing ones. You'll have to create two sets of icons in *.bmp* format: one set for the smaller logo and another set for the larger logo. Each set will have a static logo and an animated logo. The static logos should be 22×22 pixels for the smaller size and 38×38 pixels for the larger size. The animated logos have to be animated bitmaps, each of which should have a total of 10 frames. So, the smaller animated bitmap should be 22 pixels wide by 220 pixels high, and the larger animated bitmap should be 38 pixels wide by 380 pixels high.

Create the static bitmaps with any graphics program, including the version of Paint that comes with XP. You can also use special icon-creation programs to create your icons, such as Microangelo (*http://www.microangelo.us/*). See "Make Your Own Cursors and Icons" **[Hack #19]** for more details. (Make sure when using Microangelo to choose Tools → New Image format, which will let you create the icons with the proper pixel dimensions, as explained in the previous paragraph.)

To create the animated bitmaps, you'll need special tools. Microangelo does a great job of creating them, and that's your best bet. If you prefer, though, you can create the 10 separate frames for the animated bitmaps in a graphics program such as Paint and then stitch the 10 separate frames together using the Animated Bitmap Creator (*http://jsanjuan.tripod.com/download. html*), a free command-line program.

To change Internet Explorer's static logos to your new ones, run the Registry Editor **[Hack #83]** and go to:

```
HKEY_LOCAL_MACHINE\SOFTWARE\Microsoft\Internet Explorer\Main
```

Create two string values named SmallBitmap and BigBitmap and give them each the value of their filename and location, including the full path—for example, *C:\Windows\IEbiglogo.bmp* and *C:\Windows\IEsmalllogo.bmp*. As you might guess, the SmallBitmap value points to the smaller logo, and the BigBitmap value points to the larger logo.

To use your new animated logos, go to:

```
HKEY_LOCAL_MACHINE\SOFTWARE\Microsoft\Internet Explorer\Toolbar
```

Create two string values named SmBrandBitmap and BrandBitmap and give them each the value of their filename and location—for example, *C:\ Windows\IEbiganimatelogo.bmp* and *C:\Windows\IEsmallanimatelogo.bmp*. Once again, as you might guess, SmBrandBitmap is for the smaller animated logo and BrandBitmap is for the larger logo.

Exit the Registry and close Internet Explorer. When you next start up Internet Explorer, it should display your new logos. To revert to the default logos, simply delete the values you've created.

Add a Background to the Internet Explorer Toolbar

The Internet Explorer toolbar that sits at the top of Internet Explorer is about as dull as it gets—a plain, solid background, like the rest of Internet Explorer. But it doesn't have to be that way. You can add any background you want.

First, create the background or use an existing one. The background should be in *.bmp* format. Create it using a graphics program such as Paint Shop Pro (available from *http://www.jasc.com*) or Microangelo. See "Make Your Own Cursors and Icons" **[Hack #19]** for more details.

You'll also find a variety of *.bmp* files in the *C:\Windows* folder, so check them out to see if you like any. You might try *FeatherTexture.bmp*, which you can see in use as an Internet Explorer toolbar background in Figure 4-1. Whatever you choose, though, make sure it's light enough to show black text and it's not so busy that you can't read the menu text that will be on top of it. If you create or use a file that's too small, Internet Explorer will tile it for you. However, don't use a bitmap smaller than 10×10 pixels, because all the work Internet Explorer has to do to tile images that small will slow down your web browsing.

Figure 4-1. Internet Explorer with FeatherTexture.bmp as its toolbar background

Once you have a bitmap, run the Registry Editor and go to:

```
HKEY_CURRENT_USER\Software\Microsoft\Internet Explorer\Toolbar
```

Create a new string value named BackBitmapIE5 and give it the value of the filename and location of the background you're going to use, such as *C:\Windows\FeatherTexture.bmp*. Exit the Registry and close Internet Explorer. When you next start up Internet Explorer, it will display the background on the toolbar. To take away the background, simply delete the BackBitmapIE5 key.

You can change the background of the Internet Explorer toolbar without having to edit the Registry; you can use Tweak UI [Hack #8]. Run Tweak UI, click Internet Explorer, and click the box next to "Use custom background for Internet Explorer toolbar." Then, click the Change button and choose the file you want to use as the background. You'll see a sample of how the toolbar will look, so change the file until you find one you want to use. When you find it, click OK, close Internet Explorer, and restart it. The new toolbar will be there.

Change the Text of Internet Explorer's Titlebar

Internet Explorer's titlebar displays the text "Microsoft Internet Explorer," along with the title of the page you're currently visiting. However, you can change the "Microsoft Internet Explorer" text to any text you want. Run the Registry Editor and go to:

    HKEY_CURRENT_USER\Software\Microsoft\Internet Explorer\Main

Add a new string value named Window Title and give it a value of whatever text you want displayed in the titlebar. Exit the Registry and close Internet Explorer if it's open. The next time you open Internet Explorer, the titlebar will have your new text.

If you want your titlebar to have no text in it, aside from the title of the page you're currently visiting, create the Window Title string value but leave the Value field empty.

Stop Pop Ups with SP2—and Without It
#33   You don't have to be victimized by obnoxious pop-up ads and web sites on the Internet. Fight back with these tips and tools.

Surfing the Web used to be such a simple, enjoyable experience. Go to the web site of your choice, enjoy the page, and head somewhere else.

No longer. At times, it now seems like a sleazy carnival midway, complete with flashing lights and loud music, barkers pleading at you to venture into the sideshows, scamsters promising you big payoffs if you try three-card Monte, and no-goodniks lurking in the shadows.

For that, we have *pop ups* to thank. Pop ups are ads that, as the name implies, pop up over your browser, usually in a smaller window, and frequently contain flashing messages and other kinds of obnoxious come-ons. The infamous X10 surveillance camera pioneered this insufferable form of advertising, and now it's everywhere.

Pop ups are more than just insufferable annoyances, however. They can be dangerous as well. Click one of their come-ons, and you might unwittingly download spyware or a Trojan horse onto your PC.

> For more details about combating spyware, see "Kill Spyware and Web Bugs" **[Hack #34]**.

You don't have to be victimized by them, though. As you'll see in the rest of this hack, there are things you can do to keep your PC from resembling a virtual midway.

Use SP2's Built-In Pop-Up Blocker

If you haven't upgraded to Windows XP Service Pack 2 (SP2), there's at least one good reason why you should: Internet Explorer's built-in pop-up blocker. It does an exceptional job of blocking pop ups, and it lets you allow pop ups from some sites while banning them from all others.

> If the pop-up blocker isn't turned on, choose Tools → Pop-up Blocker → Pop-up Blocker Settings, check the box next to "Show Information Bar when a pop-up is blocked," and click Close.

By default, the pop-up blocker is turned on. Visit a site with a pop up, and you'll see a screen like the one shown in Figure 4-2.

There are two things of note here. First, at the top of the screen, you'll see what's called the Information Bar, which tells you a pop up was blocked. Then, right in the middle of the screen, you'll see a screen telling you to look at the Information Bar. Clearly, that notification is unnecessary, so select "Do not show this message again" and click OK.

Normally, you don't want to see a pop up, so you wouldn't need to do anything else at this point, beyond breathing a sigh of relief that a pop up was blocked. But in some instances, you want to let a pop up through. On occasion, a site will use pop ups for some good purpose—for example, to deliver more information in a small window.

If you want to allow pop ups through from the site, click the Information Bar, and you'll see the screen shown in Figure 4-3. Choose Temporarily Allow Pop-ups to allow pop ups from the site on just this visit, and choose Always Allow Pop-ups from This Site if you want to always let pop ups from the site through. Whichever you choose, the pop up will be let through immediately.

Figure 4-2. Internet Explorer's notification of a blocked pop up

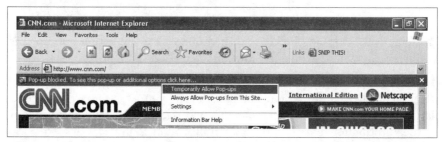

Figure 4-3. Allowing pop ups just for this visit

If you want to turn off the pop-up blocker altogether, choose Settings →
Turn Off Pop-up Blocker. And if you'd like to turn off the Information Bar
so that it doesn't appear when a pop up is blocked, choose Settings and
select Show Information Bar for Pop-ups to remove the check next to it.

But what happens if you've chosen to permanently allow pop ups from a site
and later decide you no longer want to let them through? It's easy to tell the
pop-up blocker to no longer let those pop ups through.

Installing SP2 has been known to cause problems on some XP systems and, in some cases, has stopped people from getting operating system updates via the Windows Updates site. For help in fixing the problems see "Fix SP2 Upgrade Woes" **[Hack #114]**.

Choose Tools → Pop-up Blocker → Pop-up Blocker Settings. The Pop-up Blocker Settings dialog appears, as shown in Figure 4-4.

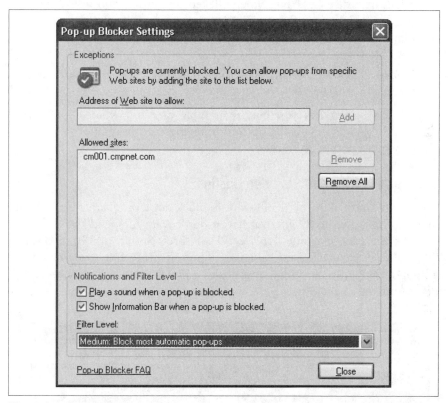

Figure 4-4. Customizing your pop-up settings

All the sites you've decided to allow pop ups from are in the "Allowed sites" box. To no longer allow pop ups from any of those sites, highlight the sites and click Remove. If you want to allow more sites than those shown here, type each site into the "Address of Web site to allow" box and click Add.

You can also tell Internet Explorer how aggressively to block pop ups, by choosing a different filter level from the Filter Level drop-down box. There are three levels you can choose:

Low

Allows pop ups from secure sites—that is, sites that use SSL encryption, such as banking sites. You'll know you're at a secure site if its URL begins with *https://*.

Medium

The default level, which blocks most pop ups. It will allow a few pop ups, through—notably, if it detects the pop up is one you might want to be allowed. What kind of pop up might that be? In some cases, a site might include a link that, when clicked, initiates a pop up—for example, launching a small map in a pop-up window. At the medium level, that pop up will get through.

High

Blocks all pop ups of any type, even if you've clicked a link to initiate them.

Finally, the screen lets you choose to play a sound when a pop up is blocked. It also gives you the option of having the Information Bar be displayed when a pop up is blocked.

Download Software to Stop Pop Ups in IE

If you don't have SP2, you'll still want to block pop ups, of course. There are many for-pay pop-up killers, but if you don't want to spend the cash, you can get an excellent one for free: EMS Free Surfer mk II, shown in Figure 4-5. It lets you set several levels of pop-up protection—you can block all pop ups or only those that appear to be unwanted—and you can turn it on and off with a click.

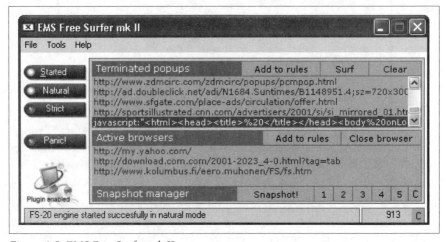

Figure 4-5. EMS Free Surfer mk II

It has other helpful tools as well, such as letting you shut every open instance of Internet Explorer with a single click, and it includes an add-in that will clean out your system cache and list of recently visited sites. Get it at *http://www.kolumbus.fi/eero.muhonen/FS/fs.htm*. (Don't confuse it with a related product, EMS Free Surfer Companion, which offers more features than the free version and costs $20.) Another good pop-up blocker is Pop-Up No-No!, available from *http://www.popupnono.com*. It blocks Flash animation ads, as well as pop ups. (For more details, see "Surf the Internet Ad-Free" [Hack #42].)

Ditch IE: Use a Different Browser to Stop Pop Ups

Here's one way to get rid of pop-up annoyances: skip Internet Explorer altogether! Opera, Mozilla, and Firefox all include built-in pop-up killers as a menu option.

Opera. Download Opera from *http://www.opera.com*. To enable its pop-up killer, choose File → Preferences → "Refuse pop-up windows." You can also have the program open pop-up windows in the background instead of on top of your browser.

Mozilla. Download Mozilla from *http://www.mozilla.org*. To enable its pop-up killer, choose Edit → Preferences → Privacy & Security → Pop-ups → and check "Reject pop-up windows."

Firefox. Download Firefox from *http://www.mozilla.org/products/firefox*. To enable its pop-up killer, choose Tools → Options and check the box next to Block Popup Windows.

Stop Messenger Service Pop Ups

A year or more ago, the most obnoxious pop ups of all started to appear on computer users' screens: pop ups that aren't connected to a browser, that appear even when you're not surfing the Web, and that show up in a text-message window for no apparent reason. You've taken no conceivable action that could have caused them to appear, such as visiting a web site. And yet there they are.

These text pop ups use XP's Messenger service, which was designed for sending notifications over internal local area networks—for example, when a network administrator wants to notify network users that a server is about to go down, or when you're notified that a printer has completed a job of yours.

The Messenger service is not related to Windows Messenger, Microsoft's instant-messaging program.

But spammers took hold of the technology and now blast out text pop ups to IP addresses across the Internet. How ubiquitous are these pop ups becoming? When I bought a new laptop, within 10 minutes of turning it on for the first time I had received my first Messenger service pop up.

To kill these pop ups, disable the Messenger service. Run the Services Microsoft Management Console by typing services.msc at a command prompt or the Run box and pressing Enter. Double-click the entry for Messenger, choose Disabled as the Startup type from the screen that appears, and click OK. Pop ups will no longer get through. Unfortunately, neither will any network messages from administrators if you're on a LAN.

If you're running a router at home that allows you to block ports, you can kill these messages by disabling port 135. How you do this varies according to your router. To do it on some models of Linksys routers, go to the router administrator screen and choose Advanced → Filters. In Filtered Private Port Range, choose Both, and for the range, type 135 twice. Click Apply. The pop ups should now be disabled.

By the way, another good reason to download and install SP2 is that it automatically turns off Messenger Service pop ups.

See Also

- "Kill Spyware and Web Bugs" [Hack #34]
- "Don't Get Reeled In by Phishers" [Hack #37]
- "Surf the Internet Ad-Free" [Hack #42]

HACK #34 Kill Spyware and Web Bugs

You don't have to be victimized by obnoxious applications that spy on you, hijack your browser, or worse. Fight back with these tips and tools.

For most people, *spyware* has replaced viruses or worms as the most-feared and obnoxious danger on the Internet. A relatively few number of people become infected by viruses or worms, but it seems as if almost everyone you know has been hit by some kind of spyware.

Spyware is a catch-all phrase that encompasses many different types of obnoxious programs. The least intrusive of the bunch report on your surfing activity to a web site, which tracks what you do and then delivers ads to your

PC based on your interests. But increasingly, they are becoming more intrusive. Some of them spawn pop-up swarms of ads that appear so quickly they overwhelm your PC, slowing it down and making it unusable. Others hijack your browser home page so that no matter what you do, you're sent to a home page of the hijacker's choosing, which might be a pornographic site, or perhaps a web site that spawns even more pop ups. And some kinds of spyware, called *keyloggers*, literally spy on you by watching every keystroke you make, and then send that information to someone on the Internet.

Web bugs are invisible bits of data, frequently a single pixel in size (sometimes called *clear GIFs*), that can track all your activities on a web site and report them back to a server.

You don't have to be victimized, though. As you'll see in the rest of this hack, there are things you can do to keep spyware and web bugs at bay.

Watch Out for Web Bugs

Web bugs are one of the more pernicious ways your online activities can be tracked, no matter which browser you're using. Sometimes, the web site the bugs send information to isn't the one that contains the web bug; for example, a web bug might send information back to an online advertising network.

Web bugs are surprisingly common. The Cyveillance technology and analysis company found that their use grew nearly 500% between 1998 and 2001. Web bugs can send the following information back to a server:

- The IP address of your computer
- The URL of the page on which the web bug is located, so they know you visited the page
- The time the web bug was viewed, so they know exactly when you visited the page
- The URL of the web bug image
- The type of browser you have
- Your cookie values

A free piece of software called Bugnosis (*http://www.bugnosis.org*) will alert you whenever it comes across web bugs on pages you visit. It reports on the URL the bug reports to, and, for some bugs, it will let you click a link it creates so that you can send an email of complaint to the web site that runs the bug. It runs inside Internet Explorer as a toolbar, and doesn't work with any other browsers.

The software can't actually protect you against web bugs, but it can alert you when you visit pages that use them, so you'll know if you want to stay away from them in the future. When you visit a site, the Bugnosis toolbar reports on the number of suspicious items that might be web bugs. To see detailed information about each suspicious item and web bug, click the down arrow next to the Bugnosis logo and choose Bugs Found in This Session. You'll see a list of every suspicious web bug, as you can see in Figure 4-6. Click the item, and you'll see a more detailed description, and an analysis on whether the item is truly a web bug, or only suspicious.

Figure 4-6. Bugnosis in action

Bugnosis can't actually block web bugs; it can only alert you to their presence. If you want your privacy protected when you surf the Web, your best bet is to surf anonymously [Hack #36].

Protect Yourself Against Spyware

Spyware is becoming ubiquitous and nastier as well. But you don't have to be a victim; there's a good deal you can do to protect yourself:

Get a free spyware detector and eradicator. One of the best and most popular free ones is Ad-Aware, available from *http://www.lavasoft.de*. It checks your system for spyware, finding not only program files, but also

Registry entries and cookies, as shown in Figure 4-7. After it does a check, you can choose which spyware problems you want the program to fix, and it'll go about its work, deleting files, folders, and cookies, and fixing Registry entries. Because no one spyware-killer is perfect, I suggest getting another free one, Spybot Search & Destroy, from *http://www.safer-networking.org/en/index.html*. Use both of them regularly to keep your system clean.

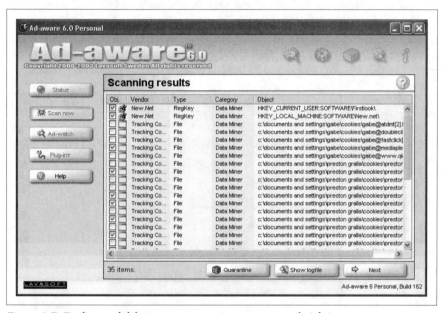

Figure 4-7. Finding and deleting spyware on your system with Ad-Aware

Keep in mind that when you delete spyware, you can disable software as well, so it's a good idea to always create a restore point before deleting spyware. Choose Control Panel → Performance and Maintenance → System Restore and follow the instructions. For example, if you remove the Cydoor spyware program, the Kazaa file-sharing program will no longer work. Alternatives to Kazaa include Shareaza (*http://www.shareaza.com*), a frontend to the popular Gnutella file-sharing network that also can hook into other file-sharing networks, such as the one Kazaa uses.

Get a for-pay spyware-killer. Ad-Aware and Spybot Search & Destroy do good jobs of finding and killing spyware after it's already infected your system. But better still is to get software that will stop the infection altogether. An excellent one is Webroot Spy Sweeper, available from

Webroot Software at *http://www.webroot.com*. You can download it and try it for free; if you continue to use it, you have to pay $19.95 per year. It does an excellent job of warning you when spyware tries to infect your system, and then stops it. It will also warn you when any program tries to start up automatically when XP starts, and when any program tries to change your home page. And like Ad-Aware and Spybot Search & Destroy, it will scan your system for spyware and then eradicate it as well. Figure 4-8 shows the program's configuration screen.

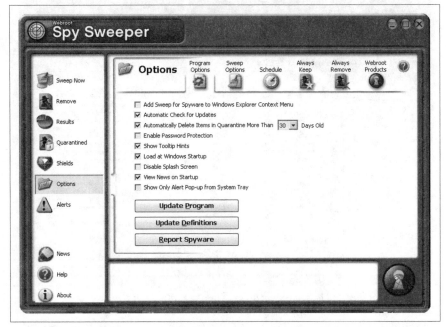

Figure 4-8. The Spy Sweeper configuration screen

 Microsoft also has an excellent spyware killer, Microsoft Windows AntiSpyware, that stops spyware from infecting your system and also scans it for threats. Get it at *http://microsoft.com/spyware*.

Be vigilant about what you download.   Ad-supported programs can include spyware, though not all do. Check out the Index of Known Spyware page run by Gibson Research at *http://grc.com/oo/spyware.htm* for a list of spyware programs.

Use a personal firewall such as ZoneAlarm [Hack #78].   A   personal   firewall will let you block any program on your system from contacting the

Internet without your approval, so you can use it to block spyware. XP's Windows Firewall doesn't have this capability, so you can't use it to block spyware.

Kill pop ups. Pop-up ads are a common way of delivering spyware. Click a pop up, and you might get infected with spyware. So, kill pop ups. For details, see "Stop Pop Ups with SP2—and Without It" [Hack #33].

Stop drive-by downloads. A web site might attempt to download software to your PC without your knowledge, and it might carry a spyware payload. Install SP2; it includes a download blocker. Additionally, the Firefox browser [Hack #43] includes a download blocker as well.

Keep your antivirus software up-to-date. Antivirus software protects you against some spyware, so make sure you run antivirus software and keep it updated.

See Also

- "Stop Pop Ups with SP2—and Without It" [Hack #33]
- "Take a Bite Out of Cookies" [Hack #35]
- "Surf Anonymously Without a Trace" [Hack #36]
- "Don't Get Reeled In by Phishers" [Hack #37]

Take a Bite Out of Cookies

Protect your privacy and keep your surfing habits to yourself with proper cookie-handling.

Cookies are small text files that web sites put on your hard disk to personalize the site for you or to track and then record your activities on the site. Cookies have gotten a lot of press—most of it bad—but the truth is, not all cookie use is bad. As a means of site customization, they're a great way of helping you get the most out of the Web. They can also carry information about log-in names and passwords, which is a timesaver, since you won't have to log into each site every time you visit. If you delete all your cookies, you won't automatically get your Amazon wish list the next time you visit that site.

 Cookies are big timesavers when it comes to logging you into web sites automatically, but they can also be security holes as well. If you use them to log you in automatically, anyone who uses your computer will be able to log in to those sites with your username and password.

But cookies can also be used to track your online activities and identify you. Information about you, based on what cookies gather, can be put in a database, and profiles of you and your surfing habits can be created.

Because cookies can be privacy-invaders, XP gives you a number of ways to restrict how web sites place and use cookies on your PC. To understand how to restrict the ways cookies are used on your PC, first you need to understand three cookie-related terms:

First-party cookie
> A cookie created by the site you're currently visiting. These cookies are often used by sites to let you log on automatically—without having to type in your username and password—and customize how you use the site. Typically, these kinds of cookies are not invasive.

Third-party cookie
> A cookie created by a site other than the one you're currently visiting. Frequently, third-party cookies are used by advertisers or advertising networks. Some people (including me) consider these kinds of cookies invasive.

Compact privacy statement
> A publicly posted policy that describes the details of how cookies are used on a site—for example, detailing the purpose of cookies, how they're used, their source, and how long they will stay on your PC. (Some cookies are automatically deleted when you leave a web site, while others stay valid until a specified date.)

To protect your privacy, you also need to know the difference between implicit consent and explicit consent. *Explicit consent* means you have specifically told a site it can use personally identifiable information about you. It's the same as *opting in. Implicit consent* means you haven't specifically told a site not to use personally identifiable information. It's the same as not having *opted out*, or specifically requesting to be taken off a list.

Internet Explorer lets you customize how it handles cookies. You can choose from six levels of privacy settings, from Accept All Cookies to Block All Cookies. When choosing, keep in mind that some sites won't function well or at all at the higher privacy settings, particularly if you choose to reject all cookies. I generally find that Medium High is a good compromise between protecting privacy and still being able to personalize web sites.

To customize your cookie settings in Internet Explorer, choose Tools → Internet Options → Privacy. Move the slider (shown in Figure 4-9) to your desired level.

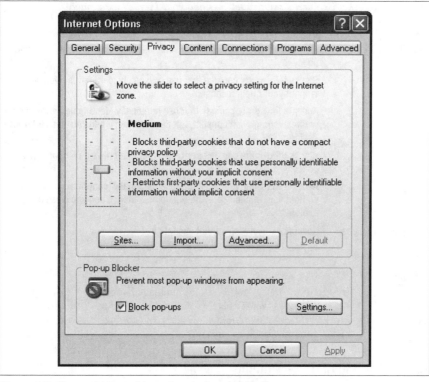

Figure 4-9. Customizing cookie settings in Internet Explorer

Table 4-1 shows how each setting affects Internet Explorer's cookie-handling.

Table 4-1. Internet Explorer's privacy settings and your privacy

Setting	How the setting affects your privacy
Block All Cookies	Blocks all cookies, without exception.
	Does not allow web sites to read existing cookies.
High	Blocks cookies from all web sites that don't have a compact privacy policy.
	Blocks all cookies that use personally identifiable information without your explicit consent.
Medium High	Blocks third-party cookies from sites that don't have a compact privacy policy.
	Blocks third-party cookies that use personally identifiable information without your explicit consent.
	Blocks first-party cookies that use personally identifiable information without your implicit consent.

Table 4-1. Internet Explorer's privacy settings and your privacy (continued)

Setting	How the setting affects your privacy
Medium (Default)	Blocks third-party cookies from sites that don't have a compact privacy policy. Blocks third-party cookies that use personally identifiable information without your implicit consent. Accepts first-party cookies that use personally identifiable information without your implicit consent, but deletes them when you close Internet Explorer.
Low	Blocks third-party cookies from sites that don't have a compact privacy policy. Accepts third-party cookies that use personally identifiable information without your implicit consent, but deletes them when you close Internet Explorer.
Accept All Cookies	Accepts all cookies, without exception. Allows web sites to read existing cookies.

> In Firefox, pretty good cookie management is built in. Access settings via Tools → Options → Privacy. You can block cookies, allow cookies on a site-by-site basis, set expiration times for cookies, and more.

Customizing IE Cookie-Handling

You're not locked into IE's preset levels of cookie-handling. If you like, you can customize how it handles cookies so that you can, for example, accept or reject cookies from individual sites, or accept or reject all first-party and third-party cookies.

To accept or reject all cookies from a specific site, choose Tools → Internet Options → Privacy → Sites. You'll see the Per Site Privacy Actions dialog box, as shown in Figure 4-10. Type in the name of the site you want to accept or block cookies from, and click either Block or Allow.

To customize how you handle first-party and third-party cookies, choose Tools → Internet Options → Privacy → Advanced. Check the "Override automatic cookie handling" box, as shown in Figure 4-11. You can accept or reject all first-party or third-party cookies, or be prompted whether to accept them. You can also decide to always allow *session cookies*, cookies that last only as long as you're on a specific web site and are deleted once you leave the site.

Figure 4-10. The Per Site Privacy Actions dialog box

Figure 4-11. The Advanced Privacy Settings dialog box

Export, Import, or Back Up Your Cookies

Although some cookies can be intrusive, some can be helpful. They can log you into web sites automatically and customize the way you use and view the site. So, when you buy a new PC, you might want to export cookies from an older computer to it. If you have more than one PC, you might want all of them to have the same cookies. And you might want to back up your cookies for safe-keeping in case you accidentally delete the wrong ones.

To export or back up cookies from IE, choose File → Import and Export. The Import/Export Wizard will launch. Choose Export Cookies and follow the directions. A single text file containing all your cookies will be created in My Documents, though you can choose a different location for them. To import cookies, launch the Import/Export Wizard, choose Import Cookies, and browse to the location where the cookie file has been stored.

Examine and Delete Cookies Manually

You can't examine and delete your cookies from within Internet Explorer. However, because XP stores each IE cookie as an individual text file, you can read them and delete them just as you would any other text file. Go to *C:\Documents and Settings\<Your Name>\Cookies* in Windows Explorer, and you'll see a list of individual cookies in a format like this:

```
your name@abcnews.com[1].txt
```

As a general rule, the name of the web site or ad network will be after the @, but not always—sometimes it will merely be a number. Open the file as you would any other text file (in Notepad, WordPad, or another text editor). Usually, there will be a list of numbers and letters inside, though you might find other useful information in there—for example, your username and password for the web site. If you don't want the cookie on your hard disk, simply delete it as you would any other text file.

Netscape Navigator and Mozilla handle cookies differently than Internet Explorer. They store all cookies in a single file, *cookies.txt*, typically found in *C:\Documents and Settings\<Your Name>\Application Data\Mozilla\Profiles\ default********.slt*, where ******** is a random collection of numbers and letters. So, the directory might be *C:\Documents and Settings\Name\Mozilla\ Profiles\default\46yhu2ir.slt*. If you've set up different Netscape/Mozilla profiles (Tools → Switch Profile → Manage Profiles → Create Profile), *cookies.txt* won't be in the *default* subfolder, but under each profile's name. You can open the file and see each individual cookie. You can't however, delete individual entries from the file by editing this file. Instead, use Netscape's built-in Cookie Manager (at Tools → Cookie Manager → Manage Stored Cookies) to read and delete cookies.

In Firefox, you'll find the *cookies.txt* file in *C:\Documents and Settings\<Your Name>\Application Data\Mozilla\Firefox\Profiles\default.xxx*, where *xxx* is a random collection of three letters. Use Firefox's built-in Cookie Manager (Tools → Options → Privacy) to read and delete cookies.

Get a Third-Party Cookie Manager

The tools built into XP for managing cookies are reasonable, but for the most flexibility in handling cookies you should get a third-party cookie manager. My favorite (and my editor's favorite) is Cookie Pal, available at *http://www.kburra.com*. It lets you easily customize which sites you'll allow to put cookies on your PC, and it includes a cookie manager that lets you read and delete cookies. It also lets you accept or reject cookies on a case-by-case basis as you browse the Web. If you use browsers other than IE, you might be out of luck, though. As of this writing, Cookie Pal works only with Versions 3 and 4 of Netscape Navigator and Versions 4, 5, and 6 of Opera. (Mozilla and later Netscape versions have similarly good managers built in, as mentioned earlier.)

Opt Out of Cookie-Based Ad Networks

Online ad networks have the potential to create in-depth, privacy-invading profiles of your web travels and personal interests because they can place a single cookie on your hard disk that will track you across multiple sites. Normally, sites can't share cookie information with each other, but ad networks have found a way around this, so they can aggregate your behavior from many web sites.

You can fight back by opting out of some of the biggest online ad networks. You'll have them place an opt-out cookie on your hard disk that will tell the various sites not to track what you're doing; this will go a long way toward protecting your privacy.

To opt out of the DoubleClick online advertising network, go to *http://www.doubleclick.com/us/corporate/privacy/privacy/ad-cookie/* and click the Ad Cookie Opt-Out button at the bottom of the page.

To see whether the opt-out worked, if you're an Internet Explorer user, go to your cookies folder, which is typically *C:\Documents and Settings\<Your Name>\Cookies*. Look for a cookie named *your name@doubleclick[1].txt*—for example, *preston gralla@doubleclick[1].txt*. The contents of the cookie should look something like this:

```
id OPT_OUT doubleclick.net/ 1024 468938752 31583413 3447013104 29418226 *
```

In Netscape Navigator, your *cookies.txt* file is typically found in *C:\ Documents and Settings\<Your Name>\Application Data\Mozilla\Profiles\ default********.slt*, where ******** is a random collection of numbers and letters. So, the directory might be *C:\Documents and Settings\Name\Mozilla\ Profiles\default\46yhu2ir.slt*. Look in the file for an entry that looks like this:

```
.doubleclick.net    TRUE    /    FALSE 1920499138    id    OPT_OUT
```

You can instead use Netscape's built-in Cookie Manager to examine the cookie, by choosing Tools → Cookie Manager → Manage Stored Cookies.

Some other advertising networks let you opt out as well. For details, go to *http://www.networkadvertising.org/optout_nonppii.asp* and follow the instructions for opting out. To verify that you've successfully opted out of the other ad networks, click the Verify Cookies menu item on the left part of the page.

See Also

- "Stop Pop Ups with SP2—and Without It" [Hack #33]
- "Kill Spyware and Web Bugs" [Hack #34]
- "Surf Anonymously Without a Trace" [Hack #36]
- "Don't Get Reeled In by Phishers" [Hack #37]

HACK #36   Surf Anonymously Without a Trace

Feel like people are watching you? On the Web, they probably are. Protect your privacy by using anonymous proxy servers.

Whenever you surf the Web, you leave yourself open to being snooped upon by web sites. They can track your online travels, know what operating system and browser you're running, find out your machine name, peer into your clipboard, uncover the last sites you've visited, examine your history list, delve into your cache, examine your IP address and use that to learn basic information about you such as your geographic location, and more. To a great extent, your Internet life is an open book when you visit.

Don't believe me? Head to *http://www.anonymizer.com/privacytest/*. This page, run by the Anonymizer.com web service, tells you your IP address and machine name. And that's just a start. Click the links such as Exposed Clipboard and Geographical Location. You'll see just a small sampling of what web sites can learn about you. Figure 4-12 shows a web site reporting on my IP address, the contents of my clipboard, my browser information, and my geographic location. It's close enough; I live in Cambridge rather than Boston, and we generally require that people turn over their passports at the border.

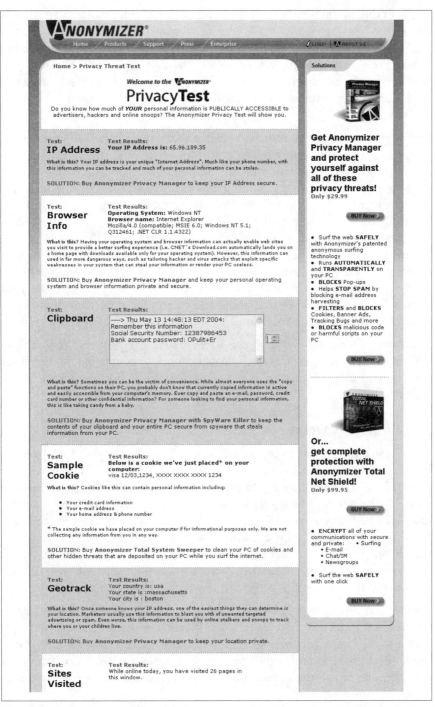

Figure 4-12. The Anonymizer.com web service, exposing my current geographic location

Much of the reason why web sites can find out this information about you is due to the trusting nature of the Internet's infrastructure and is inherent in the open client/server relationship between your web browser and the servers on the sites you visit. But a lot of it also has to do with the ability to match up information from your PC to information in publicly available databases—for example, databases that have information about IP addresses.

The best way to make sure web sites can't gather personal information about you and your computer is to surf anonymously; use an anonymous proxy server to sit between you and the web sites you visit. When you use an anonymous proxy server, your browser doesn't contact a web site directly. Instead, it tells a proxy server which web site you want to visit. The proxy server then contacts the web site, and when you get the web site's page you don't get it directly from the site. Instead, it's delivered to you by the proxy server. In that way, your browser never directly contacts the web server whose site you want to view. The web site sees the IP address of the proxy server, not your PC's IP address. It can't read your cookies, see your history list, or examine your clipboard and cache because your PC is never in direct contact with it. You're able to surf anonymously, without a trace.

There are two primary ways to use anonymous proxy servers. You can run client software on your PC, which does the work of contacting the server for you, or you can visit a web site, which does the work of contacting the server.

Web-Based Anonymizer

If you don't want to go to the hassle of installing a client—and if you don't want to pay for software—to surf anonymously, go to Anonymizer.com (*http://www.anonymizer.com*). In the box near the top of the page, type the name of the site to which you want to surf, and you'll head there anonymously. The proxy server will grab the page for you, and you'll get the page from the proxy server. You can also download a free version that runs as a toolbar in Internet Explorer. Surf as you would normally, and you'll visit those web sites directly. When you want to visit a site anonymously, click a button and the anonymous proxy server will do the work for you.

A fuller version of the program is available on a subscription basis for $29.95 per year or $9.95 for three months. It blocks banner ads, stops pop ups, encrypts the URLs you type so that they can't be read by your ISP or network administrator, and adds a few other features as well. I don't find the extra features worth the money, but if these kinds of things are important to you, go ahead and spend the money. (To learn how to block pop ups, turn to "Stop Pop Ups with SP2—and Without It" **[Hack #33]**.)

 When you use this site, some sites will appear broken, with text and graphics displaying oddly. But it's a small price to pay for your privacy.

Use Internet Explorer for Anonymous Surfing

If you want to surf anonymously, you don't have to pay a service. With a bit of hackery, you can use Internet Explorer, or any other browser. To do it, you use an anonymous proxy server to sit between you and the web sites you visit.

To use an anonymous proxy server in concert with your browser, first find an anonymous proxy server. Hundreds of free, public proxy servers are available, but many frequently go offline or are very slow. To find the best one, go to *http://www.atomintersoft.com/products/alive-proxy/proxy-list*. The web site lists information about each server, including its uptime percentage and the last time the server was checked to see if it was online.

Find the server with the highest percentage of uptime. Write down the server's IP address and the port it uses. For example, in the listing 24.236. 148.15:80, the IP address is 24.236.148.15, and the port number is 80.

In Internet Explorer, select Tools → Internet Options, click the Connections tab, and click the LAN Settings button. Check the "Use a proxy server for your LAN" box. In the Address field, type in the IP address of the proxy server. In the Port field, type in its port number. Check the "Bypass proxy server for local addresses" box, as shown in Figure 4-13; you don't need to remain anonymous on your local network.

Click OK and then OK again to close the dialog boxes. Now when you surf the Web, the proxy server will protect your privacy. Keep in mind that proxy servers can make surfing the Web much slower.

Get Software for Anonymous Surfing

If you prefer to install software, get Steganos Internet Anonym 5 (*http:// www.steganos.com/en/sia*). In addition to anonymous proxy serving, it kills pop ups and manages cookies. You can try it for free, but if you want to keep it you'll have to pay $29.95.

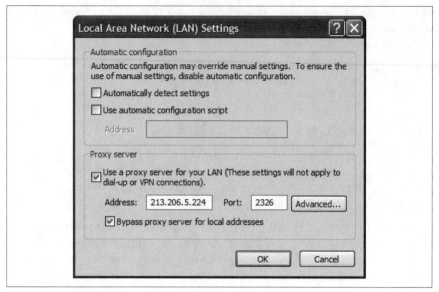

Figure 4-13. Setting up Internet Explorer to surf the Web anonymously

See Also

- Go to *http://www.gilc.org/speech/anonymous/remailer.html* to send email anonymously so that it can't be traced to you as the sender. Whistle-blowers might want to use this feature, but others should make sure not to abuse it.

- For shareware that cleans out your cached files, destroys your history trail, and uses a variety of other methods to clean all traces of where you've surfed, try SurfSecret Privacy Protector (*http://ww.surfsecret.com*).

- "Stop Pop Ups with SP2—and Without It" **[Hack #33]**

- "Kill Spyware and Web Bugs" **[Hack #34]**

- "Take a Bite Out of Cookies" **[Hack #35]**

- "Don't Get Reeled In by Phishers" **[Hack #37]**

Don't Get Reeled In by Phishers

HACK
#37

Watch out the next time your bank, eBay, or PayPal sends you an email asking for account information; it might be a scammer on a "phishing" expedition that will send you to a web site to steal your account information. Here's what you can do to make sure you don't become the catch of the day.

Of all the obnoxious scams circulating on the Internet, the worst might be *phishing* attacks, in which you're sent a spoofed email that appears to be from a bank, eBay, PayPal, or other financial institution. Often, the email address appears to be a valid email address, and the email includes the institution's logo and looks exactly like any other email you might get from it. Many of the links in the email will lead to the real site as well.

The email tells you that you need to log into your account for some reason—perhaps to verify your personal information—although often, you're told you need to log in because the institution's fraud-detection team has found suspicious activity in your account and needs you to provide information about it.

These emails can be exceedingly convincing. For example, the email shown in Figure 4-14 looks real, but in fact, it isn't from PayPal. If you click the link at the bottom of the message, you'll be sent to a site that looks like PayPal.

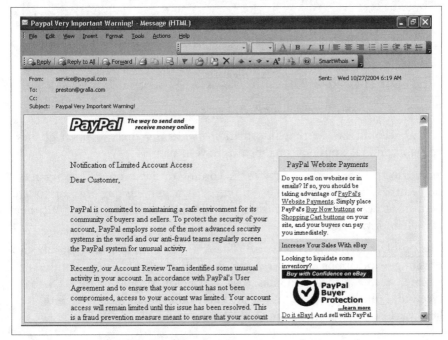

Figure 4-14. A phishing email, made to look like a message from PayPal

The site shown in Figure 4-15 looks just like the regular PayPal site. With such fraudulent sites, the design and logo will be the same, and in some instances, even the URL will look authentic.

But the site is a fraud. When you log in, the phisher steals your username and password. Then he can empty the bank account associated with your

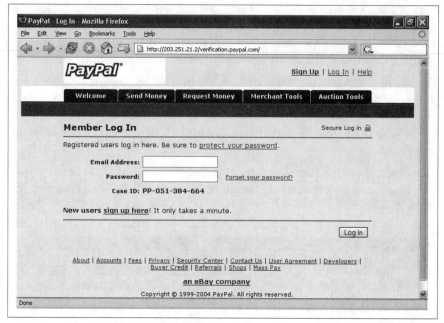

Figure 4-15. A spoofed version of the PayPal site

PayPal account or use that information in identity theft to open up new accounts and take out new credit cards in your name.

How effective are phishing attacks? According to the antiphishing organization Anti-Phishing Working Group (*http://www.antiphishing.org*), up to five percent of people who get phishing emails are fooled into giving out their private information.

The problem is only getting worse. The Anti-Phishing Working Group says phishing expeditions are increasing at a rate of 50% per month. The research firm Gartner estimates that 57 million people in the U.S. have received a phishing email. And according to the Truste web site, $500 million was lost in 2003 alone due to phishing attacks.

It can be excessively difficult for law-enforcement officials to track down the source of phishing attacks. That's because often, the emails aren't sent directly by the scammers. Instead, the scammers use so-called *zombie networks* to send the phishing attacks. These networks are made up of hundreds or thousands of PCs, whose unwitting owners have no idea their PCs are being used in this manner. Trojans have been planted on them and are then used to send out the phishing attacks. The security firm Ciphertrust estimates that as few as five zombie networks are responsible for most of the phishing email on the Internet. The best way to protect against Trojans is to keep your antivirus software up-to-date and to use a personal firewall. For details about how to use a firewall, see "Protect Your Computer with the New Windows Firewall" **[Hack #77]** and "ZoneAlarm: The World's Best Free Firewall" **[Hack #78]**.

Increasingly, phishing attacks aren't conducted by lone individuals. Instead, they are tied to organized crime. In November 2004, for example, a suspected member of the Russian mob was arrested for allegedly participating in phishing fraud.

What You Can Do About It

Phishing attacks are scary stuff, but you don't have to be victimized. In fact, there are several things you can do to make sure you never get reeled in.

First, you can use a simple bit of JavaScipt code to find out the real URL of the site you're visiting. Type the following JavaScript into your browser, and press Enter:

```
javascript:alert("Actual URL address: " + location.protocol + "//" +
location.hostname + "/");
```

A small window will pop up in the middle of your browser, telling you the actual web site you're visiting, as shown in Figure 4-16. Examine the URL, and you'll see whether you're really visiting the site you think you're visiting. If the address in the window doesn't match what you see in your browser, get thee somewhere else because it's a phishing attack.

You can also use this JavaScript code, which will do the same thing as the previous code, but adds a little bit of extra information:

```
javascript:alert("The actual URL is:\t\t" + location.protocol + "//" +
location.hostname + "/" + "\nThe address URL is:\t\t" + location.href + "\n"
+ "\nIf the server names do not match, this may be a spoof.");
```

Figure 4-16. JavaScript proof of a fraudulent site

As shown in Figure 4-17, this pop-up window includes the real URL of the site you're visiting, as well as the URL displayed in the address bar.

Figure 4-17. More information from more JavaScript

Of course, it's unlikely that you're going to memorize either piece of code and have it on hand every time you visit a web site you worry might be a spoof. So, there's a simpler solution. You can get a nifty, free add-in that will report to you on the real URL of the site you're visiting.

SpoofStick (*http://www.corestreet.com/spoofstick*) is a free add-in to both Internet Explorer and Firefox that detects phishing attacks. It installs as a toolbar in either browser, so you can turn it on and off when you want. When you're on a site and you're not sure whether the site is a spoof, turn on the SpoofStick toolbar by choosing View → Toolbars → SpoofStick in either browser. The SpoofStick toolbar will appear, as shown in Figure 4-18, displaying the site's real URL. If the site is a spoof, leave it as quickly as you can; you're about to be victimized by a phishing scam.

You can customize the size and color of the "You're On" message by clicking the Options button, choosing Configure SpoofStick, choosing the size (small, medium, or large) and color of the message, and clicking OK.

To turn off the toolbar, choose View → Toolbars → SpoofStick.

EarthLink, a popular Internet Service Provider (ISP), also offers a free anti-phishing toolbar, though it works only with Internet Explorer, not Firefox.

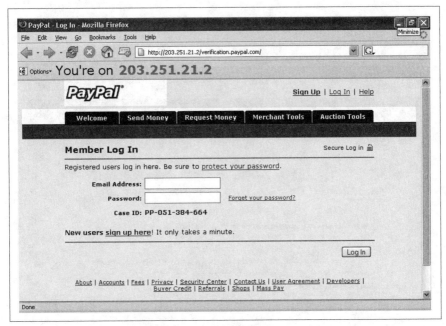

Figure 4-18. SpoofStick's evidence of a phishing scam

Head to *http://www.earthlink.net/home/tools* and download and install the EarthLink Toolbar. Whenever you visit a site that might be fraudulent, you'll be redirected away from the phishing site and instead sent to the web page shown in Figure 4-19.

If you want to live dangerously by visiting the site even after receiving this warning, click the button at the bottom of the page that reads "Continue to this potentially dangerous or fraudulent site." Even if you click, you won't be sent there unless you also turn off the toolbar's ScamBlocker feature (click the ScamBlocker button so that it turns red).

> Even if you don't have the EarthLink Toolbar turned on, it
> will still stop you from visiting phishing sites.

Which toolbar should you use? I prefer SpoofStick. EarthLink's toolbar works by checking to see whether the site you're visiting is on a list it has of potential spoof sites. And if you're one of the first potential victims and the site hasn't yet been added to the list, you'll be allowed through, but you'll think you're safe.

Of course, the paranoid among us might prefer to use both.

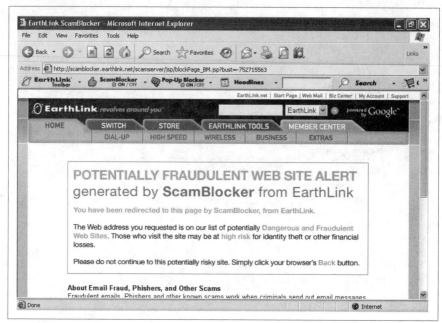

Figure 4-19. EarthLink Toolbar's ScamBlocker

Hacking the Hack

The tools in this hack will go a long way toward making sure you're never the victim of a phishing scam. But you should also take these precautions as well:

- Never respond to unsolicited mail from anyone purporting to be your credit card company, bank, eBay, or other financial institution; in other words, don't click any links in those emails. Most financial institutions have gotten savvy to phishing scams, so they won't send out emails with links to your log-on page. If you get a message that you think might be real, head to its web site on your own, not via an email link, or call your financial institution and speak with a representative.

- Don't enter your Social Security number on any web site, unless a reputable financial institution requires it for you to open an account. Again, enter your Social Security number only if you go to the site yourself to open an account, not in response to an email message.

- Don't fill out forms in email messages that ask for personal financial information or passwords. Again, the email can be forged.

To help protect others and set the law enforcement dogs on the phishers, forward the email to the Anti-Phishing Working Group at *reportphishing@antiphishing.com*, send a copy to the Federal Trade Commission at *spam@uce.gov*, and file a complaint with the FBI's Internet Fraud Complaint Center at *http://www.ifccfbi.gov*.

See Also

- Microsoft has a useful Knowledge Base Article that explains how to protect yourself against spoofed sites. Go to *http://support.microsoft.com/default.aspx?scid=kb;en-us;833786*. For advice on what to do if you've been victimized by identity theft, go to the Federal Trade Commission's site about identity theft: *http://www.consumer.gov/idtheft*.

Read Web Pages Offline
HACK #38

Take the Web with you wherever you go, and put it into an easily searchable database on your PC.

One of the main problems with doing research on the Web is that there's no easy way to save all the information you find and no simple way to read web pages when you're offline. Internet Explorer includes some basic tools for saving web pages and reading through them when you're not connected to the Internet. If you need to save only occasional pages and don't need to do searches through those pages, these tools will work reasonably well for you. But if you want to store pages in categories and folders and need to do full-text searches, you'll need a third-party program. This hack shows you how to do both.

Reading Web Pages Offline Using IE

To save your current web page to your hard disk so that you can read it again in Internet Explorer when you're not connected to the Internet, choose File → Save As. You'll be given several options for how to save it. If you're not planning to edit the HTML of the file, your best bet is to save it as a "Web Archive, single file" (*.mht*). That way, you don't clutter up your hard disk with extra folders and files stored in different locations; everything is saved to a single file. Saving it as a "Web Page, complete" stores the HTML file as well as associated graphics, in a folder structure. Saving it as a "Web Page, HTML only" saves just the HTML file itself, with no associated graphics and no folder structure. You can also save it as a text file, but if you do, expect to spend time cleaning it up because it saves all the text on the page, often in an unstructured way. To read the page after you've saved it to your disk, choose File → Open, browse to the directory where you've saved the page, and open it.

There are times when you want to save not just the page you're on, but also the pages linked off it. To do that, you'll have to save your pages another way. First, save the page to your Favorites list by pressing Ctrl-D or choosing Favorites → Add to Favorites. Then, right-click the page where it's listed in Favorites and choose Make Available Offline. A wizard will appear. Follow its instructions, and when you get to the screen shown in Figure 4-20, tell it how many links deep you want pages saved. Be very careful when doing this, because even choosing to keep one link level can take up a substantial amount of hard-disk space.

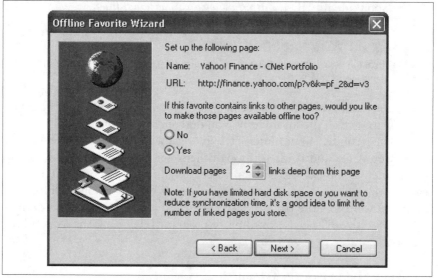

Figure 4-20. Saving web pages offline several links deep using the Offline Favorite Wizard

When you finish the wizard, you're asked how you want to synchronize the page or pages you've chosen to save to disk. When you synchronize a web page, IE grabs the latest version of the page or pages and overwrites your existing page or pages. If you want to keep a permanent copy of the page or pages, and you don't want them updated, choose "Only when I choose Synchronize from the Tools menu." Then, simply don't synchronize the page. If you do want to synchronize the page so that a more current version is available on your hard disk, choose "I would like to create a new schedule," and follow the instructions for creating a schedule.

Save Web Pages in an Offline Database with Add-Ins

If you need to save many web pages and want to be able to search through them by full-text or keyword searches, you'll have to use a third-party program. A very good one is SurfSaver, available from *http://www.surfsaver.com* (see Figure 4-21). It integrates directly into Internet Explorer and lets you save pages in separate folders within the program. You can add keywords and notes to each page, and then search by keyword or full text, or browse by folder.

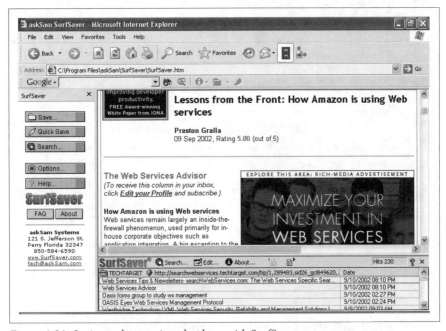

Figure 4-21. Saving web pages in a database with SurfSaver

When you visit a web page you want to save locally, right-click the page, choose SurfSaver Save, and choose which SurfSaver folder you want to save it in. You can save the page with or without graphics. When you want to search, right-click the page, choose SurfSaver Search, and then search by keyword, through notes, or through the full text on the page to easily find the page and information you want. SurfSaver also integrates directly with the freeform askSam database. It's shareware; you can try it out for free, but if you continue to use it, it costs $19.95.

My current favorite of these programs is Onfolio, shown in Figure 4-22. Like SurfSaver, it integrates with Internet Explorer, although it also integrates with Firefox, and it can work independently of a browser as well. It's more visually pleasing than SurfSaver, makes it easier to organize your pages in folders and subfolders, and it includes excellent search tools. When you want to save a web page locally, press F9, or drag the address bar to Onfolio.

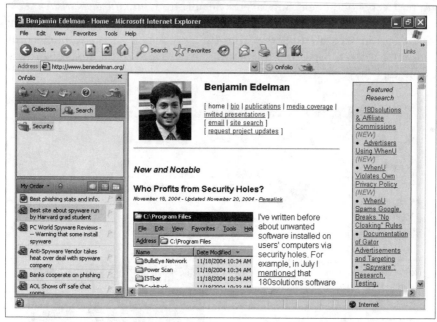

Figure 4-22. Onfolio, which makes it easy to browse to pages you've saved offline

Onfolio is shareware, and is free to try, but it costs $49.95 if you decide to keep it. Get it from *http://www.onfolio.com*.

HACK #39   Hack Internet Explorer with the Group Policy Editor

XP Professional's Group Policy Editor lets you tweak Internet Explorer in countless ways—from changing its logo and background, to changing its titlebar text, and beyond.

XP Professional owners have a reason to feel good about spending the extra $100 or so they forked over for their version of the operating system: the Group Policy Editor, available only in Professional, can make all kinds of secret tweaks to Internet Explorer. This tool, used primarily for setting network and multiuser policies and rights, can also be used to customize the way XP and Internet Explorer look and work. It makes it easy to customize many different aspects of Internet Explorer's behavior and appearance from one central place, without having to edit the Registry or delve deep into menus, dialog boxes, and options. You can customize how Internet Explorer looks and works for each individual account on the machine, or just for a single account if there is only one.

That means you'll be able to create customized versions of IE for a variety of different purposes. For example, you can create customized browsers for your children, or for a business if you run or administer a small business.

Run the Group Policy Editor by typing gpedit.msc at a command line or in the Run box and pressing Enter. When it opens, go to User Configuration\ Windows Settings\Internet Explorer Maintenance. There are five categories of Internet Explorer settings you can modify:

- Browser User Interface
- Connection
- URLs
- Security
- Programs

To change individual settings, browse to any of the categories, then from the right pane choose the setting you want to configure—for example, the browser title. Double-click the setting, and then fill out the dialog box, such as the one shown in Figure 4-23, which lets you change Internet Explorer's static and animated logos.

You can change quite a few settings with the Group Policy Editor. Next, we'll take a look at what the best of each category can do.

Browser User Interface

As the name implies, this section lets you customize Internet Explorer's interface. This section, as a whole, lets you create your own customized version of Internet Explorer. For example, you can create a version of IE specifically for one of your children—take a digital photo of her and use it as the background for the toolbar, crop a headshot photo of her and use it as the animated custom logo, and change the browser title to put her name on it. You can make three types of tweaks in this section:

Browser Title
> This option lets you customize Internet Explorer's titlebar text, though only to a limited degree; you can add your name or your company's name to a text string of "Microsoft Internet Explorer provided by." For example, you can have the titlebar read "Microsoft Explorer provided by Preston Gralla." When you do this, Outlook Express will have the same title as well. Because you need to have that initial text string, this

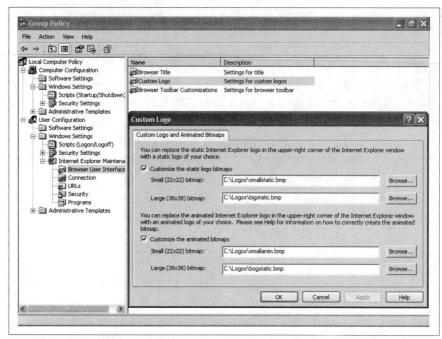

Figure 4-23. Using the Group Policy Editor to change Internet Explorer's settings

isn't a great hack unless you're a computer manufacturer and want to brand the browser.

Custom Logo

This setting lets you replace Internet Explorer's static and animated logo with logos of your own. Note that to do this, you'll first have to create the logos yourself. It's easier to use the Group Policy Editor to change your logo than to use the Registry.

Browser Toolbar Customizations

You can use your own bitmap as the background to the Internet Explorer toolbar. Additionally, you can delete the existing toolbar buttons and add buttons of your own. You don't have to worry if the bitmap you want to use is not the same size as the toolbar. XP will accommodate it—for example, by tiling a graphic that is smaller than the toolbar so that it appears multiple times.

Connection

This section lets you customize Internet Explorer's connection settings, which you would otherwise have to go to several places to set:

Connection Settings

This lets you customize your existing Internet connection settings and import them for another use on the PC. It doesn't have any use if you're the only user of the machine; it's intended to help you set up other accounts' connection settings. If you have a network at home, for example, you could copy the settings from one machine to every other machine on the network.

Automatic Browser Configuration

This is purely an administrator's tool. It lets you automatically change browser configurations on users' machines.

Proxy Settings

This lets you tell Internet Explorer to use proxy servers. You can also set up proxy servers from within Internet Explorer. For more details on setting up proxy servers, see "Protect Your Computer with the New Windows Firewall" [Hack #77].

User Agent String

This lets you customize the user agent string that is sent to web sites whenever you visit them. The user agent string gives out basic information about your operating system and browser to the web site so that the site can better track usage statistics. Using this setting lets you append a specific text string to your PC's user agent string.

URLs

This section is mainly for administrators, so if you don't need administrative tools you can pretty much forgo it. If you are an administrator, it will let you specify IE settings for multiple machines, such as setting a home page for all, specifying a URL they will go to when Help is chosen, and populating their Favorites with those of your choice. If you run a small business, you can use these settings to build a business-specific browser for all your employees. For example, set the home page to be your company's home page or populate Favorites with intranet pages or other pages your employees need to access regularly, such as benefits information:

Favorites and Links

This lets you create a Favorites folder and links, or import them. It's primarily an administrator's tool, since it doesn't add much extra functionality to the normal way you can manage Favorites.

Important URLs

You can specify the starting page, create your own customized Search bar, and create a Help page that will display when someone clicks Help → Online Support. Again, this is primarily an administrator's tool.

Security

Here's where to set Internet Explorer security settings. You can change these settings from directly within Internet Explorer just as easily as changing them here—unless you need to change the settings for several accounts, in which case this is the place to go.

Security Zones and Content Rating
>   You can customize both security zones and content ratings, which limit sites with objectionable content from being visited. This is primarily an administrator's tool, since these settings can be edited easily from inside Internet Explorer by choosing Tools → Internet Options → Security and Tools → Internet Options → Content. But it's ideal for parents who have networks at home and want to customize different security settings for their children's computers. You can set a higher level of security for children's computers and a lower level for parents' PCs.

Authenticode Settings
>   This lets you designate specific credential agencies and software publishers as trustworthy. This is primarily an administrator's tool, since these settings can be edited easily from inside Internet Explorer by choosing Tools → Internet Options → Security and Tools → Internet Options → Content → Certificates.

Programs

Once again, this section is mainly for administrators. It lets you change default programs for multiple machines. So, for users who require only a simple email program, you can set the default to be Outlook Express. For other users, you can set it as Outlook or a third-party email program.

Programs
>   This lets you change the default programs to be used for purposes such as email, HTML editing, and others. This is primarily an administrator's tool, since these settings can be edited easily by choosing Tools → Internet Options → Security and Tools → Internet Options → Programs.

HACK
#40   Speed Up File Downloads

Don't wait any longer for slow file downloads. Use this free program to accelerate them, regardless of your connection speed.

No matter how fast your Internet connection is, it's not fast enough. Whether it's a pokey dial-up or a broadband connection, you always have complaints and you always have a greater need for speed.

This is particularly true when you're downloading files, especially large ones. While there might be no way to physically change your connection speed, you can get the free Download Accelerator Plus (DAP) program from SpeedBit (*http://www.speedbit.com*) to speed up your downloads significantly, whether via FTP or HTTP.

The program accelerates your downloads in two ways. When you start to download a file, DAP does a mirror search of all the servers that carry the same file, identifies the fastest servers closest to you, and then starts downloading from those servers instead of the one you originally chose. It also sets up a multiconnection download, downloading portions of the file from multiple fast servers simultaneously and then reassembling the file when all the pieces are on your PC. This makes the most efficient use of your available bandwidth because normally there are pauses and hesitations when you download, and if you're downloading with multiple connections there will be fewer of those pauses.

The program also resumes broken downloads; if for some reason your connection is broken, it'll pick up where you left off when you next connect to the Internet. Also useful is the zip preview feature that lets you preview the contents of zip-compressed files before you download. And it'll schedule downloads for you as well. For example, you can schedule downloads to take place overnight, when you're away from your computer.

DAP is free, but the free version delivers ads inside the program. For $29.95 you can get a version without the ads that also includes a few minor extras, such as the ability to extract individual files from within *.zip* archives, instead of extracting the whole archive.

HACK #41   Secrets of Web Site Hosting with Internet Information Services (IIS)

XP Professional includes a free, built-in web server. If you're planning on using it, check out these tips to improve your site's performance, cut down on bandwidth, deliver pages faster, and reduce Page Not Found errors.

If you've wanted to host a web server but don't want to go to the trouble of configuring a separate machine and server, XP Professional has help for you. Windows XP Professional comes with Internet Information Services (IIS) Version 5.1, which lets you host web sites and FTP sites and run a Simple Mail Transfer Protocol (SMTP) service for sending email. (The Home Edition doesn't include any of these capabilities.) It's not something you'll use to build a substantial web site because it has some significant drawbacks. The web server and FTP server allow only 10 simultaneous connections, for example, and the SMTP server isn't a full-blown mail server; it can act as only a relay.

Still, if you want to host a small web site for friends, family, or internal use for a small business, or if you want to build a "staging server" to test out sites before publicly posting them on a different server, IIS is a good bet.

IIS isn't installed by default in XP Professional. To install it, choose Control Panel → Add or Remove Programs → Add/Remove Windows Components and, from the Windows Component Wizard that appears, highlight Internet Information Services (IIS) and click Details.

Administer your web site by using the Microsoft Management Console (MMC) IIS snap-in. Choose Control Panel → Administrative Tools and double-click Internet Information Services. The console tree, shown in Figure 4-24, shows the structure of your web and FTP sites and gives you control over those sites.

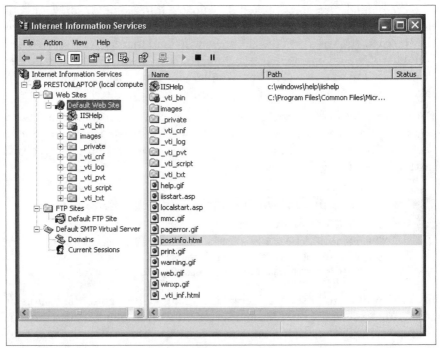

Figure 4-24. The console tree for the MMC IIS snap-in

In this hack, I'll assume you know the basics of building a web site with IIS, so I'll instead clue you in to secrets of IIS.

Change the Directory and Do a Redirect

By default, IIS uses the *C:\Inetpub\wwwroot* directory for your web site. However, you'll most likely want to change that directory to one that better matches your own PC setup. To change it, launch the MMC snap-in as detailed earlier in this hack, then right-click Default Web Site and choose the Home Directory tab, shown in Figure 4-25. In the Local Path box, type in or browse to the directory you want to use.

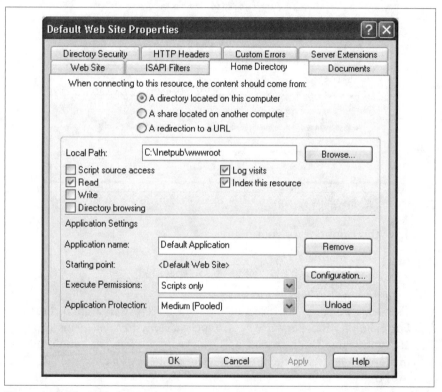

Figure 4-25. The Default Web Site Home Directory tab

If you want to use a directory on another computer located on the network, select "A share located on another computer." The Local Path box changes to Network Directory, and the Browse button changes to a Connect As button. Type in the directory information from the other computer, then click Connect As to use your logon credentials to use the network share.

This tab also lets you do a redirect of your web site so that when people visit your web site they'll be redirected to another site. That site doesn't have to be on your network; it can be any location on the Internet. This option is most useful when you move your web site to another URL but want those who use the old URL to be able to access it. To do a redirect, select "A redirection to a URL." The screen will change to the screen shown in Figure 4-26.

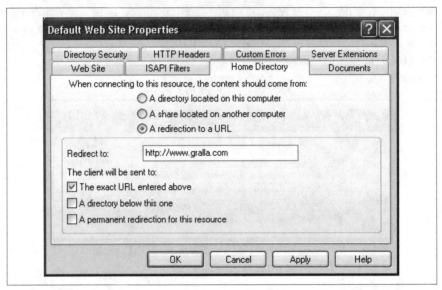

Figure 4-26. Redirecting to a URL

You have three options for your redirect:

The exact URL entered above
   This redirects all traffic to the URL you specified.

A directory below this one
   This lets you force a redirect of a parent directory to a child directory. For example, if a person was to type *www.mysite.com* in his browser, and you wanted him to end up at *www.mysite.com/pics*, you'd choose this option and have the location *www.mysite.com/pics* in the "Redirect to" box.

A permanent redirection for this resource
   When this option is chosen, a "301 Permanent Redirect" message will be sent to the visiting browser. This can be used by some browsers to automatically update their bookmarks or Favorites list with your new site location.

Redirect Incorrect Incoming URLs

They're the bugaboo of every web site administrator—people who mistype URLs and get the dreaded "404 The page cannot be found" error. For example, if a person wanted to visit *http://www.gralla.com/mybio.htm*, but instead typed *http://www.gralla.com/myboi.htm* into his browser, he'd get an error message. And I'd lose a visitor.

Solve the problem with URLSpellCheck for IIS (*http://www.port80software. com/products/urlspellcheck/*). It redirects misspelled URLs to the right page so that your visitors don't get error messages. It fixes instances in which an extra character is put into the URL, characters are transposed, a character is missing, or the wrong character is typed. It will also fix instances when the incorrect extension is typed.

 URLSpellCheck can't fix problems when someone types in the wrong domain—for example, *http://www.grala.com* rather than *http://www.gralla.com*. Domains are handled by the Domain Name System (DNS), so add-in software can't solve the problem. To solve it, you'd have to own the various misspellings of your domain and then have DNS redirect the visitor to the proper domain.

The program runs as a snap-in to the MMC. Highlight your web site in the MMC, right-click the Properties button, and click the URLSpellCheck tab. From there, you'll be able to enable or disable the program.

URLSpellCheck is shareware and free to try, but if you use it for more than 30 days you're expected to pay $49.95.

Use Caching for Better Performance

When you run a web site, three issues top your list of concerns: how to preserve bandwidth, how to reduce the performance load on your PC, and how to make the site load faster for visitors.

Here's a three-for-one solution: use caching properly. When visitors come to your site, have them use cached images such as logos, navigation bars, and similar content from their own PC, instead of hitting your server every time. When you do this, after they retrieve the image for the first time, each subsequent time they need to get the image it's retrieved from their own PC, rather than your server. Their pages load faster, your PC doesn't have to serve up as much content, and you don't use as much bandwidth.

To make sure your site uses caching, try CacheRight (*http://www. port80software.com/products/cacheright/*). Like URLSpellCheck, it runs as a snap-in to MMC. To use it, highlight your web site in MMC, right-click the Properties button, and click the CacheRight tab. From there, you'll be able to enable or disable the program, as well as set options for how the cache should be used. The main option you'll set is expiration policies for the cache—in other words, at what point the visiting browser should check your web site to see whether the content the browser has cached is old and needs to be updated. You set the amount of time, such as a week, and set when that time should start, either the last time the browser visited your site or the last time you modified the cached content. I prefer to use the start time as the last time I modified the cached content; that way, browsers won't unnecessarily try to get content from my site.

CacheRight is shareware and free to try, but if you use it for more than 30 days you're expected to pay $149.95.

See Also

- The IISFAQ site (*http://www.iisfaq.com*) is a great source for tips, advice, and downloads related to IIS.

Surf the Internet Ad-Free

HACK #42   Cruising the Internet these days feels like a trip down the Las Vegas strip. Here's how you can turn off the ads and surf in peace.

There once was a day when advertising on the Web was limited to relatively small, discreet banners ads at the top of pages.

Those days are gone. Now ads are everywhere—big ones embedded in the middle of the page, large ones running down the right column, and monster ones that seem to take up entire pages. Ads can be more than just annoying; web sites can also use them to track your surfing activities.

But you don't have to put up with it. You can surf the Internet ad-free. There are several ways to do it: either use ad-blocking software, or do some hacking of your system for free. Either way, you'll whack the ads.

Use a HOSTS File to Kill Ads

If you're looking for a free way to kill ads, using a *HOSTS* file is a great solution. This technique takes advantage of the fact that few web sites host their own ads. Instead, they generally use ad servers that deliver the ads. There aren't very many of these ad servers, so if you block those servers from delivering content to your PC, you'll block most of the ads on the Internet.

First, some background about *HOSTS* files. When you type in a URL such as *http://www.oreilly.com*, your PC needs to translate those letters into a numeric IP address that it can understand, such as 208.201.239.37. Doing this is called *name resolution*. DNS servers on the Internet provide name resolution automatically and behind the scenes as you surf the Web.

When you type in a URL, before your PC contacts a DNS server it looks at a *HOSTS* file on your PC. If it finds the domain name and IP address there, it uses the IP address it finds. If it doesn't find the domain name and IP address, it goes out to a DNS server. Because your PC first looks to the *HOSTS* file for name resolution, you can use that file to block ads.

The *HOSTS* file is a plain-text file you can create or edit with a text editor like Notepad. The file has no extension; it is named only *HOSTS*. You'll find an existing *HOSTS* file in *C:\Windows\System32\Drivers\Etc\HOSTS*. (In Windows XP Professional, it is located in *C:\Winnt\System32\Drivers\Etc\HOSTS*).

Each line in the file consists of an IP address and a domain name, like this:

```
208.201.239.37        oreilly.com
216.92131.107         simtel.net
```

When you type in an address such as *http://www.oreilly.com*, your PC looks in the file, sees that its IP address is 208.201.239.37, and then sends you there.

Every *HOSTS* file also has one default entry:

```
127.0.0.1      localhost
```

127.0.0.1 is a special IP address called a *loopback* because it refers back to your local computer, not to the Internet or a network. It's used by developers to test network software without having to be being physically connected to a network. But you can also use the loopback address to prevent web ads from displaying.

To use the *HOSTS* file to block ads, you edit the file by adding individual entries for each ad server, and then associating those entries with the loopback address—your own computer. So, when you visit a site with ads, your PC looks at the *HOSTS* file, finds the entry for the ad server, but never visits the ad server because it's instead redirected to the loopback address. So, the ads are never displayed, and your travels aren't tracked.

For each ad server you find, create a line in your *HOSTS* file, like this:

```
127.0.0.1      ads.doubleclick.net
```

Double-click is one of the largest ad servers on the Internet, so this entry will block a significant number of ads.

How to find ad servers? In your browser, right-click an ad and select Copy Shortcut. That'll put the ad's URL into the Windows Clipboard. Then you can paste it into your *HOSTS* file. Make sure to include only the domain name portion. So, for example, when you right-click an ad and copy its location, you might get a very long entry, like this:

```
http://ar.atwola.com/link/93182535/html?badsc=B0Q0AoVXYvX-nBcuskw4IZTGAt-
b7n1Q2V6vctHpvtzTK5RxgZIq9FU6ESe4QfJ7ELVJ3ENBHgvUkPknRBjhXGQIU32DP3fv_uj-
LT3lA5W-A3k5mRc7pQl6QXJ6G9mgrNblbJDXkPLBNqQXvIwmZby-bDLeZvaX9kP33XkoXAO5jQ-
u5hUSd4k7tpzXK8soyJBOZQ3lNAt5qcj8tMoKpLG_tKzaoJSChRrO8af31JSM5-
UX69B1BFEpSfUmp4ZfT5XLEI35bYTQoHS6tbTvZRcK7C8YjgqxdH
```

In your *HOSTS* file, though, use only the domain name. So, this would be your entry in the *HOSTS* file:

```
127.0.0.1      ar.atwola.com
```

It can be almost impossible to compile a list of most of the ad servers on the Internet like this. And because the servers change constantly, you'd have to constantly try to keep it up-to-date. So, instead of trying to do it yourself, you can go to a web site that has a *HOSTS* file with hundreds of entries Go to *http://everythingisnt.com/hosts*, and you'll see a page filled with *HOSTS* entries for ad servers. Copy and paste it into your own *HOSTS* file. (For more information about *HOSTS* files and ad blocking, see *http://www.everythingisnt.com/hosts.html*.)

How well does it work? Take a look at before-and-after screenshots. Figure 4-27 shows a CNN page with no ad blocked; Figure 4-28 shows the same page with the banner ad blocked by a *HOSTS* file. Also note that the browser's built-in pop-up blocker blocked a pop up.

Figure 4-27. A normal CNN page, with no ad blocking

Figure 4-28. A CNN page with ads blocked by the HOSTS file

Use Ad-Blocking Software

The *HOSTS* file does a good job of blocking ads, but it's far from perfect. If, for example, ads are being delivered from the same domain as the web page you're visiting, ads won't be blocked. Also, if the ad server is not on your *HOSTS* list, you won't be able to block it. Furthermore, the technique might not block some of the more obnoxious ads on the Internet, such as Flash-based animations.

You can buy ad-blocking software for more effective ad blocking, or download free ad-blocking software. But you might not need to buy or download extra software because your software might already include it. For example, if you use the for-pay version of the ZoneAlarm firewall [Hack #78], ad blocking is built in. To block ads, run ZoneAlarm, and click Privacy on the left-hand side of the screen. On the page that appears, in the Ad Blocking section, choose High to block all ads. Choose Medium to block most ads, but to allow banner and *skyscraper ads* (ads that take up the vertical column on the right side of a web page). You can also customize the types of ads to let through by clicking Custom and choosing which ads to block, and which to let through.

If you don't have ZoneAlarm, the following free and for-pay programs block ads to varying degrees:

Webwasher Classic

This free program blocks many types of ads, including banners and Flash animations. Get it from *http://www.webwasher.com*. When you get there, look for the Webwasher Classic area, and click the "Download free version" link.

AdSubtract Pro

This is the most comprehensive ad killer you'll find. It blocks pretty much every type of ad you can name, and can even filter out for-pay search listings on sites like Google. (For details, see the following section "Hacking the Hack.") It's shareware, and available at *http://www.intermute.com/adsubtract*. It's free to try, but you'll have to pay $29.95 if you decide to keep it.

Pop-Up No-No

This free software, available from *http://www.popupnono.com*, will block pop ups, as its name implies, but also blocks Flash animation ads.

Ad Muncher

This one uses an interesting technique to block ads: it filters HTML it receives from an ad server and replaces it with benign content. It's shareware, and available at *http://www.admuncher.com*. It's free to try, but you'll have to pay $25 if you decide to keep it.

Hacking the Hack

The worst ads of all might well be the ones you don't even realize are ads, but rather, are sponsored results in search engines that look much like regular results. But there is a way to filter out even these types of ads; you can use the Search Sanity feature in AdSubtract Pro.

When you use AdSubtract, Search Sanity isn't turned on by default. But it's easy to turn it on. Double-click the AdSubtract icon in the Windows system tray, choose Search Sanity, and check the boxes next to the search engines whose results you want to filter. Click OK, and sponsored results and ads will be banished. Figure 4-29 shows the normal Google search results; Figure 4-30 shows the Google page with the sponsored search results filtered out by AdSubtract.

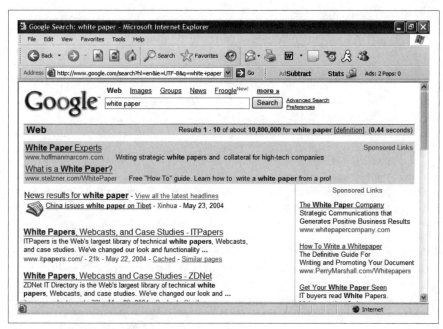

Figure 4-29. Normal Google search results

Figure 4-30. Sponsored search results filtered out by AdSubtract

See Also

HACK #43 Hack Firefox

The free browser Firefox has gained millions of adherents since its release because of its security features, customizability, and features that Internet Explorer lacks, such as tabbed browsing. Here's a grab bag of hacks for powering it up.

Internet Explorer has some serious problems. Because it's intimately tied to Windows XP, it's become a favorite source of malware-writers, who use its security holes not just to harm the browser itself, but also to get into the guts of the operating system. And it has a variety of security holes that never seem to get plugged.

In addition, it hasn't gotten a face-lift or significant new features for years (other than pop-up blocking in SP2), and it's starting to show its age. It doesn't, for example, let you browse the Web with tabs, letting you visit multiple sites simultaneously by putting each site in its own tab.

Because of this, the free, open source browser Firefox (available for download from *http://www.mozilla.org/products/firefox*), shown in Figure 4-31, has gained millions of followers. It's more secure than Internet Explorer, includes features such as a pop-up blocker, lets you browse to multiple web sites using tabs, and much more.

Many people consider Firefox superior to Internet Explorer for another reason as well: it's much more customizable, and hundreds of free add-ins are available that extend its power and features. In this hack, you'll learn how to add new features with Firefox extensions, and how to hack the interface with a hidden style sheet.

Using Firefox Extensions

Perhaps the most remarkable feature of Firefox is its ability to use *extensions*. Extensions are free add-ins that give the browser all kinds of new features. Because Firefox is open source, anyone can write an extension, and developers all over the Internet have put their creativity to use. There are hundreds of them, and new ones are added every day (by the time you read

Figure 4-31. Browsing multiple sites at once, using tabs

this, more than 1,000 extensions could be available). They add a mind-bog-gling array of capabilities, such as telling you the real URL of a site you're visiting so that you can't be the victim of a phishing exploit; letting you navigate the Web using *mouse gestures* so that you can browse by moving your mouse rather than by clicking; blocking ads; and much more.

How to find extensions? In Firefox, choose Tools → Extensions → Get More Extensions. You'll be sent to a web page that lists extensions by category, and also lists the most popular and most recent one. This is the official Firefox extensions site, but it's not the only place you can find extensions. You can find them on other places on the Web as well, notably at *http://texturizer.net/firefox/extensions* and *http://extensionroom.mozdev.org*.

Browse to the extension you want to install and click Install. If you want more information about the extension before you install it, click the title of the extension, and you'll be sent to a page with more information about it; from there, you can also download the extension (see Figure 4-32).

After you click Install, the screen shown in Figure 4-33 appears.

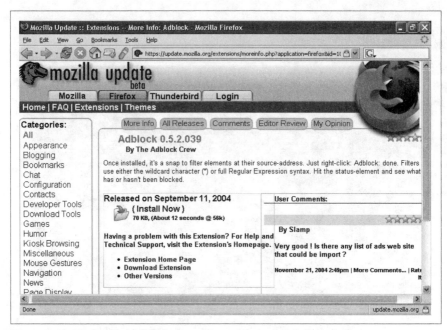

Figure 4-32. Finding the Adblock extension

Figure 4-33. Starting to install the extension

Click Install Now, and after several moments, the extension will be installed and will appear in your Extensions window, as shown in Figure 4-34. The extension won't work yet; first you have to close Firefox and restart it.

Figure 4-34. The installed extension

When you restart Firefox, the extension will start working. Many extensions allow you to customize their options. So, immediately after installing an extension, you should do that. To customize the options for an extension, choose Tools → Extensions, select the extension you want to customize, and choose Options. If you want to uninstall an extension, select it, click Uninstall, and then click OK. You'll have to close Firefox and restart for the extension to uninstall.

Hundreds of extensions are available, and everyone has their favorites. Here are a few of mine:

Googlebar
> This installs the equivalent of the Google toolbar in Firefox. (For more information about the Google toolbar, see "Better Internet Searching from Your Desktop" [Hack #47].)

BugMeNot
> Many web sites require free registration before you can read their content. This nifty add-in supplies you with login information and logs you into most of those web sites so that you don't have to fill out registration forms.

SpoofStick

A great antiphishing tool, SpoofStick displays the real URL of a web site you're visiting so that you can't be fooled by spoof sites. For more information about the tool and about stopping phishing attacks, see "Don't Get Reeled In by Phishers" **[Hack #37]**.

Autofill

When you buy online, or register with a web site, you have to fill out long forms, which can be tedious and time-consuming. With this extension, you click a button, and the form is filled in automatically.

Mouse Gestures

Instead of clicking your way around the Web, you can use mouse gestures. Hold down the mouse button and make a gesture with your mouse, and you can open and close windows, navigate from page to page, and more. So, for example, to close a tab, you would hold down the right-mouse button and move the mouse in a reverse "L" motion, and the tab would close.

Bandwidth Tester

What's the true speed of your Internet connection? Install this extension and find out. Figure 4-35 shows it at work.

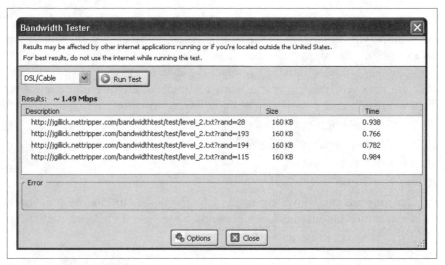

Figure 4-35. Bandwidth Tester in action

Hacking the Firefox Interface

It's easy to apply *themes* to Firefox, which give it different colors and graphics. To apply a theme, choose Tools → Themes → Get More Themes, and you'll be sent to a web site with many different themes. When you find a theme you want, click Install. For more information about a theme, click the title, and you'll be sent to a page with more information, which sometimes includes a preview. You can install the theme from that page as well.

After you click Install, the theme will be available to use. Click Tools → Themes, choose the theme you want to use, as shown in Figure 4-36, and then choose Use Theme. You'll have to restart Firefox for the new theme to take effect. If you want to uninstall a theme so that it's no longer available, select Uninstall from the screen shown in Figure 4-36.

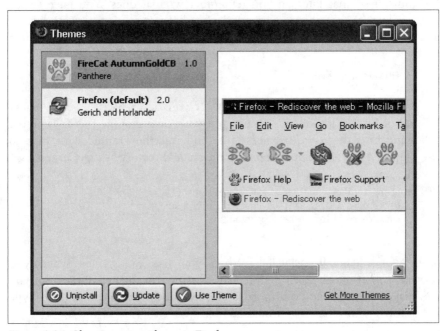

Figure 4-36. Choosing a new theme in Firefox

But Firefox lets you do more than just change the theme. You can also hack the interface. Firefox's interface can be controlled by a cascading style sheet (CSS), a file that contains instructions on how Firefox should display. By editing that file, you can change Firefox's appearance.

The file is named *userChrome.css*, and for it to work, it needs to be located in the folder *C:\Documents and Settings\<Your Name>\Application Data\ Mozilla\Firefox\Profiles\default.xxx\chrome*, where *<Your Name>* is your XP account name, and the *.xxx* will be three random characters.

When you install Firefox, there is no *userChrome.css* file in that folder. Instead, you can find it in *C:\Documents and Settings\<Your Name>\ Application Data\Mozilla\Profiles\Default\xxxxxxxx.slt\chrome*, where *xxxxxxxx* is a random collection of characters. Copy the file to *C:\ Documents and Settings\<Your Name>\Application Data\Mozilla\Firefox\ Profiles\default.xxx\chrome*. Once it's there, you can edit it to change Firefox's interface. It's a plain-text file, so you can edit it with Notepad. Following are some of the hacks you can make by editing the file. If you don't already have a *userChrome.css*, you can start off with a blank text file, and name it *userChrome.css*.

Note that it's a good idea, when putting in this code, to put in a reminder for yourself so that later on you remember what it does. You have to tell *userChrome.css* to ignore your reminder so that it doesn't try to interpret it as code. So, surround your comments with /* to begin and */ to end, like this:

```
/* This is a comment */
```

Put your own graphic on the Firefox toolbar. If you don't like the plain background of Firefox's toolbar, you can put your own graphic there. Type the following into the *userChrome.css* file, and put the graphic you want to use—for instance, *background.gif*—in the same directory as *userChrome.css*:

```
/* Change the toolbar graphic */
menubar, toolbox, toolbar, .tabbrowser-tabs {
    background-image: url("background.gif") !important;
    background-color: none !important;
    }
```

Make it easier to find the active tab. When you use many tabs when you browse, sometimes it can be difficult to distinguish the active one. So, you can make that tab stand out more, and gray out the background tabs. Type the following into the *userChrome.css* file:

```
/* Change color of active tab */
tab{
    -moz-appearance: none !important;
}
tab[selected="true"] {
    background-color: rgb(222,218,210) !important;
    color: black !important;
}

/* Change color of normal tabs */
tab:not([selected="true"]) {
    background-color: rgb(200,196,188) !important;
    color: gray !important;
}
```

Change the width of the search bar. You can change the width of the search bar on the upper-right corner of Firefox. (To hack the search bar, see "Build Your Own Firefox Search Engine" [Hack #44].) You do it by specifying the width of the bar in pixels. This code tells the search bar to be 400 pixels wide:

```
/* Make the Search bar wider
   (in this case 400 pixels wide) */
 #search-container, #searchbar {
   -moz-box-flex: 400 !important;
}
```

Move the sidebar to the right. Firefox lets you use a sidebar when you want to view your history or your bookmarks. The sidebar displays on the left side when you choose View → Sidebar. If you prefer, you can have the sidebar appear on the right, by typing this code into the *userChrome.css* file:

```
/* Place the sidebar on the right edge of the window  */
window > hbox {
    direction:rtl;
}
window > hbox > * {
    direction:ltr;
}
```

Naturally, you wouldn't necessarily use all these hacks in concert with one another. But you could, of course. Figure 4-37 shows what Firefox looks like after we've added the hacks to the *userChrome.css* file.

You can hack Firefox using the *userChrome.css* file in several additional ways. For more, go to *http://www.mozilla.org/support/firefox/tips* and *http://www.mozilla.org/unix/customizing.html*.

See Also

- "Build Your Own Firefox Search Engine" **[Hack #44]**
- "Better Internet Searching from Your Desktop" **[Hack #47]**
- "Give Internet Explorer a Face-Lift" **[Hack #32]**

HACK
#44

Build Your Own Firefox Search Engine

Firefox's built-in search box lets you search Google from wherever you are. You don't have to settle for that built-in searching, though, because you can build your own Firefox search engine plug-in to search through any site from the Google search box.

Take a look at the upper-right corner of your Firefox browser [Hack #43]. You'll see a nifty search box called the Search Bar that lets you search Google by

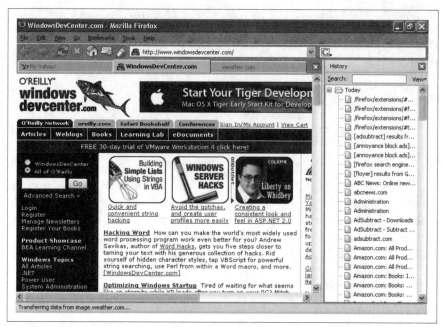

Figure 4-37. Firefox, after the userChrome.css file has been edited

typing in a search term. Better yet, you don't have to settle for searching just Google that way. You can search through other sites as well by installing a specific search engine add-in for that site to the Search Bar. So, instead of using Google to search the Internet, for example, you can use Ask Jeeves (*http://www.ask.com*) or A9 (*http://www.a9.com*).

And you're not limited to search sites. You can also search through an individual site. So, for example, you can search through Amazon.com (*http://www.amazon.com*), eBay (*http://www.ebay.com*), Dictionary.com (*http://www.dictionary.com*), or the health site WebMD (*http://www.webmd.com*) from that box as well. All you need to do is find and add the right search engine plug-in.

To do so, click the down arrow next to the G in the search box, and choose Add Engines. You'll be sent to *http://mycroft.mozdev.org/download.html*, which is a directory of hundreds of search engines you can use in Firefox. Browse or search until you find one you want; then click its link. You'll get a dialog box like that shown in Figure 4-38, asking whether you want to add it to the Search Bar. Click OK, and it'll be added.

To choose which search engine to use in the Search Bar, click the down arrow next to the G in the Search Bar and choose your search engine from

Figure 4-38. Confirming the addition of a new search engine to the Firefox Search Bar

the list. Then, type in a search term, and you'll search using that engine. The engine will stay there as your default until you choose another one.

All that's well and good. But why settle for a search engine that's already been written? It's not that hard to write a plug-in of your own.

To get started, open a new file in a text editor such as Notepad. Give it the name of the site for which you're building a search engine, and give it the extension *.src*. In our instance, we're going to build a search engine for searching the federal government's White House site, so we'll call it *White House.src*. Save it in the folder *C:\Program Files\Microsoft Firefox\ searchplugins*.

The first line of the plug-in should be the search tag <search, and the next line should indicate which version of Netscape the plug-in was written for. Now, I know Firefox isn't Netscape, but both are based on common code, called Mozilla, and for reasons not quite understandable, you need to include the most current version number of Netscape. At the time of this writing, it's 7.1, so that's the version we'll put here. Enter the text version="7.1" underneath the search tag so that the first two lines of your file look like this:

```
<search
version="7.1
```

Next, name your plug-in by using this syntax:

```
name="My Plugin"
```

But replace *My Plugin* with the name of the plug-in you're writing. In our instance, we're calling it White House.

Now, describe your plug-in by using this syntax:

```
description="My Plugin - My First Search Plugin"
```

Our plug-in now looks like this:

```
<search
version="7.1"
name="White House"
description="Search www.whitehouse.gov"
```

Now you have to tell the plug-in what action to take when you type in a search term and press Enter. What you're doing here is telling it how to search the site. To get this information, go to the site for which you want to build a search engine. Do a search, and look at the first part of the resulting URL, the portion before the first question mark (?). That's what will tell what action your search engine should take. For the *http://www.whitehouse. gov* site, that first part of the URL before the ? is *http://www.whitehouse.gov/ query.html*.

Here's the syntax:

```
action="http://myplugin.faq/search"
```

So, in our instance, the line looks like this:

```
action="http://www.whitehouse.gov/query.html"
```

Now you need to put in the name of the search form. This will be the name of the site you're on, written with the following syntax:

```
searchForm="http://myplugin.faq"
```

Again, in our instance, this is:

```
searchForm="http://www.whitehouse.gov"
```

Underneath that, put the following code:

```
method="GET"
```

This tells the plug-in to use the GET method of searching, which is the only method supported, so there's no choice here. After that line, close off the search tag with a closing tag:

```
>
```

So, here's what our plug-in looks like so far:

```
<search
version="7.1"
name="White House"
description="Search www.whitehouse.gov"
action="http://www.whitehouse.gov/query.html"
searchForm="http://www.whitehouse.gov"
method="GET"
>
```

Now you need to add a line that tells the site's webmasters and site administrators someone is searching the site using the plug-in. So, put in this line:

```
<input name="sourceid" value="Mozilla-search">
```

Next, you need to tell your plug-in what syntax to use when searching for the text you'll type into the Search Bar. This varies from site to site. Again, take a look at the URL that results after you search the site. Look for whatever falls between the first ampersand (&) and your search term. For the *www.whitehouse.gov* site, it is qt.

Here's the syntax for this line:

```
<input name="query" user="">
```

So, in our instance, the line looks like this:

```
<input name="qt" user="">
```

Now you need to close off the entire search section with a closing </search> tag:

```
</search>
```

Here's what our final file looks like:

```
<search
version="7.1"
name="White House"
description="Search www.whitehouse.gov"
action="http://www.whitehouse.gov/query.html"
searchForm="http://www.whitehouse.gov"
method="GET"
>

<input name="sourceid" value="Mozilla-search">
<input name="qt" user="">

</search>
```

That's it; you're done. Close Firefox and restart it. Click the down arrow at the Search Bar, and your search engine plug-in will show up. Select it, type in your search term, press Enter, and you'll search the site.

Hacking the Hack

When you right-click the down arrow on the Search Bar, you'll see that many plug-ins have a small icon next to them. Yours doesn't, however. That's because you haven't created an icon for it. Create a 16×16 pixel icon, give it the same name as your plug-in, and save it as either a *.jpg* or *.png* graphics file. Then, put it in the *C:\Program Files\Microsoft Firefox\searchplugins* folder. So, in our instance, we create one called *White House.jpg*.

For information about how to create icons, see "Make Your Own Cursors and Icons" **[Hack #19]**. You can also find ready-made icons in the right size, although not the right format, right on the Web. When you visit many web sites, you'll see in your web browser a small icon to the left of the *http://*; that same icon might show up next to the *http://* on your Favorites list because the sites use something called a *favicon* which the browser displays.

You can find the favicon for the site, save it to your PC, convert it to *.jpg* or *.png* format, and use it for your search engine plug-in. To find the favicon for a site, go to *http://www.website.com/favicon.ico*, where website is the Favorite you want an icon for. For example, go to *http://www.oreilly.com/favicon.ico* for the O'Reilly icon. Keep in mind, though, that not all web sites have favicons, so you won't be able to do this for every site.

If you're using Firefox to get the icon, a dialog box will open, asking what to do with the file. Save it to your hard disk. If you're using Internet Explorer, you'll open the icon itself in your browser. Right-click it, choose Save Picture As…, and save it on your hard disk.

It'll be in *.ico* format, so you need to convert it to *.jpg* or *.png*. An excellent program for doing this is IrfanView, available from *http://www.irfanview.com*. For details about how to do the conversion, see "Image Conversion in a Pinch" **[Hack #99]**. When you store the file, make sure it's in *C:\Program Files\Microsoft Firefox\searchplugins*.

See Also

- If you'd like, you can share your plug-in with others and have it available for download from the *http://mycroft.mozdev.org/download.html* site. To do so, you'll have to add some code to your plug-in. For details, go to *http://mycroft.mozdev.org/deepdocs/quickstart.html#firstplugin*. The page also has more detailed instructions for creating your search plug-in.

Google Your Desktop
HACK
#45
Google your desktop and the rest of your filesystem, mailbox, and instant messenger conversations—even your browser cache.

Not content to help you find things just on the Internet, Google takes on that teetering pile on your desktop—your computer's desktop, that is.

The Google Desktop (*http://desktop.google.com*) is your own private little Google server. It sits in the background, slogging through your files and folders, indexing your incoming and outgoing email messages, listening in on your instant messenger chats, and browsing the Web right along with you. Just about anything you see and summarily forget, the Google Desktop sees and memorizes: it's like a photographic memory for your computer.

And it operates in real time.

Beyond the initial sweep, that is. When you first install Google Desktop, it makes use of any idle time to meander your filesystem, email application, instant messages, and browser cache. Imbued with a sense of politeness, the indexer shouldn't interfere at all with your use of your computer; it springs into action only when you step away, take a phone call, or doze off for 30 seconds or more. Pick up the mouse or touch the keyboard and the Google Desktop scuttles off into the corner, waiting patiently for it's next opportunity to look around.

Its initial inventory taken, the Google Desktop server sits back and waits for something of interest to come along. Send or receive an email message, strike up an AOL Instant Messenger (AIM) conversation with a friend, or get a start on that PowerPoint presentation and it'll be noticed and indexed within seconds.

The Google Desktop performs full-text indexes of:

- Text files, Microsoft Word documents, Excel workbooks, and Power-Point presentations living on your hard drive
- Email handled through Outlook or Outlook Express
- AIM conversations
- Web pages browsed in Internet Explorer

Additionally, any other files you have lying about—photographs, MP3s, movies—are indexed by their filename. So, while the Google Desktop can't tell a portrait of Uncle Alfred (*uncle_alfred.jpg*) from a song by "Uncle Cracker" (*uncle_cracker__double_wide__who_s_your_uncle.mp3*), it'll file both under "uncle."

And the point of all this is to make your computer searchable with the ease, speed, and familiar interface you've come to expect of Google. The Google Desktop has its own home page on your computer, shown in Figure 4-39, whether you're online or not. Type in a search query just like you would at Google proper and click the Search Desktop button to search your personal index. Or click Search the Web to send your query out to Google.

But we're getting a little ahead of ourselves here.

Let's take a few steps back, download and install the Google Desktop, and work our way back to searching again.

Figure 4-39. The Google Desktop home page

Installing the Google Desktop

The Google Desktop is a Windows-only application, requiring Windows XP or Windows 2000 SP3 or later. The application itself is tiny, but it'll consume about 500MB of room on your hard drive and works best with 400MHz of computing horsepower and 128MB of memory.

Point your browser at *http://desktop.google.com*, download, and run the Google Desktop installer. It'll install the application, embed a little swirly icon in your taskbar, and drop a shortcut onto your desktop. When it's finished installing and setting itself up, your default browser pops open and you're asked to set a few preferences, as shown in Figure 4-40.

Click the Set Preferences and Continue button and you'll be notified that the Google Desktop is starting its initial indexing sweep. Click the Start Searching button to get to the Google Desktop home page (Figure 4-39).

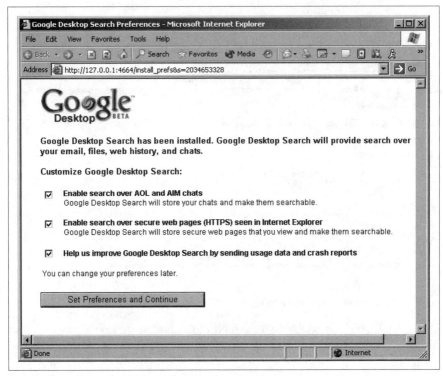

Figure 4-40. Setting Google Desktop search preferences

Searching Your Desktop

From here on out, any time you're looking for something on your computer, rather than invoking Windows search and waiting impatiently while it grinds away (and you grind your teeth) and returns with nothing, double-click the swirly Google Desktop taskbar icon and Google for it. Don't bother combing through an endless array of Inboxes, Outboxes, Sent Mail, and folders, or wishing you could remember whether your AIM buddy suggested starving or feeding your cold. Click the swirl.

Figure 4-41 shows the results of a Google Desktop search for hacks. Notice that it found 16 email messages, 2 files, 1 chat, and 1 item in my IE browsing history matching my hacks query. As you can probably guess from the icons to the left of each result, the first three are an AIM chat, an HTML file (most likely from my browser's cache), and an email message. These are sorted by date, but you can easily make a switch to relevance by clicking the "Sort by relevance" link at the top right of the results list.

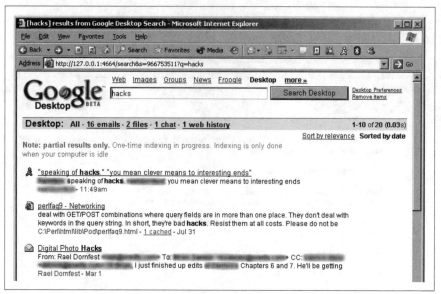

Figure 4-41. Google Desktop search results

Figures 4-42, 4-43, and 4-44 show each individual search result as I clicked through them. Note that each is displayed in a manner appropriate to the content.

Click the "Chat with..." link shown in Figure 4-42 to launch an AIM conversation with the person at hand.

Cached pages are presented, as shown in Figure 4-43, in much the same manner as they are in the Google cache.

The various Reply, Reply to All, Forward, etc., links associated with an individual message result (Figure 4-44) work; click them and the appropriate action will be taken by Outlook or Outlook Express.

Google Desktop Search Syntax

It just wouldn't be a Google search interface if there weren't special search syntax to go along with it.

The Boolean OR works as expected (e.g., hacks OR snacks), as does negation (e.g., hacks -evil).

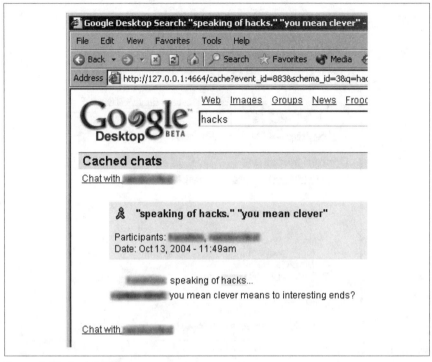

Figure 4-42. An AIM instant message

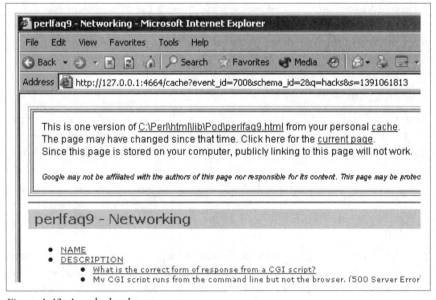

Figure 4-43. A cached web page

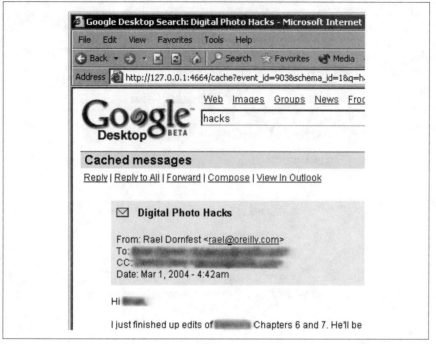

Figure 4-44. An email message

A filetype: operator restricts searches to only a particular type of file: filetype:powerpoint or filetype:ppt (*.ppt* being the PowerPoint file extension) find only Microsoft PowerPoint files, while filetype:word or filetype: doc (*.doc* being the Word file extension) restrict results to Microsoft Word documents.

Searching the Web

Now you'd think I'd hardly need to cover Googling—and you'd be right. But there's a little more to Googling via the Google Desktop than you might expect. Take a close look at the results of a Google search for hacks shown in Figure 4-45.

Come on back when you're through with that double take.

If you missed it, notice the new quick links "27 results stored on your computer."

Yes, those are the same results (and then some, given my indexer was hard at work) returned in my earlier Google Desktop search of my local machine. As an added reminder, they're called out by that Google Desktop swirl.

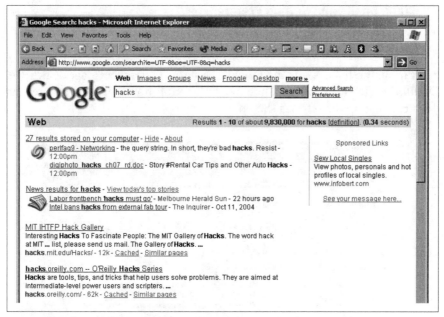

Figure 4-45. Google Desktop web search results

Click a local result and you'll end up in the same place as before: all 27 results, an HTML page, or Microsoft Word document. Click any other quick link or search result and it'll act in the manner you'd expect from any Google search results.

Behind the Scenes

Now, before you start worrying about the results of a local search—or indeed your local files—being sent off to Google, read on. What's actually going on is that the local Google Desktop server is intercepting any Google web searches, passing them on to the Google web server in your stead, and running the same search against your computer's local index. Then it's intercepting the web search results as they come back from Google, pasting in local finds, and presenting them to you in your browser as a cohesive whole.

All work involving your local data is done on your computer. Neither your filenames nor your files themselves are ever sent on to the Google web server.

For more on Google Desktop and privacy, right-click the Google Desktop taskbar swirl, select About, and click the Privacy link.

Twiddling Knobs and Setting Preferences

There are various knobs to twiddle and preferences to set through the Google Desktop browser-based interface and taskbar swirl.

Set various preferences in the Google Desktop Preferences page. Click the Desktop Preferences link on the Google Desktop home page or any results page to bring up the settings shown in Figure 4-46.

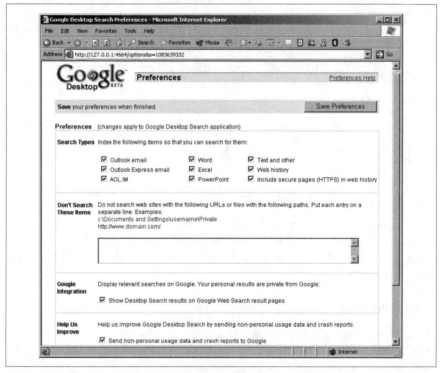

Figure 4-46. The Google Desktop Preferences page

Hide your local results from sight when sharing Google web search results with a friend or colleague by clicking the Hide link next to any visible Google Desktop quick links. You can also turn Desktop quick-link results on and off from the Google Desktop Preferences page.

Click the "Remove results" link next to the Search Desktop button on the top right of any results page and you'll be able to go through and remove particular items from the Google Desktop index, as shown in Figure 4-47. Do note that if you open or view any of these items again, they'll once again be indexed and start showing up in search results.

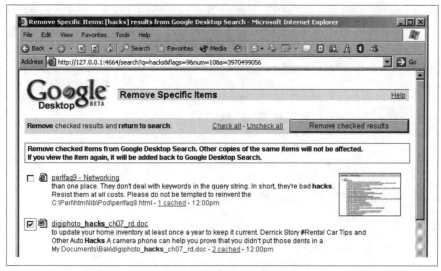

Figure 4-47. Removing items from your Google Desktop index

Search, set preferences, check the status of your index, pause or resume indexing, quit Google Desktop, or browse the "About" docs by right-clicking the Google Desktop taskbar swirl and choosing an item from the menu, as shown in Figure 4-48.

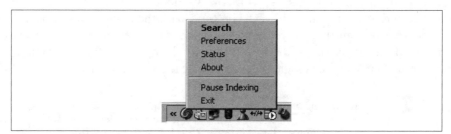

Figure 4-48. The Google Desktop taskbar menu, which gives you the knobs to twiddle and preferences to set

When evaluating the Google Desktop as an interface to finding needles in my personal haystack, one thing sticks in my mind: I stumbled across an old email message I was sure I'd lost.

See Also

- The Google Desktop Proxy (*http://www.projectcomputing.com/resources/desktopProxy*) takes desktop searching beyond your very desktop. A little proxy server sitting on your computer accepts queries from other machines on the network, passes them to the Google Desktop engine running locally, and forwards the results.

- X1 (*http://www.x1.com*) is another desktop search engine. It searches through more types of files than Google Desktop, and lets you more easily fine-tune your searches. But it takes up more RAM and system resources, and costs $74.95 (you can download a trial for free). It's also more difficult to use than the Google Desktop.

- "Out-Google Google with MSN Desktop Search" **[Hack #46]**

—Rael Dornfest

HACK #46 Out-Google Google with MSN Desktop Search

Think the Google Desktop is nifty? MSN Desktop Search leaves it in the dust and lets you fine-tune your PC searches to an amazing degree.

"Google Your Desktop" **[Hack #45]** shows all the ways you can use Google's great desktop search tool to search through your computer in the same way Google lets you search through the Web.

Surprise! Microsoft has beat Google at its own game. MSN Desktop Search does a far better job of finding email and files on your computer because it hooks directly into Windows, Outlook, Outlook Express, and Microsoft Office and lets you search in ways you can't with the Google Desktop. And it does more than that as well; once you find files or email, you can move them, delete them, copy them, respond to them—pretty much anything Windows lets you do. Google Desktop merely lets you view them.

At the time of this writing, you can download MSN Desktop Search at *http://beta.toolbar.msn.com*, but most likely it will be at a different location soon. Check *http://www.microsoft. com* for details.

In fact, this great search tool is one of the best utilities of any kind you can find, and it's free.

Microsoft didn't build MSN Desktop Search from scratch. The heart of the search tool is a program called Lookout created by a company that Microsoft bought. Microsoft changed and tweaked Lookout to build MSN Desktop Search.

At first blush, the Google Desktop and MSN Desktop Search have some basic similarities. MSN Desktop Search, like the Google Desktop, sweeps through your PC, indexing all your email, your files and folders, and your Outlook appointments and tasks. When you do a search, it searches through that index rather than through your PC, so search results are returned lightning-quick.

It performs full-text indexes of:

- Text files, Microsoft Word documents, Excel workbooks, PowerPoint presentations, OneNote documents—in fact, all Microsoft Office documents—living on your hard drive
- Email handled through Outlook or Outlook Express
- All Outlook data, including contacts, your calendar, your tasks—pretty much the whole Outlook shebang
- Keywords in the titles of music, image, and video files
- Web pages on your computer, although not web pages that you've browsed to

Unlike the Google Desktop, it has a full-blown interface rather than a simple web page, as shown in Figure 4-49.

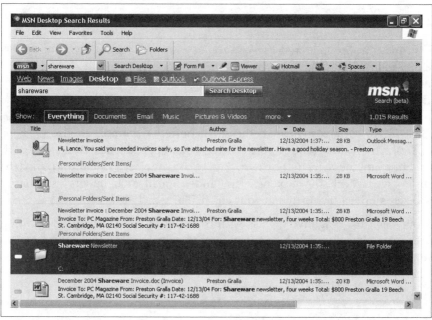

Figure 4-49. MSN Desktop Search, a full-blown utility with its own interface

We'll take a closer look at the interface later in this hack, but let's reign ourselves in for now and take a look at installation.

Installing MSN Desktop Search

MSN Desktop Search is a free download that runs on Windows XP only. Installation is straightforward. Download it (see the note at the beginning of this hack) and run the installer. It will install itself in several places, including as a small input box on the taskbar and as a toolbar in Outlook.

 To make it visible in Outlook if it's not already visible, choose View → Toolbars → MSN Toolbar.

When it's on the taskbar, it appears as an input box with a butterfly to the left, as shown in Figure 4-50. In addition to that, in the Notification area (the far-right portion of the taskbar) you'll see a small magnifying glass with a butterfly on it. That's the indexer portion of the utility.

Figure 4-50. The MSN Desktop Search input box on the Windows taskbar

If it doesn't pop open and ask you to set your preferences, set your preferences right away. The most important one concerns what it should index. For some odd reason, by default, it indexes your email and your *My Documents* folder only. That means it won't be able to find anything on the rest of your hard disk, so rectify that oversight right away. On the taskbar, click the down arrow next to the small butterfly symbol, choose Options → Deskbar Options, and from the screen that appears click Desktop Search to bring up the screen shown in Figure 4-51. Select "Email and all hard disks" and check the box next to "Index email attachments" so that it indexes all the attachments in your email. Then click OK.

Now, click the magnifying glass with the butterfly on it in the Notification area, and choose Index Now. It will start indexing. It could take from an hour to the better part of a day to complete its index, depending on how many files you have and how fast your processor is.

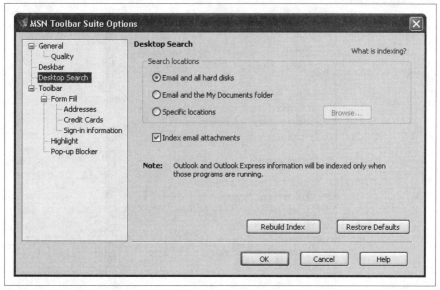

Figure 4-51. Telling MSN Desktop Search to index your entire hard disk, not just your email and My Documents folder

Defragment your hard disk before installing MSN Desktop Search and having it index your hard disk. If you defragment first, indexing will go much more quickly because files will be contiguous to one another when indexing occurs, which will speed up the indexing process.

Searching Your PC

When you want to search through your PC, click inside the search box shown in Figure 4-52 and type in your search term. (To instantly put your cursor in the search box, press Ctrl-Alt-M.) MSN Desktop Search literally starts searching with each keystroke and can display results as you type. As you type, the results pop up in a box, as shown in Figure 4-52.

This instant searching and sorting is great, but even more useful is what you can do once you find results. Right-click any result and you'll get a menu that lets you take action on the file or message, depending on the file type or

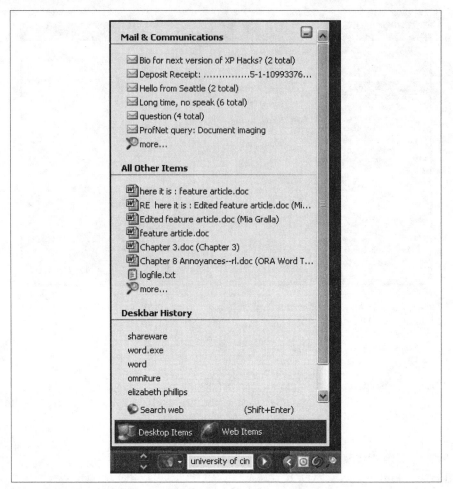

Figure 4-52. Results as you type, neatly sorted by category

whether it's an email. For example, as shown in Figure 4-53, if you right-click an email, you can open the message in Outlook, print it, reply to it, forward it, copy it, delete it, or move it to a different folder—the same options you have from inside Outlook. And Outlook doesn't have to be running for you to do it; for example, if you want to read the message, Outlook will launch automatically.

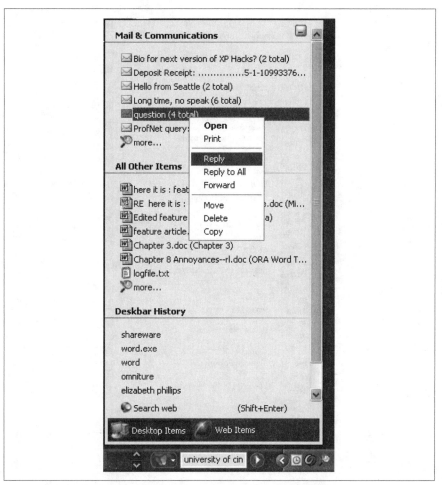

Figure 4-53. Right-clicking a file or email message to get a context-relevant menu of choices for what you can do with the file or message

Similarly, if you right-click a Word document, you get a much wider choice of options, as shown in Figure 4-54—in essence, the same set of options you'd get if you right-clicked the file in Windows Explorer.

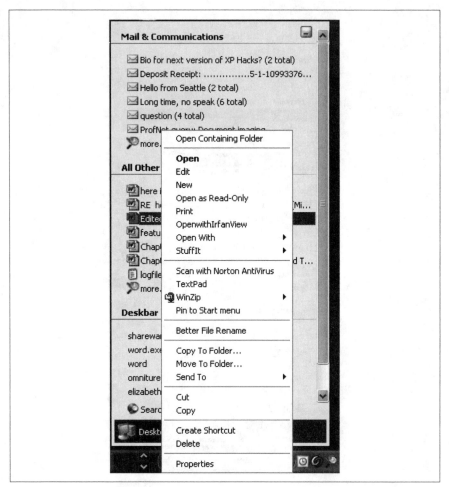

Figure 4-54. Right-clicking a Word document to get a list of options

This is the quick way to use the MSN Search Bar. If you want to get the full power of the tool, after you type in your search term, press Enter, or click the arrow to the right of the input box, and you'll come to the screen shown in Figure 4-55.

Right-click any file and you get the same menu of options you get when the results pop up.

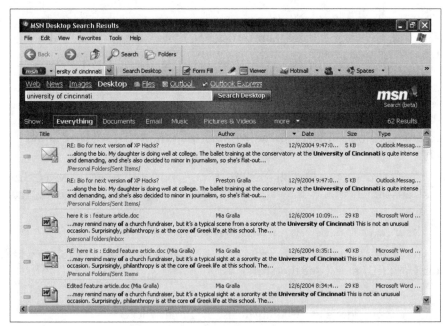

Figure 4-55. The more complete results shown in the MSN Desktop Search program

But this screen gives you far more options than that. Sort the results in different ways by clicking Title, Author, Date, Size, or Type, and sort them in ascending or descending order. Better yet, you can see your search broken down by category. Click Email, for example, and you'll see all email-related results; click Music, and you'll see any results in music files; click Documents, and you'll see results in Microsoft Office documents; and so on.

Some people with two computers who copy their Outlook *.pst* file back and forth between them might run into problems with MSN Desktop Search; it might return multiple results of the same item. Some people copy their *.pst* file from one computer to the other so that they can always have the latest version of their Outlook data on whatever PC they're currently using. But when you copy *.pst* files over one another, MSN Desktop Search might get fooled and list individual emails multiple times in a search. If that happens to you, your best bet is to rebuild your index. From MSN Desktop Search, choose Options → Desktop Options → Desktop Search, and click the Rebuild Index button. Your PC will be reindexed (which will most likely take several hours), and the new index will replace the old one, so you should no longer see multiple copies of the same item in the search results.

MSN Desktop Search Syntax

The true power of the program comes not in its basic searches—although those, as you can see, are quite powerful—but in the search syntax you can use. The syntax has been explicitly created to help you search through documents on your PC. So, unlike with the Google Desktop, you'll be able to search inside specific folders. And you can also search by the author of a document, by the sender and recipient of email, and so on. And, of course, it can handle Boolean searches, so you can use OR, AND, wildcards, and so on.

Let's say you want to find all email that was sent to you from Joe Metz, that had attachments, and that contained the word *budget*. You'd issue this search:

```
kind:email from:Joe Metz has:attachment budget
```

If you want to find every PowerPoint presentation in the *Money* folder with the word *ROI* in it, issue this search:

```
kind:presentation folder:Money ROI
```

Table 4-2 provides a more complete list of search syntax.

Table 4-2. MSN Desktop Search syntax

Syntax	Meaning
Has:attachment	Search for emails with attachments
Before:	Search for items created before a specific date
After:	Search for items created after a specific date
Author:	Search for documents created by a specific person
From:	Search for email from a specific person
To:	Search for email sent to a specific person
Kind:Contacts	Search through contacts
Kind:email	Search through email
Kind:meetings	Search through meetings in Outlook
Kind:Tasks	Search through tasks in Outlook
Kind:Notes	Search through notes in Outlook
Kind:text documents	Search through text documents
Kind:email	Search through email
Kind:spreadsheet	Search through spreadsheets
Kind:music	Search through music files
Kind:pictures	Search through graphics files
Kind:videos	Search through videos
Kind:favorites	Search through favorites

Table 4-2. MSN Desktop Search syntax (continued)

Syntax	Meaning
Store:Outlook	Search through Outlook
Store:oe	Search through Outlook Express
Folder:	Search through a specific folder

This is just a small sample of the syntax. For a more complete listing, click the arrow next to the butterfly icon on MSN Desktop Search, choose Help → Desktop Search Help, go to the Tips and Tricks section of Help, and click Advanced Query Reference.

Turning Indexing On and Off

There's one thing Google Desktop has that MSN Desktop Search doesn't, and that's real-time indexing. In Google Desktop, after the initial indexing, your files and email are instantly indexed in real time as you create them or receive them. That's not the case with MSN Desktop Search. After its initial indexing, it indexes only when your computer is idle. That means that when you do a search, it won't include information added since the last indexing.

 MSN Desktop Search will index Outlook or Outlook Express only when those programs are open, so open them if you want them indexed.

You can manually tell it to index while you're working, however. Right-click the magnifying glass with a butterfly on it in the Notification area and choose Index Now. You'll see the magnifying glass slowly flashing as it indexes, and it will continue to index as you work.

If you're not sure whether your index is up-to-date, click the magnifying glass with a butterfly on it and choose Indexing Status. The screen shown in Figure 4-56 appears. You'll see the total number of items that have already been indexed, and how many items are waiting to be indexed. To start indexing, click Index Now.

This screen also lets you tell MSN for how long it should wait while your PC is idle before it starts indexing your PC. From the drop-down box next to Snooze, choose the amount of time you want it to wait before indexing. Your choices are from 15 seconds to one day.

Figure 4-56. Checking the status of your indexing

  MSN Desktop Search doesn't completely index all the content in large files. For files larger than 1MB, it indexes only the first 1MB. That means that if you're searching, and the term you're searching for is found only after the first 1MB of a large document, MSN Desktop Search won't find it. At this point, there's no way to change the option to completely index the contents of large documents.

Hacking the Hack

When MSN Desktop Search sits on the Taskbar, there's one niggling annoyance that won't go away. The butterfly image (which Microsoft insiders call a *jellybean* because it's shaped like one) takes up precious Taskbar space, as does the small arrow to the right of it, as shown previously in Figure 4-50. They become a problem when you run a lot of programs at the same time. With the jellybean there, because there's less space on the Taskbar, you won't be able to see the tiles of all the programs that are currently running.

There's a simple Registry hack that will kill the jellybean and arrow, but still gives you the features of search. First, run the Registry Editor [Hack #83] and go to `HKEY_CURRENT_USER\Software\Microsoft\MSN Apps\DB`. Create a new DWORD value called `Buttons` and give it a value of 1. Exit the Registry.

Now, take MSN Desktop Search away from the Taskbar by right-clicking the Taskbar, choosing Properties, and removing the checkmark from MSN Deskbar. Then, right-click the Taskbar again, choose Properties, and put a checkmark next to MSN Deskbar. MSN Desktop Search will appear again on the Taskbar, this time without the jellybean, as shown in Figure 4-57.

Figure 4-57. No jellybean in the Taskbar

See Also

- "Google Your Desktop" [Hack #45]

Better Internet Searching from Your Desktop

Internet Explorer's default search features are anemic at best. Do better Internet searching by installing a Google Toolbar and other specialized search toolbars and powering up the default search.

Was there ever a Web before Google? Yes, but it was a heck of a lot harder to find anything in it. Internet Explorer's default search feature leaves a lot to be desired, not the least of which is its use of MSN Search instead of Google. But there's a lot you can do to do better Internet searching from your desktop. You can get search toolbars that integrate into your browser, and you can customize the Internet Explorer search feature as well.

Google Toolbar

The best way to empower Internet searches is by installing special toolbars from two popular search engines, Google and Ask Jeeves. The Google Toolbar is the better of the two, and not just because it's a better search engine. It also has several extra features.

The great thing about the Google Toolbar is, well, that it's Google. It gives you all of Google's functionality without even having to visit the site. To get the Google Toolbar for IE, go to *http://toolbar.google.com* and follow the installation instructions. It works only with Internet Explorer. Once you install it, you'll be able to search Google without having to visit the search site; just type your search term in the toolbar. In fact, you even get an extra on the toolbar that you don't get on Google itself—the PageRank feature that tells you how popular the current site you're visiting is.

The Mozdev.org site (*http://www.mozdev.org*) has written a third-party Google Toolbar called the Googlebar (*http://googlebar.mozdev.org*) for use with Netscape 7/Mozilla browsers. It emulates most of the features of the Google Toolbar except for PageRank. If you're a Firefox user, you can use a Googlebar extension [Hack #43].

The best of the Google Toolbar's features is that it lets you do a Google search through the site you're currently on, a particularly useful tool if the site doesn't have a search box, or if the search on the site is a poor one. In fact, I rarely use sites' search boxes and prefer to use the Google Toolbar instead. Among other features, the Google Toolbar also lets you find sites related to the one you're currently visiting, and it will translate foreign-language sites into English. The Google Toolbar will also highlight your search terms on the page results if you tell it to.

> If you're at the Google web site, you can do a targeted search of only one specific site instead of the entire Web. In the Google search box, type site:www.nameofsite.com searchterm. For example, if you want to search the *www.newscientist.com* site for the word "cloning," type site:www.newscientist.com cloning. You'll get results showing all the web pages on the site containing the word "cloning." For more Google tips and tricks, see *Google Hacks* or the *Google Pocket Guide* (both from O'Reilly).

Using the Google Toolbar is simplicity itself: type a search term into it and press Enter. If you want to search the current site instead of the entire Web, click a small button on the toolbar that pictures two pairs of googly eyes on a magnifying glass.

> If you'd prefer to search Google directly from your desktop rather than from within your browser, there's a workaround for you. Download the free program GAPIS from *http://www.searchenginelab.com/common/products/gapis*. To use it, you'll need to get a Google developer's key. You don't actually need to be a developer to get a key, though, and it's free. To get the key, go to *http://www.google.com/apis/*. The page recommends that you download the Google developer's kit, but you don't need to do that to get your free key. Instead, click Create a Google Account and follow the instructions. Once you have the account, you have to type the key into GAPIS the first time you use the program. After that, you'll be able to do Google searches by running GAPIS rather than using the Google Toolbar or visiting the Google site.

If you're concerned about your privacy, you should disable the PageRank option. When you enable this option, the Google Toolbar tracks the page you're on. If the option is disabled, the Google Toolbar doesn't track the page.

Yahoo! and Ask Jeeves both have similar toolbars. Find the Yahoo! Companion toolbar at *http://toolbar.yahoo.com*. In addition to letting you search Yahoo!, it includes other features, such as letting you check your Yahoo! mail account and blocking pop ups. The Ask Jeeves toolbar (*http://sp.ask. com/docs/toolbar*) lets you search Ask Jeeves regardless of where you are on the Web, and includes links for weather forecasts, news, and more.

Mastering the Search Companion

If you decide to forgo the Google and Ask Jeeves search toolbars, you still can do things to power up Internet Explorer's Search Companion, which you get to by pressing Ctrl-E or clicking the Search button. Of course, first you'll want to get rid of the cloyingly cute animated dog that normally appears, by choosing Change Preferences when the Search Companion appears and then choosing "Without an animated screen character."

But the Search Companion has bigger problems than stray dogs. It forces you through a step-by-step search, and, worse still, it clutters up the search area with "sponsored links" from advertisers. Type in the name Preston, for example, and you'll get sponsored links such as "Hotels near Preston," "Buy Fine Wines and Beer at Libation.com," and "Preston, Idaho Travel Information." No, thank you. I prefer my search results straight up.

A better bet is to use what Microsoft calls the Classic Internet Search Companion, which previous versions of Internet Explorer used. From the Search Companion choose Change Preferences → Change Internet Search Behavior → With Classic Internet Search. You'll have to close Internet Explorer and restart it for the changes to take effect. As you can see in Figure 4-58, it's simpler and allows you to perform more focused searches, specifically for web pages, addresses, business names, and maps, as well as perform a previous search. Click the More button to search for pictures and definitions of words.

By default, Internet Explorer uses MSN as its search engine, but after you perform a search, if you don't find what you want you can send the same query to other search engines by clicking "Send search to more search engines" and then picking the engine you want to use. You can also change the default search engine by opening the Search Companion, choosing Change Internet Search Behavior, scrolling down the page that appears, and choosing a new default search engine from the list of 13.

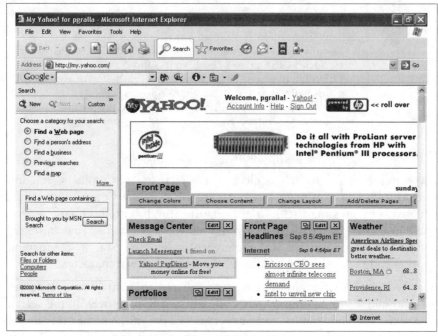

Figure 4-58. The Classic Internet Search Companion

See Also

- WebFerret by FerretSoft (*http://www.ferretsoft.com*) is free metasearch software that will send your search to multiple search engines simultaneously and display all the results, collated, in a single window.

- Copernic Agent Basic, a metasearch tool from Copernic (*http://www. copernic.com*), lets you perform more-targeted searches by sending your search to specialized search engines in a variety of categories when you choose a targeted search.

- "Google Your Desktop" [Hack #45]

- "Out-Google Google with MSN Desktop Search" [Hack #46]

HACK
#48

Run Java Applets Without Crashes or Problems

To get the most out of surfing the Web, you need the most recent version of Java. That can be harder to get than you think, but this hack will show you how.

Running a Java applet when you visit a web site should be a no-brainer; click a link and the application should run. Unfortunately, XP users have found out that isn't always the case. You might visit Java sites only to find that you can't play games, log into interactive stock and weather sites, or do any of the other things Java can be used for.

Unfortunately, there's no single fix for all Java woes. There are many potential causes, ranging from display errors, to running an old version of Java, and more. Here, though, are the primary ways you can fix Java on your machine.

Make Sure You Have a Java Virtual Machine (JVM) Installed

To run Java applets, you need a Java Virtual Machine (JVM) installed on your system. Microsoft and Sun have, in the past, had competing JVMs. Applets written for one JVM might or might not work with the other JVM.

To make things more confusing, Microsoft and Sun have been locked in a bitter legal battle about Java, which rivals the Jarndyce and Jarndyce court case at the center of Dickens' novel *Bleak House*. Fully explaining the Microsoft/Sun fight would take about as many pages as Dickens' 1,000-plus-page novel did. The upshot is this, however: because of a court ruling, Microsoft stopped distributing and supporting its JVM (which it calls Microsoft VM) in January 2004. And the Microsoft VM might or might not be enabled in your version of XP.

So, if you're having problems with Java, the first thing to do is to see whether you have a JVM installed and whether you're using the Sun version, the Microsoft version, or both versions. To see whether Microsoft VM is enabled, from Internet Explorer choose Tools → Internet Options → Security. Highlight the Internet Zone, choose Custom Level, and then scroll down until you come to the Microsoft VM section, shown in Figure 4-59.

If the Disable Java button is chosen, it means the Microsoft VM is disabled on your system.

To check whether you have the Sun JVM and whether it's enabled, from Internet Explorer choose Tools → Internet Options → Advanced and scroll down. If you see a Java (Sun) entry with a checkbox next to it, as pictured in Figure 4-60, the Sun JVM is installed.

If you don't have the Microsoft VM or the Sun JVM installed, the solution is simple: install and enable one of them. Because Microsoft stopped supporting its VM after January 2004, your best bet is to install the Sun JVM from *http://www.java.com/en/download/windows_automatic.jsp*.

If the Microsoft VM or the Sun JVM shows up (as in Figure 4-59 or Figure 4-60, respectively), but it's not enabled, you'll need to enable it. To enable the Microsoft VM, in the screen pictured in Figure 4-59 choose High

Figure 4-59. Checking to see whether you're using the Microsoft VM

Safety. That will enable the VM but will take security precautions against rogue Java applets. To enable the Sun JVM, select the checkbox under Java (Sun), as shown in Figure 4-60.

Uninstall Older JVM Versions

Your problem might be that you have an older JVM or Microsoft VM installed, and you need to update it. Go to *http://java.sun.com* and check the version number against the version number displayed in Figure 4-60. If your version number is older, you should install a newer JVM. Additionally, if you're using the Microsoft VM, you might instead want to install the Sun JVM in its place, since Microsoft discontinued support for its VM.

People have reported problems when installing a newer JVM over an older one, so I suggest first uninstalling the old JVM or Microsoft VM and then installing the new one from *http://www.java.com/en/download/windows_ automatic.jsp*. Unfortunately, uninstalling the Sun JVM or Microsoft VM is not a simple process and requires Registry editing as well as manually deleting files. Here's how to do each.

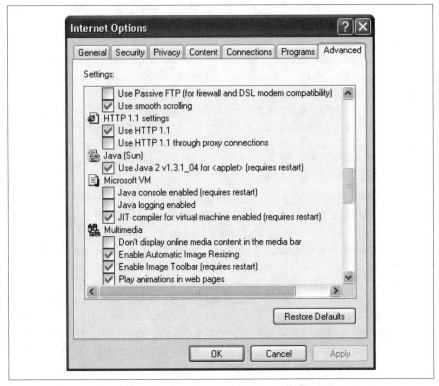

Figure 4-60. Checking to see whether the Sun JVM is installed

Uninstalling an old Sun JVM. There's good news and bad news about uninstalling an old Sun JVM. The good news is that it might go off without a hitch and take only a single step. The bad news is that you might not be so lucky, and then it'll be time to head to the Registry.

To uninstall an old Sun JVM, choose Control Panel → Add/Remove Programs. Select the Java Runtime Environment entry, click Change/Remove, and follow the uninstallation wizard. The JVM will be—or should be—uninstalled.

Sometimes, however, even after you do that, the Java Runtime Environment entry remains in the Add or Remove Programs screen. Theoretically, this should not cause a problem—because the underlying JVM has been uninstalled—but it's not clear whether in practice it will cause problems. So, you'll be best off to remove the entry in the Add or Remove Programs screen. You'll do it by deleting Registry entries and a folder.

Run the Registry Editor [Hack #83] and go to HKEY_LOCAL_MACHINE/Software/
Microsoft/Windows/CurrentVersion/Uninstall. You'll find many keys

enclosed in curly brackets, like this: {B7915B05-FC28-11D6-9D24-00010240CE95}. One of these keys is the Java uninstall Registry entry, and you need to delete it. You won't be able to know which entry to delete by the key name because the keys aren't descriptive and each is a string of long numbers enclosed in curly brackets. To find which to delete, you need to find the one that has a DisplayName with a String value that starts with Java, such as Java 2 SDK, SE v1.4.1_02. To find out which key to delete, search for the word Java by pressing Ctrl-F in the Registry, typing the word Java, and then doing a search for it. You'll be brought to the key that needs to be deleted. Before deleting the key, write down its entire name because you'll need it for the next step. Then you'll delete it.

Next, go to the uninstall folder for Java and delete that folder. Delete *C:\ Program Files\InstallShield Installation Information\{<Java 2 clsid key>}*, where *{<Java 2 clsid key>}* is the value of the registry key you deleted. After you do that, when you restart Add or Remove Programs the Java entry will be gone.

Uninstalling the Microsoft VM. Uninstalling the Microsoft VM takes a bit of work as well. From the Run box, enter the command RunDll32 advpack. dll,LaunchINFSection java.inf,UnInstall. You'll get a warning box asking if you want to go through with the uninstallation process. Click Yes to continue, and reboot your PC when prompted.

After you reboot, delete these items:

- The *C:\Windows\java* folder
- The *java.pnf* file from the *C:\Windows\inf* folder
- The *jview.exe* and *wjview.exe* files from the *C:\Windows\system32* folder
- The Registry subkey HKEY_LOCAL_MACHINE\SOFTWARE\Microsoft\Java VM
- The Registry subkey HKEY_LOCAL_MACHINE\SOFTWARE\Microsoft\Internet Explorer\AdvancedOptions\JAVA_VM

That will completely remove the Microsoft VM. Now you can install the Sun JVM from *http://www.java.com/en/download/windows_automatic.jsp*.

Change Your Display Settings

Java applets won't run unless you have a minimum color setting of 256 colors. If you don't use that minimum setting, you'll crash when you visit a web page with a Java applet. To change your display settings, right-click the desktop, choose Properties → Settings, and in the Color Quality drop-down box choose a display setting of at least 256 colors.

If you use at least 256 colors and you still experience problems, the cause might be a buggy video driver. To help find out if this is the cause of the problem, change your current display settings to a lower resolution and color depth than you're currently using—for example, bring it from 1,024×768 to 800×600, and the colors from Highest (32bit) to 256 colors. If that doesn't solve the problem, you might have a display driver with bugs in it. Go to the manufacturer's web site and download a new driver.

Networking
Hacks 49–58

XP is the most network-savvy of Microsoft's operating systems. Not only does it automatically recognize your network when you first install it, but it also includes a variety of wizards and other features that make it easy to connect to new networks and devices. Plus, it includes a variety of built-in command-line tools that help you diagnose and troubleshoot network problems.

In this chapter, you'll get networking hacks, including command-line tools for troubleshooting networks, tweaking settings for faster Internet access, and optimizing a home network, among others.

Tweak DNS Settings for Faster Internet Access

#49 Here's a handful of DNS hacks for speeding up access to web sites.

You use the Web by typing in hostnames such as *www.oreilly.com*, but web servers and Internet routers can't understand plain English words, so they need those letters translated into numeric IP addresses. Whenever you type in a hostname, such as *www.oreilly.com*, it needs to be resolved to its IP address, such as 208.201.239.37. DNS servers provide that name resolution automatically and behind the scenes as you surf the Web.

There are several ways you can hack your DNS settings so that you can get faster web access.

Speed Up Web Access with a HOSTS File

It takes time to send your request to a DNS server, have the server look up the proper IP address to resolve the name, and then send the IP address back to your PC. You can eliminate that delay by creating or editing a local *HOSTS* file on your own PC that contains hostnames and their corresponding IP addresses. When you create a *HOSTS* file, XP will first look in that to see if there's an entry for the hostname, and if it finds it, it will resolve the address itself. That way, you won't have to go out to a DNS server and wait for the response before visiting a web site. The *HOSTS* file is a plain-text file you can create or edit with a text editor like Notepad.

You'll find an existing *HOSTS* file in *C:\Windows\System32\Drivers\Etc\ HOSTS* (in Windows XP Professional, it's located in *C:\Winnt\System32\ Drivers\HOSTS*). The file has no extension; it is named only *HOSTS*. Open it in Notepad and enter the IP addresses and hostnames of your commonly visited web sites, like this:

```
208.201.239.37      oreilly.com
216.92131.107       simtel.net
```

Each entry in the file should be on one line. The IP address should be in the first column, and the corresponding hostname in the next column. At least one space should separate the two columns. You can add comments to the file by preceding the line with a #, in which case the entire line will be ignored by the file, or by putting a # after the hostname, in which case only the comment after will be ignored. You might want to comment on individual entries—for example:

```
130.94.155.164          gralla.com      #still in beta
```

When you're finished editing the file, save it to its existing location.

> Make sure to check your *HOSTS* file regularly and keep it up-to-date, or else you might deny yourself access to certain web sites. For example, if the *http://www.gralla.com* web site were to change its IP address but your *HOSTS* file kept the old, incorrect address, your browser would not be able to find the site because it would be given the wrong addressing information.

Adjust XP's DNS Cache Settings

As a way of speeding up DNS, when you visit a site XP puts the DNS information into a local DNS cache on your PC. So, when you want to go to a site, XP first looks in its local DNS cache, called the *resolve cache*, to see whether the DNS information is contained there. That way, if it finds the information locally, it doesn't have to query a remote DNS server to find IP information. The cache is made up of recently queried names and entries taken from your *HOSTS* file.

The cache contains both *negative* and *positive entries*. Positive entries are those in which the DNS lookup succeeded, and you were able to connect to the web site. When XP looks in the cache, if it finds a positive entry it immediately uses that DNS information and sends you to the requested web site.

Negative entries are those in which no match was found, and you end up getting a "Cannot find server or DNS" error in your browser. Similarly, when XP looks in the cache and finds a negative entry, it gives you the error message without bothering to go out to the site.

Negative entries can lead to problems. When you try to make a connection to a site that has a negative entry in your cache, you'll get an error message, even if the site's problems have been resolved and it's now reachable.

You can solve this problem, though, using a Registry hack. By default, XP caches negative entries for five minutes. After five minutes, they're cleared from your cache. But if you'd like, you can force XP not to cache these negative entries so that you'll never run into this problem. Run the Registry Editor [Hack #83] and go to HKEY_LOCAL_MACHINE\SYSTEM\CurrentControlSet\ Services\Dnscache\Parameters. Create a new DWORD value with the name NegativeCacheTime and give it a value of 0. (The value might already exist. If it does, edit its value to 0.) The DWORD determines how much time, in seconds, to keep negative entries in the DNS cache. If you like, you can have the entries stay alive for one second by giving the DWORD a value of 1.

After you're done editing, exit the Registry. To make the change take effect, restart your computer, or flush your cache by issuing the command ipconfig /flushdns at a command prompt.

 For more information about using ipconfig, see "Troubleshoot Network Connections with ping, tracert, and pathping" [Hack #51].

That command will flush your DNS cache—all the entries, both positive and negative, will be flushed, and it will be empty until you start visiting web sites. Negative entries, however, will not be added to the cache if you've given the DWORD a value of 0.

You can also use the Registry to control the amount of time positive entries are kept in the DNS cache. By default, they are kept for 24 hours. To change the default, go to HKEY_LOCAL_MACHINE\SYSTEM\CurrentControlSet\Services\ Dnscache\Parameters again and create a DWORD value called MaxCacheEntryTtlLimit. (If it's already present, just edit the value.) For the value, enter the amount of time you want the entry to remain, in seconds, making sure to use Decimal as the base.

Fix DNS Problems

Sometimes, when you can't connect to a web site, the cause is a DNS problem. There are things you can do to solve these problems, though. If you're having trouble connecting to a site, to find out if DNS is a potential culprit first ping [Hack #51] the site to which you can't connect by issuing the ping command at the command prompt or in the Run box, like this:

    ping www.zdnet.com

If the site is live, you'll get an answer like this:

```
Pinging www.zdnet.com [206.16.6.252] with 32 bytes of data:

Reply from 206.16.6.252: bytes=32 time=119ms TTL=242
Reply from 206.16.6.252: bytes=32 time=79ms TTL=242
Reply from 206.16.6.252: bytes=32 time=80ms TTL=242
Reply from 206.16.6.252: bytes=32 time=101ms TTL=242

Ping statistics for 206.16.6.252:
    Packets: Sent = 4, Received = 4, Lost = 0 (0% loss),
Approximate round trip times in milli-seconds:
    Minimum = 79ms, Maximum = 119ms, Average = 94ms
```

If it's not, you'll get a response like this:

    Ping request could not find host. Please check the name and try again.

If you ping a site and it's live, but you can't connect to it with your browser, a DNS problem might be the reason. If you suspect you're having a DNS problem, take the following actions:

Check your HOSTS file. If your *HOSTS* file contains an incorrect or outdated listing, you won't be able to connect. Even if you don't recall adding listings to a *HOSTS* file, it still might contain listings because some Internet accelerator utilities edit them without telling you. Open your *HOSTS* file with Notepad and see if the site you can't connect to is listed there. If it is, delete the entry, and you should be able to connect.

Check your DNS settings. Make sure your DNS settings are correct for your ISP or network. Find out from your ISP or network administrator what yours are supposed to be. Then, to find out your current DNS settings, double-click the problem connection in the Network Connections folder, choose Support → Details, and look at the bottom of the tab to find your DNS servers. If they don't match what they're supposed to be, right-click the problem connection and choose Properties. Then, highlight Internet Protocol (TCP/IP) and choose Properties. Change the DNS servers to the proper ones, or choose "Obtain DNS server address automatically" if your ISP or network administrator tells you to.

Flush your DNS cache. The problem might be related to your DNS cache, so flush it out. To flush the cache, type ipconfig /flushdns at a command prompt.

Find out if your ISP is having DNS problems. The cause might be your ISP. One possibility is that one of its DNS servers is down, and you're trying to access the down server. Ping each of your ISP's DNS servers and, if any of them don't respond, remove them from your DNS list, as outlined earlier in this hack.

HACK #50 Optimize Your Home Router

Home routers let you share broadband Internet access and build a home network. Here's how to get the most out of your router.

It's quite easy to set up an inexpensive router for a home network. But the default settings aren't always optimal because no network is one-size-fits-all. And frequently, the documentation for the routers is so poor that it's hard to tell what the settings are and what options you have.

Home router options differ somewhat from model to model. Here's advice for how to customize the most common and most important settings:

Connect on Demand and Maximum Idle Time settings
  Depending on your ISP, you might become disconnected from the Net after you haven't used the Internet for a certain amount of time. To solve the problem, if your router has a Connect on Demand setting, enable it; that will automatically reestablish your Internet connection when you use an Internet service, even if your ISP has cut you off. If there is a Maximum Idle Time setting, set it to 0 so that your router will always maintain an Internet connection, no matter how long you haven't used the Internet. As a practical matter, you should need to use only one of these two settings; either one will maintain a constant Internet connection for you.

Keep Alive setting
  Use this setting to maintain a constant Internet connection, even if your PC is idle. It's similar to the Connect on Demand and Maximum Idle Time settings, except that it doesn't let your connection disconnect, so it is an even better setting to enable, if your router has it.

Router Password
  Your router requires a password for you to use its administrator account. It comes with a default password. For example, Linksys routers come with a default password of admin. Change the password for maximum security.

Enable Logging
  For security reasons, it's a good idea to enable logging so that you can view logs of all outgoing and incoming traffic. Depending on your

router, it might save permanent logs to your hard disk or allow only the viewing of temporary logs. You might also be able to download extra software from the manufacturer to help keep logs. For example, Linksys routers use temporary logs, but if you want to save permanent logs, you can download the Linksys Logviewer software from *http://www.linksys. com*. You can view logs using a text editor, like Notepad, or a log analysis program, such as the free AWStats (*http://awstats.sourceforge.net*).

Special Hub/Router Settings for DSL Access

If you have DSL access, you might need to customize your router's settings to provide your network with Internet access; sometimes the router's settings block Internet access. Here are the settings you'll need to change so that you can get onto the Internet:

PPPoE (Point to Point Protocol over Ethernet)
Some DSL ISPs use this protocol when offering Internet access. By default, this protocol is disabled on routers because it's normally not required for Internet access. However, if you have DSL access, you might need to enable it in your router.

Keep Alive setting
Some DSL ISPs will automatically disconnect your connection if you haven't used it for a certain amount of time. If your router has a Keep Alive setting, enable it by clicking the radio button next to it; this will ensure that you are never disconnected.

MTU (Maximum Transmission Unit)
As a general rule, DSL users should use a value of 1492 for their MTU. The MTU sets the maximum size of packets a network can transmit. Any packets larger than the MTU setting will be broken into smaller packets. DSL ISPs often set the MTU to 1492, so if you set a packet size larger or smaller than that, you might slow down Internet access.

You should also check with your DSL provider, as these settings can vary somewhat from provider to provider.

Settings for Using a VPN

If you use a Virtual Private Network (VPN) [Hack #82] to connect to your corporate network from home and you use a router, you might run into difficulties and not be able to connect to the VPN. Some routers, such as those from Linksys, are specifically designed to work with VPNs and have specific setup screens for them; if you have one of those, you shouldn't have any problems. Make sure to get the proper encryption, authentication, and similar information about the VPN from your network administrator, and then use those settings for the VPN setup screen in your router.

However, you might run into problems running a VPN with a router that doesn't have specific VPN settings, even if the device claims it will work with VPNs. In particular, one default setting, hidden fairly deeply in most router setup screens, can disable VPN access; some routers, such as those made by Linksys, include an option called Block WAN Request. By default, this option is enabled and blocks requests into the network from the Internet; for example, it stops ping requests into the network. However, enabling this option also blocks VPN access. VPN access requires that requests get into the network from the Internet, so if you block those requests the VPN won't work. If you have a Linksys router, disable this setting by logging into your administrator's screen, choosing Advanced → Filters, selecting Disable Block WAN Request, and clicking Apply. For other routers, check the documentation.

VPNs use a variety of protocols for tunneling through the Internet, such as IPSec and the Point-to-Point Tunneling Protocol (PPTP). Make sure these settings are enabled on your router if you want to use it in concert with a VPN.

Enable Specific Internet Services: Port Forwarding

Residential routers often use Network Address Translation (NAT), in which the router's single, external IP address is shared among all the computers on the network, but each computer has its own internal IP address, invisible to the Internet. For example, to the Internet each computer looks as if it has the address of 66.32.43.98, but internally they have different addresses, such as 192.168.1.100, 192.168.1.101, and so on. The routers have built-in Dynamic Host Configuration Protocol (DHCP) servers that assign the internal IP address. These internal IP addresses allow the PCs to communicate with each other and to connect to the Internet, and they also offer protection to PCs on the network. To the rest of the Internet, each PC has the IP address of the router, so each PC's resources can't be attacked or hijacked—they're invisible. The router itself doesn't have resources that can be used to attack your PCs, so you're safe.

But if you have servers on your network that need to provide Internet-related services (perhaps you have an FTP or web server), or if you need to allow certain PCs to be connected to the Internet for specific purposes (such as for playing multiplayer games), you'll run into trouble because they don't have IP addresses that can be seen by the rest of the Internet.

However, with this trick, you can use your router to forward incoming requests to the right device on your network. For example, if you have a web server, FTP server, or mail server and you want people to be able to connect to them, you'll be able to route incoming requests directly to those servers. PCs on the Internet will use your router's IP address, and your router will then route the requests to the proper device on your network. Normally, the devices would not be able to be connected to because the IP addresses they are assigned by the router are internal LAN addresses, unreachable from the Internet.

Not all routers include this capability. To use this feature in a Linksys router, log into your administrator's screen and choose Advanced → Forwarding to get to the screen shown in Figure 5-1.

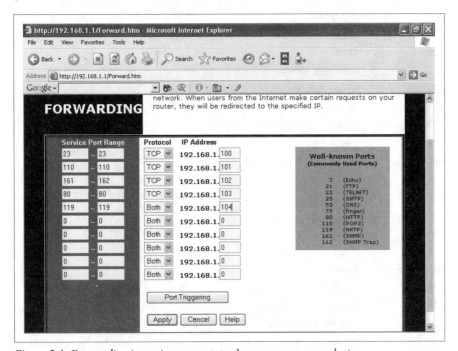

Figure 5-1. Forwarding incoming requests to the proper server or device

When this feature is enabled, the router examines incoming requests, sees what port they're directed to (for example, port 80 for HTTP), and then routes the request to the proper device.

Fill in each device's IP address, the protocol used to connect to it, and the port or port range you want forwarded to it. It's also a good idea to disable DHCP on each device to which you want to forward requests and instead give them static internal IP addresses. If you continue to use DHCP instead of assigning them a static IP address, the IP addresses of the servers or devices might change and would therefore become unreachable. Check your router's documentation on how to force it to assign static IP addresses to specific devices.

Table 5-1 lists port addresses for common Internet services. For a complete list of ports, go to *http://www.iana.org/assignments/port-numbers*.

Table 5-1. Common Internet TCP ports

Port number	Service
7	Echo
21	FTP
22	PCAnywhere
23	Telnet
25	SMTP
42	Nameserv, WINS
43	Whois, nickname
53	DNS
70	Gopher
79	Finger
80	HTTP
81	Kerberos
101	HOSTNAME
110	POP3
119	NNTP
143	IMAP
161	SNMP
162	SNMP trap
1352	Lotus Notes
3389	XP's Remote Desktop
5010	Yahoo! Messenger
5190	America Online Instant Messenger (AIM)
5631	PCAnywhere data
5632	PCAnywhere
7648	CU-SeeMe
7649	CU-SeeMe

Cloning a MAC Address for Your Router

There once was a time when cable companies banned home networks, or when they charged extra when you ran one at home. The theory was that because you were using so much extra bandwidth for multiple computers, you should be charged extra.

Thankfully, those days are gone—or at least they should be. If you're one of the unlucky few who has a cable or DSL company that charges extra for a home network, there's something you can do to get around the problem.

This hack will help with that, and it will help if you have a cable or DSL provider that requires that you provide the Media Access Control (MAC) address of your network adapter for your connection to work. If you had a single PC when you began your broadband service, but you've since installed a router at home to set up a network and share Internet access among several PCs, you'll have to provide the ISP with your new router's MAC address.

There is a way to use your existing MAC address with your new router by cloning the address. To your ISP, it looks as if your MAC address hasn't changed. You might want to do this even if your cable provider doesn't charge extra for several PCs because it will save you from having to call up the cable company's tech-support line to provide a new MAC address.

Note that not all routers have this capability, so yours might not be able to do it. Most Linksys routers let you do this, so if you have a Linksys, do the following to clone your MAC address. Depending on your model, the exact steps might vary:

1. Find out your current network adapter's MAC address (the MAC address your broadband provider already has) by opening a command prompt, typing `ipconfig /all`, and looking under the entry for "Ethernet adapter Local Area Connection." You'll see an entry like this:

   ```
   Physical Address. . . . . . . . . : 00-08-A1-00-9F-32
   ```

   That's your MAC address.

2. Log into your administrator's screen for the Linksys router and choose Advanced → MAC Addr. Clone. A screen similar to Figure 5-2 appears.

3. Type in the name of the MAC address you've obtained from your network adapter and click Apply. Your router will now be recognized by your ISP. Note that you might have to power down your cable modem and then power it back up for the router to be recognized.

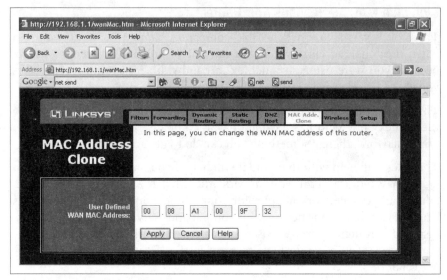

Figure 5-2. Cloning an existing MAC address

 If your ISP requires a MAC address and you don't clone an existing one, you'll have to provide your ISP with your router's address. Make sure you give them the right one. Your router typically has two MAC addresses, a LAN MAC address and a WAN MAC address. The LAN address is used only for the internal network, so make sure to provide your ISP with the device's WAN MAC address. If you give the LAN address, you won't be able to access the Internet.

Manage Your Network's Bandwidth

There's one problem with home networks that share a single Internet connection: one PC can hog all the bandwidth. For example, if someone in your house uses file-sharing software, that can suck up just about all of a network's spare bandwidth, and everyone else who's connected might see their connections slow to a crawl.

There's a simple answer for the problem. Use software that will limit the bandwidth that any single PC on your network can use. So, if you have a 3-megabit-per-second connection, you could limit any PCs to .5 megabits per second, for example. That way, anyone can still share files with others at a reasonable rate, but still let others get high-speed connections.

NetLimiter (*http://www.netlimiter.com*), shown in action in Figure 5-3, is a great program for doing this.

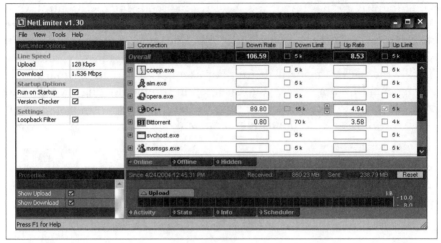

Figure 5-3. Setting bandwidth limits on a PC-by-PC basis on your network with NetLimiter

Not only will you be able to set bandwidth limits per PC, but you'll also be able set upload and download transfer rates for individual programs on a PC. So, you could give more of an individual PC's bandwidth to file sharing, for example, and less to email. NetLimiter is shareware; you can try it out for free, but after 28 days, you're expected to pay $29.95 to the developer.

HACK #51 Troubleshoot Network Connections with ping, tracert, and pathping

When you need help tracking down network connection problems, the command line is the place to go.

If you're having problems with your network and network connections and you need troubleshooting help, forget XP's GUI; it doesn't offer you enough help. To get to the root of the problems, you're going to have to get down and dirty with command-line tools. ping and tracert are familiar tools that you might have used on occasion, but you might not know the depth of their power or the switches available to use with them. And you probably haven't heard of pathping, a quasi-combination of the two commands.

Troubleshoot TCP/IP Problems with ping

The quickest, most commonly used, and, frequently, most helpful TCP/IP troubleshooting tool is the command-line tool ping. Use ping to find out whether the resource or server you're trying to connect to on your network or the Internet is active, and to see if there are any problems with the hops along the way to that resource or server. ping sends Internet Control Message Protocol (ICMP) Echo Request messages to the destination you're checking on, receives responses in return, and reports to you information about the connection path between you and the destination and how quickly the packets made their trip. For example, if you are having trouble getting email from a server, your first step in troubleshooting should be to ping the server to see whether the server is live, and to see how responsive it is. To use ping, get to a command prompt and type:

> ping *target*

where *target* is either a hostname or an IP address—for example, *pop3. catalog.com*, *zdnet.com*, or *209.217.46.121*. In response, you'll get information in this format:

```
Pinging zdnet.com [206.16.6.208] with 32 bytes of data:

Reply from 206.16.6.208: bytes=32 time=83ms TTL=242
Reply from 206.16.6.208: bytes=32 time=73ms TTL=242
Reply from 206.16.6.208: bytes=32 time=91ms TTL=242
Reply from 206.16.6.208: bytes=32 time=72ms TTL=242

Ping statistics for 206.16.6.208:
    Packets: Sent = 4, Received = 4, Lost = 0 (0% loss),
Approximate round trip times in milli-seconds:
    Minimum = 72ms, Maximum = 91ms, Average = 79ms
```

If the host isn't active, instead of getting this report you'll get the message "Request timed out."

If you enter a hostname, ping reports back with its IP address and then gives details about its four attempts to contact the host, a measurement of how long (in milliseconds) the packet took to make the round trip between your PC and the host, the Time To Live (TTL) information about each packet, and a summary of its findings.

The TTL field can tell you how many hops the packets took to get from your PC to its destination. TTL initially specified the amount of time a packet could live, in seconds, before it expired, as a way to make sure packets didn't simply bounce around the Internet forever and create traffic jams. However, it has been reinterpreted to mean the maximum number of hops a packet will be allowed to take before it reaches its destination. The default number is 255. Each time a packet takes another hop, its TTL is reduced by one. The TTL number that ping reports is the packet's final TTL when it reaches its destination. To find out the number of hops a packet takes, subtract its initial TTL (by default, 255) from the TTL reported by ping. In our example, the packets took 13 hops to get to their destination.

You can use ping with switches, like so:

```
ping -a -l 45 208.201.239.237
```

This command changes the packet size sent from its default size of 32 bytes to 45 bytes, and resolves the IP address to a hostname—in other words, it lists the IP address's hostname.

ping has a wide variety of useful switches that you can use for all kinds of troubleshooting. You use the basic ping command to check whether an Internet or network resource is live and to see if there are any delays in reaching it. But, as Table 5-2 shows, you can use ping and its switches for many other purposes as well—for example, to find out the IP address of a hostname, and vice versa.

Table 5-2. Useful ping switches

Switch	What it does
-a	Resolves an IP address to a hostname.
-f	Turns on the Don't Fragment flag for a packet. This lets you send packets that don't get broken up, and it can be useful for when you want to test whether packets of a certain size are getting through.
-i *value*	Sets the value of the TTL field, using a number from 0 to 255. When you use this field, even though the field will be set to the number you specify, note that the ping report will report back as if it were set to 255. For example, if you set a TTL of 20 and the packet takes 15 hops, the TTL value ping reports will be 240.
-l *value*	Pings using the value specified, in number of bytes.
-n *count*	Specifies the number of ICMP Echo Request messages sent, instead of the default number of 4.
-r *count*	Displays the IP addresses of the hops taken along the route to the destination. Specify a number between 1 and 9. If the number of actual hops exceeds the number you specify, you will get a "Request timed out" message.
-s *count*	Displays a timestamp for the Echo Request and the Echo Reply Request for hops along the route. Specify a number between 1 and 4. If the number of actual hops exceeds the number you specify, you will get a "Request timed out" message.
-t	Keeps sending the Echo Request message continually until stopped by pressing Ctrl-Break, Pause, or Ctrl-C.
-w *value*	The maximum amount of time (in milliseconds) to wait for an Echo Reply message for each Echo Request message before issuing a timeout message. The default is 4000 (4 seconds).

Trace Your Network and Internet Data Path with tracert

Frequently, you have a connection problem over your network or the Internet not because your final destination is down, but because there's a problem with a router somewhere between you and your final destination. For troubleshooting those kinds of problems, use tracert. It displays the path that data takes en route to the server or service you're trying to reach, either on your network or across the Internet. As with ping, it does this by sending ICMP Echo Request messages to the destination you're checking on. To use it, type tracert *destination* at a command prompt, where *destination* can be either an IP address or a hostname. Following is a typical response from a tracert command:

```
Tracing route to redir-zdnet.zdnet.com [206.16.6.208]
over a maximum of 30 hops:

  1     9 ms   11 ms    10 ms  10.208.128.1
  2     8 ms    8 ms     7 ms  bar02-p0-1.cmbrhe1.ma.attbb.net [24.128.8.53]
  3     9 ms     *       32 ms  bar03-p7-0.wobnhe1.ma.attbb.net [24.147.0.193]
  4     8 ms   14 ms     9 ms  12.125.39.213
  5    12 ms   10 ms     9 ms  gbr2-p70.cb1ma.ip.att.net [12.123.40.102]
  6    25 ms   26 ms    24 ms  gbr4-p80.cb1ma.ip.att.net [12.122.5.65]
  7    36 ms   39 ms    64 ms  gbr4-p40.cgcil.ip.att.net [12.122.2.49]
  8    33 ms   33 ms    48 ms  gbr3-p60.cgcil.ip.att.net [12.122.1.125]
  9    72 ms   80 ms    78 ms  gbr3-p30.sffca.ip.att.net [12.122.2.150]
 10    72 ms   77 ms    73 ms  idf26-gsr12-1-pos-6-0.rwc1.attens.net [12.122.
255.222]
 11    76 ms   78 ms    79 ms  mdf3-bi4k-2-eth-1-1.rwc1.attens.net [216.148.
209.66]
 12    73 ms   72 ms    74 ms  63.241.72.150
 13    72 ms   74 ms    71 ms  redir-zdnet.zdnet.com [206.16.6.208]
```

If the destination can't be reached, you will get the message "Destination unreachable."

As you can see, tracert shows the IP address and hostname address of each hop, along with timing data for each hop. If you're having problems on your network, this can help you locate the source of the problem; if a hop has a particularly long delay, you know that's the cause.

You can use several switches with tracert, like this:

```
Tracert -d -h 45 zdnet.com
```

This command traces to *zdnet.com*, displaying only the IP addresses of each router and specifying a maximum number of 45 hops en route to the destination. Table 5-3 shows the most useful tracert switches.

Table 5-3. Useful tracert switches

Switch	What it does
-d	Does not display the hostname of each router
-h *value*	Sets a maximum number of hops for the trace to the destination
-w *value*	Sets the maximum amount of time in milliseconds to wait for a reply

Troubleshoot Network Problems with pathping

The pathping command works like a combination of ping and tracert. Type pathping from the command line, like this:

    pathping target

where target is either a hostname or an IP address—*pop3.catalog.com* or *209.217.46.121*, for example. You then get a two-part report: first a list of every hop along the route to the destination, and then statistics about each hop, including the number of packets lost at each hop. It uses switches—for example:

    pathping -n -w 1000 oreilly.com

This command tells pathping not to resolve the IP addresses of routers, and to wait one second (1,000 milliseconds) for an Echo Reply message. Table 5-4 lists the most important pathping switches.

Table 5-4. Useful pathping switches

Switch	What it does
-n	Does not display the hostname of each router.
-h value	Sets a maximum number of hops for the trace to the destination. The default is 30 hops.
-w value	Sets the maximum amount of time (in milliseconds) to wait for a reply.
-p	Sets the amount of time (in milliseconds) to wait before a new ping is issued. The default is 250.
-q value	Sets the number of ICMP Echo Request messages to transmit. The default is 100.

See Also

- "Troubleshoot Network Connections with netsh, netstat, and ipconfig" [Hack #52]

HACK #52 Troubleshoot Network Connections with netsh, netstat, and ipconfig

Here are a few more command-line tools for tracking down problems with your network connection.

In addition to well-known command-line network utilities such as ping, tracert, and pathping [Hack #51], three additional all-purpose utilities can help you troubleshoot network connections: netsh, netstat, and ipconfig.

Use netsh to Troubleshoot Network and Internet Connections

netsh is a wide-ranging command-line diagnostic tool that has an exceedingly large number of commands available. (For a complete list of available commands, use Windows XP Help and Support and search for netsh.) Here you'll learn the most interesting.

Perhaps the most useful of the netsh commands are the netsh diag commands. Use them to find out information about your PC's network setup, such as finding the IP address of its mail server, newsgroup server, DNS server, and similar resources.

There are two ways to use netsh: directly from the command line with all its switches, or first getting to the netsh console by typing netsh at the command line and then typing the command from the netsh> prompt that appears. For example, you could type netsh diag show adapter at the command line, which lists every network adapter on your PC, or you could get to the netsh> prompt and type diag show adapter.

Use the netsh command to connect to the resources and then get information about them. For example, to find out the IP address of your DNS servers, type netsh diag show dns; to find out the IP address of your mail server, type netsh diag connect mail.

Table 5-5 lists the most useful of the netsh diag commands. Precede each of them with netsh diag. Note that they each have many switches associated with them. For more details, use Windows XP Help and Support and search for netsh.

Table 5-5. Useful netsh diag commands

Command	What it does
connect ieproxy	Establishes a connection to Internet Explorer's proxy server, if one exists
connect mail	Establishes a connection to the default Outlook Express mail server
connect news	Establishes a connection to the default Outlook Express newsgroup server
ping adapter	Establishes a connection with the named adapter
ping dhcp	Establishes a connection with a DHCP server
show adapter	Lists all the adapters on the PC
show all	Lists all the network objects defined for the local PC, such as adapters, network clients, servers, modems, and other objects
show dhcp	Lists all the DHCP servers for the specified adapter
show dns	Lists all the DNS servers for the specified adapter
show gateway	Lists all the gateways for the specified adapter

Use netstat to Get Information About Open Network Connections

If you want to get a snapshot of all incoming and outgoing network connections, use the netstat command. At a command prompt, type netstat. It lists all connections, including the protocol being used, the local and Internet addresses, and the current state of the connection, like this:

```
Active Connections
  Proto  Local Address         Foreign Address           State
  TCP    PrestonGralla:1031    localhost:2929            ESTABLISHED
  TCP    PrestonGralla:2887    192.168.1.103:netbios-ssn TIME_WAIT
  TCP    PrestonGralla:2899    www.oreillynet.com:http   ESTABLISHED
  TCP    PrestonGralla:2900    www.oreillynet.com:http   ESTABLISHED
  TCP    PrestonGralla:2932    mail.attbi.com:pop3       ESTABLISHED
  TCP    PrestonGralla:2936    vmms2.verisignmail.com:pop3 ESTABLISHED
```

It will help you know whether connections are live, the network or Internet device to which they're connected, and which local resource is making the connection. It's best suited for when you're troubleshooting network problems and want to find out whether certain ports are open, why certain computers on the network are having connection problems, and similar issues. You can use command-line switches with netstat. For example, display open ports and open connections with this syntax: netstat -a. Table 5-6 lists netstat switches.

Table 5-6. Useful netstat switches

Switch	What it does
-a	Displays all open connections and ports.
-e	Displays Ethernet statistics about packets transmitted and received. Can be combined with the -s switch.
-n	Displays the addresses and ports in numeric, IP address form.
-o	Displays the process identifier (PID) that owns each connection.
-p *proto*	Displays the connections used by the protocol, which can be IP, IPv6, ICMP, ICMPv6, TCP, TCPv6, UDP, or UDPv6.
-r	Displays the network's routing table.
-s	Displays statistics for each protocol. It lists all statistics for all protocols, but you can list only those for a specified protocol if you combine it with the -p switch.
interval *value*	Runs netstat repeatedly, pausing *value* seconds between each new display. To stop the display, press Ctrl-C.

Use ipconfig to Troubleshoot TCP/IP

One of the most powerful tools for analyzing and troubleshooting TCP/IP problems is the ipconfig command-line utility. It provides information about each of your adapters, including the assigned IP address, subnet mask, default gateway, MAC address, DNS servers, whether DHCP is enabled, and a variety of other data. To see basic information about your adapters, type `ipconfig` at a command prompt, and you'll see information like this:

```
Windows IP Configuration
Ethernet adapter Local Area Connection:
        Connection-specific DNS Suffix  . : ne1.client2.attbi.com
        IP Address. . . . . . . . . . . : 192.168.1.100
        Subnet Mask . . . . . . . . . . : 255.255.255.0
        Default Gateway . . . . . . . . : 192.168.1.1
PPP adapter {6A724E76-AB59-4ABC-BBF5-41CA4410EB8D}:
        Connection-specific DNS Suffix  . :
        IP Address. . . . . . . . . . . : 172.165.155.106
        Subnet Mask . . . . . . . . . . : 255.255.255.255
        Default Gateway . . . . . . . . :
```

As you can see, `ipconfig` provides basic information about your IP address, subnet mask, default gateway, and a connection-specific DNS suffix, if any. However, you can get much more detailed information by using the `/all` switch, like this: `ipconfig /all`. For most troubleshooting purposes, use the `/all` switch. You get a much more comprehensive listing, as shown here:

```
Windows IP Configuration
        Host Name . . . . . . . . . . . : PrestonGralla
        Primary Dns Suffix  . . . . . . :
        Node Type . . . . . . . . . . . : Hybrid
        IP Routing Enabled. . . . . . . : No
        WINS Proxy Enabled. . . . . . . : No
Ethernet adapter Local Area Connection:
        Connection-specific DNS Suffix  . : ne1.client2.attbi.com
        Description . . . . . . . . . . : CNet PRO200WL PCI Fast Ethernet
Adapter
        Physical Address. . . . . . . . : 00-08-A1-00-9F-32
        Dhcp Enabled. . . . . . . . . . : Yes
        Autoconfiguration Enabled . . . . : Yes
        IP Address. . . . . . . . . . . : 192.168.1.100
        Subnet Mask . . . . . . . . . . : 255.255.255.0
        Default Gateway . . . . . . . . : 192.168.1.1
        DHCP Server . . . . . . . . . . : 192.168.1.1
        DNS Servers . . . . . . . . . . : 204.127.202.19
                                          216.148.227.79
        Lease Obtained. . . . . . . . . : Saturday, December 28, 2002 8:
53:40 AM
        Lease Expires . . . . . . . . . : Sunday, December 29, 2002 8:53:
40 AM

PPP adapter {6A724E76-AB59-4ABC-BBF5-41CA4410EB8D}:
        Connection-specific DNS Suffix  . :
        Description . . . . . . . . . . : WAN (PPP/SLIP) Interface
        Physical Address. . . . . . . . : 00-53-45-00-00-00
        Dhcp Enabled. . . . . . . . . . : No
```

```
IP Address. . . . . . . . . . . . : 172.165.155.106
Subnet Mask . . . . . . . . . . . : 255.255.255.255
Default Gateway . . . . . . . . . :
DNS Servers . . . . . . . . . . . : 64.12.104.134
NetBIOS over Tcpip. . . . . . . . : Disabled
```

You can also use `ipconfig` to release and renew IP addresses, and to perform other troubleshooting functions as well. For example, to renew an adapter's IP address, use this command:

```
ipconfig /renew "adapter name"
```

where *adapter name* is the name of the adapter whose IP address you want to renew. Make sure to put quotes around the adapter name and use spaces if there is more than one word in the adapter name. Table 5-7 lists other switches you can use with `ipconfig`.

Table 5-7. Command-line switches for ipconfig

Switch	What it does
/all	Displays complete TCP/IP configuration information
/displaydns	Displays information from the DNS resolver cache [Hack #49]
/flushdns	Clears the DNS resolver cache [Hack #49]
/registerdns	Refreshes all DHCP leases and reregisters DNS names
/release "adapter"	Releases the IP address for the specified adapter
/renew "adapter"	Renews the IP address for the specified adapter
/setclassid "adapter" newclassid	Resets the DHCP Class ID for the specified adapter
/showclassid "adapter"	Displays the DHCP Class ID for the specified adapter

See Also

- "Troubleshoot Network Connections with ping, tracert, and pathping" [Hack #51]

Speed Up Network Browsing
#53
Speed up your network browsing by tweaking your Registry.

When you use My Network Places to browse for other machines on your network, it usually takes a long time to display the list of shared resources for the target machine. This is because Windows XP first checks for the scheduled tasks on the target machine before listing the shared resources present on the computer.

> To schedule a task using Windows XP's Scheduled Tasks, choose Start → Programs → Accessories → System Tools → Scheduled Tasks.

This unnecessary checking can easily add 30 seconds of delay. You can decrease the time browsing takes by modifying the Registry to turn off this checking:

1. Invoke the Registry Editor by typing regedit [Hack #83] at the command line.

2. Open the following Registry key:

   ```
   HKEY_LOCAL_MACHINE\SOFTWARE\Microsoft\Windows\CurrentVersion\Explorer\
   Remote Computer\NameSpace
   ```

3. Delete the following key (the value for it is the Scheduled Tasks, as shown in Figure 5-4):

   ```
   {D6277990-4C6A-11CF-8D87-00AA0060F5BF}
   ```

4. Close the Registry and reboot.

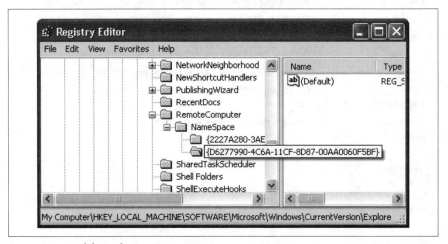

Figure 5-4. Modifying the Registry

That's it! You should now be able to browse to another computer on the network without much delay.

—*Wei-Meng Lee*

Control Another PC with Remote Access

You can control a computer—virtually moving its mouse and typing on its keyboard—over the Internet, using either Windows XP's built-in features or a third-party program.

When you are at work, wouldn't it be nice if you could log on to your home computer to check your email or find a file you took home? How about using your home or office desktop computer from your laptop on the road? You can use a remote control program to use another computer over the Internet, viewing its screen on your screen and giving commands via your mouse and keyboard. Windows XP comes with a feature called Remote Desktop, or you can use a third-party program. Windows Messenger [Hack #97] also enables people who are chatting to share control of each other's computers.

The computer you will control is called the *remote server*, and the computer you are actually sitting in front of is the *remote client*. Windows XP comes with a remote client program (Remote Desktop Connection), and Windows XP Professional comes with a remote server (Remote Desktop) that works with one client at a time—that is, one computer can "take over" your computer remotely (with luck, it'll be you doing the takeover!).

> Remote Access Server (RAS) on Windows NT or 2000 servers and the Routing and Remote Access utility on Windows Server 2003 both act as remote servers that allow multiple remote clients to connect.

Windows XP Home Edition can't act as a remote server; if you need to be able to access a Home Edition system remotely, you need to upgrade to Windows XP Professional or use a third-party program. We recommend VNC, the small, free, open source program available at *http://www.realvnc. com.*

Configuring the Windows XP Remote Server

If you want to be able to control your Windows XP Professional system remotely, set it up as a remote server. Using an administrator user account, choose Start → Control Panel → Performance and Maintenance → System (or press the Windows-Break key), click the Remote tab, select the "Allow users to connect remotely to this computer" checkbox in the Remote Desktop section of the tab to enable incoming connections, and click Select Remote Users if you want to control which user accounts can be used by remote clients. (Windows automatically allows connections from the current user, along with all user accounts in the local Administrators and Remote Desktop Users groups.)

Normally, remote clients connect to the server via a local area network or a permanent Internet connection. However, you can also configure the remote server to accept incoming phone calls if you have a dial-up modem. Create a dial-up connection that accepts incoming calls by running the New Connection Wizard (click "Create a new connection" from the task pane in the Network Connections window). Choose "Set up an advanced connection" as the Network Connection Type, choose "Accept incoming connections," choose your modem, choose whether to accept VPN connections [Hack #82], and choose which user accounts the incoming connection can connect to.

Firewalls usually refuse remote access connections [Hacks #77 and #78], so if you want your remote server to be accessible from the Internet, you need to open a port in your computer's firewall. Remote Desktop uses port 3389. If you use Windows XP's built-in Windows Firewall, display the Network Connections window, right-click the Internet connection, choose Properties from the shortcut menu, click the Advanced tab, and click Settings to display the Advanced Settings dialog box. Click the Remote Desktop checkbox; if the Service Settings dialog box appears, just click OK.

> If you want to change the Remote Desktop server port to a number other than 3389 (perhaps to decrease the likelihood of hackers breaking through it), see the Microsoft Knowledge Base Article Q187623 (at *http://support.microsoft.com*, type the article number in the "Search the Knowledge Base" box).

When you connect from your remote client (described later in this hack), you need to provide a domain name or IP address. If your computer connects via a dial-up, DSL, or cable connection, its IP address changes each time you connect, and the computer doesn't have a domain name. One solution is to have someone at the remote server display the Network Connections window, right-click the Internet connection, choose Status from the shortcut menu, click the Support tab, and call, IM, or email you with the IP address that appears. However, this solution is no good if no one is available to do this. Instead, you can sign up for a dynamic DNS service [Hack #55] at *http://www.dyndns.org* or *http://www.tzo.com*. The dynamic DNS service at DynDNS.org gives you a free domain name in the form <*yourname*>. *dyndns.org* (they offer several dozen domain names to which you can add your name). TZO.com provides a subdomain at <*yourname*>.*tzo.com* for $25 per year. You install a small utility on your computer that automatically tells the dynamic DNS whenever your computer's IP address changes.

One final configuration note: when a client connects to your server via Remote Desktop, the user logs into one of the Windows XP user accounts. You can't log into accounts that have no password. Choose which account you plan for remote users to log into, and give it a password.

Setting Up the Remote Client

To set up the remote client software that comes with Windows XP, connect to the Internet and then choose Start → All Programs → Accessories → Communications → Remote Desktop Connection. (If it's not there, you need to install it from your Windows CD.) In the Remote Desktop Connection window, type the domain name or IP address of the server computer and click Connect. Log on with the Windows XP user account and password for the remote server. Your computer screen now shows what's on the screen of the server computer. A connection bar appears as a button on the screen, showing the IP address of the remote server, along with Minimize, Restore, and Maximize buttons you can use to resize the remote client window.

Once you're connected, you can cut and paste information from the remote client window to other windows. You can also use local files in your remote session; your local disk drives appear in My Computer (Windows Explorer). When you print from the remote client, the print job goes to your default local printer, not to the printer on the server.

—Margaret Levine Young

HACK #55 Make Servers Always Available by Mapping a Hostname to a Dynamic IP Address

Make sure the web site or other kind of Internet server you run at home is always available to the world.

If you run your own web server, mail server, or other kind of server at home and are connected to the Internet via a cable modem or DSL modem, people frequently might not be able to connect to your server. That's because, typically, broadband ISPs assign you a dynamic IP address that changes regularly, even if you don't turn off your PC. Because your IP address constantly changes, there is no way for people to connect to you. One day its IP address might be 66.31.42.96, the next it might be 66.41.42.136, and if people don't know your server's current IP address they won't be able to find it. You won't be able to solve the problem by getting your own domain (such as *www.gralla.com*) and publishing that because DNS servers won't be able to keep track of your changing IP address either. If people type in your domain name, the servers won't be able to report on your IP address—and again, your server won't be able to be reached.

There is a way to solve the problem, however: you can map your server's hostname to a dynamic IP address. When you do this, it doesn't matter that your IP address changes; when people type in your web site's URL, they will be forwarded to your new IP address automatically.

You can do this for free by signing up with a service that provides automatic mapping. A number of services will do it for free, such as No-IP.com (*http:// www.no-ip.com*). When you sign up for the service, you choose a hostname for your server and give that hostname out to people who want to connect to the server. Whatever name you choose will end in *.no-ip.com*—for example, *grallasite.no-ip.com*.

After you get your hostname, you download client software that continually monitors your IP address. It reports on your server's current IP address to the No-IP.com site. Whenever the IP address changes, it reports that new IP address to the site. The client checks your IP address every three seconds.

Whenever a PC tries to connect to your server, it first goes to a No-IP.com server, which looks up your server's current address and then redirects the PC to your server, based on your current IP address. The person contacting your site will not have to do anything different from what he normally does; he just types in your URL and is connected to your site.

If you own a domain and want to map that hostname to a dynamic IP address instead of using a No-IP.com address, you'll have to sign up for No-IP.com's No-IP Plus service for $24.95 a month.

If you're using a router at home to share Internet access among several PCs, you might run into problems using the service. Many routers use NAT, in which all PCs on the network share a single external Internet address but are assigned internal network addresses. The No-IP.com client will track your external address, but because that single address is used by all PCs on the network, not just the server, incoming traffic won't be routed to your server. You can fix the problem by using the port forwarding feature of your router to send the incoming traffic to the server **[Hack #50]**.

You might run into another problem as well: when you try to test your server by connecting to it from a PC inside your network, you might not be able to connect to it. That's because you might not be able to connect to the external IP address from inside the network. If this happens, the only solution is to connect to the site from a PC outside your network or ask a friend to connect to it.

One more thing to watch out for: if you're behind a firewall, the No-IP.com client might have trouble connecting back to the No-IP.com site to report on your changing IP address. If you're using a firewall like ZoneAlarm [Hack #78] or a similar one that blocks outbound connections, tell it to allow the client to make outbound connections. Also, depending on the firewall you use, you might need to configure it to open TCP port 8245 because that's the port the client uses to contact No-IP.com with your new IP address.

See Also

- "Secrets of Web Site Hosting with Internet Information Services (IIS)" [Hack #41]

Renew Your DHCP-Assigned IP Address

H A C K
#56

Sometimes, while assigned an IP address by a DHCP server, your PC doesn't appear to be on the network and you can't get Internet or network access. Renewing your IP address often solves the problem.

If you're on a network but you can't send or receive data, use any network resources, or visit the Internet, the culprit might be a problem with your DHCP-assigned IP address. The simplest way to fix it is to renew the IP address—get rid of the old one, and ask the DHCP server to send along a new one.

Before trying this, first make sure you're using a DHCP-assigned IP address rather than a static one. Right-click My Network Places and choose Properties to get to the Network Connections folder. Right-click your current network connection and choose Properties. On the General tab, select Internet Protocol (TCP/IP) and choose Properties. On the General tab, the radio button next to "Obtain an IP address automatically" will be selected if you're using DHCP.

After you've confirmed you're using DHCP, release your current IP address by typing ipconfig /release at a command prompt. The ipconfig command is an all-purpose command that lets you solve many network-related problems [Hack #52]. To renew the address and get a new IP address from the DHCP server, type ipconfig /renew at a command prompt. Your new IP address should fix the problem.

To find your new IP address, type ipconfig at a command prompt. You can also select your connection in the Network Connections folder, click "View status of this connection," and click the Support tab. You'll see the screen shown in Figure 5-5, which shows your new IP address and confirms that it was assigned by a DHCP server.

Figure 5-5. Confirming that you've gotten a new IP address

 HACK #57 Repair a Broken TCP/IP Connection

Get back onto the Internet fast if you have TCP/IP woes.

TCP/IP problems can be exceedingly difficult to troubleshoot, and at times your TCP/IP connection appears to break for no apparent reason. Everything looks like it should be working, but you're not able to connect using the protocols. If you have a broken connection, try the following:

Try automated repair.   Right-click the broken connection in the Network Connections folder and choose Repair.

Run the Network Setup Wizard.   It walks you step by step through TCP/IP and network configuration and will correct any errors you might have introduced inadvertently.

Reset your router.   If you have a home network, the problem might lie with the router or in the connection between the router and your broadband provider. Follow the directions for resetting the router.

Reset your cable modem or DSL modem.   If you have a broadband connection, the problem might lie in the assignment of your IP address by your ISP. Power off your cable modem or DSL modem, unplug its Ethernet cable, and leave it powered off for five minutes. Then restart it. This is also a good time to reset your router. You can also try releasing and renewing after you've turned the connection back on.

Reset TCP/IP to its original configuration. If all else fails, you can try to reset your TCP/IP stack to the same state that it was in when XP was first installed on the computer. Use the NetShell utility [Hack #52]. Issue this command: `netsh int ip reset [log_file_name]`, where *log_file_name* is the name of a file where the actions taken by NetShell will be recorded.

Get a new Ethernet cable. Your old cable might be nicked, the connector might be loose, or mice might have nibbled on it.

VoIP Hacks

HACK #58

The Voice over Internet Protocol (VoIP) lets you make phone calls over the Internet for less money than the normal phone system. But VoIP services can sometimes be flaky. Here's a grab bag of hacks for getting more out of your VoIP service.

VoIP technology has been around for several years, but only recently has it begun to take off and be available directly to consumers. With a VoIP service, you pay a monthly fee, just as you do to your normal telephone provider, and you get services such as call waiting, caller ID, and similar features. Typically, VoIP phone plans are less expensive than traditional phone plans, and they're often much less expensive for when you make overseas calls. They also offer low-priced "all-you-can-eat" plans for making phone calls in the U.S. They require that you have a broadband Internet connection such as a DSL modem or cable modem because lower-speed service doesn't have a high enough bandwidth to deliver good enough voice quality.

When you use a VoIP service, you plug a special VoIP phone into your home router, DSL modem, or cable modem via an Ethernet cable.

> If you plug the phone into your DSL modem or cable modem, you then plug your PC into a port on your phone via an Ethernet cable so that your PC can also get Internet access.

Calls made over VoIP travel over the Internet, as do any other Internet packets. They are then transferred to the normal phone system via a gateway so that you can call any phone in the world as you would with any telephone. You receive calls in the same way. Someone makes a call on a normal telephone, and that call travels over the normal telephone system, then is sent to a gateway where the call is broken into IP packets and delivered over the Internet to your telephone. With this type of VoIP service, you get your own phone number, just like any phone number. In fact, you might even be able to keep your existing phone number.

There are also software-only VoIP services, in which you don't use any special hardware or equipment. Instead, you download a piece of software and use your PC's speakers and microphone to talk, or else plug a headset into your PC's microphone jack. Generally, these only let you call others who use the same software that you do; in other words, you can't make calls to normal telephones, but can make them to those who also use the same VoIP software you're using. In this scenario, the phone call travels over the Internet. It never actually travels to the normal phone system because the calls aren't made to normal telephones.

These VoIP services are typically free. They don't offer full service plans, and so don't have caller ID, call waiting, and similar features. In fact, instant messenger programs such as AOL Instant Messenger, Yahoo! Messenger, and Windows Messenger let you make calls this way. Some of these services let you make phone calls to regular telephones as well, although for that they charge you a fee. And for now, anyway, you can't receive normal phone calls on them; you can make phone calls only. But that is expected to change.

The best-known full-featured VoIP service that lets you make phone calls to anyone and receive phone calls is Vonage (*http://www.vonage.com*). It offers a variety of service plans—for example, $14.99 per month for 500 minutes of calls per month to anywhere in the U.S or Canada, or $24.99 per month for unlimited calls per month to anywhere in the U.S. or Canada. All plans include a variety of free services, such as voicemail, caller ID, call waiting, call forwarding, call transfer, and three-way calling. And international calls are as low as 2 cents per minute to London, Paris, Rome, and Hong Kong. A variety of other companies are entering the VoIP market, including ISPs and AT&T. The best-known software-only VoIP service is Skype (*http://www.skype.com*), which is available for free when you make calls to other Skype users.

But using VoIP can sometimes be a frustrating experience. So, use these hacks to solve some common VoIP woes.

Troubleshoot VoIP Phone/Home Router Problems

Some people have had problems when using Vonage VoIP service with their home routers. Instead of incoming calls being sent to their phones, the calls go directly to voicemail. How you solve this varies from router to router, but here's how to do it with the popular Linksys router line. Other routers should have similar fixes.

You're going to set up your router so that it uses its port forwarding feature to send calls directly to your IP telephone. First, turn off your cable modem or DSL modem, all the computers on your network, your router, and your IP telephone. Then, turn your cable modem or DSL modem and your router back on. Turn on your IP telephone, and make sure that turn it on before turning on any PCs on your network. This will make sure it is given the network's first IP address via DHCP.

Your caller ID service on either your normal telephone or VoIP phone can easily be subject to caller ID spoofing so that the caller ID number you see before you pick up the phone isn't really the person calling you. Normally, in caller ID, whenever someone makes a phone call his Calling Party Number (CPN) is sent along with it. Sent along with the CPN is a privacy flag; if the caller has requested that his number not be shared, the flag tells the phone network to block the CPN from being sent.

But VoIP changes all that. Using the open source Linux-based PBX software Asterisk with certain VoIP providers, someone can change the CPN sent along with his call, making it appear to come from any number he wants. So, keep in mind that increasingly, caller ID is being subject to spoofing and hacks.

Once you've turned on your IP telephone and your PCs, log into the Linksys administrator's setup screen by opening your browser, typing http://192.168.1.1, and pressing Enter. Leave the username blank, and use the password admin and press Enter. (That's the default password for the router; if you've changed it, use the password you've changed it to.)

From the setup screen, choose Advanced → Forwarding. You'll come to the port forwarding screen. Set up port forwarding to route these port ranges to your IP telephone. Forward each port to the IP address of your IP phone, such as 192.168.1.101. (The IP address will be the first one assigned by your network.) Set the protocol to UDP. Use the port settings in Table 5-8.

Table 5-8. Port ranges for your IP telephone

Port range	Protocol	IP address
53 to 53	UDP	Your phone's IP address
5060 to 5061	UDP	Your phone's IP address
123 to 123	UDP	Your phone's IP address
69 to 69	UDP	Your phone's IP address
10000 to 20000	UDP	Your phone's IP address

Your screen will look like Figure 5-6.

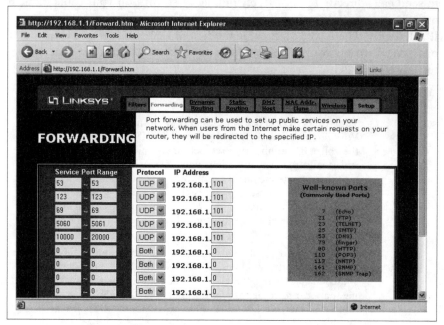

Figure 5-6. *Setting up a Linksys router to work with a Vonage IP phone*

If you're not sure of your Vonage phone's IP address, it's easy to find out. Take the phone off the hook. The red function button on the top of the phone will light up. Press the illuminated red button and then dial 80#. Your IP address will be displayed.

When you're done, click Apply. The port forwarding will take effect immediately, so your problems should be solved.

Get Your Vonage IP Phone to Work with DSL

The nature of some DSL services cause conflicts with Vonage IP telephones, so when you use DSL, you might not be able to get your IP phone to work. Even if the phone previously worked with a cable modem, when you switch to DSL it might stop working.

The problem is that DSL services often require the use of PPPoE, but if you don't also turn on PPoE in your Vonage phone, the phone won't work. To turn on PPPoE in your Vonage phone, open a web browser in the computer that has the phone connected to it. Go to *http://192.168.102.1* and press

Enter. (That's the default address for configuring Vonage phones. If you have another type of phone, or if your Vonage phone has a different configuration address, use that instead.)

The phone's Basic Configuration screen will appear. Select the Enable PPPoE option, and type the DSL service name, username, and password that your DSL provider gave to you. Click Save Changes. You'll get the message "This will require a reboot of the unit. Are you sure?" Click OK. Your phone will reboot. Wait five minutes, and pick up your phone. It will now work.

Is VoIP a Telephone or Internet Service?

When you use VoIP, are you making a phone call or using the Internet? The logical answer, of course, is both. But state and federal governments are not logical, so that question makes an enormous difference in how VoIP services will be regulated. If VoIP is treated as if it were a telephone service, for example, VoIP companies could be required to provide Enhanced 911 emergency phone services and pay into federal and state universal service funds that are used to help pay for telecommunications service to low-income areas, schools, and libraries. Also unclear is whether VoIP services must comply with federal wiretap laws.

At the time of this writing, the Federal Communications Commission hasn't made a definitive decision on the matter, but it has made a series of rulings related to VoIP. It ruled that software-only VoIP that makes PC-to-PC phone calls only is not a phone service and therefore does not have to comply with phone service regulation. It also ruled that state governments do not have regulatory authority over VoIP services that use the telephone system to let you make and receive phone calls to anyone, anywhere, as a phone service. Instead, the federal government has that authority. But as of this writing, it still hasn't ruled on whether it will treat that service like a telephone call, like Internet access, like some hybrid of the two, or in some other way.

Cut Your DSL Costs with VoIP

Many DSL services let you make phone calls as well as get high-speed Internet access over the same telephone line. So, if you use VoIP in concert with DSL, you're paying double for your phone service—once for DSL, and the second time for VoIP.

There's a solution: get a DSL service that offers only Internet access, not phone service. It's sometimes called Naked DSL. Qwest and Verizon both offer Naked DSL, and other DSL providers might follow suit.

A federal law says that when you switch telephone providers, you should be allowed to keep your existing phone number. But you'll have to ask for it; it doesn't happen automatically. And there might be circumstances in which you can't keep your existing phone number. If you're switching to Vonage, go to *http://www.vonage.com/identity/vonage/includes/lnploa.pdf* and fill out the form online. You'll be told whether you can transfer your phone, as well as the steps you have to take to have it switched. The change might not take effect immediately, and you might get a temporary phone number that you can use with your Vonage phone while the changeover happens.

Make Skype Calls at Work

If you try to make Skype calls at work, you might get a "Skype error #1102" and be unable to make a connection. If that happens, it means your business's firewall won't let you through. To make the calls, you'll have to tell the system administrator to open up unrestricted outgoing TCP access to all destination ports above 1024, or to port 80. (Destination ports above 1024 is a better bet, however.) That will let you make the connection. If you want better voice quality, tell the administrator to also open up outgoing UDP traffic to all ports above 1024, and to allow UDP replies to come back in.

CHAPTER SIX

Email

Hacks 59–64

If you're like a lot of people, email is a big part of your life. For many, it's replaced the telephone for keeping in touch with friends and family—and, of course, it's absolutely vital for work as well.

But the odds are you're not getting the most out of your email. You might be bedeviled by spam, you might be blocked from opening specific files sent to you via email, and you might not know how to back up your mail programs. In this chapter, you'll find hacks for all that and more, including great Registry hacks for getting the most out of Outlook and Outlook Express, as well as Outlook alternatives. And you'll find out how to hack Google's Gmail email service by doing things such as using it as a virtual hard drive.

Slam That Spam

#59 You don't have to be bedeviled by unwanted mail. Use this hack to kill as much as 90% (or much more, in my case) of your spam.

People who have certain body parts they'd like enlarged, who expect Nigerian strangers to shower several million dollars upon them, who favor spending boatloads of money for semiworthless goods, and who enjoy vile, pornographic come-ons littering their email box love spam.

Everyone else, like you and I, hate the stuff.

While there's no foolproof way of stopping all the spam that makes its way into your mailbox, I've found ways to block at least 90% of what I don't want headed my way. To get such an effective blocking rate, you'll need to use downloadable software; the antispam features built into Outlook and Outlook Express simply don't cut it. (However, if you're bent on trying to use Outlook and Outlook Express's antispam features, head to the end of this hack to learn how.)

You can use two primary kinds of software to block spam. One type sits between your email program and the mail servers where you pick up your email. It checks your mail, marks email that it considers spam, and then (depending on the program) lets you handle that spam in a variety of ways, such as automatically deleting it, letting you manually delete it, or marking it in a way that will alert your normal email program that it's spam—and letting the email program filter or kill the spam. In all cases, you'll be able to read the messages before they're deleted, if you want.

The other type of software integrates directly into Outlook or another email program and kills spam from directly within the program. I favor this kind because it's a simpler, one-step process. But I've used both types, and both work well.

For the kind of spam killer that sits between your email program and your mail server, I suggest the free program MailWasher (*http://www.pcworld. com/downloads/file_description/0,fid,20000,00.asp*). It imports your existing email server account settings so that you don't have to set them up from scratch, and it lets you read and preview messages before deleting spam. I especially like its bounced mail feature; it will send a false "address not found" message to the sender so that it will appear as though your email address doesn't exist. While not all spammers bother to clean up their lists of addresses, this could lead to less spam ultimately coming into your mailbox. As with most spam killers, you can add addresses to a list of known spammers, though spammers so frequently spoof their addresses that this might not be of much help. You can also create filters with specified words or groups of words that MailWasher will look for in email, and if it finds them it will consider the message spam.

A more powerful, for-pay version of the program is available for $37 from *http://mailwasher.net*. Its primary benefit is that it will check multiple email accounts for spam; the free version will check only one. If you need to check only a single account, stay with the free version.

One of the tricks spammers use is to target a site and send a dictionary attack to many potential email accounts on a server. They will send to "bob," "nancy," etc., as well as to "asmith," "bsmith," "csmith," etc. Most of the emails will bounce, but the spammer doesn't care. He encodes the email in HTML with an embedded <IMG> tag. The tag has information encoded within it to uniquely identify the valid email addresses. For example, say *cjones@mycompany.com* gets an email in HTML format. Inside the email is:

```
<img src=83.48.123.74/img/jojo_jpg_cjones_mycompany_com.jpg>
```

The web server at 83.48.123.74 will load the image named *jojo.jpg* to an email in cjones' email program. When the user sees the advertisement for herbal Viagra or whatever, she will delete it. However, the damage has already been done. The spammer knows *cjones@mycompany.com* exists because he knows the image was downloaded. Soon the user cjones will be getting more than just offers for herbal Viagra.

One way to prevent this type of attack is to turn off displaying HTML or displaying graphics in emails. In Outlook 2003, displaying graphics is turned off by default. Instead of a graphic, you'll see an X for each graphic. To view the graphic, you have to right-click the X and choose Download Pictures. If you're receiving email from a spammer, obviously you don't want to view the graphic.

If, for some reason, Outlook 2003 is displaying graphics in your email, you can easily tell it to stop. Choose Tools → Options → Security and in the Download Pictures area, click Change Automatic Download Settings. The screen shown in Figure 6-1 appears.

Figure 6-1. Blocking graphics being displayed in Outlook 2003

Check the box next to "Don't download pictures or other content automatically in HTML e-mail." If you want to automatically display pictures from people on your Safe Senders and Safe Recipients lists (see details later in this hack), check the appropriate boxes. You should also check the box next to "Warn me before downloading content when editing, forwarding, or replying to email." You should check this box because when you forward, edit, or reply to an email, Outlook will display and include the graphic, unless you tell it not to when you're warned. Checking this box tells Outlook to warn you first.

Unfortunately, there's no direct way to do this in Outlook if you have a version earlier than 2003, but there's a hack that will do the trick for you. When you're in your Inbox, turn off Outlook's Preview Pane by choosing View → Preview Pane. (To restore the pane, choose View → Preview Pane again.) HTML email will grab pictures from web servers only when you've opened the mail or viewed it in the Preview Pane, so all you have to do is delete spam without opening it—by using spam killers as outlined earlier in this hack—and you'll be safe. In Outlook Express, you can do the same thing by choosing View → Layout and unchecking the box next to "Show preview pane."

If you use Outlook 2002 with at least Service Pack 1 installed, you can use a Registry hack to turn off the display of HTML. Close Outlook. Then run the Registry Editor [Hack #83] and go to HKEY_CURRENT_USER\Software\Microsoft\Office\10.0\Outlook\Options\Mail. Create a new DWORD value whose name is ReadAsPlain. Double-click the new value to open it. In the Value Data box, type 1, and then click OK. Open Outlook and notice that any new *unsigned* emails are read as plain text, not HTML.

> In Eudora, this is done by selecting Tools → Options → Display and then unchecking "Automatically download HTML graphics" (this turns off the display of HTML email); by selecting Tools → Options → Display and unchecking "Allow executables in HTML content"; and by selecting Tools → Options → Styled Text and checking "Send plain text only" (this turns off the sending of HTML email, which is just a polite thing to do).

Peer-to-Peer Technology Fights Spam

I've tried quite a few Outlook add-in spam killers, and my favorite is Safety-Bar (*http://www.cloudmark.com*). I've found that it blocks well over 95% of the spam I receive. It uses peer-to-peer technology to gather the collective intelligence of thousands of other email users to fight spam. When you install it, it creates a *Spam* folder in Outlook and routes any spam into that folder, where you can review it and then delete it. If you get spam that isn't automatically routed to the folder, you can mark it as spam. Not only is the mail then sent to the *Spam* folder, but also, SafetyBar servers are told you consider that piece of mail spam. That information goes into a database, along with similar information from hundreds of thousands of other people who use the program. A variety of algorithms are used to determine what is spam and what isn't, and that's what ultimately blocks spam on everyone's system. It uses collective intelligence, which might be the ultimate spam killer.

You can also block and unblock messages as spam, so if mail is accidentally marked as spam it won't be blocked in the future. I've used the program for more than six months, and I've found it increases in effectiveness over time. By now, I estimate that it blocks more than 95% of spam, though that changes on a daily basis.

SafetyBar runs as a small toolbar in Outlook, as shown in Figure 6-2. (It runs as a toolbar in Outlook Express as well.) A nice little touch is the message bar that tells you how much spam the program has blocked, how much time it's saved you, or how much spam it's blocked in a day. Depending on my mood, when I see the total amount of spam it's blocked I'm either depressed that there's so much spam in the world or pleased at how much spam I've been able to avoid.

Figure 6-2. SafetyBar running on the Outlook toolbar

SafetyBar costs $39.95 for a one-year subscription. Admittedly, that's a hefty price for a spam killer, considering that others are available for free. But if you get enough spam, you might consider it worth the money.

> One of the more intriguing features of SafetyBar is that it keeps a running count of all the emails you've received and what percentage is spam. It shows that more than half of all the mail I receive is spam. As of this writing, I've received 149,465 emails while using SafetyBar, and 84,622 of them were spam.

Slam Spam Before It Starts

The best way to fight spam is to make sure it never gets sent to your email box in the first place. So, how do you end up on spam lists? There are many ways, but the most common, according to a comprehensive study done by the Center for Democracy & Technology, is that your email address is harvested by spammers who use programs to automatically scan web pages and gather email addresses from them. Those addresses are then sold to other spammers, so you could end up on dozens of lists.

You might need to have your email address on a public web site for many reasons, so removing your address from sites might not be an option. However, there are ways to hide your address from spammers, even when it's in plain view.

One way used to be to spell out your email address—for example, post "preston at gralla dot com" instead of *preston@gralla.com*. Automated harvesting programs won't be able to grab your address that way.

At least you *used* to be able to use that trick. Some spammers have figured it out by now. My new favorite trick is to use a bit of inline JavaScript to generate my email address at page load time. Harvester bots see a `<script>` tag, but users see *bob@bob.com*.

```
<script type="text/javascript" language="javascript">
<!--
      {     document.write(String.
fromCharCode(60,97,32,104,114,101,102,61,34,109,97,105,108,116,111,58,98,111
,98,64,98,111,98,46,99,111,109,34,62,98,111,98,64,98,111,98,46,99,111,109,60
,47,97,62))
      }
//-->
</script>
<noscript>
<a href = "mailto:%62%6F%62%40%62%6F%62%2E%63%6F%6D">email me</a>
</noscript>
```

I got the JavaScript generator from *http://www.u.arizona.edu/~trw/spam/spam.htm*. You feed it your email address, and it generates the JavaScript.

Another solution is to use HTML characters for your address rather than plain-text characters. That way, a person who visits the page can see the email address, since HTML translates the underlying code into a readable address, but an automated harvester won't be able to read it. To use HTML characters, you need to use the ANSI characters and precede each character with &#. Separate each HTML character by a ; and leave no spaces between characters. For example, in HTML, the *preston@gralla.com* address is:

```
&#112;&#114;&#101;&#115;&#116;&#111;&#110;&#64;&#103;&#114;&#97;&#108;&#108;
&#97;&#46;&#099;&#111;&#109
```

Keep in mind, though, that if you use HTML characters to spell out your email address, you won't be able to include automated HTML "MailTo" links; that requires you to actually spell out the text instead of using HTML characters.

Table 6-1 lists the common ANSI codes you'll need for most email addresses.

Table 6-1. Common ANSI codes

A	65	Q	81	g	103	w	119
B	66	R	82	h	104	x	120
C	67	S	83	i	105	y	121
D	68	T	84	j	106	z	122
E	69	U	85	k	107	@	64
F	70	V	86	l	108	.	46
G	71	W	87	m	109	0	48
H	72	X	88	n	110	1	49
I	73	Y	89	o	111	2	50
J	74	Z	90	p	112	3	51
K	75	a	97	q	113	4	52
L	76	b	98	r	114	5	53
M	77	c	99	s	115	6	54
N	78	d	100	t	116	7	55
O	79	e	101	u	117	8	56
P	80	f	102	v	118	9	57

For a more comprehensive list of ANSI codes and special HTML characters, go to *http://www.alanwood.net/demos/ansi.html*.

You can do several other things to keep your address out of spammers' hands. When registering at a site, always read the fine print to see whether you're also signing up to get unsolicited mail. I also suggest using multiple email addresses, including those from free mail services like Hotmail and Yahoo, and to use those addresses when registering at sites. That way, any spam will be sent to them rather than your normal mail address.

Viewing Mail Header Information in Outlook and Outlook Express

As a general rule, spammers spoof their email addresses so that you won't be able to find them. However, not all do, and if you examine email header information you might be able to trace spam to its source. Once you find the originating mail server, you can send a message to the ISP's administrator, asking to block mail from the sender. It might not always work, but it's worth a try.

The problem for Outlook and Outlook Express users is that those programs don't show mail header information—information such as the original sender of the message, the original mail server, and relay information in your messages. However, there is a way to view it.

In Outlook, right-click the message whose header you want to view, and choose Options. Header information appears at the bottom of the screen, as shown in Figure 6-3. You can scroll through it and copy and paste from it. You can also view this information if you're reading a message, by choosing View → Options.

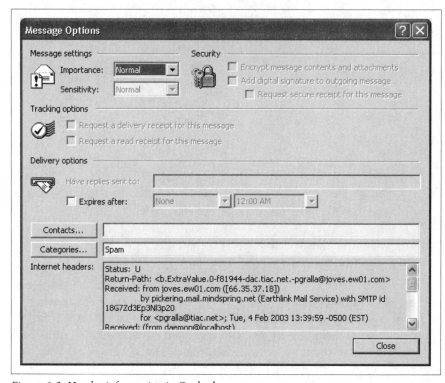

Figure 6-3. Header information in Outlook

Note that if you use logic when trying to view header information in Outlook, it won't work. If you choose View → Message Header, for example, you won't see your header information. Instead, that option toggles the To:, Cc:, and Subject: lines on and off.

In Outlook Express, right-click a message and choose Properties → Details, and you'll see header information, as shown in Figure 6-4.

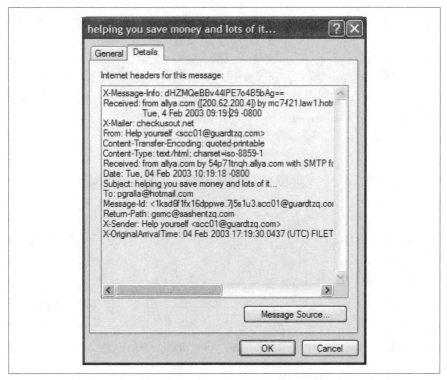

Figure 6-4. Displaying header information in Outlook Express

Handling Spam in Outlook Express

Both Outlook and Outlook Express include ways to handle spam. Outlook Express doesn't do a particularly effective job because it requires that you manually determine what spam is and then block future spam based on that. Because spam comes in from so many different email addresses and includes so many different subject lines, it's difficult to control spam in this way. However, you can give it a try. Here's how to do it in Outlook Express.

Outlook Express handles spam by letting you add email addresses and domains to a Blocked Senders list. Then, every time a message comes in from the address or domain, the mail is automatically sent to the *Deleted Items* folder. To add an address or domain to the list, choose Tools → Message Rules → Blocked Senders List. The Blocked Senders tab of the Message Rules dialog box appears. Click Add, and you'll see the screen pictured in Figure 6-5. Type in the email address or domain you want to block. You can block mail, newsgroup messages, or both. Click OK when you're done.

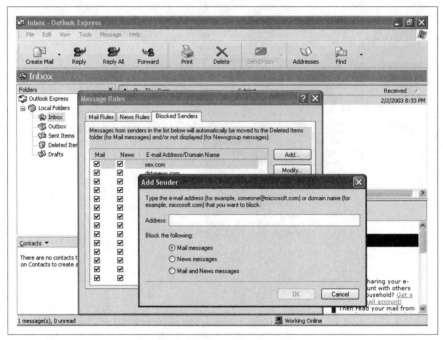

Figure 6-5. Blocking spam in email and newsgroup messages using Outlook Express

Handling Spam in Outlook

Outlook handles spam differently than Outlook Express, and different versions of Outlook handle spam differently.

Outlook 2003 includes a surprisingly good spam killer. It checks incoming messages, and if it decides they're spam, it routes them to a *Junk E-mail* folder, where you can then examine and delete them.

To make sure its spam-killing capability is turned on, choose Tools → Options and click the Junk E-mail button in the E-mail section of the screen. The screen shown in Figure 6-6 appears.

You can choose among several options:

Low

> This moves only the most obvious spam to the *Junk E-mail* folder. This means some spam will get through, but it's not likely that it will accidentally tag legitimate email as spam.

High

> This is the most aggressive spam fighter. It catches a higher percentage of spam, but also will most likely tag legitimate email as spam.

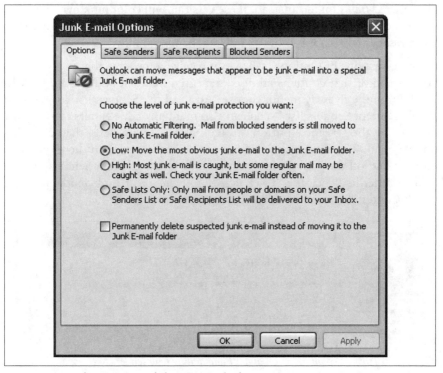

Figure 6-6. Configuring spam-fighting in Outlook 2003

Safe Lists Only

This will allow mail to come through only from people or domains that you have specifically said are safe—what Outlook calls Safe Senders. All other mail will be tagged as junk. As a practical matter, this isn't a particularly good setting because it will tag almost all of your mail as spam.

You can add senders to the Safe Senders list by clicking the Safe Senders tab, clicking the Add button, typing in the email address or domain, and clicking OK. You can also add senders to the list when you receive email. Right-click the message in Outlook and choose Junk E-mail → Add Sender to Safe Senders List.

You can similarly put senders on a Blocked Senders list, which will block all email from them. Click the Blocked Senders tab, click the Add button, type in the email address or domain, and click OK. You can also add senders to the list when you receive email. Right-click the message in Outlook and choose Junk E-mail → Add Sender to Blocked Senders List.

Previous versions of Outlook aren't nearly as effective in fighting spam. They don't have a *Junk E-mail* folder, and don't automatically send spam to the *Deleted Items* folder. Instead, these versions will color junk mail gray and color messages with adult content maroon. You can then scan your Inbox for messages with those colors and delete them manually.

In these versions of Outlook, when you receive a message that you consider to be spam or that contains adult content, right-click it and choose Junk E-mail. From the flyaway menu, choose "Add to Junk Senders list" or "Add to Adult Content Senders list." You can also manually add senders to either list by clicking the Organize button on the Outlook toolbar and then choosing Junk E-mail. The screen shown in Figure 6-7 appears. From here, you can turn on and off the Junk Senders list and the Adult Content Senders list. To add to either list, click the "Click here" link, click Edit Junk Senders or Edit Adult Content Senders, and add addresses to either list.

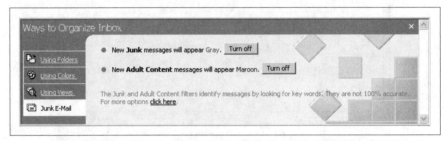

Figure 6-7. Turning spam filters on and off and adding new senders to the spam lists

 You can also use Outlook's normal filters to handle spam. You can define a rule that will route messages from certain senders, or that contains certain content, to folders that you define, or to the *Deleted Items* folder. To create rules for doing this, choose Tools → Rules Wizard and follow the instructions. Keep in mind, though, that because spammers use different email addresses constantly, this won't help you a great deal.

See Also

- You can download the Center for Democracy and Technology's report on how spam is generated and how to avoid it at *http://www.cdt.org/speech/spam/030319spamreport.shtml*.
- SpamPal (*http://www.spampal.org*) is a free spam fighter that marks email as spam before it gets to your email program. Then you use your email program's filters to filter out the resulting spam.
- An excellent resource for news and information about spam and what you can do to stamp it out can be found at *http://spam.abuse.net*.

Open Blocked File Attachments in Outlook and Outlook Express

Force Outlook and Outlook Express to let you open a wide variety of file attachments that they normally block.

The world is full of nasty email-borne worms and viruses, and everyone certainly needs to be protected from them. But Microsoft, in the latest versions of Outlook and Outlook Express, takes a Big Nurse, draconian approach to the problem; it refuses to let you open a wide variety of file attachments sent to you via email, including those ending in *.exe*, *.bat*, and many other common file extensions. (Eudora doesn't do this!) The theory is that it's possible a file with one of those extensions might be dangerous, so you shouldn't be allowed to open *any* file with that extension. That's like banning all cars because some people sometimes get into accidents.

When you try to open a file with one of those blocked extensions, you get the following error message: "Outlook blocked access to the following potentially unsafe attachments." Then you get a list of the attachments in your email that you can't open.

Depending on your version of Outlook/Outlook Express, and whether you've applied a Service Pack update to either of them, your version might or might not exhibit this behavior. Some older versions don't act this way; all newer versions do, including SP2.

The simplest way to know whether your version acts this way is to see what happens when you get one of the blocked file attachments. If it's allowed to go through, there's no need to use this hack. If it's blocked, get thee to the keyboard. Outlook and Outlook Express handle the problem differently, so we'll take a look at each.

Force Outlook to Let You Open Blocked File Attachments

Outlook assigns a level of risk to every file attachment sent to you. Level 1 is considered unsafe, so Outlook blocks your access to Level 1 attachments; you won't be able to open these files. Level 2 is considered a moderate risk, and you won't be able to open those files directly. Instead, you have to save the files to disk, and then you'll be able to open them. I'm not clear on how that increases security, but that's what Microsoft has done. Oh, and there's another oddball fact about Level 2: no file types are considered Level 2 risks. The only way for a file to be considered at that risk level is if you use Outlook in concert with a Microsoft Exchange Server and the administrator uses his administration tools to put file extensions into that risk category. The administrator is also the only person who can take file extensions out of the category. So, you can pretty much ignore that category, unless you have some convincing official reason for changing your company's policy. Any file types not in Levels 1 and 2 are considered "other" and you can open them normally.

To force Outlook to let you open blocked file attachments, use this Registry hack. Before starting, you need to know the list of Level 1 file attachments that Outlook blocks. They're listed in Table 6-2. Just to make things more confusing, depending on your version of Office and what Service Pack you've installed, not all of these extensions can be blocked.

Table 6-2. Blocked file extensions in Outlook

Extension	File type
.ade	Microsoft Access project extension
.adp	Microsoft Access project
.app	Visual FoxPro application
.asx	Windows Media audio/video
.bas	Microsoft Visual Basic class module
.bat	Batch file
.chm	Compiled HTML Help file
.cmd	Microsoft Windows NT Command script
.com	MS-DOS program
.cpl	Control Panel extension
.crt	Security certificate
.csh	Unix shell extension
.exe	Executable program
.fxp	Visual FoxPro compiled program
.hlp	Help file
.hta	HTML program
.inf	Setup information
.ins	Internet Naming Service
.isp	Internet Communications settings
.js	Jscript file
.jse	Jscript Encoded Script file
.ksh	Unix shell extension
.lnk	Shortcut
.mda	Microsoft Access add-in program
.mdb	Microsoft Access program
.mde	Microsoft Access MDE database

Table 6-2. Blocked file extensions in Outlook (continued)

Extension	File type
.mdt	Microsoft Access workgroup information
.mdw	Microsoft Access workgroup information
.mdz	Microsoft Access wizard program
.msc	Microsoft Common Console document
.msi	Microsoft Windows Installer package
.msp	Microsoft Windows Installer patch
.mst	Microsoft Windows Installer transform; Microsoft Visual Test source file
.ops	Office XP settings
.pcd	Photo CD image; Microsoft Visual compiled script
.pif	Shortcut to MS-DOS program
.prf	Microsoft Outlook profile settings
.prg	Visual FoxPro program
.reg	Registry entries
.scf	Windows Explorer command
.scr	Screen saver
.shb	Shell Scrap object
.shs	Shell Scrap object
.url	Internet shortcut
.vb	VBScript file
.vbe	VBScript Encoded script file
.vbs	VBScript file
.wsc	Windows Script Component
.wsf	Windows Script file
.wsh	Windows Script Host Setting file

Decide which file extension you want to be able to open from within Outlook, and close Outlook if it's running. Then run the Registry Editor [Hack #83] and go to HKEY_CURRENT_USER\Software\Microsoft\Office\10.0\Outlook\ Security, which, as its name implies, handles Outlook security. Create a new String value called Level1Remove. In the Value Data field, type the name of the file extension you want to be able to open, for example, *.exe*. You can add multiple file extensions. If you do, separate them with semicolons, but no spaces, like this: .exe;.bat;.pif. Use Table 6-2 as a guide for which blocked file extensions you want to be able to open.

When you're done, exit the Registry and reboot. Now you'll be able to open the file extensions you specified.

There's also an Outlook add-in that will let you open blocked email attachments without having to edit the Registry. The Attachment Options add-in, available from *http://www.slovaktech.com/attachmentoptions.htm*, lets you visually change which attachments you can open, and it also lets you set an additional option—having Outlook ask you whether you want to open certain file extensions on a case-by-case basis, instead of blocking them or automatically opening them. The author asks that you send a $10 donation if you use the add-in.

> If you know the person sending you a certain attachment, you can also have him zip the file and resend it to you. That way, you're getting a file with a *.zip* file extension, which will get through.

Force Outlook Express to Let You Open Blocked File Attachments

Depending on your version of Outlook Express, it might prevent you from opening certain email file attachments in the same way Outlook blocks certain files.

> If you have installed Windows XP Service Pack 1 or Service Pack 2, Outlook Express Service Pack 1, or Internet Explorer 6 Service Pack 1, you'll be blocked from opening certain email file attachments. Also, if you have a newer version of XP, you might be blocked.

With Outlook Express, unlike with Outlook, you won't be able to determine on an extension-by-extension basis which attachments you can open. Instead, you can tell the program to let you open all blocked extensions or you can tell it to stop you from opening any blocked extensions.

To tell Outlook Express to let you open blocked attachments, choose Tools → Options → Security to open the dialog box shown in Figure 6-8. Clear the box next to "Do not allow attachments to be saved or opened that could potentially be a virus."

You might have to close Outlook Express and restart it for the settings to take effect.

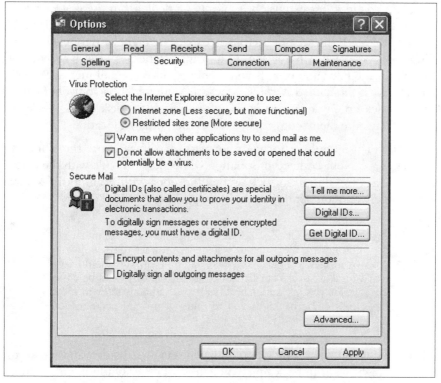

Figure 6-8. Forcing Outlook Express to let you open all email attachments

Back Up and Restore Outlook and Outlook Express Datafiles

#61

If email and contact lists are your lifeblood, you need to back them up regularly, but there's no easy way to do that using Outlook or Outlook Express. This hack tells you how to do it in each program.

There are two ways to back up and restore Outlook and Outlook Express datafiles: the easy way and the hard way. In the hard way, you manually back up all the datafiles, which can be a long and laborious process because those files are kept in so many different places. Do it once and you might not do it again. In the easy way, you get an add-in that does the backup for you.

Backing Up Outlook Manually

If all you want to do is back up your Outlook messages and contacts, it's a breeze. Outlook keeps all messages, contacts, and your calendar in a single file that ends in a *.pst* extension, typically *Outlook.pst* in the *C:\Documents and Settings\<Your Name>\Local Settings\Application Data\Microsoft\Outlook* folder. If they're not there, you can locate them by right-clicking the Outlook Today icon in Outlook, choosing Properties → Advanced, and looking in the Filename box. If you archive your old email messages, there will also be a file named *Archive.pst* in the same folder as your *Outlook.pst* file. To back up Outlook, just back up these files to a disk or another computer. To restore them, copy them back to their original locations.

If you don't use Outlook for your contacts, and instead use the Windows Address Book, your contact information will be kept in a file with the extension *.pab*. So, you'll need to back up that file along with your *.pst* file to have a backup of your contact list.

If you use Outlook on an Exchange Server, there might not be any *.pst* files on your system. If you want to back up your messages, contacts, and calendar yourself, you should do a local archive. Your Exchange administrator should be doing it for you, as well. Check with your administrator to see if he's doing backups, and to find out how to make a local archive.

That's fine if you want to back up only your email, calendar, and messages. But you might want to back up a whole host of other Outlook information, including your Outlook bar shortcuts; the mail rules you've created; your customized toolbar settings; your stationery, signatures, and templates; and other customizations and files. These files might be in the same folder as *Outlook.pst*, in *C:\Documents and Settings\<Your Name>\Application Data\Microsoft\Outlook*, or in another folder. Various flavors and versions of Outlook are notorious for keeping their files in different locations. Back up these files as you do your *Outlook.pst* file, to a disk or another computer, and restore them by copying them back into their original folders.

Table 6-3 describes what each of Outlook's files does. Depending on how you use Outlook, some of these files might not be present on your system.

Table 6-3. Outlook files and their extensions

Type of file	Extension
Personal Folders	*.pst*
Personal Address Book	*.pab*
Outlook Bar shortcuts	*.fav*
Rules Wizard rules (Outlook 2000 and earlier)	*.rwz*

Table 6-3. Outlook files and their extensions (continued)

Type of file	Extension
Nicknames for AutoResolution	*.nick*
Nicknames for AutoComplete (Outlook 2002)	*.nk2*
Customized print settings	*OutlPrnt*
Customized toolbar settings	*Outcmd.dat*
Customized system folder views	*Views.dat*
Macros and VBA programs	*VbaProject.otm*
Send/Receive group settings (Outlook 2002)	*.srs*
Stationery	*.htm* files
Templates	*.oft* files
Dictionary	*.dic* files
Junk Senders lists	*Junk Senders.txt*
Adult Senders list	*Adult Senders.txt*

If you have a laptop and a desktop PC, you've already found you apparently can't synchronize Outlook between them; they each have different data stores of your email messages. To keep them in sync, simply copy the *Outlook.pst* file from one to the other. For example, when you're working normally at home or the office, your desktop PC should have the complete, current version of the *Outlook.pst* file. When you travel with your laptop, copy the file over to it, and your laptop will have the current version of your file. When you return home or to the office, copy the file back to your desktop PC.

Backing Up Outlook Express Manually

Outlook Express has a different data structure than Outlook does, so you'll need to back up different files. Express is messier than Outlook; it stores your email in multiple files, and you'll have to back up all of them, rather than just a single file, as you do with Outlook. And you'll have to back up Registry keys as a way to save your personal settings.

Mail messages in Outlook Express are kept in files with *.dbx* extensions. To find out their locations, open Outlook Express and chose Tools → Options → Maintenance → Store Folder. You'll see a dialog box (shown in Figure 6-9) that will tell you the location of the *.dbx* files. Go to that folder and back up all the *.dbx* files. Expect to see a lot of them; two dozen or more are not that uncommon, depending on how many mail folders you have. Then, to restore them, just copy them back to their original folders.

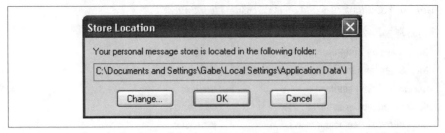

Figure 6-9. Finding the location of Outlook Express's .dbx files so you can back them up

The information about your mail settings, accounts, and preferences is stored on a single Registry key, HKEY_CURRENT_USER\Software\Microsoft\ Internet Account Manager. Back up the entire key and its subkeys to a single *.reg* file. When you want to restore them, restore the key as you would using any other *.reg* file.

> For information on backing up to *.reg* keys, restoring using *.reg* keys, and other ways to back up the Registry, see "Safely Edit the Registry Using .reg Files" **[Hack #85]** and "Better Registry Backups" **[Hack #86]**.

Outlook Express uses the Windows Address Book for contact information, so you need to back up the *.dbx* file or files. Typically, *.dbx* files are stored in *C:\Documents and Settings\<Your Name>\Application Data\Microsoft\ Address Book*, but you might have to look elsewhere. Restore the *.dbx* file by copying it back to its original location.

Mail rules are stored in the Registry, in the HKEY_CURRENT_USER\Identities key and its subkeys. As outlined earlier in this hack, back up this key and its subkeys to a *.reg* file, and restore back to the Registry if you need to.

Backing Up Outlook and Outlook Express Using Add-In Software

If you don't want to go through the trouble of manual backups and restores, you can try out Outlook Express Backup and Genie Outlook Backup from Genie-Soft (*http://www.genie-soft.com*), which will automate your backups for you. You get a wide variety of backup options, including backing up multiple identities and information, viewing emails from inside the backup and copying text from them, using an automated backup scheduler, encrypting your backups, spanning multiple disks when you back up, and compressing your backups. Both are shareware and free to try, but if you continue to use either of them, you are expected to pay $29.95.

See Also

- Microsoft has a free add-in for Outlook, called the Personal Folders Backup tool, that will automatically back up and restore your *.pst* files. It won't, however, back up any other Outlook settings. For details, go to *http://office.microsoft.com/en-us/assistance/HA010875321033.aspx.*

 Retrieve Web-Based Email with Your Email Software

There's no longer a need for Hotmail and Yahoo! mail users to be forced to abandon their desktop email software when checking their email. This hack lets you use your email client to gather web-based email from them.

I have more email accounts than any person has any right to. In addition to my normal POP3-based email accounts, I have web-based accounts on Yahoo! and Hotmail. This means there's no apparent way to get all my email in one location; I use Outlook for POP3-based email and the Web for Yahoo! and Hotmail. It also means I can never have all my email on my hard disk because Yahoo! and Hotmail store it on the Web. But I like to keep all my outgoing and incoming email in one location. What to do?

I've found two free add-ins that let you use your normal email program with Yahoo! mail and Hotmail, whether it's Outlook, Outlook Express, Eudora, or any other. YahooPOPs! lets you send and receive Yahoo! email, and Hotmail Popper does the same for Hotmail.

Getting Yahoo! Mail with YahooPOPs!

Several years ago, you had the free option of getting your Yahoo! mail using the Yahoo! POP mail server. No longer. Today, if you want to do that directly from Yahoo!, you have to pay a fee.

But with the simple-to-set-up YahooPOPs! (*http://yahoopops.sourceforge. net*), you can treat Yahoo! like any other mail server and get email from it without having to pay. It's open source software that has a POP3 interface on one end to talk to your email client, and on the other end it uses an HTTP interface to talk to Yahoo! and get your mail.

 If you use Linux or Mac OS X on another computer, you can use Linux- and Mac-specific versions of YahooPOPs! on those computers and get your Yahoo! mail on them as well.

Getting it to work requires two steps. First, configure the program itself; then, configure your email client to work with it. If you like, you don't have to configure the program itself; you can leave its defaults, but I recommend making a few changes to the defaults before using it.

After you install the program and run it, it sits in your system tray. To configure it, double-click its icon. While there's a good deal you can configure, I recommend leaving most defaults in place—with one exception: in Receiving Email under Email Preferences, uncheck "Download emails from the Bulk Mail folder," as shown in Figure 6-10. If you leave that box checked, you'll receive all the spam Yahoo! has filtered into your *Bulk Mail* folder.

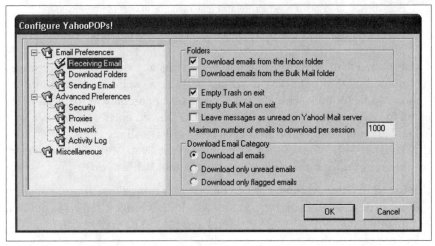

Figure 6-10. Making sure you don't download email from your Bulk Mail folder

As you can see in Figure 6-10, you can configure other preferences here as well, such as whether to download all email or only flagged or unread emails. I stay with the defaults, but you can change them if you wish.

Now it's time to configure your email program to work with it. How you do that varies from program to program, so check the program's documentation on the Web for how to do it for individual mail clients. Essentially, though, you create a new mail account in your mail client and call both the incoming mail server and outgoing mail server "localhost." That configures your client to get the mail from YahooPOPs!. As such, the client doesn't contact Yahoo! directly. Instead, YahooPOPs! does that; then your client gets the email from YahooPOPs!.

To configure Outlook to work with YahooPOPs!, select Tools → E-mail Accounts. Click "Add a new email account" and then Next, and then select POP3 as the Server Type. Click Next and enter your username and Yahoo! email address under User Information. Under Logon Information, enter your Yahoo! login ID and password. Select "localhost" as your Incoming mail server, and "localhost as the SMTP server" as your outgoing mail server. Then, select More Settings → Advanced and increase the Server Timeout to 10 minutes. Select the Outgoing Server tab and enable "My outgoing server (SMTP) requires authentication." Then, select "Log on using" and enter your Yahoo! Mail address as the username and your Yahoo! Mail password as the password. Click OK to close the More Settings dialog box. Click Next and then click Finish.

Once you do that, all your outgoing and incoming Yahoo! email will show up in Outlook, just as if the mail were being delivered by any POP3 mail server.

Getting Hotmail Mail with Hotmail Popper

Hotmail Popper (*http://www.boolean.ca/hotpop/*) works in the same way as YahooPOPs! to let you retrieve and send mail via your Hotmail account. It retrieves mail from Hotmail, and then your email client retrieves it from Hotmail Popper.

There's one caveat, though. As of this writing, if you're using the free version of Hotmail you won't be able to use Hotmail Popper to get your email. You'll have to have a Hotmail Plus or equivalent MSN account; in other words, you need a for-pay Hotmail account. You used to be able to use Hotmail Popper with the free version of Hotmail, but then Microsoft pulled the plug on it. However, Microsoft is well known for repeatedly changing its mind, so there's a chance Hotmail Popper will once again work with the free version of Hotmail.

Setup is similar as well. First, configure Hotmail Popper to get your mail; then configure your email client to retrieve it. You shouldn't need to change the defaults of the program after you install it because by default it won't retrieve bulk mail from Hotmail. It runs in the Notification area, so if you need to configure it, right-click its icon and choose Properties.

Once it's running, you have to configure your email client to work with it. Configuration is almost identical to the way you need to configure your mail client for YahooPOPs!, so see the previous section for more information. You create a new POP3 account and set your username and password as you do normally. For your incoming and outgoing mail, use the address 127.0.0.1 as the server. You won't need to increase the server timeout as you do with YahooPOPs!, though if you experience trouble retrieving mail from the server you can try doing that as a way to solve the problem.

Gmail, Google's free email service, lets you retrieve email from it with your normal email software such as Outlook or Outlook Express. You won't need any add-ins to do it. For details, see "Gmail Hacks" [Hack #63].

Once you've configured it, use it as you would any other POP3 mail account.

HACK #63   Gmail Hacks

The best search engine on the planet now has the best web-based email on the planet. Here's how to get more out of it.

If you're looking for a free, web-based email service, the best one, hands down, is Gmail. It offers more storage than any of the others (as of this writing, a whopping 1GB's worth), lets you search through your mail using all of Google's searching syntax, lets you use your normal email software to receive mail via POP3...the list could go on. Suffice it to say, it's the one to use.

Because there's so much to Gmail, you might not know all of its features, or how to get the most out of it. In this hack, you'll learn how to import contacts from your existing email software into Gmail, how to use your normal email software to receive Gmail, and how to use Gmail as a virtual drive so that you can use the service as if it were an extension of your hard drive.

Import Your Contacts into Gmail

You've most likely got dozens or hundreds of contacts in your existing email software. It would be nice to get them into Gmail. It's not that tough to do; it's essentially a two-stage process. Gmail can import contacts in the comma-separated values (CSV) format, so first you have to export your contacts into a CSV file and then import them into Gmail.

How you export your contacts varies according to your email software. In Outlook, choose File → Import and Export, and the Import and Export Wizard launches. Choose "Export to a file," click Next, and from the screen that appears choose Comma Separated Values (Windows). From the next screen, choose your *Contacts* folder, as shown in Figure 6-11, and click Next.

From the next screen, give the file a name (a *.csv* extension will be automatically added to it), browse to the folder where you want to save it, and click Next, and then Finish.

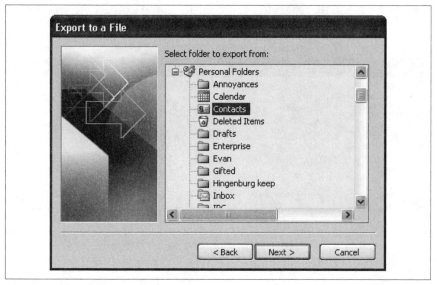

Figure 6-11. Choosing the Contacts folder

Now that you have the file ready, go to your Gmail account and click Contacts on the left side of the screen. Click Import Contacts from the upper-right side of the page that appears. Click the Browse button, then navigate to the folder where you've exported your contacts, select it, and click Open. Now you should be at the screen pictured in Figure 6-12, with your information filled in. Click Import Contacts.

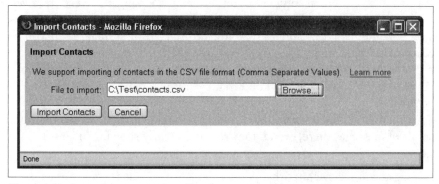

Figure 6-12. Importing contacts into Gmail

After a minute or more, depending on the speed of your Internet connection and how many contacts you're importing, you'll get the message shown in Figure 6-13, telling you that your contacts have been imported, and listing the total number of contacts you've imported. Click the Close button. Now your contacts will be available. To see them, on the Contact screen click All Contacts.

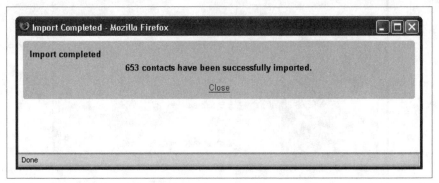

Figure 6-13. All of your contacts exported into Gmail

Use Gmail as a POP3 Account

Unlike other web-based email services, you can use your regular email software to receive mail using a POP3 mail server. (To do this with Yahoo! Mail or Hotmail, you'll need add-in software [Hack #62].) You'll first have to configure Gmail to let you do it, and then you'll have to tell your email software to retrieve the mail.

In Gmail, click Settings and then click the Forwarding and POP link at the top of the page. The screen shown in Figure 6-14 appears.

If you want your email software to retrieve all the email you've ever received on Gmail, choose Enable POP for all mail. Be very careful before making this selection. Remember, Gmail gives you up to 1GB of storage, so if you've received a lot of mail, you could end up downloading hundreds of megabytes of mail when you make your first connection to Gmail using your email software. Also keep in mind that even if you have only a little mail in your Inbox, that's not all the email you have in your Gmail account. Most of your mail is in the *Archive* folder, and you might have hundreds or thousands of messages there, even if they're not currently showing in your Inbox.

If you choose Enable POP only for mail that arrives from now on, only those messages you receive after this point will be downloaded to your email software. It's a much safer choice. If you want some old mail downloaded, you can always go into your Gmail account and forward the mail to yourself. That way, the forwarded mail will be treated as new mail and will be downloaded, while all the rest of your old mail won't be downloaded.

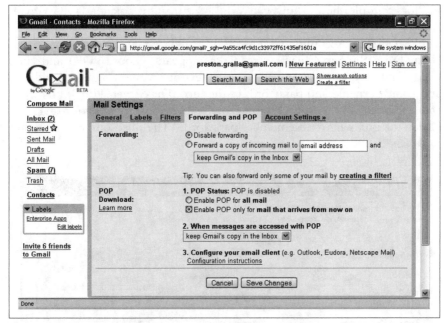

Figure 6-14. Configuring Gmail for POP3 access

Next, make your choice about what should happen to your Gmail messages: should they be kept on the Gmail server, and if they are, should they be kept in the Inbox or in the Archived mail? Here are your choices:

Keep Gmail's copy in the Inbox. This will leave all new mail on the Gmail server, and leave it in your Inbox. That way, even after you download it to your PC, it will stay in the Gmail Inbox on the Web, as if you hadn't read it.

Archive Gmail's copy. This will leave all new email on the Gmail server, but instead of putting it into your Inbox, it will move it to your Archived mail. So, whenever you visit Gmail on the Web, if you want to see the mail, go to your Archive.

Trash Gmail's copy. This will move all the messages to your Trash, where it will be cleaned out by Gmail on a regular basis.

Now it's time to configure your email program to get your Gmail mail. You set it up as you do any other new mail account. For your POP3 server, use pop.gmail.com, and for your SMTP server, use smtp.gmail.com. When setting it up, make sure to tell your software to use a secure connection (SSL) for both SMTP and POP3.

So, for example, here's how you would set up Outlook for POP3 Gmail. After you've enabled POP3 access in Gmail, launch Outlook and choose Tools → E-mail Accounts. Choose "Add a new e-mail account" and click Next. From the Server Type screen that appears, choose POP3 and click Next. On the screen that appears next, enter your name, your email address, and your username and password. In the Incoming Server (POP3) box, type pop.gmail.com and in the Outgoing mail server box, type smtp.gmail.com. Check the box next to "Remember password." The filled-out screen should look like Figure 6-15.

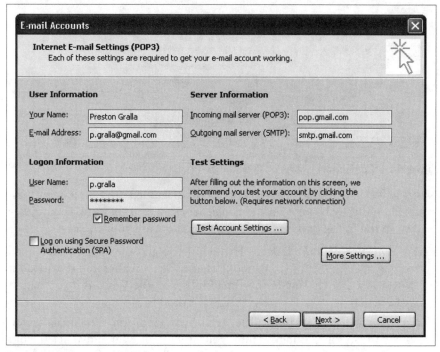

Figure 6-15. Setting up POP3 access in Outlook 2003

Now, click More Settings and then choose the Advanced tab. In both the POP3 and SMTP sections, check the box next to "This server requires an encrypted connection (SSL)." When you do that, the port numbers for the servers will change. For POP3, the port number should change from 110 to 995. If it doesn't, type 995 in the Incoming Server (POP3) box. For SMTP, type 465 in the Outgoing Server (SMTP) box. Now click the Outgoing Server tab. Check the box next to "My outgoing server (SMTP) requires authentication." Select "Use same settings as my incoming mail server." Click OK. You'll come back to the screen pictured in Figure 6-15. Click

Next and then Finish. Now you should be able to send and receive mail using Gmail.

Use Gmail as a Virtual Hard Drive

With all of that extra space on Gmail, wouldn't it be nice to use some of it for storage rather than mail?

You can, with a free piece of software called GMail Drive shell extension. Download it from *http://www.viksoe.dk/code/gmail.htm* and install it. (It works only with Internet Explorer, Version 5 and above.)

After you install it, run Windows Explorer. Under My Computer, a new drive will have been created, called the Gmail Drive. Click it, and type in your Gmail password and username. If you don't want to have to log in every time you click the drive, check the box next to Auto Login.

You can use the Gmail drive as you can any other folder on your hard drive. (You'll of course have to be connected to the Internet for it to work.) This means you can copy files to it using Windows Explorer in the same way that you do any other files, and you can create subfolders as well.

> The Gmail drive looks like any hard drive on your system, but remember that it's a virtual drive and you're connected to it over the Internet. So, you can transfer files to it only at the speed of your Internet connection. On a dial-up connection, this will be exceedingly slow.

But when you view the contents of your Gmail drive, the icons for the files won't look like the normal ones, as you can see in Figure 6-16. Instead of showing the native icons for each file type (such as pieces of paper for Word files), they'll show as gear-type icons.

When you copy a file to your Gmail drive, you're actually creating an email and posting it to your account. The email will appear in your Inbox, with the file as an attachment, as shown in Figure 6-17. If you want to open any of the files from inside Gmail, click the email to view it, and then click the Download button. The file will be downloaded to your PC. Of course, you don't want to do this because the file is *already* on your PC.

As you can see from Figure 6-17, using Gmail as a virtual drive can make your Inbox pretty messy. Luckily, you can create a filter that will automatically route the files to your archived mail folder. That way, you'll never see them in your Inbox, and they'll be in your archives.

Figure 6-16. The Gmail drive in action

The emails with the files attached to them all show up preceded by the letters GMAILFS. So, create a filter that will move all files with that prefix to your archived mail by first clicking Create a Filter from the top of the Gmail screen. In the Subject box, type GMAILFS, check the box next to "Has attachment," and then click Next Step. Then check the box next to Skip the Inbox (Archive it) and then click Create Filter, and all your files will be sent straight to your Archive, bypassing the Inbox.

You can also have them labeled so that you know at a glance which files you copied from your hard disk. Before clicking Create Filter, check the box next to "Apply the label." From the drop-down box next to it, select New Label, and from the screen that appears, type in the label name (such as Hard Drive), and click OK. From the drop-down list, choose your new label. Now click Create Filter. The files will be archived, but will also have the label next to them, so you can easily view only your files by clicking the Hard Drive label when you log in to Gmail.

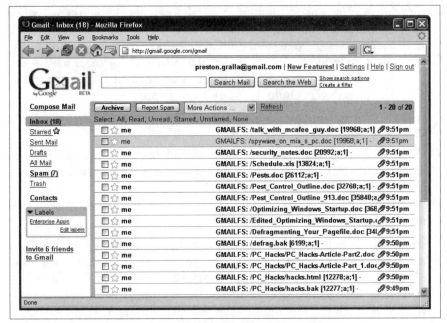

Figure 6-17. What the files look like from within Gmail

 It's not a good idea to use Gmail as your hard drive if you're going to be using POP3 to retrieve your email from Gmail with your email software. If you do that, whenever you retrieve email from Google, you'll also retrieve all the files you've copied to Google when you used it as a virtual hard drive, which can be hundreds of megabytes.

See Also

- Many other free add-ins extend the functionality of Gmail—for example, to notify you when you have mail in Gmail, to keep a to-do list, and so on. Find them at *http://www.marklyon.org/gmail/gmailapps.htm*.

 ## HACK #64 Fire Outlook and Outlook Express

Contrary to popular belief, Microsoft doesn't make the only two email programs on the planet. Eudora, Thunderbird, and Pegasus are great, free alternatives.

Strange, but true: before Outlook and Outlook Express, there was email software. I know this because I used it all the time. That email software is still around, and some believe it is superior to Outlook and Outlook Express in some ways. While many alternative email programs are out there, two of my favorites, Eudora and Pegasus, have both been around a very long time. And Thunderbird is an open source alternative that's been developed in concert with the great Firefox browser [Hack #43]. While all of them have some drawbacks, they each have enough unique features that they might make you want to throw away Outlook and Outlook Express.

Check Your Mood with Eudora

Once upon a time, Eudora ruled the roost. In the pre-Outlook and pre-Outlook Express days, you'd find it on the desktops of power users everywhere. Although it's not nearly as popular today, it has its fans, and with good reason, because it has some unique features you won't find in any other email software.

Foremost is one of the all-time great features in an email program, a feature that will be welcomed gladly by anyone who has ever blasted out a red-hot email in a fit of anger. As you type, Eudora's MoodWatch feature analyzes your messages for their degree of aggressiveness and rates them on a scale of one ice cube all the way up to three chili peppers. You see the rating as you write and you get a warning before sending the message if it might be offensive.

Another goody is the ability to share files on a peer-to-peer basis with other Eudora users, through the Eudora Sharing Protocol (ESP). You define groups of people with whom you want to share files, and they're the only ones who can access those files. In turn, you can share files with people who give you access to files on their computers. The New ESP Share Group Wizard walks you through setting up a share group. Choose Tools → ESP Groups → New, click "Create a brand new share group," and then click Next.

You can customize many features of this tool, including the ability to set up a new mailbox just for users in this group so that the messages from users in your new group will be filtered automatically into the appropriate mailbox. The wizard prompts you for this and other options, including share group name, share group description, transfer to new or existing mailbox, share group folder (choose where the files to be shared with the group will live), and even the choice of which Eudora personality—dominant or otherwise—should be associated with the file share group.

You can also set all Eudora preferences for each file share group (right-click the group's name and choose Options) and set filtering options for messages from the file share group with the ESP Settings button. You can specify each user's role within the group (can they send updates, only receive updates, or both?). Once you've set your preferences, you can share files across machines and collaborate on any sort of document (see Figure 6-18). It's pretty amazing, and might even convince non-Eudora users to make the switch.

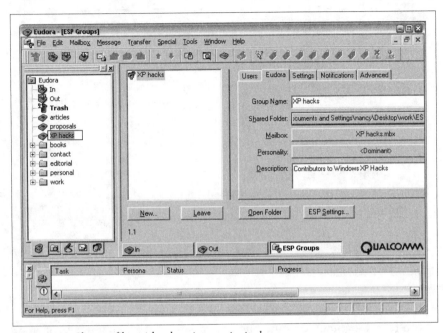

Figure 6-18. Sharing files with others in your invited group

Also included is a way to send voice messages via email, as well as very powerful filtering and searching capabilities. If you're a statistics hound, you'll find a usage stats area (Tools → Statistics) that analyzes and displays statistics, such as how much time you've spent using the program and the time of day you send and receive the most messages. Email addicts will love it (see Figure 6-19).

An ad-supported version of Eudora is available for free from *http://www. eudora.com*. If you want to do away with the ads, you can either pay $49.95 or switch to the "light" version, which lacks some of the program's features.

> If you want to amaze friends and acquaintances with little-known technology facts, here's one for you. Eudora was named after the well-known fiction writer Eudora Welty because of a short story she wrote in 1941, "Why I Live at the P.O.," about a woman who moves into her post office.

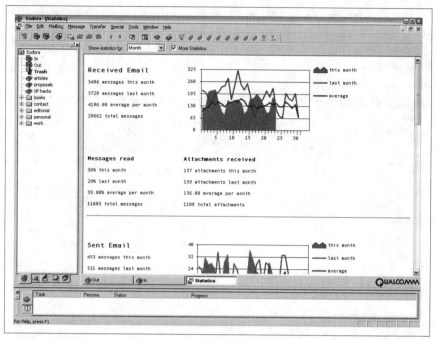

Figure 6-19. Email usage statistics

Move Forward to the Past with Pegasus

If you're a longtime computer user, Pegasus might remind you of your youth, when there were no common interface standards and a program reflected the personality of individual programmers rather than focus groups and user interface whizzes. In part, that's because this program was first released in 1990, in the days of Windows 3.0. Its eccentric layout and tiny icons will whisk you back in the Wayback Machine to those days gone by.

That is this program's strength and its weakness. Good luck trying to figure out this program when you first install it; it's bristling with often-undecipherable icons. Even the tool tips that appear when you hold your mouse cursor over these icons don't necessarily help. For example, can anyone explain to me what "Open a list of local people on your system" means?

However, the strength is that these eccentricities carry over into the list of the program's features, and it's a very powerful program. The way in which it handles rules for how to automatically process incoming messages is extremely sophisticated. For example, you can use it to create a set of rules that will let you automatically allow people to subscribe to listserv email discussion groups that you run using Pegasus.

Its message-viewing capabilities are also exceptional. You can choose a view that lets you quickly switch between displaying an HTML message either as plain text or as full-blown HTML, and in the "Raw view" you can see the entire message, including all the header information showing you the path the email took to reach you.

Some decidedly odd features also are buried deep in this program. For example, one feature lets you send an email that includes preformatted text telling someone he's received a phone call. Somehow, I don't think that one came out of a focus group.

Pegasus is free and available from *http://www.pmail.com*. If you want manuals and support, you can pay $29.95.

Use Open Source Thunderbird

Thunderbird (shown in Figure 6-20) is a remarkably powerful program, particularly because it's free. It's open source software and is being developed by Mozilla.org, which also develops the Firefox and Mozilla browsers.

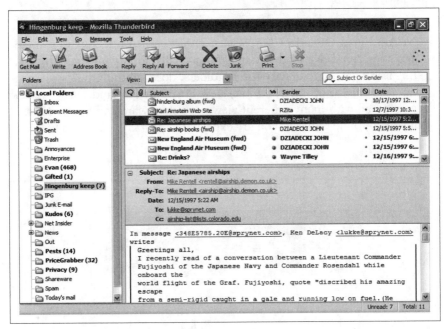

Figure 6-20. The Thunderbird email client

You'll find just about everything you want in an email program here: a spam killer, the ability to get and read RSS feeds, the ability to read newsgroups, the ability to handle multiple email accounts, excellent search tools, very good filters that make it easy to find the email you want fast—there's lots more here as well. For example, it also includes built-in encryption for more secure emails. Particularly useful is the ability to group mail in your folders by several criteria, including date, priority, sender, recipient, status, subject, or label.

When you install it, it will import your messages and contacts from other email programs, including Outlook, Outlook Express, Netscape Mail, and Eudora. If you've got a lot of mail, this can take some time.

Like Firefox, Thunderbird can use *extensions*, free add-ins that give it extra features. Some extensions, for example, let you use mouse gestures to open, close, and send email, as well as accomplish other tasks; you hold down the right mouse button and move your mouse in a certain way, and it accomplishes the task. Other add-ins let you read RSS feeds, control your music player, and more.

It's free; get it at *http://www.mozilla.org/products/thunderbird.*

See Also

- If you decide to stick with Outlook but want a way to improve it, try Nelson Email Organizer (*http://www.caelo.com*). It offers ways to manage your email overload better, automatically sorts your email by putting it into a variety of easy-to-use folders, does lightning-quick searches on your mail, notifies you when new email arrives, and lets you view your email with many different views. It's shareware and free to try, but if you continue to use it, you are expected to pay $39.95.

Wireless
Hacks 65–74

It's an unwired world, and XP is at the center of it. XP was built with wireless in mind. Because it includes a built-in wireless discovery of networks, it's easy to set up home and corporate wireless networks, as well as connect to hotspots when people travel with their laptops or PDAs.

In this chapter, you'll learn about wireless hacking—everything from wardriving to find wireless networks, to protecting your home wireless network, using wireless encryption, solving hotspot woes, and more.

Go War-Driving for WiFi Access

#65 WiFi networks are everywhere, it seems; you can get free Internet access on wireless community FreeNets armed with your laptop, a car, and software called Network Stumbler.

One of the coolest technological advances in popular use today is the wireless network. Wireless networks based on the WiFi standard (802.11x) are becoming increasingly common across the country—not only in people's homes, but also in universities, corporations, coffee shops, airports, and other public places. Now you can bring your email to Starbucks.

Frequently you'll find dozens of hotspots in one location, particularly in certain urban neighborhoods and suburban office parks that house high-tech companies. Where I live—in Porter Square in Cambridge, Mass.—there are dozens of wireless networks in private homes, apartment buildings, and businesses within a very short walk from my home. There are at least a half dozen on my three-block street alone, in addition to mine. From my back porch, I not only get access to my own wireless network, but can also often pick up signals from four nearby WiFi networks.

The widespread availability of these inexpensive WiFi networks has led to a grassroots community wireless networking movement. The idea is simple:

allow people passing by to use your WiFi network to hop onto the Internet, and they in turn let you and others use their WiFi networks for Internet access when you pass near their homes or places of business. These wireless grassroots organizations are often called *FreeNets*. You'll find them in cities including New York, Seattle, Houston, and the San Francisco Bay area, as well as others. For more details about them and how to participate, go to the Free Networks.org web site (*http://www.freenetworks.org*). In fact, some cities are creating free wireless zones in downtown business areas to allow anyone with a wireless-enabled computer to get Internet access. Paris, for example, might soon be known for more than its beauty, culture, good food, and disdain for tourists; it might turn into one giant wireless zone, allowing Internet access anywhere in the city, though for a price.

How do you find these wireless networks? The best way is by doing what has become known as *war-driving*: driving through neighborhoods with your laptop, special software, and, if you want to pick up more networks, an antenna hooked up to your WiFi card.

> The extremely environmentally conscious prefer to go *war-walking*, though walking around with a laptop is not particularly easy. A better way is with a WiFi-equipped PDA, like the Palm Tungsten C using a product called NetChaser (*http://www.bitsnbolts.com*).

Run the software, and it not only locates the network, but also provides a variety of information about it that you can use to connect to it, such as its SSID (network name), whether it uses encryption, and the wireless channel it's on. Armed with that information, you should be able to connect to it if it's a FreeNet—for example, if it is set to allow anyone to connect to it, or if it uses a commonly agreed-upon security scheme that everyone in the FreeNet uses for their WiFi networks.

If you walk in certain urban neighborhoods, you might notice strange symbols on the sidewalk that look something like those pictured in Figure 7-1. Yes, it's a conspiracy, but in the positive sense. These are *war-chalking* symbols that tell passersby that a WiFi network is nearby. The left symbol means the wireless network is open; the middle one means it is closed; and the right one means it uses WEP encryption.

Figure 7-1. War-chalking symbols

Sometimes you'll find additional information next to the symbol that gives information on how to connect to the network, such as the SSID. The symbols were inspired by the practice of hoboes, who during the Great Depression would make chalk marks near homes that were friendly to hoboes and would give them food. For more information about war-chalking, go to *http://www.blackbeltjones.com/warchalking/index2.html*.

To go war-driving, download the free Network Stumbler program (*http://www.netstumbler.com*), which shows you detailed information about any nearby wireless networks. Figure 7-2 shows what happens when I run the software on my back porch. I can detect signals from four nearby WiFi networks in addition to my own.

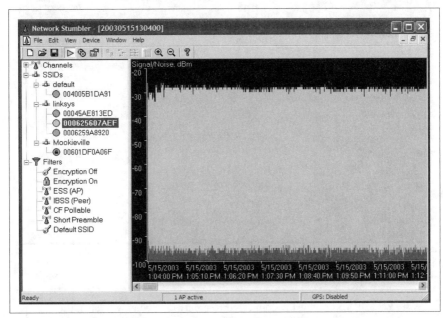

Figure 7-2. Detecting nearby wireless networks with Network Stumbler

For each WiFi network it uncovers, Network Stumbler tells you the network's SSID, name, manufacturer, channel, type, signal strength, signal-to-noise ratio, and whether the network's encryption is enabled, among other details. Armed with that information, you can try to connect to the network.

> If a network uses encryption, a small lock appears next to it; look closely at the Mookieville network in Figure 7-2 and you might be able to see it.

Once you've found a network, exit Network Stumbler. Then, to connect to the network, click the small network icon in the system tray (officially known as the XP Notification Area—the area of the taskbar where XP corrals little icons). The Wireless Network Connection screen appears. Click the network to which you want to connect, and after a few moments, you'll be connected, as shown in Figure 7-3.

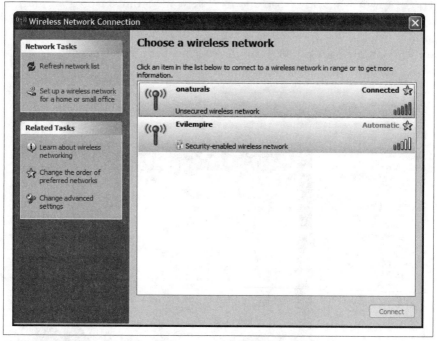

Figure 7-3. *The Wireless Network Connection Properties screen*

 If you're already connected to a network, when you click the small network icon you'll be sent to the Wireless Network Connection Status screen, which will show you the current state of your connection. To look for the other network or networks that Network Stumbler found, click View Wireless Networks from that screen, and you'll see a list of all wireless networks within range. Click any wireless network to connect to it.

If this screen doesn't show you the network uncovered by Network Stumbler, click Refresh Network List. If the network still doesn't show up, that's because the signal is too weak for you to connect to it.

Not everyone will be able to use Network Stumbler, because it won't work with all wireless network cards. As of this writing, it works with the following cards (and possibly some others not listed here): Lucent Technologies WaveLAN/IEEE (Agere ORiNOCO); Dell TrueMobile 1150 Series (PCM-CIA and mini-PCI); Avaya Wireless PC Card; Toshiba Wireless LAN Card (PCMCIA and built-in); Compaq WL110; Cabletron/Enterasys Roam-about; Elsa Airlancer MC-11; ARtem ComCard 11Mbps; IBM High Rate Wireless LAN PC Card; and 1stWave 1ST-PC-DSS11IS, DSS11IG, DSS11ES, and DSS11EG. For more information, go to *C:\Program Files\ Network Stumbler\readme.html*, assuming you've installed the program in *C: \Program Files\Network Stumbler*.

Network Stumbler will find all wireless networks near you, not just those that are part of FreeNets. So, you might well find the wireless networks of people who don't realize others outside of their homes or businesses can tap into their networks. Some law enforcement officials will tell you that tapping into those people's networks is illegal, so be forewarned.

Mapping Wireless Networks

Network Stumbler lets you save your war-driving information in a file, and you can then upload that information to a web site (such as *http://wifimaps. com*) that uses your information and information provided by many other war-drivers to create maps of WiFi networks across the country. You can zoom in and out on these maps, so you can get a view of the concentration of WiFi networks in a metropolitan area, or you can see individual WiFi networks on individual streets, as shown in Figure 7-4.

Go to *http://wifimaps.com* to view the maps or to upload your Network Stumbler information. Be aware that the site is a volunteer effort, and, not uncommonly, you'll find the maps aren't working. If that happens, check back again in a few days; it usually gets up and running after a while.

Building a Homemade Wireless Cantenna for War-Driving

One way to increase the range of your war-driving and the strength of the signal when you connect to WiFi networks is to build your own wireless antenna. You can build one for a few dollars using a tin can and other stray parts, as long as you're willing to do a little bit of soldering. Because they're built out of tin cans, they're frequently called *cantennas*.

My 15-year-old son, Gabe, built several for his seventh-grade science fair project several years ago and compared the effectiveness of each. The results were clear: the giant 34.5-ounce coffee cans were far superior to normal-size coffee cans and Pringle's cans.

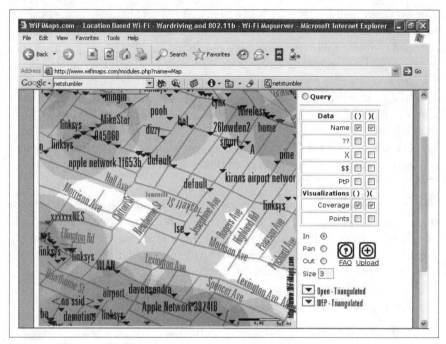

Figure 7-4. A map of WiFi networks in my neighborhood

If you haven't bought a WiFi card yet and are considering building one of these cantennas, I suggest buying an Orinoco card. It has a small connector in its side through which you connect a *pigtail connector*, which can then be hooked up to a small antenna you build out of copper wire and a small connector, which goes inside the tin can. You can buy a pigtail and the required connectors at a number of places, including HyperLink Technologies (*http://www.hyperlinktech.com*). If you don't have a WiFi card with a small connector, building one of these cantennas becomes much more difficult.

You can find good directions for making cantennas at numerous web sites. Three good places to start are *www.oreillynet.com/cs/weblog/view/wlg/448*, *www.netscum.com/~clapp/wireless.html*, and *www.turnpoint.net/wireless/cantennahowto.html*. Just so that you get the idea of how to build one, though, I'll give you an overview here. First you empty and wash the can. Next, you build the small antenna that will go inside the can by soldering a short piece of thick copper wire to a small piece of hardware called an *N connector*. Then, drill a hole in the can and insert the small antenna you just soldered. Attach the antenna to the can by securing it with small screws and bolts. Attach one end of the pigtail to your wireless card, attach the other end to the N connector, and *voilà!* You have a cantenna.

See Also

- "Check WiFi Network Performance with Qcheck to Help Improve Throughput" **[Hack #67]**
- "Troubleshoot Network Connections with netsh, netstat, and ipconfig" **[Hack #52]**

Extend the Range of Your Wireless Network

HACK #66

The efficiency and throughput of WiFi networks can vary dramatically. Make sure you get maximum throughput from your wireless network.

If you have more than one PC at home, the best way to hook them together and share a high-speed Internet connection is via a wireless network—in particular, one based on the WiFi standard, which is actually a family of standards known under the umbrella term of 802.11x.

The biggest problem in setting up a home network usually involves running the wires between PCs and a residential gateway. If your PCs are on different floors of your house, you might have to drill holes in your walls, ceiling, and floors and run wire through them. Even when PCs are on the same floor, you have to deal with the problem of wires snaking along the floor.

That's the problem I've had in my 150-year-old home in Cambridge. Drill through a wall, ceiling, or floor here, and you never know what you'll find (horsehair insulation was only one of our many surprises). Even my electrician shudders when he has to take out the drill.

So, for me, a wireless network was a no-brainer. I now have a half dozen PCs and laptops and four printers situated in various parts of the house, all connected via a combination wired/wireless network and sharing a single broadband Internet connection. And when the weather is nice here (twice a year, by my last calculation), I take my laptop out on my back porch and work from there while still connected to the Internet and other PCs and printers in the house.

But there's a catch with all wireless networks, including mine. Wireless networks rarely deliver data at their rated bandwidth speed. One factor affecting bandwidth speed is the distance between the access point and the wirelessly equipped PC. Compaq, for example, notes that at a distance of 150 feet the throughput of its wireless access point drops from 11Mbps to 5.5Mbps, and at a distance of 300 feet it drops to 2Mbps. Even that significantly understates the drop-off in speed, and most people find that the drop-off is much more dramatic than that, most commonly by a factor of two.

WiFi and Buying New Equipment

There are several versions of the 802.11x WiFi standard, so before you buy WiFi gear, you should know what you're paying for because some are much faster than others. The 802.11b standard was the first one to be ratified, and equipment that adheres to it is the least expensive. (This is the standard commonly used by public wireless *hot spots* in coffee shops, airports, hotels, and other locations.) It operates in the 2.4GHz part of the spectrum and its maximum throughput is 11Mbps.

The newer standard, 802.11g, operates in the same part of the spectrum and has a maximum throughput of 54Mbps, significantly faster than 802.11b. You won't pay much extra for 802.11g gear compared to 802.11b, so if you're buying all your equipment from scratch, it's the best bet.

802.11b and 802.11g equipment work with each other, although with one "gotcha" you need to watch out for. If you mix and match 802.11g and 802.11b equipment, the entire network will operate at the lower 802.11b speed. So, if you have an 802.11g router and 802.11b adapters, the network will run at the slower speed. In fact, if you have an 802.11g router, three 802.11g adapters, and one 802.11b adapter, the entire network will *still* run at the lower speed, even between the 802.11g adapters and the 802.11g router. The upshot: if you're going with 802.11g, make sure every piece of your equipment is 802.11g, not 802.11b.

You also might come across 802.11g routers and adapters that promise speeds far greater than 802.11g, commonly at 108Mbps. That works only when you buy all the hardware from the same manufacturer because they use proprietary protocols to reach those speeds. If you mix and match components from different manufacturers, you'll get normal 802.11g speeds, not the faster ones.

Distance is only one factor affecting performance. Interference from other devices and the exact layout of the house or office can also affect it dramatically. However, there are things you can do to extend the range of your network and get more throughput throughout your home:

Centrally locate your wireless access point. This way, it's most likely that all your wirelessly equipped PCs will get reasonable throughput. If you put your wireless access point in one corner of the house, nearby PCs might get high throughput, but throughput for others might drop significantly.

Orient your access point's antennas vertically. As a general rule, transmission will be better when antennas are vertical rather than horizontal. Keep in mind, though, that this is only a starting point for positioning the antenna. The exact layout of your house might alter the best positioning of the antenna.

Point the antennas of your wireless PCs toward the access point. Although 802.11 technology does not require a direct line of sight, pointing antennas in this way tends to increase signal strength. USB wireless cards generally have small antennas that can be positioned, but frequently wireless PC cards don't, so you might have trouble figuring out the antenna orientation in a wireless PC card. If you have a wireless PC card that doesn't have what appears to be an antenna, the antenna is generally located at the periphery of the card itself, so point that at the access point.

Don't place your access point next to an outside wall. If you do that, you'll be broadcasting signals to the outside, not the inside, of the house. That's nice if you want to give your neighbors access to your network, but not great if you want to reach all the PCs in your house.

Avoid putting your access point or PCs near microwave ovens or cordless phones. Many microwave ovens and cordless phones operate in the same 2.4GHz part of the spectrum as 802.11b WiFi equipment does. So, microwave ovens and cordless phones can cause significant interference. Cordless phones tend to be the bigger problem.

Avoid placing the antennas of access points or PCs near filing cabinets and other large metal objects. They can cause significant interference and dramatically reduce throughput.

Consider using external and booster antennas. Some PC cards, notably Orinoco cards, will accept external antennas that you can buy or build on your own. They have a small connector to which you attach a pigtail and wire and then attach that wire to an antenna. (For information about building your own antenna, see "Go War-Driving for WiFi Access" [Hack #65].) Some access points often accept booster antennas that you can buy as well.

If you have a Linksys wireless network and are looking to improve its signal strength, you can buy a number of different add-ons that promise to extend its range and strengthen its signal. The WRE54G Wireless-G range expander, for example, is able to take a WiFi signal and *bounce* it further along, expanding your network's range. It works with both 802.11g and 802.11b routers. And Linksys High Gain Antennas will strengthen your network's signal. Unscrew the antennas from your existing Linksys router, and screw these new ones into place. It also works with 802.11b and 802.11g routers.

Other manufacturers sell similar products, so check your router manufacturer's web site for details.

Try and try again. The ultimate way to find the best placement for your access point and wireless PCs is to continuously experiment and see what kind of throughput you get. Each house and office is so different that no single configuration can suit them all.

Carefully monitor your throughput as you make these changes so that you determine the best positioning for your access point and PCs. To determine your true throughput, use the free network analysis program Qcheck [Hack #67].

See Also

- "Check WiFi Network Performance with Qcheck to Help Improve Throughput" [Hack #67]
- "Go War-Driving for WiFi Access" [Hack #65]

HACK #67 Check WiFi Network Performance with Qcheck to Help Improve Throughput

XP can't tell you the true throughput on your wired or wireless network. For that, you'll need free, third-party software that can help you improve throughput.

When you buy network hardware, including a hub/router and network cards, you're told that hardware's rated speed—for example, 100Mbps for an Ethernet network, or 11Mpbs for an 802.11b WiFi network.

But those numbers only tell you how your network might perform in ideal conditions; as the saying goes, "your mileage may vary," and it usually does. WiFi networks are particularly finicky and are especially prone to being affected by interference and other factors. Where you place your wireless access point and PCs and how you position their antennas [Hack #66] can make a dramatic difference in the actual speed of your network. So, you'll want to know the true connection speed of your network, WiFi networks in particular, so that you can optimize their performance when you troubleshoot them.

But how can you find out your true network performance? If you have a WiFi card, you can find information about your connection by clicking the small network icon in the Notification Area (also called the system tray). When you do that, the Wireless Network Connection Status screen appears, as shown in Figure 7-5.

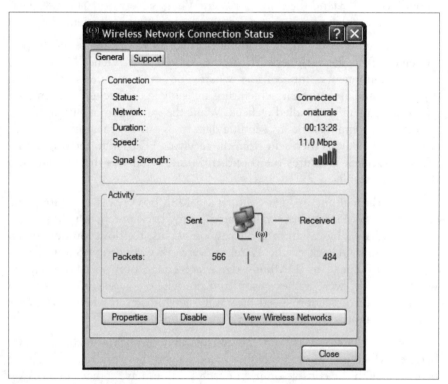

Figure 7-5. The Wireless Network Connection Status screen

There's only one problem with that screen: it's highly inaccurate. True, its little green bars and Signal Strength indication give you a broad picture of the relative strength of your network connection. But the Speed indication isn't an actual measurement as far as I can tell; it appears to tell you only your maximum theoretical connection speed, given the nature of your hardware, and doesn't reflect your true current connection speed. When I use my

WiFi network, it always tells me the speed is 11Mbps, even when actual, real-time measurement shows my true throughput is less than half of that.

So, how do you measure the true speed of a network in your real-world conditions? Get the free program Qcheck (*http://www.ixiacom.com/products/ performance_applications/pa_display.php?skey=pa_q_check*). It performs a series of tests, including throughput and response time, and gives you a good snapshot of your network's real performance. When trying to optimize a WiFi network, run Qcheck on each PC on the network to get baseline performance results for each. Then run the test for each PC after you move the base station and PCs, change the positioning of the antennas, and so forth, as outlined in "Extend the Range of Your Wireless Network" **[Hack #66]**. That way, you'll be able to fine-tune your network for optimum efficiency.

Once installed on every machine in your network, Qcheck measures the performance of the network between any two of your PCs. Qcheck is made up of two components: the console where you run your tests, shown in Figure 7-6, and an endpoint, which runs invisibly in the background on each PC on which you've installed Qcheck. While the exact metrics vary from test to test, the program works by sending data from one PC to another on your network. The data is then sent from the receiving PC back to the originating PC, and Qcheck measures the round-trip time, calculates throughput, and displays the results.

Note the throughput in Figure 7-6; it's 5.128Mbps. I was measuring the speed of my WiFi network while seated on my back porch, which is about 30 feet and a wall away from my access point. Just to show you how much more accurate Qcheck is, the Wireless Network Connection Status screen reported my speed as 11Mbps—the exact connection speed my laptop would have if I were inches away from the wireless access point. (And in actuality, the connection speed of a WiFi network, even when devices are next to one another, is much slower than 11Mbps.)

To run the Qcheck tests, run the console and then choose the two PCs between which you want to measure speed on your network. Only one must be the PC with the console on it, but each PC does have to have Qcheck on it. You don't need to run the console on each machine because the endpoints are running on them invisibly in the background; during Qcheck's installation the endpoints are configured to launch on startup.

You'll need to know the IP addresses of the PCs you want to test. If one of the PCs you're testing is the one running the console, choose *localhost* for that endpoint. To find the IP address of other PCs on your network, first go to that PC, right-click My Network Places, then double-click your network

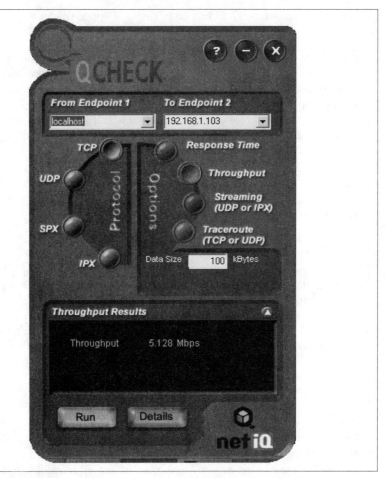

Figure 7-6. The Qcheck console

connection (it might read Local Area Connection, for example, or Wireless Network Connection). Click the Support tab, and you'll see your IP address.

Once you choose the PCs you want to test, choose the specific test to run. The best overall benchmark will be the Throughput test using either the TCP or UDP protocols. If you happen to use IPX or SPX on your network (some people still use these older protocols rather than TCP/IP), you can do benchmark throughput tests using them as well, though few home networks use those protocols. If you run any kind of streaming media across your network—for example, if you will be using your network to play MP3 files or other digital music on a PC and then stream it to another location in your house—choose the UDP streaming test. Streaming media use the UDP protocol, so the only way to test how they will perform on your network is to use the test for that protocol.

Make sure to run your test multiple times, and to be safe, run them a half hour or more apart. Because of the fickle nature of wireless transmissions, you can find dramatic differences in throughput from one moment to the next. For example, a few minutes after running the throughput test shown in Figure 7-6, I ran it again and was shown a throughput of 1.602Mbps. That one test was an anomaly, and other tests were more in keeping with my initial ones.

See Also

* "Go War-Driving for WiFi Access" [Hack #65]

HACK #68   Protect Your Home WiFi Network

The bad guys don't just target corporate networks. If you have a WiFi network at home, intruders are after you as well. Here's how to keep your network and all your PCs safe.

Your home WiFi network is an open invitation to intruders. It's like leaving your front door wide open and putting a sign out front saying, "Come in and take anything you want."

That's because WiFi broadcasting doesn't stop at your front door, or even the walls of your house or apartment. It leaks out through them. Anyone with a WiFi-connected device passing by can detect the signal and easily connect to your network [Hack #65]. And once they've connected, they can do much more than just steal your bandwidth; if you've enabled folder-sharing on any PCs, they can get at your personal information and files, delete files, and wreak a lot more havoc than that.

But there's a lot you can do to keep out intruders and protect your network and PCs. First, make sure you use encryption on your network [Hack #69]. If you've set up PCs on your network for sharing folders, you can require anyone who tries to get into those folders to have a password. Open Windows Explorer, right-click each folder on which you've enabled sharing, choose Properties, and click the Sharing tab. (This works in XP Professional only.)

But that's just the basics. There's a lot more you need to do. No single hack will keep your network protected, so you should use all of what follows.

Stop Broadcasting Your Network's SSID

Your service set identifier (SSID) is your network's name, and if people know what your SSID is, it's easier for them to find your network and connect to it. Your router broadcasts its SSID, and that broadcast tells passersby there's a network there. It also gives out the name, which makes it easier to connect to.

So, if you turn off SSID broadcasting, you'll go a long way toward protecting your network. But doing that, by itself, won't necessarily solve the problem. Even if you stop broadcasting your network's name, people might still be able to connect to your network. That's because manufacturers generally ship their wireless routers with the same generic SSID; for example, Linksys routers all have the SSID "Linksys" by default. So, even if you stop broadcasting your SSID, intruders can easily guess your router's name and log on.

The answer? First change your SSID's name, and then hide it. That way, passersby won't see it, and they won't be able to guess it either. How you do this varies from manufacturer to manufacturer, and even from model to model from the same manufacturer. But for many models of Linksys routers, here's what to do.

To change your SSID name and stop broadcasting it, log in to the setup screen by opening your browser and going to *http://192.168.1.1*. When the login screen appears, leave the username blank. In the password section type admin, and then press Enter.

Click the Wireless tab and look for the Wireless Network Name (SSID) box. Enter the new name of your network. On the same screen, scroll down to SSID Broadcast and choose Disabled, as shown in Figure 7-7. Then, click Save Settings. If you are doing this from a wireless PC, you will immediately lose your connection to the access point and the Internet.

 Make sure you don't disable your wireless network—just disable SSID broadcasting. If you choose Disable under the Wireless setting, you'll disable your wireless network.

After you change your network name, reconnect each WiFi computer to the network, using the new network name. To reconnect in Windows XP SP2, right-click the small wireless icon in the Windows system tray. From the screen that appears, click Change Advanced Settings, and then click the Wireless Networks tab. Click the Add button in the Preferred Network section, type the network name, click OK, and then OK again. In installation of Windows XP prior to SP2, click the small wireless network icon in the Windows

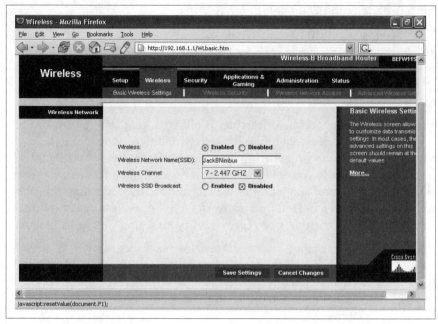

Figure 7-7. Changing your SSID name from the default

system tray and select the Wireless Networks tab. Click the Add button, type in the network name, click OK, and then OK again.

 Not all Linksys routers let you disable SSID broadcasting.

While you're at the Wireless screen, there's something else you can do to help keep your network invisible to outsiders. You should regularly change the channel over which your router transmits. That way, if someone has tapped into it before, she won't know on which channel it's now broadcasting. Choose a new wireless channel from the Wireless Channel drop-down list, and then click Save Settings.

Limit the Number of IP Addresses on Your Network

Your wireless router uses DHCP to hand out network addresses to each PC on your network. So, another way to stop intruders from hopping onto your network is to limit the number of IP addresses it hands out to the number of computers you actually have. That way, no one else will be able to get an IP address from your network's DHCP server because your PCs will use up all the available IP addresses.

Your router's built-in DHCP server hands out IP addresses whenever a computer needs to use the network, and the router lets you set the maximum number of IP addresses it hands out. To limit the number on a Linksys router, go to the Setup screen and scroll to the bottom. In the Number of Address box, type the number of computers that will use your network and click Save Settings, as shown in Figure 7-8. If you add another computer to your network, make sure you go back to the screen and increase the number of DHCP users by one.

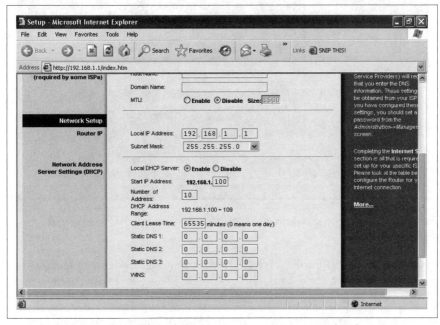

Figure 7-8. Limiting the number of IP addresses your DHCP server hands out

If you use this technique, you'll also have to change the number of IP addresses your router hands out if you turn off one of your PCs or take it away from the network. For example, if you take a laptop with you on the road, remember to change the number of IP addresses your router hands out and decrease the number by one.

Check and Filter MAC Addresses

The simplest way to check if you have an intruder is to see a list of every PC on your network. If you see an unfamiliar PC, it means you have an intruder.

To see all the computers currently on your network and their MAC addresses, log on to the router, click Status, and then click Local Network. Click the DHCP Client Table button, and you'll see a list of all the PCs on your network, their IP addresses, and their MAC addresses, as shown in Figure 7-9. If you see an unfamiliar computer listed there, you have an intruder. To kick the intruder off the network, check the box next to its listing and click Delete.

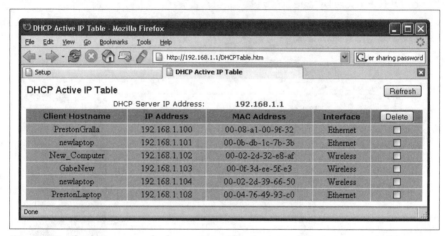

Figure 7-9. Checking to see whether any intruders have made it onto your wireless network

That will only temporarily solve the problem, though. The intruder can simply reconnect to your network and get a new IP address. You can, however, permanently ban any specific PC from ever connecting.

When you see an intruder, write down his MAC address. Then click Security, and from the screen that appears click Edit MAC Filter Setting. From the MAC Address Control Table that appears, type the MAC address onto a line and click Apply. The PC with that MAC address will now be permanently banned from your PC.

For even more security, you can allow only PCs with certain MAC addresses onto your network—just those who you want to let in. How you do this varies from router to router, but on a Linksys, from the main setup screen choose Wireless → Wireless Network Access to get to the Wireless Network Access screen. Select Restrict Access. Scroll to the bottom of the screen and click Wireless Client MAC List. You'll see a list of every wireless PC on your network, including their MAC addresses. Check the Enable MAC Filter box for each computer and click Save. You'll be sent back to the Wireless Network Access screen, and the MAC addresses of each PC will be put in a box next to MAC 01, MAC 02, and so on. Click Save Settings. Now, only computers you specify will be allowed onto your network.

If you want to allow a new computer with a different MAC address onto your network, you need to add that MAC address. To find out the computer's network adapter's MAC address, at a command prompt type `ipconfig /all` and press Enter. The screen will display information. Look for the numbers next to `Physical Address`, such as `00-08-A1-00-9F-32`. That's the MAC address. Copy that number into a MAC box on the Wireless Network Access screen, and that computer will be allowed to connect to your network. When you copy the number, don't include the hyphens.

Check Your Router Logs and Traffic

Your router keeps logs that track all the activity on your network. So, if you regularly check those logs, you can find out whether you've been targeted, or whether an intruder has made his way onto your network.

How you check the logs varies from router to router. But on many Linksys routers, you can examine both your incoming and outgoing logs. Log on to the router, click Administration, and then click Log. You'll see two buttons: Incoming Log and Outgoing Log.

Click Incoming Log to display a screen that shows the most recent inbound traffic, including the source IP where the traffic is coming from and the destination port number on a PC on your network. It's tough to decipher this screen, and there's not much immediately useful information here. Much more useful is the Outgoing Log, which shows all outbound traffic. It shows the LAN IP address of each piece of originating traffic, as well as the destination and the port number used. If you see unfamiliar destinations and LAN IP addresses, you have an intruder.

These two screens provide only a current snapshot of your network use, and they don't provide immediately useful information. But there's downloadable software that examines your router logs in much more detail and which can give you much useful information, including whether you're under attack, where the attack is coming from, the type of attack you're under, and similar information.

The best of the bunch is shareware, rather than freeware. Link Logger (*http://www.linklogger.com*) works with routers from Linksys, Netgear, and ZyXEL. When you run it, it automatically gathers information from your router logs, monitors your network, reports on what exploits and weaknesses are being targeted, and provides a wide range of reports and graphs. If you do find you're being attacked, it will list the attacker's IP address and computer name and identify the ports on his PC where the attack is coming from, as well as the IP address, computer names, and ports on your network being attacked, as shown in Figure 7-10. It will also specifically identify the type of attack.

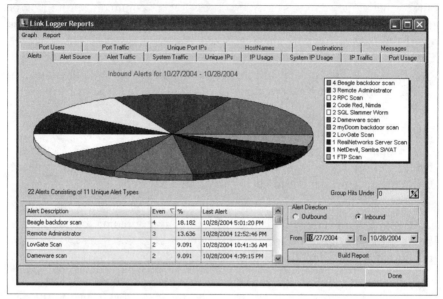

Figure 7-10. The Link Logger Reports screen

So, for example, you can create a report, like the one shown in Figure 7-10, which lists for you all the attacks and alerts over a given period of time and includes a breakdown of the number of each type of attack.

Get Back at the Attacker

You can also use Link Logger to try to get back at your attackers, by asking that their ISPs investigate them and possibly take action against them. First you need to find out the attacker's ISP. Then, send an email to the ISP and include the log files in the message.

On the Link Logger main screen, scroll until you find an attack or group of attacks from the same person, as shown in Figure 7-11. (Each attack will have an icon of a skull and crossbones next to it.) Do a Whois search, which will match the IP address with its ISP. Then, do an ARIN Whois Database Search at *http://network-tools.com* by typing the IP address into the box near the bottom of the screen and pressing Enter.

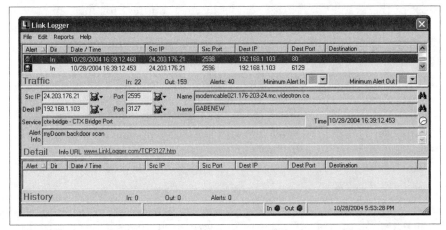

Figure 7-11. Using Link Logger to find out the IP address and other information identifying an attacker

You'll see the name and contact information for the ISP, as shown in Figure 7-12.

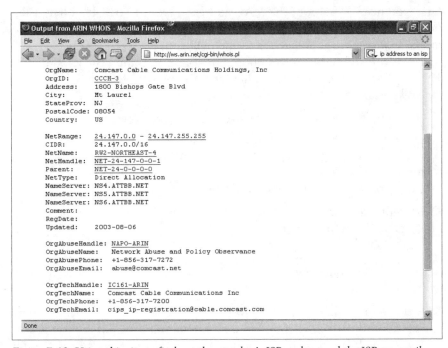

Figure 7-12. Using this site to find out the attacker's ISP and to send the ISP an email, including the Link Logger log

Most of the time, it will also include an email address for the person you should contact if you discover you've been attacked by someone who uses the ISP. Often, it's an address such as *abuse@comcast.net*. (This is the address that would appear if the attacker uses the Comcast ISP.)

Now that you have the right email address, you need to send an email to it and paste log information into the email. Right-click the listing or group of listings that originated the attack and choose Copy. That will copy the log information to the Windows Clipboard. Paste the information into an email, and send it to the ISP of the attacker.

Hacking the Hack

Despite all your precautions, there's a chance that someone has broken into your network, or at least uncovered information about it. People who go war-driving [Hack #65] often tell the whole world about unprotected WiFi networks they've found. So, there's a chance that information about your network is listed on a publicly available web site, for all the world to see. If so, someone can use that information to try and get into your network.

First, you need to find out the MAC address of your router. It's often listed on one of your router's screens, but if you don't know it, it's easy to find. To find it, first go to the command line and ping your router's IP address. You'll find it in your router documentation. For a Linksys router, the IP address is 192.168.1.1. So, for a Linksys router, at the command line type the following and press Enter:

```
ping 192.168.1.1
```

Strictly speaking, you don't need to ping the router. But it's a good idea to do it because when you ping it, the router's MAC address information will be put into your PC's Address Resolution Protocol (ARP) cache. Then it's easy to grab the information out of the cache.

After you ping your router, stay at the command prompt, issue the following command, and press Enter:

```
Arp -a
```

A screen like the one shown in Figure 7-13 will appear. Your MAC address will be listed directly under Physical Address.

Now that you know your router's MAC address, you can see whether information about your router is posted on a public web site. Go to *http://www.wigle.net*. Click the Search link on the lefthand side of the screen. You'll have to register at the site, but it's free, so before you search for your MAC address, fill out the registration information.

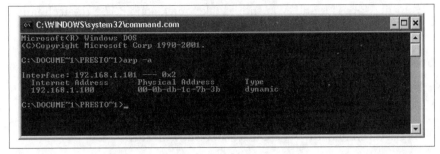

Figure 7-13. Finding out your router's MAC address

Once you've registered, log in, and the screen shown in Figure 7-14 appears. In the BSSID or MAC box, type in the MAC address of your router, making sure to put colons between the numbers, instead of the hyphens that Arp shows you. For example, you would type in a MAC address like this:

    00:0b:db1c:7b:3b

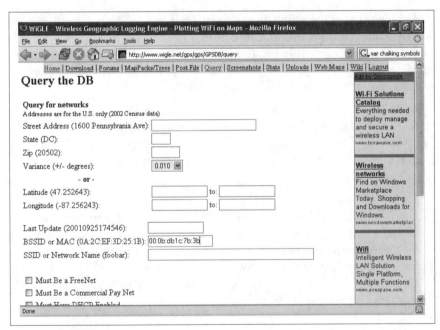

Figure 7-14. Checking the WiGLE web site to see whether a wireless network has been "outed"

Click Query. If a blank screen comes up, information about your network hasn't been posted to the site. But if your network is there, there will be a great deal of information about it, including its SSID, the channel it is broadcasting on, and other identifying information.

If your network is found, you should take quick action. Use the techniques in this hack and also turn on wireless encryption **[Hack #69]**.

See Also

- For a list of freeware and shareware that will help you decipher your router's logs, head to *http://lists.gpick.com/pages/Firewall_Log_Tools. htm*. That page lists a dozen or more pieces of software and includes reviews and links to where they can be downloaded.
- "Enable WiFi Encryption" **[Hack #69]**

HACK #69 Enable WiFi Encryption

Using an unencrypted WiFi network is like putting a big sign on your front door saying, "Burglars: the door's open and no one's home. Come in and help yourself." Here's how to put a virtual lock on your WiFi network to stop snoopers from coming in.

WiFi networks are incredibly convenient—and incredibly easy to snoop on. All that data going out over the air between your PCs and between your PCs and the Internet can easily be snooped on by anyone nearby using simple, off-the-shelf software such as packet sniffers. Virtually every keystroke and piece of data that goes out across your network can be read.

"Protect Your Home WiFi Network" **[Hack #68]** discusses a variety of precautions that will help protect your wireless network. Those hacks will help keep out most snoopers. But the most determined ones might be able to bypass them, so your best bet for the most security is to use *encryption*.

You can use two encryption standards to protect your network: Wireless Equivalent Protocol (WEP) and WiFi Protected Access (WPA). The WEP protocol is older and less secure than the WPA protocol. But you might be forced to use WEP because older hardware doesn't support WPA. Keep in mind that all your hardware has to support the encryption standard you choose. So, for example, if you have a newer router that uses WPA, but your WiFi network adapters don't support it, you won't be able to use WPA. Instead, you'll have to use WEP.

> If your current hardware doesn't support WPA, check the manufacturer's web site to see whether any firmware upgrades are available that offer WPA support. Some routers might have firmware upgrades for WPA, but WiFi network adapters usually are not upgradeable for WPA support.

How you turn on encryption varies from manufacturer to manufacturer, and even from model to model from the same manufacturer. It also varies depending on your wireless adapter. This hack shows how to set up encryption on a Linksys router.

If your hardware supports both WEP and WPA, choose WPA because it's a more secure form of encryption. But even though WEP has gotten a bad name among security experts because it isn't as secure as WPA, for most home networks it's perfectly suitable. Home networks are not targeted by serious, dedicated intruders, so WEP is perfectly suitable for keeping out passersby. Business networks, though, should upgrade to WPA hardware because valuable information is sent across their networks.

Setting Up WEP Encryption

To use WEP encryption, you must configure your router to use it, choose an encryption key, and then configure all your wireless network adapters to use the encryption with the proper key.

First, go to the Setup screen of your router. For a Linksys router, open a browser, type http://192.168.1.1 in the address bar, and press Enter. A login screen appears. Leave the "User name" field blank; in the Password field, type admin and press Enter. If you've changed the username and password, use those instead.

From the Setup screen, choose Wireless → Wireless Security. Select Enable next to Wireless Security. The Wireless Security options, which will have been grayed-out when you came to the page, will now be live so that you can fill them out.

Select WEP from the Security Mode drop-down list. In the Default Key section, choose any key from 1 through 4. (It doesn't matter which you choose.)

Next, select the wireless encryption level you want to use. You have a choice of 64 bits or 128 bits. Using 128-bit encryption is much more secure than 64-bit encryption, although it will slow down your network to a certain extent. Businesses should absolutely use 128-bit encryption, and home users should consider using it as well, despite potential network slowdowns. But before choosing 128-bit encryption, make sure your WiFi adapter supports it. Some WiFi adapters support only 64-bit WEP encryption. Check your documentation or the manufacturer's web site for details.

You might come across some confusing and apparently mis-
leading information when choosing WEP encryption on your
router. Some hardware manufacturers give you the choice of
40-bit or 104-bit encryption, rather than 64-bit and 128-bit
encryption. In fact, though, 40-bit WEP encryption and 64-
bit WEP encryption are two terms for the same thing, and
104-bit and 128-bit WEP encryption are similarly terms for
the same thing. WEP uses a 24-bit *initialization vector*, which
means you don't control that part of the key. So, some manufacturers refer to the standard as 40-bit or 104-bit, and others call it 64-bit or 128-bit.

From the Wireless Encryption Level drop-down box, choose either "64 bits
10 hex digits" or "128 bits 26 hex digits." Depending on which you choose,
the form you have to fill out will change, as illustrated in Figures 7-15 and
7-16.

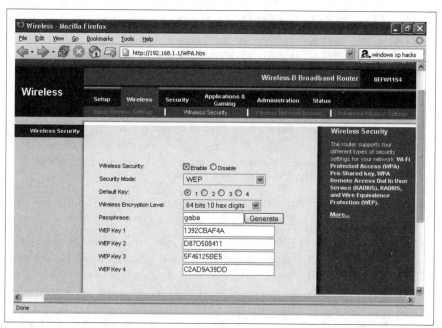

*Figure 7-15. Using 64-bit WEP encryption rather than 128-bit (for WiFi network
adapters that don't support 128-bit encryption)*

If you chose 64-bit encryption, type a phrase in the Passphrase box and click
Generate. That will generate the WEP key you'll use on your router and
each PC on the network. Four keys will be created in the WEP Key boxes.
You'll use only one of these keys at a time, but you generate four of them

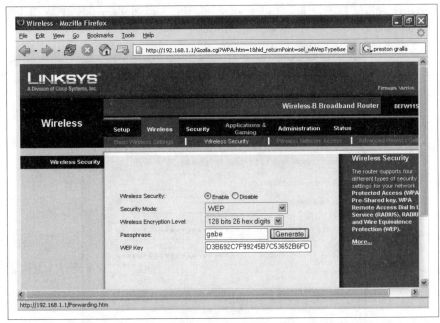

Figure 7-16. Choosing 128-bit WEP (a better bet than 64-bit because of its increased security, despite slight network slowdowns)

because you can manually switch between them at regular intervals, for added security. You don't have to generate your keys this way; you can create them yourself and type them in manually. But, chances are, it will be far easier to crack than one randomly generated by the router's software, so it's a good idea to use one the router will create for you.

If you instead selected 128-bit encryption, you'll be sent to a new screen. In the Passphrase box, type a phrase and click Generate. This will generate a 128-bit encryption key.

Regardless of whether you created a 64-bit key or a 128-bit key, copy the key (or keys, in the case of 64-bit) onto a piece of paper. You'll use this key for each PC that is going to access the network.

Click Save Settings. That applies the key to your network. From now on, only PCs that use WEP encryption and the key you just generated will be able to get onto your network.

Now that you've configured your router to use WEP, you have to configure each wireless computer on your network to use WEP and the key you just generated. On each PC, click the wireless connection icon in the system tray. Then, click Properties, click the Wireless Network tab, highlight your

network, click Properties, and then click the Association tab. The dialog
box shown in Figure 7-17 appears, although it won't yet be filled out.

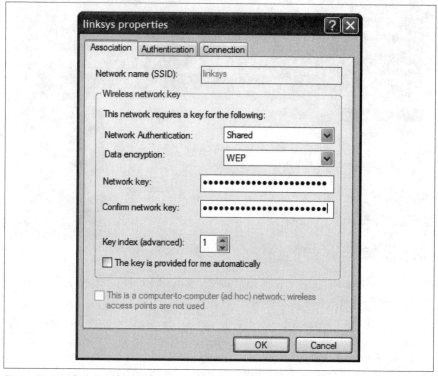

Figure 7-17. Choosing the right key number for 64-bit encryption

In the Network Authentication drop-down box, select Shared. In the Data
Encryption dialog box, choose WEP. When you do that, the box that reads
"The key is provided for me automatically" is checked. Uncheck this box.

 If you can't get WEP to work, it might be due to problems
with network authentication. Experiment with using Open
and Shared on each PC (choose this option from the Network Authentication drop-down box).

Enter your WEP key in the "Network key" box and type it again in the
"Confirm network key" box. From the Key Index, choose the key number
that you'll be using. Click OK and then OK again. Now the PC can connect
to your network using WEP encryption.

For added security, change the key number and associated network key on each PC regularly. You shouldn't need to change the number on your router because it will recognize all the keys you generated. If you use 128-bit encryption, you'll have only one key to use.

Setting Up WPA Encryption

The process for turning on WPA encryption is similar to that for turning on WEP, with a few differences along the way. First, you need to make sure your version of XP supports WPA. SP2 does; earlier versions don't. To check whether you have SP2 installed, right-click My Computer, choose Properties, and look on the General tab. If you have SP2 installed, it will tell you at the bottom of the System section near the top of the tab.

If you don't have SP2, go to *http://www.microsoft.com/downloads/details. aspx?FamilyId=009D8425-CE2B-47A4-ABEC-274845DC9E91* and download a system patch that will install WPA on your system. Or, you can update your entire system to SP2 by going to *http://windowsupdate. microsoft.com*.

Now that your system supports WPA, you need to make sure all your hardware supports it as well, by checking the documentation and manufacturers' web sites. If not, see if firmware updates are available, and download and install them. Remember, you'll have to upgrade your router and wireless networking adapters, not just a few components. Also download the latest driver for your network adapters.

Once your system and hardware are WPA-enabled, go to the Setup screen of your router. For a Linksys router, open a browser, type http://192.168.1.1 in the address bar, and press Enter. A login screen appears. Leave the "User name" field blank; in the Password field, type admin and press Enter. If you've changed the username and password, use those instead.

From the Setup screen, choose Wireless → Wireless Security. Select Enable next to Wireless Security. The Wireless Security options, which will have been grayed-out when you came to the page, will now be live so that you can fill them out.

Select WPA Pre-Shared Key from the Security Mode drop-down list. In the WPA Algorithms drop-down list, choose TKIP, which is the approved, certified algorithm for WPA. Some products support Advanced Encryption System (AES), but that hasn't been certified for interoperability among different vendors' hardware.

In the WPA Shared Key box, type a key between 8 and 63 characters in length. The longer it is and the more random the characters, the more secure it will be. Write down the key. You'll need to use this on each wireless PC on your network.

Leave the Group Key Renewal row at 3600. Click Save Settings. That applies the key to your network. Figure 7-18 shows what the screen should look like when you're done. Now, only PCs that use WPA encryption and the key you just generated will be able to get onto your network.

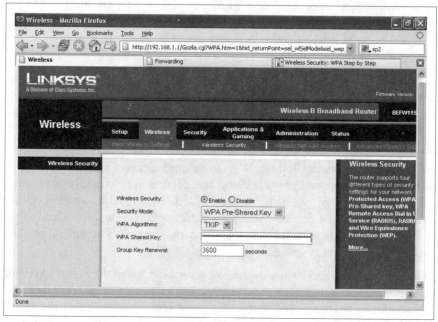

Figure 7-18. Creating a long and random WPA shared key for a more secure network

Now that you've configured your router to use WEP, you have to configure each wireless computer on your network to use WEP and the key you just generated. On each PC, click the wireless connection icon in the system tray. Then, click Properties, click the Wireless Network tab, highlight your network, click Properties, and then click the Association tab.

In the Network Authentication drop-down box, select WPA-PSK. In the Data Encryption dialog box, choose TKIP. When you do that, the box that reads "The key is provided for me automatically" is checked. Uncheck this box. Enter your WPA key in the "Network key" box, and type it again in the "Confirm network key" box. Click OK and then OK again. Now the PC can connect to your network using WPA encryption.

For both WPA and WEP, it's a good idea to change your key regularly because if someone monitors your network and captures network packets for a long enough period of time, they might be able to crack your encryption. If you regularly change your key, it will be much harder for them to crack the encryption because they'll have less time and data to do so.

See Also

- For more detailed instructions on using WPA on your network, see the *PC Magazine* article "Wireless Security: WPA Step by Step" at *http://www.pcmag.com/print_article/0,3048,a=107756,00.asp.*

- For more information about WPA, see the Microsoft Knowledge Base Article 815485 (*http://support.microsoft.com/default.aspx?scid=kb;en-us;815485*).

HACK #70 Stop Moochers from Stealing Your WiFi Bandwidth

Everyone these days seems to have a WiFi-equipped laptop or PDA. If you have a WiFi network at home or at work and you are worried that passersby might be connecting to it and stealing your bandwidth, here's what you can do.

As shown in "Go War-Driving for WiFi Access" **[Hack #65]**, if you have a WiFi network, it's a breeze for anyone passing by to detect it. And if you haven't protected yourself properly—or if someone is dedicated enough to stealing your bandwidth—moochers can get in and suck up all your bandwidth by doing things such as downloading movies and MP3s. That means there's less bandwidth for you.

There's an easy way to find out if someone is leeching your bandwidth and then to send them alerts telling them you know they're using your bandwidth and you'd like them to get off your network. Download AirSnare, a free program which monitors your network for wireless intruders, reports on who they are, shows you their activity, and sends them warnings.

Before you install AirSnare, you need to download and install a library of tools called WinPcap, an architecture that captures and analyzes network packets. Get it from *http://winpcap.polito.it/install/default.htm* and follow the installation instructions.

Next, download and install AirSnare from *http://home.comcast.net/~jay.deboer/airsnare.*

Strictly speaking, AirSnare isn't precisely freeware. Its author calls it *beggarware*. That is, he lets you use it for free, but he asks that you make a donation to him to help him develop the program further.

Before you use AirSnare, you need to know the MAC address of any network card that will be using your wireless network. The MAC address is a number that uniquely identifies a network card or other piece of communications hardware. You're going to tell AirSnare that these MAC addresses are trusted ones and shouldn't be treated as intruders.

You can find out the MAC address for your PCs in several ways. One simple way is to go to a command prompt in Windows, type `ipconfig /all`, and press Enter. In the results you get, look for the numbers next to `Physical Address`, such as `00-08-A1-00-9F-32`. That's the MAC address.

Copy down the MAC address for every PC on your network. Include the addresses for all your PCs, even if they connect to the network via Ethernet rather than wirelessly. For example, if you have a laptop that you sometimes connect to your network wirelessly and sometimes via Ethernet, when you issue the `ipconfig /all` command and press Enter you'll see two sets of entries, each of which has its MAC address. Copy down both of them.

Next, go to C:\Program Files\AirSnare, open *trustedMAC.txt* with WordPad, and add each MAC address (such as `00-08-A1-00-9F-32`) on a new line in the file. Follow it by a space, and then type in a description of the computer—for example, `00-08-A1-00-9F-32 Preston's New Laptop`.

Now go to C:\Program Files\AirSnare and run the file *AirSnare.exe*. You have to run the file from this location because the program doesn't install an icon on the desktop or show up as an entry in Windows' All Programs menu.

Not all WiFi adapters will work with AirSnare. If you get the error message `runtime error '-2147220982 (8004020a)' procedure packetsethwfilter failed. error code= 0`, it means your WiFi adapter won't work with it. Try installing the software on another computer on your network.

Choose your network adapter from the list that appears, and AirSnare will spring into action. Whenever it finds a MAC address on the network that you haven't told it is a friendly one, it sounds an alert and changes its screen color to red. Then it starts logging any traffic between the MAC address and the network in its Unfriendly MAC Watch Window. It gives details about all the traffic, including the port being used and the destination IP address. It also identifies common ports such as FTP, Telnet, email, web, DHCP, and other popular ports so that you have more information than just a port number.

You can save all the information to a log file by clicking the Stop button and clicking "Write to log file." All the information will be saved in a text file. Filenames start with *ASlog* and are followed by the date and time; for example, *ASlog031605_2305.txt* indicates the log was saved on March 16, 2005, at 23:05 (that's 11:05 p.m.).

Once you know someone is using your network, you want to warn them away, which you can do with the program's AirHorn module. Choose Window → AirHorn Window. The screen pictured in Figure 7-19 appears. In the Server box type in your computer's hostname, or its IP address. If you're not sure what those are for your PC, use the ipconfig /all command from earlier in this hack, and get the information from there.

Figure 7-19. Sending a message to intruders

In the Send To box, enter the IP address of the computer to which you're sending a warning, which you'll find in the Unfriendly MAC Watch Window. Then, in the Send From box, type your name or how you want to be identified and type the message you want to send, as shown in Figure 7-19. Click Send Message, and the warning will be sent on its merry way.

There's only one problem with this warning module: it works only if both you and the person on the other end have the Windows Messenger service turned on. The Windows Messenger *service* isn't the Windows Messenger *chat program*. Rather, it's used to send notifications over local area networks—for example, when a network administrator warns users that a server is about to be taken down. Because the Windows Messenger service has frequently been used to send spam, though, many people have turned it off. And XP SP2 turns it off by default [Hack #33]. So, don't count on this part of the program working.

Hacking the Hack

Knowing that you have a bandwidth moocher is one thing, but kicking him off your network is another thing entirely. Sometimes a warning will suffice, but if one of you isn't using the Windows Messenger service, you won't even be able to warn him. So, what to do if you can't get through, or you can get through and the moocher ignores you?

You can kick him off your network using your wireless router's built-in capabilities. How you do this varies from router to router, but here's how to do it using the Linksys BEFW11S4. Go to the administrator's screen by going to *http://192.168.1.1*. Leave the username blank, type admin for the password, and press Enter. (If you've changed the username and password from the default, use those instead.)

Next, click Status, and from the screen that appears, click Local Network. A page will appear with basic information about your router. Click DHCP Client Table, and you'll see a list of all the devices on the network with their IP addresses and MAC addresses, as shown in Figure 7-20. Check the box next to the intruder and click Delete, and he'll be kicked off your network.

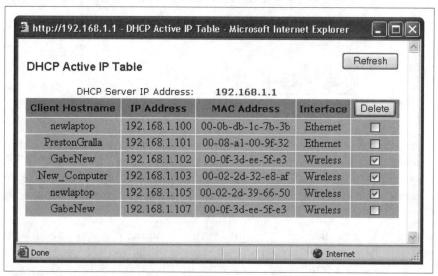

Figure 7-20. Kicking WiFi bandwidth moochers off your network by deleting them from the IP table

To make sure he can't get on again, you can tell your wireless router not to allow him onto your network. In my example of a Linksys router, log on to the administrator's screen and click Security. From the page that appears, click Edit MAC Filter Setting. On the Filtered MAC Address page that appears, you'll be able to ban devices with specific MAC addresses from getting onto your network. Type in the MAC address in an empty box, and click Apply. From now on the intruder will be barred.

Of course, someone else at some point might try to get on as well. Your best bet to keep out intruders is to use encryption and to limit the number of IP addresses on your network. Also, refer to "Protect Your Home WiFi Network" [Hack #68] for several additional security measures you can take.

See Also

- "Protect Your Home WiFi Network" [Hack #68]
- "Enable WiFi Encryption" [Hack #69]

HACK #71 Solve Hotspot Woes

Send mail at a hotspot, even if your ISP won't normally let you do it, and make sure your hotspot connection doesn't get interrupted by "stuttering."

WiFi hotspots are great ways to connect to the Internet when you're away from home. They're practically everywhere these days, from coffee shops to airports, hotels, and even entire sections of metropolitan areas.

But hotspots, despite their convenience, come with problems as well. Depending on your normal ISP, you might not be able to send mail at hotspots. And if you're in an area that has lots of hotspots close to one another, you might find your connection *stuttering*; your current connection might drop, and you might find your PC automatically trying to jump from hotspot to hotspot, leaving you in the cold.

What to do? Here's how to hack hotspots to solve those problems.

Sending Mail from Hotspots

The Internet is not the cooperative, friendly place it used to be several years ago, particularly because of the spamming scourge. When spam and scams weren't much of a problem years ago, it was easy to send mail even when you were outside of your normal ISP's network—and you're outside your ISP's network when you're at a hotspot rather than at home or an office on a broadband connection, or when you're dialing directly into your ISP.

ISPs used to allow anyone to use their SMTP servers to send mail. But when spam became a big-time problem, they cracked down on that because it allowed spammers to hide the true source of the origin of their spam. Now, most ISPs won't allow anyone outside their network to use their SMTP servers to send mail. So, when you're at a hotspot outside your ISP's network, you're treated like any outsider, and you won't be able to use the normal SMTP server to send mail.

There are several ways around this problem. The easiest is to use the SMTP server used by the hotspot. Find out the server address, configure your email software to use it, and you're ready to go.

Didn't know that hotspots have SMTP servers? Join the club. Most hotspot providers don't publicize that fact. In fact, often, their technical support departments don't even know they have SMTP servers. I made several calls to T-Mobile asking about it and was told each time the servers don't exist. In fact, though, they do.

The big national hotspot providers all have SMTP servers, although smaller mom-and-pop shops most likely don't have them. So, here are the SMTP servers for popular hotspot providers:

T-Mobile
> *myemail.t-mobile.com*

Boingo
> *mail.boingo.com*

Wayport
> *mail.wayport.net*

Surf and Sip
> *mail.surfandsip.net*

If you happen to connect to a hotspot at a hotel, ask whether the hotel has an SMTP server you can use.

How you configure SMTP varies according to the email software you use. If you use Outlook, choose Tools → Email Accounts and then click "View or change existing e-mail accounts." From the list that appears, choose your email account, and click Change. In the "Outgoing mail server (SMTP)" box, type in the name of the SMTP server you want to use (for example, *mail.boingo.com*), as shown in Figure 7-21. Click Next and then click Finish. Now you'll be able to send email at a Boingo hotspot.

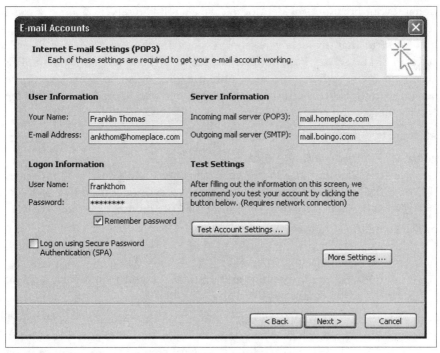

Figure 7-21. Configuring Outlook to use Boingo's SMTP server

 Before you change your SMTP server address, write down your original one. Make sure, when you leave the hotspot, that you change the address back to the original, because if you don't you won't be able to send mail when you're at your normal ISP.

If you use Outlook Express, choose Tools → Accounts, select the Mail tab, click the Properties button, and then select the Servers tab. In the "Outgoing mail server (SMTP)" box, enter the name of the hotspot's SMTP server. Click OK, then OK again, and then Close. You're all set.

 If you've followed these steps, checked that the SMTP address is accurate, and checked that your hotspot won't let you send email, the SMTP server might require authentication. If so, on the screen in Outlook or Outlook Express that requires you to enter the SMTP address, check the "My server requires authentication" box and click the Settings button. From the screen that appears, select "Log on using" and enter your hotspot account name and password where indicated.

What if your hotspot provider doesn't have an SMTP server? There are still a few solutions for you. One is to pay an SMTP relay service so that you'll be able to send mail from any hotspot, even if the hotspot provider doesn't have an SMTP server. Pay the relay service, and then you can use its SMTP server no matter where you are. Configure your email software to use the server, as outlined earlier in this hack, although you should check with the service, in case it has any special setup instructions.

Here are two reputable relay services:

AuthSMTP (http://www.authsmtp.com)
> Pricing plans start at $25 per year, which lets you send 1,000 messages or 100MB of mail per month, and go up to $169 per month, which lets you send 10,000 messages or 1GB of mail per month.

SMTP.com (http://www.smtp.com)
> Has a variety of pricing plans, including a monthly $9.99 plan, which lets you send 50 emails per day; a $29.99-a-year plan, which lets you send up to 30 emails per day; and a $149.99-a-year plan, which lets you send up to 300 emails per day.

There's one more solution you can turn to. You can install an SMTP server on your own laptop. Then, when you send mail, you configure your laptop to use that SMTP server to send mail. A simple one to set up and use is 1st SMTP (*http://www.emailarms.com/downloads/1st_smtp.html*). It's shareware, so you can try it out for free, but it costs $49 if you continue to use it.

Stop Hotspot Stuttering

Some metropolitan areas are so full of hotspots that several of them are available from the same location. When I go to Davis Square, located a few blocks from my house in Cambridge, sit at a café, and fire up my laptop, depending on which café I'm sitting at I usually see at least two hot spots, and sometimes three or more.

If you're near several hotspots and the connections are weak, your connection will *stutter* and jump; when one connection fades out, XP will automatically connect you to another one, and that one will stutter, and XP will jump to another connection, and so on. The upshot is that you're never connected to any one of them long enough to maintain a useful Internet connection.

Stuttering is caused by the very thing that allows you to easily connect to hotspots, XP's Windows Zero Configuration (WZC) applet, which runs automatically on startup. When running, WZC looks for a new network connection every three minutes, and if, at the point it's looking for a connection, your current connection fades out, it will search for a new one, and then automatically connect to it. The result is stuttering, jumping, and general uselessness.

How to hack it? Temporarily disable WZC after you've made a connection; that way, it'll stay with your one connection, even as it fades out and in. After you're finished at the hotspot, turn WZC back on so that the next time you want to connect to a hotspot or your home WiFi network, it will do its job.

To temporarily disable WZC, select Start → Run and in the Open box, type services.msc, and press Enter. This runs the Services console. Scroll down until you see the Wireless Zero Configuration entry. Right-click it and choose Stop, as shown in Figure 7-22. That turns the service off; you'll stop the stuttering and jumping. When you're done with a hotspot, repeat the steps, except choose Start.

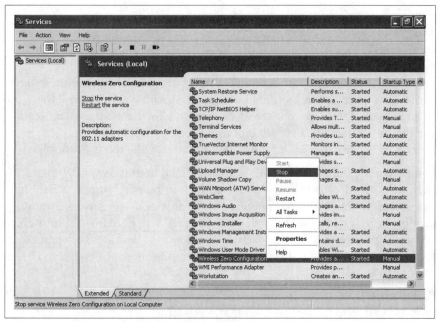

Figure 7-22. Temporarily turning off the WZC service to stop hotspot stuttering

Hacking the Hack

Turning WZC on and off can be a time-consuming chore. So, if you frequently connect to hotspots that stutter, you can speed things up by creating a desktop shortcut that, when double-clicked, will stop WZC, and creating another shortcut that, when double-clicked, will start it back up.

To do this, in Windows Explorer go to *C:\Windows\System32*. Drag the *Net.exe* file to the desktop. Right-click it and select Create Shortcut. Give the shortcut a name by right-clicking it, selecting Rename, and typing in a name, such as `Halt WZC`. Right-click the shortcut again, choose Properties, and click the Shortcut tab. The target field will read something like this: `C:\Documents and Settings\Administrator\Desktop\net.exe`. Replace this with `C:\WINDOWS\system32\net.exe`, enter a space, type `stop wzcsvc`, and click OK. Now the contents of the target field should be `C:\WINDOWS\system32\net.exe stop wzcsvc`.

Repeat these steps to create a shortcut for starting WZC. Name it `Start WZC`, and type `C:\WINDOWS\system32\net.exe start wzcsvc` in the target field.

Now, whenever you want to stop WZC, double-click the Halt shortcut. To start WZC back up, double-click the Start WZC shortcut.

HACK #72 Set Up Bluetooth on XP

The Bluetooth wireless standard is a great way to get computers and gadgets to talk to each other. Here's how to set it up on XP.

Bluetooth wireless support is showing up in all sorts of devices these days, and the software is easy to use. Few consumers know about it or know how to use it, though. This hack will expose you to the basics of Bluetooth, explain how to set up some Bluetooth devices, and point you to some good sources of information about the ways you can use Bluetooth in your life.

Some people confuse Bluetooth with the 802.11x standards (WiFi), since they are both wireless technologies. But WiFi is intended primarily for Internet data and connecting computers, while Bluetooth is used to communicate between a wide variety of devices. Where WiFi needs to get into every corner of your world to be effective, Bluetooth is best at short ranges. In fact, the effective range of most Bluetooth communications is about 32 feet (10 meters).

Bluetooth can be used to connect all kinds of different devices—PCs, cell phones, cell phone headsets, PDAs, keyboards, portable game systems, audio headphones, GPS receivers, printers, digital cameras, barcode scanners, medical equipment, and even your car. Each device supports one or more profiles that dictate what types of devices it can communicate with and how that communication will take place. If two devices share a profile, they can communicate; otherwise, they will not even make the attempt.

Installing Bluetooth

My own initiation into Bluetooth was when I needed a new mouse for my laptop. I had avoided buying one of the infrared wireless mice because of the line-of-sight issues, but a Bluetooth mouse seemed like just the ticket. I purchased a Bluetooth dongle that plugs into my laptop's USB port and a Bluetooth wireless mouse. In addition to the dongle-type adapters, you can also get permanent Bluetooth cards that go into the PCI slot of your desktop computer. The installation procedure is mostly the same.

The Plug-and-Play mechanism in Windows XP works so well that I usually just attach any new piece of hardware without bothering to use the software CD unless I have to. But due to the way that Bluetooth works, it's best to install the software first so that you have an opportunity to configure Bluetooth prior to using it.

When you install the software, you'll find the usual assortment of wizard pages asking you where you want to install the software and such. The installer might display a warning about Bluetooth devices and signed drivers. This is a security precaution and a convenience for you. If you click OK, the installer will temporarily disable the signed drivers messages to install the Bluetooth adapter. Otherwise, you would end up with a lot of messages about unsigned drivers.

Once the installer is complete, attach your Bluetooth adapter. If you have a PCI Bluetooth adapter, install the card in an open slot and restart your PC. Windows XP will detect the adapter and associate the drivers with those that you installed earlier. You will probably see several messages show up in the system tray as it installs the drivers for the Bluetooth adapter.

Once Windows XP has finished loading the drivers, you can start configuring your Bluetooth adapter. The My Bluetooth Places icon, shown in Figure 7-23, will open a window that allows you to discover and browse nearby Bluetooth devices. There is also an icon in the system tray for Bluetooth; it's a blue circle with the runic B on it. The B in the system tray icon changes color depending on the status of the Bluetooth connection—red for when no Bluetooth adapter is connected, white for when an adapter is connected, and green for when a device is communicating with your PC.

Figure 7-23. The My Bluetooth Places desktop icon

Open the My Bluetooth Places window. If you have a Bluetooth device nearby and it is turned on, it might show up on this list. Ignore any devices for the moment while we go through the configuration process. In the upper-left corner of My Bluetooth Places, there is a list of links under the heading Bluetooth Tasks. Click the link labeled Bluetooth Setup Wizard. The choices you are presented with, shown in Figure 7-24, pertain to how you want to use your Bluetooth adapter. For now, choose the last option, the one that begins with "I want to change the name...".

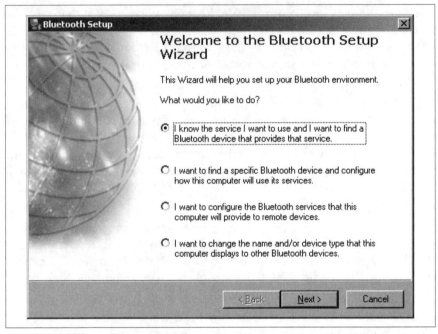

Figure 7-24. Bluetooth Setup Wizard

If you want to set up service for a particular type of device, such as a mouse or a printer, choose the button labeled "I know the service I want to use...". If you want to connect to a specific device (in case more than one person is using a Bluetooth device in your proximity), choose the button labeled "I want to find a specific Bluetooth device..." and click the Next button. In this screen, you provide the name of your computer and the type of computer you are using (laptop or desktop). I use a generic name for the computer because this value is broadcast to the world. People who attempt to hack into Bluetooth-connected computers could use this information to their advantage. Click the Finish button to go back to My Bluetooth Places.

If you haven't already done so, now would be a good time to turn on your Bluetooth device and make sure it is running properly. Click the Bluetooth Setup Wizard link again. This time, when presented with the wizard screen of choices, choose "I know the service I want to use..." and click the Next button. The wizard will present you with a complete list of items that it knows how to communicate with. This is where you will go if you want to add a printer or a headset in the future. To set up the mouse, scroll the list to the bottom, select Human Interface Device, and click the Next button.

The next screen, shown in Figure 7-25, will cause Windows XP to search for all Bluetooth devices in range. If your device does not show up, make sure it is powered on and operating correctly. There might be a Connect or Pair button on the device that you must press to start the communication with the PC. If many devices are in the area, you can use the pop-up box beneath the list to show only certain types of devices. If the device you want to connect is in the list, choose it and click the Next button.

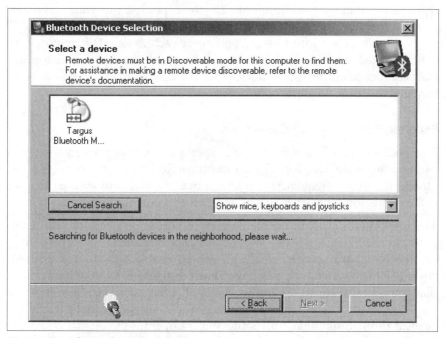

Figure 7-25. Bluetooth Device Selection screen

At this point, the Bluetooth wizard will attempt to connect with the device. If all went well, you should see the confirmation window shown in Figure 7-26. This is your way of knowing the device you are looking for is available and communicating with your computer. Once you click the confirmation button, your mouse and your PC are paired. If you ever see this window and you weren't expecting it, it could be a sign that someone nearby is attempting to communicate with your computer via the Bluetooth connection.

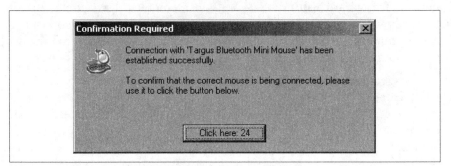

Figure 7-26. Bluetooth confirmation dialog

If you are planning to add multiple Bluetooth products to your computer, you add them by going to the Bluetooth Setup Wizard and choosing the "I know the service I want to use..." option for each device. Different devices will follow the same instructions as we've done with the mouse in this example, although there might be device-specific settings that you will have to configure once the connection is made.

Securing Your Bluetooth Connection

Bluetooth can make your computing experience more convenient by eliminating some of the need for cables. Unfortunately, because the signal is being broadcast on open frequencies, anyone is free to listen in or even participate in the discussion. That's why it's necessary for you to take precautions.

The first precaution is to enable only the services you need for your computer. In the Bluetooth Setup Wizard, the choice labeled "I want to configure the Bluetooth services..." allows you to enable and disable different types of Bluetooth communications. Disable any types of communications that you do not plan to use at that moment. Click the Finish button when you have made the changes you need. These services can be easily re-enabled through the Bluetooth Setup Wizard or from the link labeled View My Bluetooth Services.

The next precaution involves locking out other devices. Go to My Bluetooth Places and choose the link labeled "View or modify configuration." The Bluetooth Configuration dialog box, shown in Figure 7-27, allows you to choose how your Bluetooth connection communicates to the outside world.

Figure 7-27. Bluetooth Configuration screen

Click the tab labeled Accessibility. Remove the check mark from the box labeled "Let other Bluetooth devices discover this computer." This will prevent unwelcome intrusions by unknown devices. The Discovery tab allows you to configure which devices your connection can discover. This is useful if you are in an office environment with many different types of Bluetooth devices. The Local Services tab lets you configure how different types of devices interact with software services installed on your PC. This will be necessary for synchronizing a PDA, listening to music, or transferring files.

Two of the more publicized Bluetooth security problems are called *Bluejacking* and *Bluesnarfing*. Both of these exploits require the attacker to be within communication range of the victim, which is less than 32 feet (10 meters) for most phones and laptops. Bluejacking involves the unsolicited receipt of messages to a Bluetooth device, usually a phone. It's primarily used as a prank; your phone starts vibrating and you get a message criticizing your hairstyle or the brand of phone you are using. Your attacker will be close by, and chances are good that he is around 15 years old. Bluesnarfing is more dangerous because the attacker is out to retrieve datebook and contact information from your phone. In both cases, if you disable the Bluetooth features of your phone when you aren't using them, you won't have these problems.

Networking with Bluetooth

Bluetooth provides many of the same features WiFi does. Bluetooth has a maximum data transmission rate of somewhere around 100,000 bytes per second, which is much lower than 802.11. Plus, its limited range means all the parties must be in very close proximity. For these reason, it's not an effective competitor to 802.11 for day-to-day wireless networking.

There are times, however, when an ad hoc wireless network using Bluetooth could be useful. If no network is present and no one has a floppy or flash drive handy, you can use a Bluetooth connection between the computers to share files. Keep in mind that the data rate for Bluetooth is miniscule compared to 802.11, so use it sparingly. For details on how to transfer files between PCs with Bluetooth, see "Set Up an Ad Hoc WiFi Network" [Hack #74].

For details on how to pair your PC via Bluetooth with another device such as a cell phone to connect to the Internet, see "Connect to the Internet with a Bluetooth Phone" [Hack #73].

See Also

- The O'Reilly Wireless web site (*http://wireless.oreilly.com*) has a good deal of Bluetooth-related information.
- *Windows XP Unwired* by Wei-Meng Lee (O'Reilly) is a good source for Bluetooth-related advice.
- *Wireless Hacks* by Rob Flickenger (O'Reilly) contains many more Bluetooth hacks.
- "Connect to the Internet with a Bluetooth Phone" [Hack #73]
- "Set Up an Ad Hoc WiFi Network" [Hack #74]

—Eric Cloninger

HACK #73   Connect to the Internet with a Bluetooth Phone

Don't worry about normal phone dial-in connections, hotspots, or WiFi. No matter where you are, the Internet is with you, as long as you have a Bluetooth-enabled phone.

Lots of phones these days include Bluetooth connections, and if you have one, Internet access for your laptop is only a phone call away. All you'll need to do is fire up your laptop and phone, connect them to one another, and make the Internet connection. To do this, you'll of course need a laptop with Bluetooth capabilities as well.

If your laptop doesn't have Bluetooth capability, it's easy to add. You just need a USB Bluetooth adapter. Companies including D-Link, Keyspan, Belkin, and many others sell them, often for around $30. Just plug the little device into your USB port, follow installation instructions, and you'll be set.

Don't expect broadband connection speeds when you do this—at least not yet. The exact connection speed you'll get varies according to the precise technology your cell phone uses and, of course, depending on the quality of your current cell phone connection. These days, though, expect 20 to 40Kbps with a GSM/GPRS cell phone, 20 to 150Kbps with EDGE, about 50 to 120Kbps with CDMA 1xRTT, and from 300 to 500Kbps with CDMA 1xEV-DO. If you don't know which technology your cell phone uses, check with your cell phone carrier, and they'll let you know.

The exact screens you'll see when you make the connection will vary somewhat from phone to phone, so for this hack, I'll show you how to do it with the Sony Ericsson T68i Bluetooth-enabled phone. The steps with other Bluetooth-enabled cell phones should be very similar.

First, turn on your cell phone and laptop, and make sure they're within range of one another. Then turn on the phone's Bluetooth radio. To do this on the Sony Ericsson T68i, press the joystick button and select Connect → Bluetooth → Options → Operation Mode → On.

Next, you'll have to make the phone *discoverable* so that your laptop can find it. On the Sony Ericsson T68i, press the joystick button, and select Connect → Bluetooth → Discoverable.

Now you need to discover the phone in XP. In XP, go to My Bluetooth Places and select View Devices in Range. You should see the Sony Ericsson T68i icon. Right-click it and select Discover Available Services. You'll get to a group of icons that show the list of available services. Right-click the Dial-Up Networking service and select Connect Dial-up Networking, as shown in Figure 7-28.

You'll be asked whether you want to accept or decline the connection or "Add to Paired." It's a good idea to select the "Add to Paired" option. That way, the next time you want to connect to the Internet using your laptop and cell phone, they'll automatically discover one another, and you won't have to go through the entire discovery process.

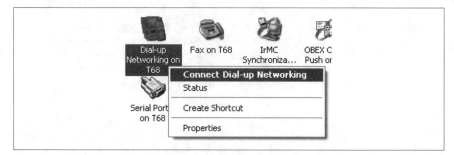

Figure 7-28. Connecting to the Internet by right-clicking the Dial-up Networking icon and choosing Connect Dial-up Networking

When you select "Add to Paired," the screen shown in Figure 7-29 will appear. The device name will already be filled in for you. Make up a PIN that you want to use for pairing the devices, and type it into the Bluetooth PIN Code box.

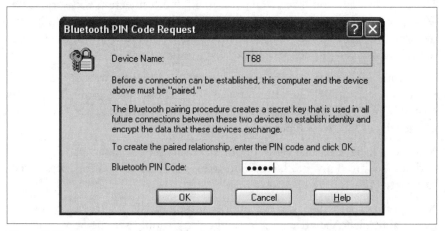

Figure 7-29. Pairing your phone and laptop

 It's a good idea to use only numbers for your PIN; otherwise, you might have problems with keying in alphabetic characters using your phone's PIN dialog box.

On your cell phone, you'll have to accept the pairing. A dialog box will appear asking if you want to accept the pairing. Select "Add to Paired," and type in the same PIN you used on your laptop.

From now on, connecting to the Internet is the same as with any other dial-up connection. The familiar dial-up connection dialog box will appear in

XP, asking for a username, password, and phone number. Enter the information you normally use to connect to your ISP, including your username, password, and phone number. Click the Dial button, and you'll dial in and connect.

Set Up an Ad Hoc WiFi Network

#74

Don't have a WiFi router handy, but want to set up a network among multiple PCs? It's easy to do using the ad hoc networking built into XP.

There are times when you don't need a network to share a single Internet connection. Instead, you just want to share files, use the printer of another PC, send and receive instant messages; in other words, do pretty much everything you can do on a network.

But what if you want to do all that and you don't have a router?

You can set up an ad hoc network, in which you connect on a peer-to-peer basis with other computers and PDAs. You don't need any extra software for it. The capability is built right into XP.

All you need are WiFi-equipped PCs. To establish an ad hoc network, first one PC does the basic setup and then the rest of the PCs connect to that ad hoc network.

On the PC that's setting up the network, double-click the Wireless Network icon in the system tray. Click the Properties button, and then click the Wireless Networks tab. Click the Add button and make sure you're on the Association tab. The screen shown in Figure 7-30 appears.

Type a name for your network in the SSID box. At the bottom of the screen, check the box next to "This is a computer-to-computer (ad hoc) network; wireless access points are not used."

If you're not using encryption to protect the ad hoc network, choose Disabled from the "Data encryption" drop-down box. If you are going to use encryption, follow the instructions in "Enable WiFi Encryption" [Hack #69].

Click OK and then OK again. Your network is now set up. Even though you've set it up, it won't be visible to you. But it will be visible to people nearby, and they can easily connect to it.

On each PC that you want to connect to the network, right-click the Wireless Network icon in the system tray and choose View Available Wireless Networks. You should see the SSID of the network you've just set up. To connect to the network, just click the Connect button. Depending on how you've set up your PC's security, you can now share files, browse each other's hard disks, send messages, use each other's printers, and so on.

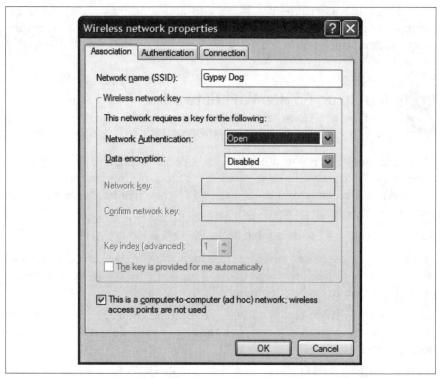

Figure 7-30. Getting an ad hoc network started

If for some reason another PC doesn't find your ad hoc network, you'll need to check that second computer's wireless settings. It might be set up to hide ad hoc networks. Double-click the Wireless Network icon in the system tray, click the Properties button, and then click the Wireless Networks tab. On that tab, click Advanced to display the dialog box shown in Figure 7-31. Make sure you haven't selected "Access Point (infrastructure) networks only." Then click Close. Now the network will show up.

Because there is no router for the network, there's no DHCP server, but all PCs on the network get temporary IP addresses called *link local addresses*, ranging from 169.254.0.0 through 169.254.0.16.

Bluetooth File Transfers

Bluetooth also allows you to set up ad hoc networks. In fact, by their very nature, Bluetooth connections are in essence ad hoc networks. So, every time you set up a Bluetooth connection, you're setting up an ad hoc network. For details, see "Set Up Bluetooth on XP" [Hack #72] and "Connect to the Internet with a Bluetooth Phone" [Hack #73].

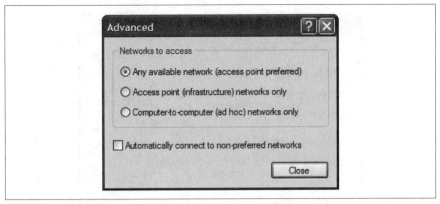

Figure 7-31. Deselecting "Access Point (infrastructure) networks only" to see any nearby ad hoc networks

To transfer files between two PCs with Bluetooth, first pair the PCs [Hack #73]. Then, from one PC, right-click the other paired PC and choose Discover Available Services. You'll see a file transfer icon. Double-click it. Depending on the security settings, you might be prompted to enter a PIN. If so, you'll use the same PIN on both PCs.

 Bluetooth is much slower than WiFi when it comes to file transfers—from 100Kbps to a maximum of 750Kbps, compared to up to 54Mbps for the 802.11g version of WiFi.

The other PC will now show up in My Bluetooth Places, and now you can navigate through it to transfer files from it to your PC.

Hacking the Hack

You can use an ad hoc network to share a single Internet connection among multiple users. In that case, the user that sets up the ad hoc network configures his PC to allow others to share his Internet connection. Then, when other PCs connect to the ad hoc network, they can get onto the Internet. Of course, to be able to do this, the PC has to have a live Internet connection, such as a broadband cable modem or DSL modem connection.

On the PC that set up the ad hoc network, right-click My Network Places and choose Properties. The Network Connections dialog box appears. Right-click the wireless connection and choose Properties. Click the Advanced tab to bring up the dialog box shown in Figure 7-32.

Check the box next to "Allow other network users to connect through this computer's Internet connection" and click OK. Don't check the box next to

Set Up an Ad Hoc WiFi Network

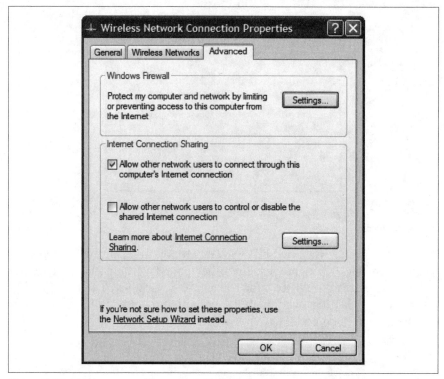

Figure 7-32. Sharing your ad hoc network's Internet connection with others

"Allow other network users to control or disable the shared Internet connection," unless you want to give them that kind of control over the connection. Then click OK again.

If you have servers or network services on your PC that you want to give others access to, such as FTP servers and mail servers, click the Settings button and put checks next to each server or service. Then click OK and OK again.

When you do all this, your PC will function like a DHCP server and hand out private network addresses to the other PCs accessing the Internet. In essence, you're turning your PC into a wireless router.

Security
Hacks 75–82

From the moment you turn on your PC and connect to the Internet or a network, you're in danger. Snoopers and intruders might try to get into your system; crackers might try to install Trojans to take control of your computer or turn it into a *zombie* and use it to launch attacks against other PCs or web sites. Day by day, the Internet and networks become increasingly dangerous places to be.

The hacks in this chapter, though, show you how you can use the Internet and networks and still be safe. You'll learn how to hide files and folders using encryption, how to test your PC's vulnerabilities, how to use firewalls to harden your PC against attacks, and more.

 Hide Folders and Files with the Encrypting File
#75 System

Protect all the information on your PC from prying eyes using XP
Professional's built-in encryption scheme.

If you have Windows XP Pro, you can use the Encrypting File System (EFS) to encrypt your files so that no one else can read them.

 Home Edition users won't be pleased to know that EFS isn't
available for Windows XP home users.

EFS lets you encrypt only the files and folders of your choice; you can encrypt a single file or folder or all your files and folders. Encrypted files and folders show up in Windows Explorer in green, so you can tell at a glance which have been encrypted. You can work with encrypted files and folders transparently. In other words, after you encrypt them, you open and close them as you normally would any other file. They're decrypted on the fly as you open them, and then decrypted as you close them. You're the only person who can read or use the files. Encryption is tied to your account name, so even other accounts on the same computer won't be able to read or use them, unless you specifically grant access to certain accounts.

> Each time you encrypt a file, EFS generates a random number for that file called the file encryption key (FEK). EFS uses that FEK to encrypt the file's contents with a variant of the Data Encryption Standard (DES) algorithm, called DESX. (DESX features more powerful encryption than DES.) The FEK itself is encrypted as well using RSA public key-based encryption.

EFS does have a few minor limitations you should be aware of:

- EFS works only on NTFS volumes. If you have a FAT or FAT32 volume, you'll have to convert it to NTFS **[Hack #30]** if you want to use EFS.

- EFS won't work on compressed files. You'll have to decompress them if you want to encrypt them. Similarly, if you want to compress an encrypted file, you'll have to decrypt it.

- EFS can't encrypt files in the *C:\Windows* folder or any files marked with the System attribute.

When you work with encrypted files and folders, they seem to behave like any other files on your hard disk. In fact, though, their behavior is somewhat different, and you might notice files you thought were encrypted suddenly become decrypted for no apparent reason. So, before you turn on encryption, you should understand the common actions you can take with encrypted files and folders, and what the results will be. Table 8-1 lists what you need to know.

Table 8-1. How encrypted files and folders behave

Action	Result
Move or copy unencrypted files into an encrypted folder.	The files are automatically encrypted.
Move or copy encrypted files from an encrypted folder to an unencrypted folder.	The files remain encrypted.
Move or copy encrypted files from an encrypted folder to a non-NTFS volume.	The files are decrypted, though first you are given a warning and a chance to cancel the move or copy operation.
Back up files using XP's backup utility.	The backed-up files and folders remain encrypted.

Table 8-1. How encrypted files and folders behave (continued)

Action	Result
Rename an encrypted file.	The file remains encrypted after it is renamed.
Delete an encrypted file.	The restorable file in the Recycle Bin remains encrypted.

Encrypting Files and Folders

To encrypt a file or folder, right-click the file or folder and choose Properties → General → Advanced. The Advanced Attributes dialog box appears, as shown in Figure 8-1.

> If no Advanced button appears on the Properties dialog box, it means you aren't using NTFS, so you can't use encryption.

Figure 8-1. Encrypting files or folders using the Advanced Attributes dialog box

Check the box next to "Encrypt contents to secure data." Note that you can't check both this box and the "Compress contents to save disk space" box. You can either compress the item or encrypt it, but not both.

Click OK and then OK again. If you're encrypting a folder, the Confirm Attributes Changes dialog box appears, as shown in Figure 8-2. You have a choice of encrypting the folder only, or encrypting the folder plus all subfolders and all the files in the folder and subfolders. If you encrypt the folder only, none of the files currently in the folder will be encrypted, but any new files you create, move, or copy into the folder will be encrypted.

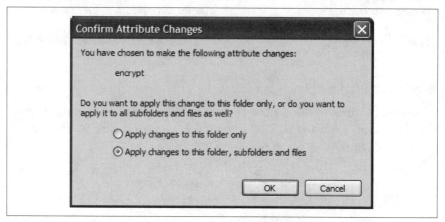

Figure 8-2. Encrypting the folder only, or all the subfolders and files as well

If you're encrypting a file in an unencrypted folder, the Encryption Warning box will appear, as shown in Figure 8-3. You have the choice of encrypting the file only, or the file and the parent folder. As a general rule, you should encrypt the folder as well as the file because if you encrypt only the file, you might accidentally decrypt it without realizing it. Some applications save copies of your files and delete the original; in those instances, the files become decrypted simply by editing them. If you encrypt the folder as well, all files added to the folder are encrypted, so the saved file is automatically encrypted. Click OK after you make your choice.

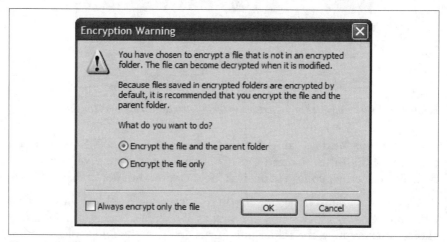

Figure 8-3. Encrypting the parent folder as well as the file

Note that you won't be able to encrypt every file on your system. Files that have the System attribute, as well as files located in *C:\Windows* and its sub-folders, can't be encrypted.

Decrypting Files and Folders

You decrypt files and folders in the same way that you encrypt them. Right-click the file or folder, choose Properties → General → Advanced, clear the check from the box next to "Encrypt contents to secure data," and click OK and then OK again.

Letting Others Use Your Encrypted Files

When you encrypt files, you can still share them with others and let them use them as if they were not encrypted—a process that XP defines as *transparent*. You'll be able to share them this way only with other users on the same computer or with others on your network. You designate who can use the files and who can't. To allow specified people to use your encrypted files, right-click an unencrypted file and choose Properties → General → Advanced. The Advanced Attributes dialog box appears. Click Details. The Encryption Details dialog box appears, as shown in Figure 8-4. It lists all the users who are allowed to use the file transparently. Click Add.

The Select User dialog box appears. Choose the user you want to be able to use your encrypted files, and click OK. Only users who have Encrypting File System certificates on the computer will show up on this list. The easiest way for someone to create a certificate is to encrypt any file; that automatically creates a certificate.

Encrypting and Decrypting from the Command Line

If you prefer the command line to a graphical interface, you can encrypt and decrypt using the *cipher.exe* command-line tool. To find out the current state of encryption of the directory you're in, type cipher without parameters at a command prompt. cipher tells you the state of the directory. For individual files, it lists a U next to files that are not encrypted, and an E next to those that are encrypted.

When used with parameters, cipher can encrypt and decrypt files and folders, show encryption information, create new encryption keys, and generate a recovery agent key and certificate.

To encrypt or decrypt a folder or file, use the complete path, filename (if you're acting on a file), and any appropriate switches, as outlined in

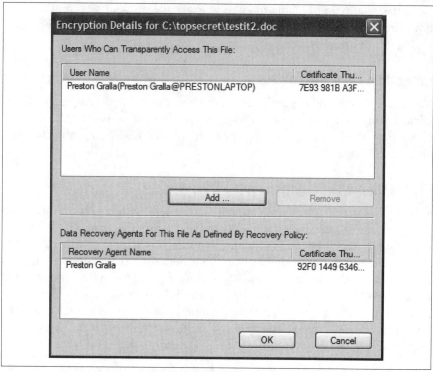

Figure 8-4. The Encryption Details dialog box

Table 8-2. The /E switch encrypts folders or files, and the /D switch decrypts them. To perform the task on multiple folders or files, separate them with single spaces. For example, to encrypt the *Secret* and *Topsecret* folders, issue this command:

```
cipher /E \Secret \Topsecret
```

Note that you can use wildcards with the cipher command. Using the command line instead of the graphical interface is particularly useful for performing bulk or batch operations—for example, simultaneously encrypting or decrypting multiple folders or files, or types of files within folders. Let's say, for example, you want to encrypt every *.doc* file in the *Secret* and *Topsecret* folders, but not touch any other files in those folders. You issue this command:

```
cipher /E  /A \Secret\*.DOC  \Topsecret\*.DOC
```

Table 8-2 lists the most useful command-line switches for cipher. For more help, type cipher /? at the command line.

Table 8-2. Command-line switches for cipher

Switch	What it does
/A	Acts on individual files within folders.
/D	Decrypts the specified folder.
/E	Encrypts the specified folder.
/F	Forces encryption on all specified objects, including those that have already been encrypted.
/H	Displays all files in a folder, including those that have hidden or system attributes. By default, hidden or system attributes are not displayed when using the cipher command.
/I	Continues to perform the specified operation, even if errors are encountered. By default, cipher halts when errors are encountered.
/K	Creates a new file encryption key for the user running cipher. If this option is chosen, all the other options will be ignored.
/R	Generates an EFS recovery agent key and certificate, then writes them to a *.pfx* file (containing the certificate and a private key) and a *.cer* file (containing only the certificate).
/S	Performs the operation on the folder and all its subfolders.
/U	Updates the user's file encryption key or recovery agent's key on every encrypted file.
/U /N	Lists every encrypted file and does not update the user's file encryption key or recovery agent's key.
/Q	Lists only basic information about the file or folder.
/W	Wipes data from available, unused disk space on the drive. Normally, when a file is deleted in XP, only the entry in the filesystem table is deleted; the data itself remains untouched until another file overwrites it. This switch deletes all the data in those previously deleted files. It does not harm existing data.

Test Your Security with Shields UP!

HACK #76

Head to this web site for a thorough, free check of your PC's vulnerabilities.

Do you *really* know how secure your PC is from intruders? Probably not. But there's a free online tool that will probe your PC for online security vulnerabilities and report to you on the results.

The Shields UP! site is run by the Gibson Research Corporation, and it tests your machine, trying to make connections to a handful of the most well-known and vulnerable Internet ports on your PC. The site runs two tests, reports to you on the results, and then explains what the reports mean—where you're vulnerable and how serious those vulnerabilities are. It also has a great deal of useful information about Internet security, as well as free and for-pay security software you can download. Visit the site at *http://www.grc.com*. You might have to do some clicking around to find the tests, but keep clicking Shields UP! and you'll eventually get there.

The best use for the site is to test your PC's vulnerabilities, then install a firewall [Hacks #77 and #78] and see the results of what you've done. It'll tell you whether there are any remaining vulnerabilities you need to fix. Figure 8-5 shows the results of a probe of a PC without a firewall. It's relatively secure, but could be more secure because the site has found ports, even though they're closed. Figure 8-6 shows that the PC is operating in "stealth mode" after the installation of the firewall—the PC doesn't even appear to exist.

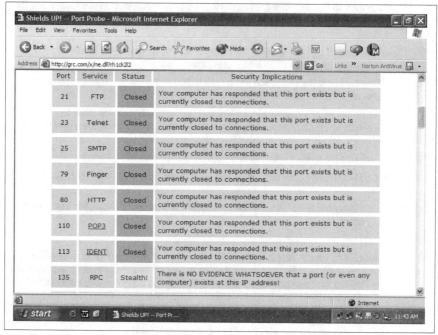

Figure 8-5. The security report on a PC before installing a firewall

Protect Your Computer with the New Windows Firewall
HACK #77

XP SP2 turns on the Windows Firewall by default, so you're automatically protected from incoming attacks. Here's how to configure the Windows Firewall for maximum protection and flexibility and use it to log potential attacks and send information about the intruders to your ISP.

The moment you connect to the Internet, you're in some danger of intrusion, especially if you have a broadband connection. PCs with broadband connections are tempting targets because their high-speed connections are ideal springboards for attacking other networks or web sites.

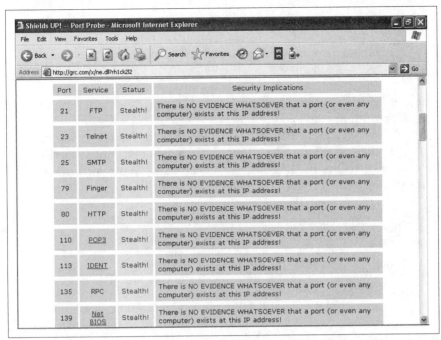

The following table appears in the image:

Port	Service	Status	Security Implications
21	FTP	Stealth!	There is NO EVIDENCE WHATSOEVER that a port (or even any computer) exists at this IP address!
23	Telnet	Stealth!	There is NO EVIDENCE WHATSOEVER that a port (or even any computer) exists at this IP address!
25	SMTP	Stealth!	There is NO EVIDENCE WHATSOEVER that a port (or even any computer) exists at this IP address!
79	Finger	Stealth!	There is NO EVIDENCE WHATSOEVER that a port (or even any computer) exists at this IP address!
80	HTTP	Stealth!	There is NO EVIDENCE WHATSOEVER that a port (or even any computer) exists at this IP address!
110	POP3	Stealth!	There is NO EVIDENCE WHATSOEVER that a port (or even any computer) exists at this IP address!
113	IDENT	Stealth!	There is NO EVIDENCE WHATSOEVER that a port (or even any computer) exists at this IP address!
135	RPC	Stealth!	There is NO EVIDENCE WHATSOEVER that a port (or even any computer) exists at this IP address!
139	Net BIOS	Stealth!	There is NO EVIDENCE WHATSOEVER that a port (or even any computer) exists at this IP address!

Figure 8-6. The security report on a PC after installing a firewall

Whenever you're connected, your system is among many constantly being scanned for weaknesses by *crackers* (malicious hackers) and wannabes (often called *script kiddies*) sending automated probes looking for vulnerable PCs. In fact, these kinds of probes are so common and incessant, you can think of them as the background radiation of the Internet.

One of the best ways to protect yourself against these probes and more targeted attacks is to use a *firewall*. Firewall software sits between you and the Internet and acts as a gatekeeper of sorts, only allowing nonmalicious traffic through.

If you have a home network, your router might offer firewall protection. For details on how to optimize that protection and get the most out of other router features, see "Optimize Your Home Router" [Hack #50] and "Protect Your Home WiFi Network" [Hack #68].

In this hack, we'll look at how to get the most out of the Windows Firewall, the firewall built into XP SP2, which is turned on by default when you install SP2.

Before SP2, the firewall was called the Internet Connection Firewall (ICF). It was much the same as the Windows Firewall although with some differences, notably in how you access the firewall and its features.

The Windows Firewall offers basic Internet security by stopping all unsolicited inbound traffic and connections to your PC and network, unless your PC or another PC on the network initially makes the request for the connection. However, it will not block outgoing requests and connections, so you can continue to use the Internet as you normally would for browsing the Web, getting email, using FTP, or similar services.

If you use the Windows Firewall or another type of firewall, you can run into problems if you run a web server or an FTP server, or if you want to allow Telnet access to your PC. Because firewalls block unsolicited inbound communications, visitors won't be able to get to your sites or get Telnet access to your PC. However, you can allow access to these resources, while still retaining firewall protection [Hack #80].

If you're sharing an Internet connection through a PC, only the PC that directly accesses the Internet should run the Windows Firewall. All the other PCs will be protected. Don't run the Windows Firewall on any of those other PCs because you'll cause connection problems. And don't use the Windows Firewall with a Virtual Private Network (VPN) [Hack #82] connection because it will interfere with various VPN functions, including file sharing.

The Windows Firewall has one serious drawback: it won't protect you against Trojans, such as the Back Orifice Trojan. *Trojans* let other users take complete control of your PC and its resources. For example, someone could use your PC as a launch pad for attacking web sites and it would appear you were the culprit, or he could copy all your files and find out personal information about you, such as your credit card numbers if you store them on your PC.

The Windows Firewall won't stop Trojans because it blocks only incoming traffic, and Trojans work by making outbound connections from your PC. To stop Trojans, get a third-party firewall. The best is ZoneAlarm [Hack #78].

When you install XP SP2, you're automatically protected because it turns on the Windows Firewall. There's a chance, though, that the firewall has been turned off. To make sure it's turned on, click Security Center from the Control Panel. When the Security Center appears, there should be a green light next to the Firewall button, and it should say ON, as shown in Figure 8-7.

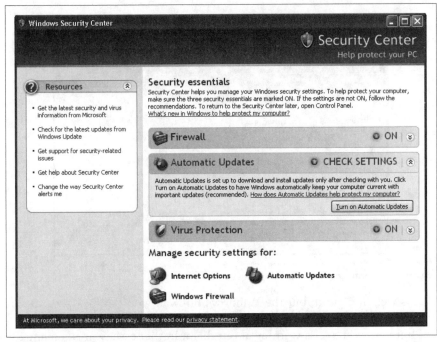

Figure 8-7. Making sure the Windows Firewall is turned on

If it's not on, click the Windows Firewall icon at the bottom of the screen, click ON, and then click OK.

Allow Programs to Bypass the Firewall

The Windows Firewall offers protection from inbound threats, but it can also cause problems. A variety of software needs to be able to accept inbound connections, so the firewall blocks them from working. Instant messaging programs and FTP programs, for example, both need to be able to accept these kinds of connections, and the Windows Firewall blocks them.

Usually, but not always, the first time you run one of these programs, you'll get the warning from the Windows Firewall shown in Figure 8-8. The warning will show you the name of the program and the publisher and will ask if you want to keep blocking the program. If you'd like to allow the Windows Firewall to let the program function, click Unblock. To keep blocking the program, click Keep Blocking. As for the Ask Me Later choice, it doesn't really ask you later. It lets the program accept incoming connections for just this one time when you run it. After you exit, the next time you run the program, you'll get the same warning.

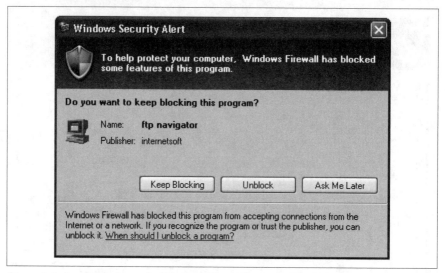

Figure 8-8. A warning from the Windows Firewall

That's well and good, but the Windows Firewall won't always pop up this alert. So, you might find that some programs don't work with the firewall on, but you won't get a warning about them. In that case, you can manually tell the Windows Firewall to let it through by adding programs to its exceptions list.

To do so, choose Control Panel → Security Center → Windows Firewall. Then, click the Exceptions tab, shown in Figure 8-9. This tab lists all the programs for which the firewall will accept inbound connections. If a program is listed here but doesn't have a check next to it, it means the firewall blocks it. To tell the firewall to stop blocking inbound connections for the program, check the box next to it and click OK.

> When you get a warning from the Windows Firewall and click Ask Me Later, the program will be listed on the Exceptions tab, with no check next to it.

To add a program to the exceptions list, click Add Program to bring up the window shown in Figure 8-10. Choose a program from the list and click OK, and then click OK again to add it to your list. If the program you want to add isn't listed in the Add a Program dialog box, click the Browse button to find it and then add it.

There might be some programs for which you want to grant access to only certain people and not others. Maybe, for example, you want to allow an

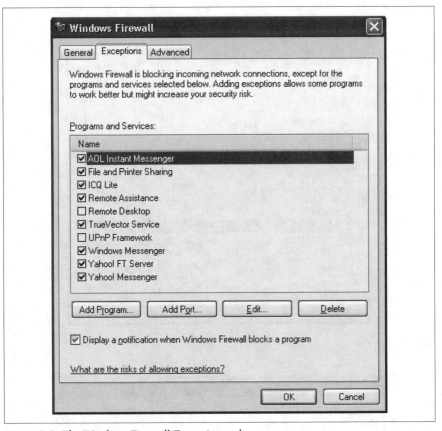

Figure 8-9. The Windows Firewall Exceptions tab

instant messenger program to work only with people on your own network. There's a way to do that.

First, add the program to the exceptions list. Then, highlight the program and click Edit → Change Scope. The Change Scope dialog box appears, as shown in Figure 8-11. Choose "My Network (subnet) only," click OK and then OK again, and the firewall will let only inbound connections from your network. To allow inbound connections for the program for only specific IP addresses, choose "Custom list," type in the IP addresses you want to allow, and then click OK and OK again.

> If you want to allow inbound connections to any servers on your system, such as web servers, or if you want to open up specific ports in the firewall, see "Punch an Escape Hole Through Your Firewall" [Hack #80].

Figure 8-10. Choosing a program to add to your exceptions list

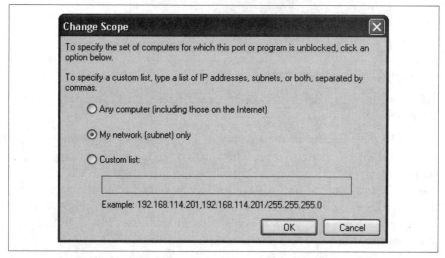

Figure 8-11. Granting access to your network to specific people only

Track Firewall Activity with a Windows Firewall Log

The Windows Firewall can do more than just protect you from intruders; it can also keep track of all intrusion attempts so that you can know whether

your PC has been targeted, and what kinds of attacks the Windows Firewall
has turned back. Then you can send that information to your ISP so that it
can track down the intruders.

> If you have a home network, you can get add-on software
> that will automatically log all intrusion attempts and help
> you track down intruders as well **[Hack #68]**.

First, create a Windows Firewall log. From the Security Center, choose Windows Firewall → Advanced, and click the Settings button in the Security
Logging section. The dialog box shown in Figure 8-12 appears.

Figure 8-12. Creating a Windows Firewall log

Choose whether to log dropped packets, successful connections, or both. A
dropped packet is a packet that the Windows Firewall has blocked. A successful connection doesn't mean an intruder has successfully connected to
your PC; it refers to any connection *you* have made over the Internet, such
as to web sites. Because of this, there's usually no reason for you to log successful connections. If you do log them, your log will become large quickly,
and it will be more difficult to track only potentially dangerous activity. So,
your best bet is to log only dropped packets.

After you've made your choices, choose a location for the log, set its maximum size, and click OK. I don't let my log get larger than 1MB, but depending on how much you care about disk space and how much you plan to use
the log, you might want yours larger or smaller.

The log will be created in a W3C Extended Log format (*.log*) that you can examine with Notepad or another text editor or by using a log analysis program such as the free AWStats (*http://awstats.sourceforge.net*). Figure 8-13 shows a log generated by the Windows Firewall, examined in Notepad.

```
pfirewall.log - Notepad
File  Edit  Format  View  Help
#Verson: 1.0
#Software: Microsoft Internet Connection Firewall
#Time Format: Local
#Fields: date time action protocol src-ip dst-ip src-port dst-port size tcpflags tcpsyn tcpack tc

2002-12-22 11:43:35 DROP UDP 192.168.1.106 239.255.255.250 1900 1900 424 - - - - - - -
2002-12-22 11:43:35 DROP UDP 192.168.1.104 239.255.255.250 1900 1900 430 - - - - - - -
2002-12-22 11:43:35 DROP UDP 192.168.1.106 239.255.255.250 1900 1900 385 - - - - - - -
2002-12-22 11:43:35 DROP UDP 192.168.1.104 239.255.255.250 1900 1900 430 - - - - - - -
2002-12-22 11:43:35 DROP UDP 192.168.1.104 239.255.255.250 1900 1900 448 - - - - - - -
2002-12-22 11:43:35 DROP UDP 192.168.1.106 239.255.255.250 1900 1900 448 - - - - - - -
2002-12-22 11:43:35 DROP UDP 192.168.1.104 239.255.255.250 1900 1900 385 - - - - - - -
2002-12-22 11:43:35 DROP UDP 192.168.1.106 239.255.255.250 1900 1900 385 - - - - - - -
2002-12-22 11:43:35 DROP UDP 192.168.1.104 239.255.255.250 1900 1900 376 - - - - - - -
2002-12-22 11:43:35 DROP UDP 192.168.1.106 239.255.255.250 1900 1900 376 - - - - - - -
2002-12-22 11:43:38 DROP TCP 207.46.248.249 192.168.1.104 80 3218 40 R 4247099263 2102237511 0 -
2002-12-22 11:43:40 OPEN UDP 192.168.1.104 204.127.202.19 1026 53 - - - - - - - -
2002-12-22 11:43:40 OPEN TCP 192.168.1.104 206.16.6.252 3221 80 - - - - - - - -
2002-12-22 11:43:41 OPEN TCP 192.168.1.104 206.16.0.136 3222 80 - - - - - - - -
2002-12-22 11:43:41 OPEN TCP 192.168.1.104 206.16.0.45 3223 80 - - - - - - - -
2002-12-22 11:43:41 OPEN TCP 192.168.1.104 206.16.0.45 3224 80 - - - - - - - -
2002-12-22 11:43:41 OPEN TCP 192.168.1.104 209.249.123.229 3225 80 - - - - - - - -
2002-12-22 11:43:42 OPEN TCP 192.168.1.104 209.249.123.229 3226 80 - - - - - - - -
2002-12-22 11:43:43 OPEN TCP 192.168.1.104 216.239.39.102 3227 80 - - - - - - - -
2002-12-22 11:43:43 OPEN TCP 192.168.1.104 209.249.123.229 3228 80 - - - - - - - -
2002-12-22 11:43:43 OPEN TCP 192.168.1.104 209.249.123.229 3229 80 - - - - - - - -
2002-12-22 11:43:43 OPEN TCP 192.168.1.104 206.16.0.45 3230 80 - - - - - - - -
2002-12-22 11:43:43 OPEN TCP 192.168.1.104 206.16.0.45 3231 80 - - - - - - - -
2002-12-22 11:43:43 OPEN TCP 192.168.1.104 206.16.0.45 3232 80 - - - - - - - -
2002-12-22 11:43:43 OPEN TCP 192.168.1.104 206.16.0.45 3233 80 - - - - - - - -
2002-12-22 11:43:43 OPEN TCP 192.168.1.104 206.16.0.147 3234 80 - - - - - - - -
2002-12-22 11:43:43 OPEN TCP 192.168.1.104 206.16.0.147 3235 80 - - - - - - - -
2002-12-22 11:43:43 OPEN TCP 192.168.1.104 206.16.0.45 3236 80 - - - - - - - -
2002-12-22 11:43:43 OPEN TCP 192.168.1.104 206.16.0.45 3237 80 - - - - - - - -
2002-12-22 11:43:43 OPEN TCP 192.168.1.104 206.16.0.45 3238 80 - - - - - - - -
2002-12-22 11:43:43 OPEN TCP 192.168.1.104 206.16.0.45 3239 80 - - - - - - - -
2002-12-22 11:43:43 OPEN TCP 192.168.1.104 206.16.0.147 3240 80 - - - - - - - -
2002-12-22 11:43:43 OPEN TCP 192.168.1.104 206.16.0.45 3241 80 - - - - - - - -
2002-12-22 11:43:43 OPEN TCP 192.168.1.104 206.16.0.45 3242 80 - - - - - - - -
2002-12-22 11:43:43 OPEN TCP 192.168.1.104 206.16.0.45 3243 80 - - - - - - - -
```

Figure 8-13. A log generated by the Windows Firewall

Each log entry has a total of up to 16 pieces of information associated with each event, but the most important columns for each entry are the first eight.

> In a text editor, the names of the columns don't align over the data, but they will align in a log analyzer.

Table 8-3 describes the most important columns.

Table 8-3. The columns in the Windows Firewall log

Name	Description
Date	Date of occurrence, in *year-month-date* format
Time	Time of occurrence, in *hour:minute:second* format
Action	The operation that was logged by the firewall, such as DROP for dropping a connection, OPEN for opening a connection, and CLOSE for closing a connection

Table 8-3. The columns in the Windows Firewall log (continued)

Name	Description
Protocol	The protocol used, such as TCP, UDP, or ICMP
Source IP (src-ip)	The IP address of the computer that started the connection
Destination IP (dst-ip)	The IP address of the computer to which the connection was attempted
Source Port (src-port)	The port number on the sending computer from which the connection was attempted
Destination Port (dst-port)	The port to which the sending computer was trying to make a connection
size	The packet size
tcpflags	Information about TCP control flags in TCP headers
tcpsyn	The TCP sequence of a packet
tcpack	The TCP acknowledgment number in the packet
tcpwin	The TCP window size of the packet
icmtype	Information about the ICMP messages
icmcode	Information about the ICMP messages
info	Information about an entry in the log

The source IP address is the source of the attack. You might notice the same source IP address continually cropping up; if so, you might have been targeted by an intruder. It's also possible that the intruder is sending out automated probes to thousands of PCs across the Internet and your PC is not under direct attack. In either case, you can send the log information to your ISP and ask them to follow up by tracking down the source of the attempts. Either forward the entire log or cut and paste the relevant sections to a new file.

Watch Out for Problems with Email and the Windows Firewall

Depending on the email program you use and how it gets notification of new email, the Windows Firewall could interfere with the way you retrieve your email. It won't stop you from getting your email, but it could disable your email program's notification feature.

The Windows Firewall won't interfere with the normal notification feature of Outlook Express because the initial request asking for notification of new email comes from Outlook Express, which is inside the firewall. When the server responds to the request, the firewall recognizes that the server is responding to the request from Outlook Express, so it lets the communication pass through.

However, if you use Outlook and connect to a Microsoft Exchange server using a remote procedure call (RPC) to send email notifications (which is usually the case with Exchange), you'll run into problems. That's because the RPC initially comes from the server, not from Outlook, so the firewall doesn't allow the notification to pass to you. In this case, you can still retrieve your email, but you'll have to check for new email manually; you won't be able to get automatic notification from the server. So, if you don't get new mail notifications after you install the Windows Firewall, it's not that co-workers, friends, and spammers are suddenly ignoring you; you'll just have to check for new mail manually.

Hacking the Hack

The Windows Firewall Exceptions tab is especially useful for anyone who uses file sharing on a home or corporate network but wants to turn file sharing off when they're on a public network connection, such as a WiFi hotspot. When you get to a hotspot, before connecting, go to the tab, uncheck the box next to File and Printer Sharing, and click OK. File sharing will be turned off. Then, when you get back to your home or business network, turn it back on again.

See Also

- For more information about the Windows Firewall, see Microsoft Knowledge Base Article 875357 (*http://support.microsoft.com/kb/875357*).
- "ZoneAlarm: The World's Best Free Firewall" [Hack #78]
- "Optimize Your Home Router" [Hack #50]
- "Protect Your Home WiFi Network" [Hack #68]
- "Punch an Escape Hole Through Your Firewall" [Hack #80]

H A C K   ZoneAlarm: The World's Best Free Firewall
#78
For the best protection, get this firewall, which is far superior to XP's Windows Firewall and keeps you safe from Trojan horses and other dangers.

The Windows Firewall that ships with XP has one very serious deficiency: it can't monitor and block outbound traffic from your PC to the Internet. Many Trojan horses do their damage by installing themselves on your system and then allowing others to take control of your PC, or by using your PC to attack web sites, servers, and other computers. The Windows Firewall won't offer you protection against these types of Trojans; it won't be able to tell when a Trojan is making an outbound connection, so the Trojan will be able to do its damage without your knowledge.

Other firewalls, however, will offer that protection. The best of them is ZoneAlarm (*http://www.zonealarm.com*). There are four versions of the program, a free version and three for-pay versions with differing levels of protection. The free version offers excellent protection against inbound threats as well as against Trojans. It also tells you whenever someone is probing your computer for security holes and gives information about the prober, often including his IP address and the nature of the probe.

ZoneAlarm with Antivirus, which sells for $24.95 for a year's subscription, adds virus and worm protection to the free firewall features. ZoneAlarm Pro, which sells for $49.95 for a year's subscription, doesn't offer worm and virus protection, but does improve on the free version's protection features, blocks pop ups and cookies, stops personal information from being sent from your computer over the Internet, and does better tracking and reporting about those who might have tried to attack your PC. ZoneAlarm Security Suite, which sells for $69.95 for a year's subscription, does everything the antivirus, free, and Pro versions do, and also protects against instant messaging dangers, protects against phishing attacks, kills spam, and adds other features as well. At a minimum, try ZoneAlarm because, well, it's free. If you feel you need more protection, you can go with a for-pay version. I've been using the free version for several years and have never felt the need to go to the paid version. Figure 8-14 shows a record of activity that ZoneAlarm Pro has monitored and blocked.

Configuring ZoneAlarm to Block Trojans

The most important feature of ZoneAlarm is its ability to block outgoing traffic from your PC. That way, you can be sure a Trojan hasn't infected your PC and can't "call out" to make contact with someone malicious, or be used to attack others from your PC. All versions of ZoneAlarm, the free as well as the for-pay, offer this protection. Since that's the most important feature, that's what's covered in most of this hack.

After you install ZoneAlarm, click Firewall in the left panel and you'll get to choose the level of protection (from Low to High) you want for the Internet Zone and the Trusted Security Zone (for computers on your network, or that you trust for some other reason). The settings are self-explanatory.

When you start using ZoneAlarm, alerts, such as the one shown in Figure 8-15, will start popping up every time a program attempts to make a connection to the Internet. It will most likely be a program you are familiar with, such as Internet Explorer, Outlook Express, or a similar program. If

Figure 8-14. Activity that ZoneAlarm has monitored and blocked

it's a program you're familiar with and you want the program to always be able to access the Internet, click the box that reads "Remember this answer the next time I use this program," and then click Yes to let the program access the Internet.

If it's a program you're unfamiliar with, or if you have no idea why it would be connecting to the Internet, click More Info. You might be asked whether you want to allow your browser to access the Internet. Click Yes, and you'll be sent to ZoneAlarm's site, which will offer some basic information about the alert. The general rule, though, is to allow only programs you are familiar with to access the Internet. If you've just launched a program that requires Internet access and you get the alert, let the program access the Internet. Or, you might want to let a program you've just installed contact the maker's web site for automatic updates and patches, if you like that sort of thing. But if the alert pops up for no reason at a random time and you're unfamiliar with the program, you should deny it access. You should also immediately run an antivirus program to see whether it can detect a Trojan.

If you allow the program to access the Internet, and you check the box so that you're not alerted next time, it will always be able to access the Internet. If you want to always be alerted when the program tries to access the Internet, don't check the box.

Figure 8-15. A ZoneAlarm warning

After you designate a program as always being allowed to access the Internet, it will be put onto a list that ZoneAlarm maintains about trusted programs. You can customize any program on that list, take programs off the list, or customize their security settings. To do this, click Program Control in ZoneAlarm's left panel, and click the Programs tab. You'll see a screen similar to Figure 8-16.

Use this screen to customize how you'll allow each program to access the Internet. By inserting a check mark in the appropriate column, you can choose whether to allow the program to access the Internet or Trusted Zone, whether you want it to act as a server in the Internet or Trusted Zone, and similar features. A check mark means the program is allowed to access the Internet; an X means it's not allowed to access the Internet; and a ? means it should ask before being allowed to access the Internet.

See Also

- "Kill Spyware and Web Bugs" [Hack #34]
- "Take a Bite Out of Cookies" [Hack #35]
- "Surf Anonymously Without a Trace" [Hack #36]
- "Punch an Escape Hole Through Your Firewall" [Hack #80]

Figure 8-16. Customizing the way a program can access the Internet

Use a Proxy Server to Protect Your PC

HACK #79

Many private businesses protect their networks with proxy servers. But you can get the same kind of protection at home—for free—without buying any new hardware.

Proxy servers protect your PC by offering a kind of relay protection. When you use a proxy server, Internet Explorer contacts the proxy instead of the web site. The proxy delivers the page to you if the page is in its cache. If the page is not in its cache, it contacts the site, grabs the page, and then delivers the page to you. In this way, you never directly contact a web site or other Internet location; instead, the proxy server does, so it, rather than you, will be the target of attack or privacy invasion by the site. Proxy servers can be configured for any kind of Internet access, not just web browsing.

Some businesses use proxy servers as part of corporate-wide security precautions, and if you work at such a business, your work PC has been specifically set up to use those servers. But even if you are not at a business with a proxy server you can still use one to protect your PC. You won't have to set up and run the proxy server yourself; instead, you can use one of the many free ones available on the Internet.

Setting up a proxy server in this way is a two-step process. First, find a free, public proxy server. Then, set up your PC to use it. To find a free, public proxy server, go to the Stay Invisible web site (*http://www.stayinvisible.com*) and click View Proxies. The site lists hundreds of free, public proxies from around the world and updates the list daily, as shown in Figure 8-17.

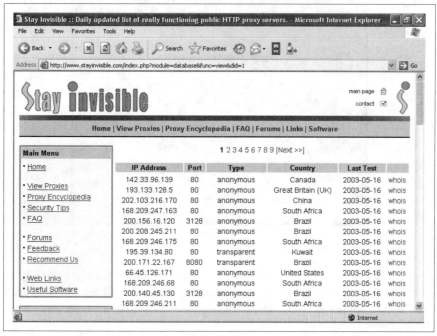

Figure 8-17. Stay Invisible's list of free public proxy servers around the world

Choose a proxy server from the list, and copy down its IP address and port number. If you want to double-check that the server is functioning, go to the Check Your Proxy section on the left side of the web page, type its IP address and port number, and click Check. If the server is functioning, a page will pop up with the server's IP address and name (often, the name is the same as the IP address). If the server is not functioning, you'll get a message telling you the connection can't be made.

Once you've confirmed a working proxy server and copied down its IP address and port number, it's time to configure Internet Explorer to use it. Open Internet Explorer, choose Tools → Internet Options → Connections, and click Settings if you use a dial-up connection and LAN Settings if you access the Internet using an always-on connection, such as over a LAN or via a cable modem or DSL modem. The options will be the same for both ways of access. Figure 8-18 shows the LAN Settings dialog box for configuring a proxy server.

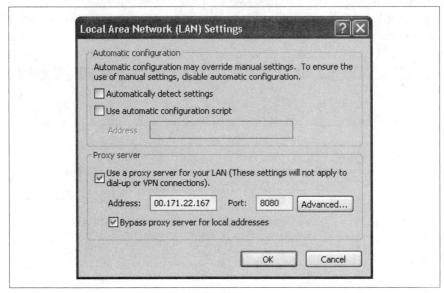

Figure 8-18. Configuring your proxy settings using the LAN Settings dialog box

Type in the address of the proxy server and its port number. For local domains, you need to use a proxy server because they will be secure. Check the "Bypass proxy server for local addresses" box if you know your local domain is secure.

If you're at work and the company uses separate proxy servers for different Internet services, such as FTP and Gopher, click the Advanced button. From there, you'll be able to fill in the specific information about proxy servers for each Internet service.

Hacking the Hack

If you have a reason for wanting to limit your PC to visiting only certain web sites and banning it from visiting any others—such as for a child's computer, which you want to have only very limited Internet access—you can hack the proxy server settings to accomplish that.

Go to the LAN Settings dialog box (shown in Figure 8-18), and enable use of a proxy server. Then, click the Advanced button and the Proxy Settings dialog screen appears, as shown in Figure 8-19.

For the HTTP entry, type in a word, such as nowhere, or type in an Internet address that doesn't exist. When you do this, you're telling Internet

Figure 8-19. Using the Proxy Settings dialog box to limit the web sites your PC can visit

Explorer to use a proxy server that isn't there. This effectively blocks access to the Internet because instead of going to a web site, Internet Explorer will go to a proxy server. But because the proxy server doesn't exist, your browser won't be able to visit any site.

Next, check the box next to "Use the same proxy server for all protocols." This will ensure that you're blocking Internet access for other services, such as FTP, not just for the Web.

Now you've effectively blocked access to the Internet for the PC. At this point you can enable a setting that will let the PC visit only specific web sites. In the Exceptions section, type the locations of the web sites you want to allow to be visited, separated by a semicolon. This Exceptions box tells Internet Explorer to bypass the proxy server for the listed sites, so it will go straight to those sites, bypassing the not-there proxy.

Once you put those settings into effect, whenever your PC tries to access the Web it will look for a proxy server that doesn't exist, so it won't be able to get onto the Internet. However, it will let you go to the web sites you've put in the Exceptions section.

See Also

- "Close Down Open Ports and Block Protocols" [Hack #81]
- "Test Your Security with Shields UP!" [Hack #76]
- "Surf Anonymously Without a Trace" [Hack #36]

HACK #80 Punch an Escape Hole Through Your Firewall

Sometimes, firewalls offer too much protection; they block unsolicited incoming traffic that you want to receive, such as if you're hosting a web site. Here's how to open a hole in your firewall to let only specific incoming traffic through.

Most firewalls block all unsolicited inbound traffic and connections, which can be a problem if you're running a web site, email or FTP server, or other service that requires you to accept unsolicited inbound packets. But you can punch a hole through your firewall to let only that traffic in, while still keeping potentially dangerous intruders out.

First, decide what kind of unsolicited inbound traffic and connections you want to let through, and then find out which ports they use. For example, if you have a web server, you'll have to allow traffic through that's bound for port 80. Table 5-1 [Hack #50] lists common ports; for a complete list, go to *http://www.iana.org/assignments/port-numbers*.

How you allow traffic through a firewall varies from firewall to firewall. To do it for XP's built-in Windows Firewall, from the Control Panel choose Security Center. (If a Security Center icon shows in the system tray, you can instead click that icon.) Then, click the Windows Firewall icon at the bottom of the screen. Click the Exceptions tab. The Windows Firewall Exceptions dialog box appears, as shown in Figure 8-20. To enable a service and allow its incoming traffic through the firewall, put a check next to the service you want to allow through and click OK.

> The Windows Firewall is built into SP2. If you have a version of Windows prior to SP2, it is called the Internet Connection Firewall (ICF). You configure it in the same general manner as you do the Windows Firewall.

For this screen, you won't have to know the port numbers for the services whose incoming traffic you want to let through; you just need to know which service you want to allow. XP will know to block or unblock the proper port.

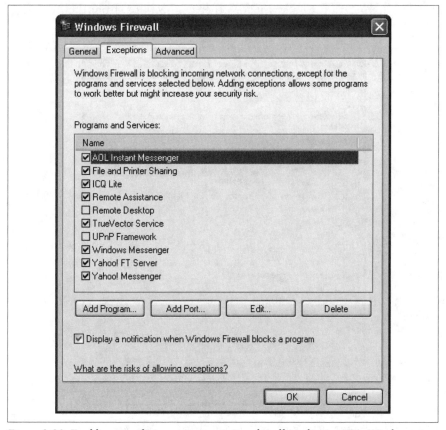

Figure 8-20. Enabling specific incoming services and traffic to bypass XP's Windows Firewall

You can easily add a new program to the Exceptions list to let it pass through the firewall [Hack #77].

In addition to programs that you allow through the firewall, you might also want to allow services through. For example, if you're running a web server, FTP server, or other server, or you have a VPN [Hack #82] that you want to allow others to use, you'll have to tell the firewall to let those requests through.

From the Control Panel, choose Security Center and click the Windows Firewall icon at the bottom of the screen. Click the Advanced tab, highlight the connection for which you want to allow the service through, and click Settings. Now, select the service you want to allow to pass through, as shown in Figure 8-21, and click OK and then OK again. That service will now be able to bypass the Windows Firewall for the connection you had selected. If you want to allow it for other connections, from the Advanced tab select a different connection and repeat the steps.

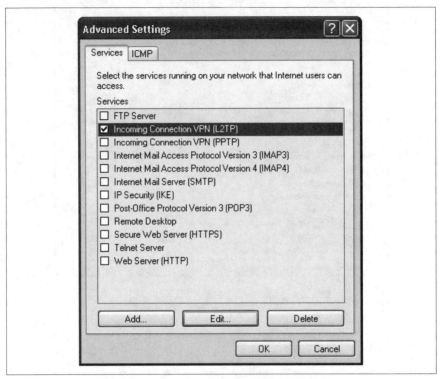

Figure 8-21. Choosing to let a service bypass the Windows Firewall

There's a chance the default settings for the services you want to allow don't work properly. If that's the case, you can edit them. Depending on the service, you can change the service's name or IP address, its description, the internal and external port numbers the service uses, and whether it uses the TCP or UDP protocol. For example, if your business uses a VPN with a different port number than the one used by the Windows Firewall, you can change the port number the Windows Firewall uses so that your VPN will work. Some services include hardcoded properties that you can't change, while others will let you edit them. For example, the Remote Desktop can use only 3389 for external and internal ports and TCP as its protocol, and those can't be edited. But a few of the services, notably the VPN connections, let you edit the ports and protocol.

To edit the properties for one of the services, select it and choose Edit, and you'll see the Service Settings screen, as shown in Figure 8-22.

Figure 8-22. Customizing an inbound service that you want to pass through the Windows Firewall

This process lets you select from a number of services that you want to bypass the Windows Firewall. Table 8-4 describes what each service does. Note that the entry msmsgs might or might not show up in your system; Windows Messenger appears if you've used Windows Messenger or Outlook Express (which uses some Messenger components). Unlike all the other services listed, it is enabled by default, so it can already bypass the Windows Firewall.

Table 8-4. Services that can be allowed to bypass the Windows Firewall

Service	What it does
FTP Server	Allows others to connect to an FTP server on your PC.
Incoming Connection VPN (L2TP)	Allows for the use of a Virtual Private Network using the L2TP tunneling technology.
Incoming Connection VPN (PPTP)	Allows for the use of a Virtual Private Network using the PPTP tunneling technology.
Internet Mail Access Protocol Version 3 (IMAP3)	Allows others to connect to an IMAP3 email server on your PC to retrieve email.
Internet Mail Access Protocol Version 3 (IMAP4)	Allows others to connect to an IMAP4 email server on your PC to retrieve email.
Internet Mail Server (SMTP)	Allows others to use an SMTP server on your PC for sending email.
IP Security (IKE)	Allows for the use of the Internet Key Exchange (IKE) security technology.

Table 8-4. Services that can be allowed to bypass the Windows Firewall (continued)

Service	What it does
Msmsgs	Allows for the use of Windows Messenger, plus any software that uses its components, such as Outlook Express.
Post-Office Protocol Version 3 (POP3)	Allows others to connect to a POP3 email server on your PC to retrieve email.
Remote Desktop	Allows others to connect to your PC and take control of your desktop using XP Professional's Remote Desktop feature. (Available in XP Professional only.)
Secure Web Server (HTTPS)	Allows others to connect to a web server on your PC that uses the HTTPS security protocol.
Telnet Server	Allows others to use a Telnet server on your PC to use your PC's resources.
Web Server (HTTP)	Allows others to connect to a web server on your PC.

Just because a service isn't listed in Table 5-1 [Hack #50] doesn't mean you can't allow its incoming traffic to bypass the Windows Firewall. You can add any service if you know its port information and the name or IP address of the PC on your network where you want the traffic routed. For example, to play some instant messenger games, you'll need to allow port 1077 to get through. To add a new service, get to the Advanced Settings dialog box shown in Figure 8-21. Then click the Add button and fill out the dialog box shown in Figure 8-23.

Figure 8-23. Adding a new service that can bypass the Windows Firewall

Fix the Windows Firewall's Disabling of File Sharing

When you use the Windows Firewall and try to browse to another computer on your network to share its files, you might get an error message and you won't be able to connect to those files. That's because the Windows Firewall closes the ports used for file sharing and server message block (SMB) communications. (SMB is used by the network to allow file and printer access.) You also might not be able to browse the Internet through My Network Places.

To allow file sharing to work across the network and to allow browsing the Internet through My Network Places, open UDP ports 135 through 139, TCP ports 135 through 139, and TCP and UDP port 445 in the Windows Firewall.

Allow Diagnostic Services to Bypass the Firewall

The Internet Control Message Protocol (ICMP) enables troubleshooting and diagnostic services, such as ping Troubleshoot Network Connections with ping, tracert, and pathping. By default, though, the Windows Firewall won't allow incoming ICMP traffic. You can allow various ICMP-enabled services to pass through your firewall by clicking the ICMP tab on the Advanced Settings dialog box shown in Figure 8-21. From the screen that appears, shown in Figure 8-24, check the boxes next to the services you want to allow. To get a description of each service, highlight it and read about it in the Description area.

Punch a Hole Through ZoneAlarm

If you use the ZoneAlarm firewall [Hack #78], you can also allow specific unsolicited incoming traffic through. Click Firewall on the left side of the screen, and then click Custom for each of your security zones. The Custom Firewall Settings dialog box appears, as shown in Figure 8-25. Click the service you want to allow through, click OK, and you'll be done.

See Also

- "ZoneAlarm: The World's Best Free Firewall" [Hack #78]

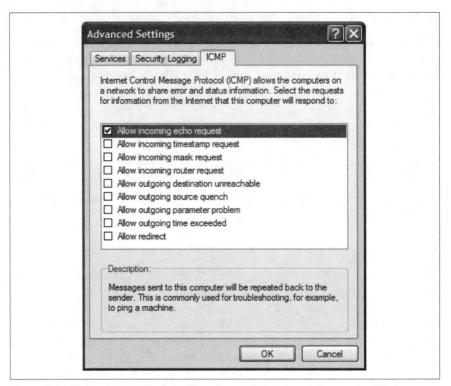

Figure 8-24. Using the ICMP tab to allow diagnostic services to bypass the Windows Firewall

Close Down Open Ports and Block Protocols

HACK
#81

You don't need a firewall to protect your PC; you can manually close down ports and block certain protocols.

As noted in "Protect Your Computer with the New Windows Firewall" [Hack #77] and "ZoneAlarm: The World's Best Free Firewall" [Hack #78], firewalls can protect your PC and your network from intruders. But if you don't want to use a firewall and you still want protection, you can manually close down ports and block protocols.

Some of these ports and protocols are more dangerous than others. For example, leaving open the port commonly used by Telnet (port 23) means someone could use that service to take control of your PC. And the infamous Back Orifice Trojan, which also can give malicious users complete control of your PC, uses a variety of ports, including 31337 and 31338, among others. For a list of which ports are used by Trojans, go to *http:// www.sans.org/resources/idfaq/oddports.php*.

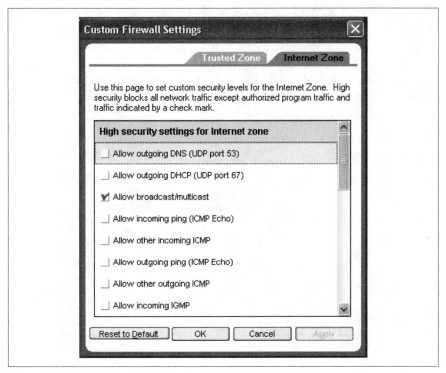

Figure 8-25. Allowing specific incoming traffic to bypass ZoneAlarm

In this hack, you'll need to know which ports you want to be open on your PC, such as port 80 for web browsing, and you'll close down all others. For a list of common ports, see Table 5-1 [Hack #50]. For a complete list of ports, go to *http://www.iana.org/assignments/port-numbers.*

To close down ports and protocols manually, right-click My Network Places and choose Properties to open the Network Connections folder. Right-click the connection for which you want to close ports and choose Properties. Highlight the Internet Protocol (TCP/IP) listing and choose Properties. On the General tab, click the Advanced button. Click the Options tab, highlight "TCP/IP filtering," and choose Properties. The TCP/IP Filtering dialog box appears. To block TCP ports, UDP ports, and IP protocols, choose the Permit Only option for each. Doing this will effectively block all TCP ports, UDP ports, and IP protocols.

You don't want to block all ports, though, so you have to add the ports you want to allow to pass—such as port 80 for web access. You need to keep port 80 open if you want to browse the Web. Click Add to add the ports or protocols you will allow to be used, as shown in Figure 8-26. Keep adding as many ports and protocols as you want to be enabled, and click OK when you're done. Only the ports and protocols that are listed will be allowed to be used.

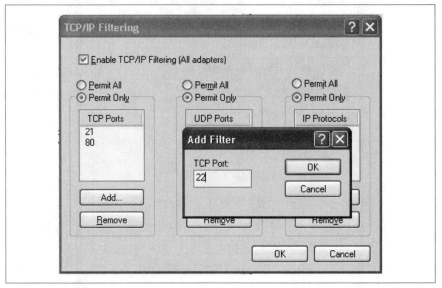

Figure 8-26. Blocking TCP ports, UDP ports, and IP protocols

Keep in mind that Internet applications and services use hundreds of TCP and UDP ports. If, for example, you enable only web access, you won't be able to use all other Internet resources, such as FTP, email, file sharing, listening to streaming audio, viewing streaming video, and so on. So, use this hack only if you want your PC to use a very limited number of Internet services and applications.

HACK #82 Set Up a Virtual Private Network

Sometimes you would like to connect to your home machine from work or while traveling. Making your home machine a virtual private network (VPN) server is a secure way to accomplish this.

If you've ever taken files home so that you can work on them on your personal computer, you've probably had the experience of arriving to work the next day only to realize you've forgotten to bring the files back with you. If the files were important enough, you probably had to drive all the way back home to get them, or you're had to make a lame excuse to your boss as to why you don't have the TPS report ready yet. Perhaps you're a road warrior who has found yourself stranded in a hotel room on a Monday morning, just hours before a big meeting, without that copy of the presentation you thought you had copied from your home machine. If either of these sounds like a situation you've been in, this is the hack for you.

It is well known that Windows XP has a VPN client built into it, which allows you to make secure connections to your company's network. Less well known is that Windows XP also has the ability to act as a VPN server, allowing you, or others you designate, to make secure connections into your home network. While you have an established VPN session with your home machine, you can access files from its hard drive or other machines on the network that have file sharing enabled. All you need is a local Internet connection and a VPN client that supports the Point to Point Tunneling Protocol (PPTP), which the client for all versions of Windows does.

Preparing your home machine to accept VPN connections is fairly straightforward. Click Start → Settings → Control Panel → Network and Internet Connections → Network Connections → Create a new connection. This will launch the New Connection Wizard. While advancing through this wizard, the options you want to enable are "Set up an advanced connection," "Accept Incoming Connections," and "Allow virtual private connections." The sixth screen of the wizard allows you to specify the users that can use the VPN; make sure you enable at least one account. If you haven't created a password for your user, now is the time to do so. You are essentially opening up a part of your machine to the Internet, so make sure you choose a good password. After the wizard is complete, nothing further needs to be done; the VPN is ready to accept incoming connections. You can test this by using a VPN client to connect to the IP address of the VPN server machine.

Most home users use a router that provides Network Address Translation (NAT), which obscures the actual IP address of the machine they want to make a VPN connection to. This means you won't be able to make a VPN connection to your machine until you configure your router to allow the VPN traffic to pass through to your VPN server [Hack #50].

CHAPTER NINE

The Registry
Hacks 83–87

When it comes to hacking XP, no other tool comes close to the Registry. It contains the underlying organization of the entire operating system, and its often-incomprehensible settings hold the key to countless hacks. In simpler days, one could hack Windows without bothering with the Registry; a solid knowledge of things like *.ini* files would suffice. But no longer. If you want to get hacking, the Registry holds the key—literally, since it's organized by way of keys.

Even if you've edited the Registry before, you'll find a lot in this chapter to help. It not only teaches the mechanics of using the Registry, but also explains its underlying organization. You'll find ways to keep your Registry safe, learn how to back it up, and find downloadable tools to make the most of the Registry. As a bonus, this chapter includes a grab bag of other great hacks.

HACK #83 Don't Fear the Registry

The Registry is the single best tool available for hacking XP. Here's an introduction to how it's organized and how to use it.

If you haven't spent much time in the Registry, you can easily be cowed by it. At first glance, it's a maze of apparently incomprehensible settings. In fact, though, there's a method to the madness. The Registry is a hierarchical database of information that defines exactly how your system works, including virtually every part of XP and its applications. Editing the Registry database is often the best way to hack XP. In fact, you can make many changes to the operating system in no other way.

Even if you've never used the Registry directly before, you've changed it without realizing it. Whenever you change a setting using the Control Panel, for example, behind the scenes a Registry change is made that puts that new setting into effect. The menus and dialog boxes you see in XP are often little more than a visual frontend to the Registry.

If you want to optimize XP and master every part of it, you'll have to use the Registry. XP contains so many different settings and customizations that it simply wasn't possible for Microsoft to build a graphical interface for every conceivable option. And many times it's easier and you get more options when you edit the Registry instead of using the graphical XP interface. You can use Windows XP without ever editing the Registry—many users do— but advanced users understand its power tool status.

The way to edit the Registry is by using the *Registry Editor*, also called RegEdit, which is shown in Figure 9-1. To run it, type regedit in the Run box or at a command line and press Enter.

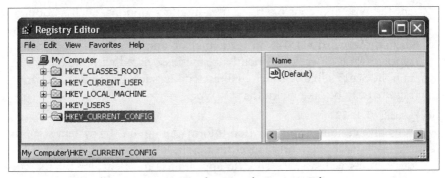

Figure 9-1. Controlling Registry settings by using the Registry Editor

Before you edit the Registry, though, first you should get a basic understanding of its structure.

Sometimes, we power users like to jump in without reading the manual. The Registry is not the best place to experiment and learn as you go until you understand at least a little of what's going on. You could render your system useless and unrecoverable with just a few changes. So, we recommend making a backup **[Hack #86]** and reading at least most of this chapter first. You'll be glad later if you do this now.

The Five Logical Registry Hives

The Registry has many thousands of settings; in fact, it often has tens of thousands of them. They are organized into five main Registry sections, called *Registry hives*. Think of each hive as a root directory. Each hive has a different purpose. When you start to delve into the Registry, you might notice that many of the settings seem to be exact duplicates of one another—in other words, the settings in one hive mirror the settings in another hive. In fact, frequently one set of settings is merely an alias (called a *symbolic link*) of another, so when you change those settings in one hive, the changes are made in both hives.

> The hives themselves are stored in the *C:\Windows\system32\ config* and *C:\Documents and Settings\{username}* files.

Following are the five hives and what each does:

HKEY_CLASSES_ROOT
> This hive contains information about file types, filename extensions, and similar information. It instructs XP on how to handle every different file type and controls basic user interface options, such as double-clicking and context menus. This hive also includes class definitions (hence the word CLASSES in its name) of unique objects, such as file types or OLE objects. Frequently, classes associated with file types contain the Shell subkey, which defines actions, such as opening and printing, that can be taken with that file type.

HKEY_CURRENT_USER
> This hive contains configuration information about the system setup of the user that is currently logged in to XP. It controls the current user's desktop, as well as XP's specific appearance and behavior for the current user. This hive also manages network connections and connections to devices such as printers, personal preferences such as screen colors, and security rights. Also included in this hive are Security Identifiers (SIDs), which uniquely identify users of the PC and which have information about each user's rights, settings, and preferences.

HKEY_LOCAL_MACHINE
> This hive contains information about the computer itself, as well as the operating system. It includes specific details about all hardware, including keyboard, printer ports, storage—the entire hardware setup. In addition, it has information about security, installed software, system startup, drivers, services, and the machine's specific XP configuration.

HKEY_USERS
> This hive contains information about every user profile on the system.

HKEY_CURRENT_CONFIG
> This hive contains information about the current hardware configuration of the system, in the same way HKEY_CURRENT_USER contains information about the current user of the system.

Using Keys and Values

Each hive is at the top of the hierarchy, and underneath each hive are keys, which can in turn contain subkeys, and those subkeys can contain subkeys, and so on, organized in folderlike fashion, much like a hard drive.

Keys and subkeys contain a value, which controls a particular setting. For example, this key:

```
HKEY_CURRENT_USER\Control Panel\Mouse\DoubleClickSpeed
```

determines the amount of time between mouse clicks that must elapse before Windows won't consider it to be a double-click. To set the amount of time, you change the key's value. In this case, the default value is 500, measured in milliseconds, and you can edit the Registry to change it to whatever value you want, as shown in Figure 9-2. You can also make the changes using the Mouse Properties dialog box (Start → Control Panel → Printers and Other Hardware → Mouse). When you make changes to that dialog box, the changes are in turn made in the Registry, which ultimately controls the setting. In essence, the dialog box is merely a convenient front-end to the Registry.

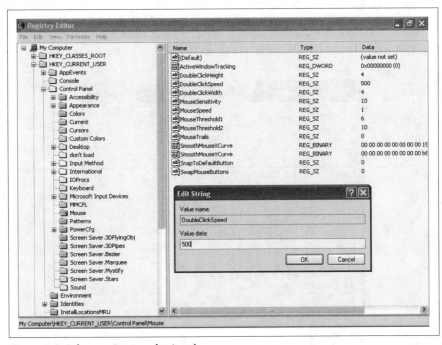

Figure 9-2. Editing a Registry key's value

A key can contain one or more values. Following are the five primary datatypes of values in the Registry:

REG_SZ *(string value)*

> This datatype is easy to understand and edit because it is made up of plain text and numbers. It is one of the most common datatypes in the Registry. The value for DoubleClickSpeed, mentioned earlier in this hack, is of this type.

REG_MULTI_SZ *(string array value)*

> This datatype contains several strings of plain text and numbers. The Registry Editor will let you edit these values, but it won't let you create them.

REG_EXPAND_SZ *(expanded string value)*

> This datatype contains variables that Windows uses to point to the location of files. For example, to point to the location of the Luna theme file, the expanded string value in the Registry is %SystemRoot%\resources\Themes\Luna.theme.

REG_BINARY *(binary value)*

> This datatype is made up of binary data: 0s and 1s. Figure 9-3 shows a typical example of a binary value. As a general rule, you won't edit binary values—instead you'll edit string values because they're made up of text and numbers, as shown in Figure 9-4.

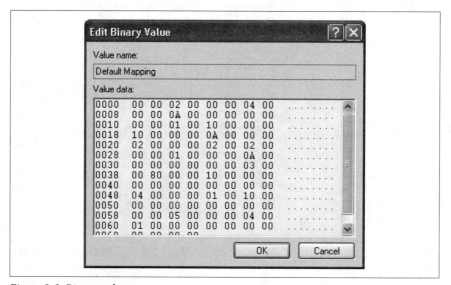

Figure 9-3. Binary values

Figure 9-4. Editing string values

REG_DWORD (DWORD *values*)

This datatype is represented as a number. Sometimes a 0 turns on the key or a 1 turns off the key, though it can use other numbers as well. While you see and edit the value as a number, such as 456, the Registry itself views the number as a hexadecimal number, 1C8. Figure 9-5 shows a DWORD value being edited.

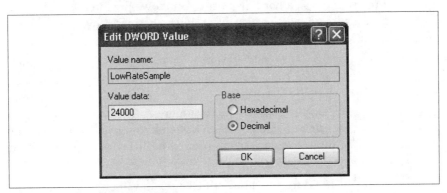

Figure 9-5. Editing DWORD values

Launching the Registry Editor

There's an upside and a downside to using XP's Registry Editor. The upside is that it's relatively simple to use. The downside is that it doesn't offer much functionality beyond basic Registry editing.

In some instances, when you make changes using the Registry the changes take effect as soon as you exit the Registry. In other instances, they'll take effect only after you log out and then log back in. And, in yet other instances, they'll take effect only after you restart Windows.

To run the Registry Editor, type regedit in the Run box or at a command prompt and press Enter. If this is the first time you've run the Registry Editor, it will open highlighting the HKEY_CURRENT_USER hive, as shown in Figure 9-6. If you've previously used the Registry Editor, it will open highlighting the last key you edited or the last place you were in the Registry.

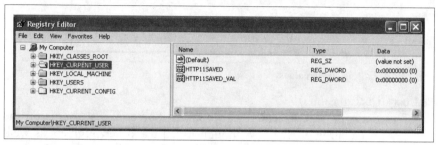

Figure 9-6. Using the Registry Editor for the first time

You can browse through the Registry with the Registry Editor in the same way you browse through a hard disk using Windows Explorer. Clicking a + sign opens a key to reveal the next level down the hierarchy. Clicking a – sign closes the key.

The Registry can be several levels deep in keys and subkeys, so navigating it using a mouse can take a substantial amount of time. (Every time you open it, it jumps to the last-used key.) You can use shortcut keys, though, to more easily navigate through the Registry. The right-arrow key opens a key to reveal subkeys; the left-arrow key closes a key and moves one level up in the key hierarchy. To jump to the next subkey that begins with a specific letter, press that letter on the keyboard.

You use the Registry Editor to edit existing keys and values, create new keys and values, or delete existing keys and values. Again, sometimes the changes take effect as soon as you make the change and exit the Registry Editor; other times, you'll have to reboot for them to take effect. Keep in mind that there is no Save button. When you modify a value, it changes right then and there. There is also no Undo button, so make your changes carefully.

If you want to edit a particular key, an even faster way to navigate is to use the Find command from the Edit menu. (You can also use the Find command by pressing Ctrl-F.) To find successive keys with the same value, press the F3 key.

To edit the data associated with a value, double-click the value in the right pane of the Registry Editor; a box appears that lets you edit the value, as shown in Figure 9-7.

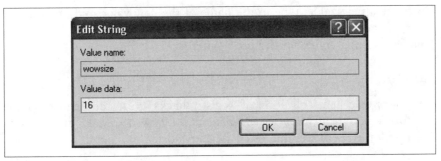

Figure 9-7. Editing a value

When you're editing the Registry, it's often hard to tell what key you're editing because the Registry Editor doesn't highlight that key. Instead, it shows only an open folder icon next to it, but it's easy to miss that icon. Check the status bar at the bottom of the Registry Editor; it should display the key you're editing. If it doesn't, choose View → Status Bar from the Registry Editor menu.

To rename a key, select it and choose Edit → Rename from the menu. You can also right-click the key and choose Edit → Rename.

Adding and Deleting Keys and Values

Editing the Registry often requires that you add and delete keys and values. To add a new key, select the new key's parent key in the left pane. Then, choose Edit → New → Key from the menu. Type in the new key's name. You can also right-click the new key's parent key and choose Edit → New → Key. To delete a key, select it and press the Delete key.

Very often, you need to add values to a key for its changes to take effect. To add a value to a key, select the new key's parent key in the left pane. From the menu, choose Edit → New, and from the submenu, select the type of value you want to create. We've already covered the five types of values you can create; as a reminder, they're detailed in Table 9-1.

Table 9-1. Values you'll encounter in the Registry

Value name	Registry datatype
String value	REG_SZ
Binary value	REG_BINARY
DWORD value	REG_DWORD
String array value	REG_MULTI_SZ
Expanded string value	REG_EXPAND_SZ

To create a new value, type in the name of the new value and press Enter. Press Enter again. The Edit String dialog box appears, as shown in Figure 9-7. Enter your data and press Enter.

See Also

- For an excellent collection of Registry hacks, go to the Registry Guide for Windows at *http://www.winguides.com/registry*. Make sure to sign up for the newsletter that offers Registry advice and hacks.

Hack Away at the Registry

#84   Here are eight great hacks that use the Registry to do their magic.

You'll find dozens of Registry hacks sprinkled throughout this book, but to give you a sense of the breadth of the kinds of hacks you can accomplish using the Registry, I've included a wide-ranging sample of Registry hacks here as well.

Automatically Close Programs at Shutdown

When you shut down Windows, if you have any programs running you'll get a message box warning you that a program is still running. Then you have to close the program and tell XP again to shut down. It's a fairly point-less warning—better yet would be if XP automatically killed the programs without issuing the warning. That way, you wouldn't get error messages and wouldn't have to close each individual application before shutting down your computer.

To have XP automatically close programs at shutdown, run the Registry Editor and go to HKEY_CURRENT_USER\Control Panel\Desktop. Edit the AutoEndTasks key so that is has a value of 1. If the key doesn't exist, create it as a DWORD value and give it the value of 1. To disable it, either delete the key, or set the value to 0.

Disable XP Shutdown

There might be times when you want to make sure XP can't be inadvert-ently shut down. You can use a Registry hack to disable the normal shut-down. Run the Registry Editor and go to HKEY_CURRENT_USER\Software\ Microsoft\Windows\CurrentVersion\Policies\Explorer. Create a new DWORD value named NoClose with a data value of 1. Exit the Registry and reboot for the change to take effect. You won't be able to shut down Windows in the normal manner from now on; you'll have to run Task Manager by pressing Ctrl-Alt-Del or right-clicking the toolbar, choosing Task Manager, and then using the Task Manager's Shut Down menu to close Windows. If you want to re-enable normal shutdowns, delete the NoClose value.

Change the Names of the Registered User and Company

When you install XP or when it comes factory-fresh on a PC, a username and company name are entered as the owner of the system. And that's the way it stays, like it or not. But a Registry hack will let you change both. Run the Registry Editor, go to HKEY_LOCAL_MACHINE\SOFTWARE\Microsoft\Windows NT\CurrentVersion, and look for the values RegisteredOwner and RegisteredOrganization. Edit their value data to whatever username and company name you want.

Change the Amount of Time Before Programs Time Out

When an application hangs and no longer responds, XP displays a dialog box that prompts you to kill the application or wait a while longer. By default, the dialog box appears after the application hasn't responded for five seconds.

This can cause problems. For example, if a program is doing heavy-duty calculations in the background, it won't respond until the calculation is done, so the operating system will report that the application is hung, even though it isn't. You can use a Registry hack to increase or decrease the amount of time it takes before XP reports that the program has hung.

Run the Registry Editor and go to HKEY_CURRENT_USER\Control Panel\ Desktop. Select the HungAppTimeout entry and edit it to input a new value in milliseconds. The default is 5000. Exit the Registry. You might need to reboot for the new setting to take effect. Try increasing the number in increments of 1,000 until you find a number that works.

Disable the Disk Cleanup Warning

If your hard disk has what XP decides is too little space left on it, the operating system will pop up a warning and recommend that you run Disk Cleanup. But you might be like me and not want a virtual nanny nagging you to clean up your mess. You can turn off the warning with a Registry hack. Run the Registry Editor and go to HKEY_CURRENT_USER\Software\ Microsoft\Windows\CurrentVersion\Policies\Explorer. Create a DWORD value called NoLowDiskSpaceChecks and give it a value of 1. Exit the Registry and reboot. You can also do this by using Tweak UI [Hack #8].

Change the Default Location for Installing Programs

XP uses the *C:\Program Files* directory as the default base directory into which new programs are installed. However, you can change the default installation drive and/or directory by using a Registry hack. Run the Registry Editor and go to HKEY_LOCAL_MACHINE\SOFTWARE\Microsoft\Windows\ CurrentVersion. Look for the value named ProgramFilesDir. By default, the value will be C:\Program Files. Edit the value to any valid drive or folder; XP will use that new location as the default installation directory for new programs.

Allow Laptops to Enter Power-Saving State (Increase the USB Polling Interval)

Some laptops' processors might not be able to enter their power-saving state, even when they're idle, because USB polling fools the processor into thinking the laptop is active. Your system polls your USB ports once every millisecond to see whether a device is present. So, even if a device isn't present, it continues polling. The problem is that some laptop processors won't go into their power-saving state because the constant polling makes them think the laptop is active.

With a Registry hack, you can increase the polling interval from the default of one millisecond, letting the processor enter its power-saving state. Run the Registry Editor and go to HKEY_LOCAL_MACHINE\System\CurrentControlSet\ Control\Class\{36FC9E60-C465-11CF-8056-444553540000}\0000. Create the new DWORD value IdleEnable and set the data value to a number between 2 and 5. This will set the polling interval in milliseconds. If there are additional sub-keys for HKEY_LOCAL_MACHINE\System\CurrentControlSet\Control\Class\ {36FC9E60-C465-11CF-8056-444553540000} (such as 0001, 0002, etc.), repeat the procedure and create the IdleEnable DWORD in each of them. Exit the Registry. You might need to reboot for the new setting to go into effect. You also might need to try several different values until you find one that works.

Change the Size of Your Mouse and Keyboard Buffer

You sometimes can get an error message telling you that you have an overflow in your mouse buffer or keyboard buffer. When that happens, it means the buffer isn't large enough and you need to increase its size. To increase your mouse buffer, run the Registry Editor, go to HKEY_LOCAL_MACHINE\ SYSTEM\CurrentControlSet\Services\Mouclass\Parameters and find the MouseDataQueueSize subkey. The default setting is 100 (64 hex). Increase the decimal number to increase the size of the buffer; then exit the Registry and reboot. You might need to try several different settings until you find the right one.

To increase the keyboard buffer, look for the KeyboardDataQueueSize subkey in HKEY_LOCAL_MACHINE\SYSTEM\CurrentControlSet\Services\Kbdclass\Parameters. The default setting is 100 (64 hex). Increase the number to increase the size of the buffer; then exit the Registry and reboot. Again, you might need to try several different settings until you find the right one.

Safely Edit the Registry Using .reg Files

Forgo the dangers and inconvenience of editing the Registry directly. Instead, use plain-text .reg files.

When you're editing the Registry, it's easy to make small errors that cause major repercussions. You might inadvertently edit the wrong key, put in a wrong value, or—given how confusing the Registry is—even make changes without realizing it. The Registry is unforgiving when this happens. It doesn't keep a backup, so you're stuck with the new setting unless you've made backups yourself [Hack #86].

When you edit the Registry directly, you're also apt to make errors if you're making multiple changes because you have no chance to look at all the changes you're making at once.

There's a way to solve both problems: use *.reg* files to edit the Registry. These are plain ASCII text files you can create or read with Notepad or any text editor and merge into the Registry to make changes. You can create a *.reg* file from scratch, or you can export it from a portion of the Registry, edit it with Notepad or another text editor, and then merge it back into the Registry. You'll find that *.reg* files are particularly useful if you're going to make changes to the Registry of several computers or if you are leery about editing the Registry directly.

You should also consider creating *.reg* files to copy the parts of the Registry you're about to edit using the Registry Editor [Hack #83]. Then, if you make a mistake with the Registry Editor, you can revert to the previous version of the Registry by merging the *.reg* file into the Registry. They're also useful if you need to do search-and-replace operations on parts of the Registry because the Registry Editor doesn't include search-and-replace functionality. You can do the search-and-replace operation in your text editor and then merge the edited file back into the Registry.

To create a *.reg* file from an existing portion of the Registry, run the Registry Editor, highlight the key or portion of the Registry you want to export, and choose File → Export. Choose a name and location for the file. You can export an individual key, a branch of the Registry, a hive, or the entire Registry. Following is an example of a *.reg* file exported from the HKEY_CURRENT_USER\Control Panel\Accessibility branch:

```
Windows Registry Editor Version 5.00
[HKEY_CURRENT_USER\Control Panel\Accessibility]
[HKEY_CURRENT_USER\Control Panel\Accessibility\Blind Access]
"On"="0"
[HKEY_CURRENT_USER\Control Panel\Accessibility\HighContrast]
"Flags"="126"
"High Contrast Scheme"="High Contrast Black (large)"
[HKEY_CURRENT_USER\Control Panel\Accessibility\Keyboard Preference]
"On"="0"
[HKEY_CURRENT_USER\Control Panel\Accessibility\Keyboard Response]
"AutoRepeatDelay"="1000"
"AutoRepeatRate"="500"
"BounceTime"="0"
"DelayBeforeAcceptance"="1000"
"Flags"="126"
[HKEY_CURRENT_USER\Control Panel\Accessibility\MouseKeys]
"Flags"="62"
"MaximumSpeed"="80"
"TimeToMaximumSpeed"="3000"
[HKEY_CURRENT_USER\Control Panel\Accessibility\SerialKeys]
[HKEY_CURRENT_USER\Control Panel\Accessibility\ShowSounds]
"On"="0"
[HKEY_CURRENT_USER\Control Panel\Accessibility\SoundSentry]
"Flags"="2"
"FSTextEffect"="0"
"WindowsEffect"="1"
[HKEY_CURRENT_USER\Control Panel\Accessibility\StickyKeys]
"Flags"="510"
[HKEY_CURRENT_USER\Control Panel\Accessibility\TimeOut]
"Flags"="2"
"TimeToWait"="300000"
[HKEY_CURRENT_USER\Control Panel\Accessibility\ToggleKeys]
"Flags"="62"
```

Edit a *.reg* file as you would any other text file. As you can see, the first line of the *.reg* file starts with Windows Registry Editor Version 5.00. Don't change this; Windows XP uses it to confirm that the file does in fact contain Registry information. Previous versions of Windows have a different first line; for Windows 95/98/Me and Windows NT 4.0, the first line reads either REGEDIT4 or Registry Editor 4.

The names of Registry subkeys are surrounded by brackets, and they include the full pathname to the subkey, such as [HKEY_CURRENT_USER\Control Panel\Accessibility\Keyboard Response] in our example. Following each subkey are the subkey values and data. Values and data are both surrounded by quotation marks. Here is the full section of a subkey, along with its associated values and data:

```
[HKEY_LOCAL_MACHINE\SYSTEM\CurrentControlSet\Services\Mouclass]
"ErrorControl"=dword:00000001
"Group"="Pointer Class"
"Start"=dword:00000001
"Tag"=dword:00000001
"Type"=dword:00000001
"DisplayName"="Mouse Class Driver"
```

As you can see, quotes surround data for String values. DWORD values, however, are preceded by dword: and don't have quotes surrounding them. Similarly, binary values are preceded by hex: and don't have quotes surrounding them.

Edit the value and data and save the file. When you've made your changes, import the file back into the Registry by choosing File → Import in the Registry Editor and opening the file. An even easier way to import it is to double-click the file. XP will ask whether you want to import it; when you answer yes, XP will import it and make the changes to the Registry. This is somewhat counterintuitive and can be confusing; at first you might think double-clicking a *.reg* file will open it for editing. But it won't; it will merge it into the Registry. To open a *.reg* file, open Notepad or another text editor and then open the *.reg* file. Alternatively, you can right-click the *.reg* file and choose Edit.

> Because double-clicking a file merges it back into the Registry, it's easy to mistakenly make Registry changes when you really just want to edit a *.reg* file. I explain how to protect yourself against this kind of mistake later in this hack.

Delete Registry Keys and Values Using .reg Files

You can use a *.reg* file not just to create new keys or values or to modify existing ones, but also to delete keys and values. To delete a key with a *.reg* file, put a minus sign in front of the key name, inside the bracket, like this:

```
[-HKEY_CURRENT_USER\Control Panel\Accessibility\Keyboard Response]
```

When you import the *.reg* file, that key will be deleted. Keep in mind that you won't be able to delete a key this way unless all its subkeys have been deleted first, so you'll have to delete them first.

You can also delete a key's value using a *.reg* file, by putting a minus sign after the equals sign in a *.reg* file, like this:

```
"BounceTime"=-
```

When you import this into the Registry, the value will be deleted but the key will still stay intact.

Protect the Registry by Changing the Default Action for Double-Clicking a .reg File

As mentioned earlier in this hack, when you double-click a *.reg* file, the file doesn't open for editing; instead, it gets merged directly into the Registry. This can easily cause serious problems because you might want to edit the file, and therefore end up double-clicking it, the way you normally open files in XP. But the file will end up merging it into the Registry and making Registry changes you didn't want to make.

To solve the problem, you can change the default action so that a *.reg* file is opened for editing in Notepad rather than merged when you double-click it. In Windows Explorer, choose Tools → Folder Options → File Types to open the File Types dialog box. Highlight the REG entry and click Advanced. Highlight the Edit action and click Set Default. The Edit action should turn bold. Click OK.

Change the Default Editor for .reg Files

Notepad is the default editor for editing *.reg* files, but if you have another text editor you'd rather use you can force that to be the default instead. First, follow the directions from the previous section to open the File Types dialog box and highlight the REG entry's Edit action. Then, click the Edit button and type in the full path and filename of the text editor you want to use to edit *.reg* files, followed by %1—for example:

```
C:\Program Files\TextPad 4\TextPad.exe %1
```

Then click OK twice.

> Never use a word processor such as Word to edit *.reg* files (unless you *make sure* to save it as a plain-text file from within the word processor!). Word processors add extra codes that the Registry can't understand. Always use a text editor such as Notepad or WordPad.

Better Registry Backups
#86

Avert disaster by backing up the Registry so that you'll always be able to revert to a clean copy.

The Registry is unforgiving; once you make a change to it, that change is permanent. There is no Undo function. To get the Registry back to the way you want it, you'll have to reedit it and remember the often arcane and complicated changes you made—if you can. And, unlike most other Windows applications, the Registry Editor doesn't ask you whether you want to save your changes. Make the change, and it's done. To paraphrase F. Scott Fitzgerald, there are no second acts when you edit the Registry.

Because of this, you should take precautions to keep your Registry safe and ensure that you can restore it to its previous safe settings whenever you want to. The best way to do that is to back up your Registry before you edit it. You should make copies of your Registry not only to protect against accidentally doing damage while you're editing it, but also to ensure that you can restore your system in the event of a system crash.

Here are the best ways to back up your Registry:

System Restore
> One of the simplest ways to back up and restore the Registry is by using System Restore. System Restore creates a snapshot of your entire system, including the Registry, and lets you revert your system to that snapshot. To use System Restore, before editing the Registry choose Start → Control Panel → Performance and Maintenance → System Restore and then follow the wizard to create a restore point. If you want to restore the Registry to its pre-edited state after you edit it, use the same wizard to do so.

Backup utility
> You can also use the Windows Backup utility to back up and restore the Registry.

> By default, the Backup program is installed in XP Professional but not XP Home Edition. If you have the Home Edition, you must install Backup manually. For more on backup strategies, see "Build a Better Backup Strategy" **[Hack #96]**.

> Run the Backup utility by choosing Start → All Programs → Accessories → System Tools → Backup. If you use the Backup Wizard, when you get to the What to Back Up screen choose "Only back up the System State data." Then, follow the Wizard's directions. It will back up the Registry as well as other system files, including boot files used to boot XP.

> If you don't use the Backup Wizard, click the Backup tab in the Backup utility, check the box next to System State, and then click Start Backup. When you want to restore your system, run the Backup utility. Click Restore and Manage Media → Start Restore.

Registry Editor
> You can also use the Registry Editor to back up the Registry. This is probably the easiest way to back up the Registry, but it won't back up

two Registry keys: the SAM and Security keys that control password policies, user rights, and related information. Unless you have a complex
system with many users, though, these keys are not absolutely vital.

Run the Registry Editor by typing Regedit in the Run box or a command prompt and pressing Enter. Highlight My Computer. If you highlight an individual Registry hive instead, only that hive will be backed
up. Next, choose File → Export. The Export Registry File dialog box
appears, as shown in Figure 9-8. Give the file a name, choose a location, and save it. For safety's sake, also make backups to another
machine and to a CD.

To restore the Registry, run the Registry Editor, choose File → Import,
and then import the file.

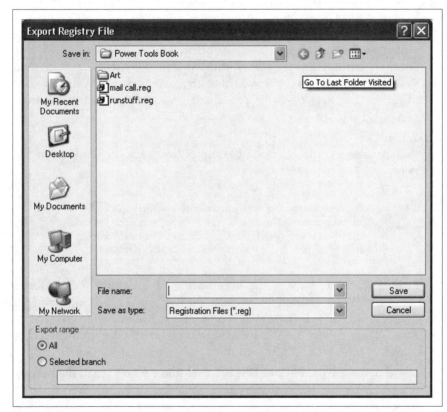

Figure 9-8. Using the Export Registry File screen to back up the Registry

Track and Restore Registry Changes with RegSpy

Protect your Registry and track changes to it made by programs with this downloadable goodie.

An excellent way to keep your Registry safe is to use RegSpy, which watches the changes programs make to the Registry, tracks and reports on those changes, and then lets you restore your Registry or use your knowledge about the changes the program makes to fine-tune the way the program runs. One of the program's more useful features is the way it lets you undo changes on a program-by-program basis by building a RollBack script for that program. When you roll back the Registry, you'll roll back changes made only by that one program, not by any others. This is far superior to XP's System Restore because System Restore makes changes en masse; there's no way to use it to save some changes and delete others.

My favorite RegSpy feature is SnapShots, which creates files in JavaScript or Visual Basic format and lets you review and repeat all the Registry changes that took place, step by step. That way, you can get a better understanding of the changes programs make during the installation process, and you can better undo or customize any changes made. It's also a great way to learn more about the Registry; watching the changes made by several different programs gives you insight into the Registry's inner workings.

RegSpy is shareware and free to try, but it costs $19.95 if you continue to use it. It's available from *http://www.utils32.com/regspy.htm*.

See Also

- Both RegCleaner and Registry First Aid (shareware from *http://www. rosecitysoftware.com*) will clean up your Registry by deleting old and unneeded Registry entries that clog up your system.

- Registry Commander (*http://www.aezay.dk/aezay/regcmd*) is a free utility that gives you a host of features that the Windows Registry Editor leaves out, such as a history list that lets you jump to recently edited keys, the ability to copy and paste entire keys and bookmark keys, and advanced search tools.

- Resplendent Registrar (*http://www.resplendence.com*) is shareware that includes even more tools that the Registry Editor leaves out, such as search-and-replace, a Registry defragmenter to reclaim wasted disk space, an activity monitor that tracks all Registry activity, and a tool that lets you compare the contents of two Registry keys, among other features.

CHAPTER TEN

Applications
Hacks 88–98

An operating system by itself is a paltry thing; applications do the real work. So, if you want to get the most out of XP, you need to hack the applications that run on top of it.

Some old programs have a hard time running under XP, so you'll see in this chapter how to get apparently incompatible programs to run under the operating system. You'll also find out how to remove applications and uninstall entries that you can't seem to get rid of, even when you thought you'd uninstalled the application. And we'll cover shortcuts for launching applications quickly and customizing them to the way you like them. There's more as well, including how to create and open Microsoft documents without having to spend hundreds of dollars for Office.

HACK #88 Remove Unruly Applications and Uninstall Entries

Uninstalling programs is sometimes tougher than you expect; even when you use built-in uninstallers, programs leave bits of themselves all over your hard disk and Registry. Here's how to remove them.

Uninstalling applications can be a tricky business. At a glance, it seems simple: choose Start → Control Panel → Add or Remove Programs, then choose the program you want to remove in the Add or Remove Programs dialog box, and click Remove.

But uninstall routines are generally only as good as the programmer who made them. And that means unruly programs commonly leave bits of themselves behind, even after you uninstall them. They might leave behind DLLs that load every time you start Windows, as well as Registry entries, even though the original program is gone. In both instances, your system performance takes a hit loading resources for programs that no longer exist. The programs also might leave behind unnecessary files and folders, which take up hard-disk space.

There's a good deal you can do to clean up after these unruly applications, though. Follow this advice:

- After you've run the uninstallation routine, run the Registry Editor [Hack #83], search through the Registry for any keys and values the program left behind, and then delete them. Frequently, you can find the settings for the program at \HKEY_LOCAL_MACHINE\SOFTWARE*Publisher*\ *Program Name*, where *Publisher* is the name of the software company that made the program and *Program Name* is the name of the software package (in the case of companies with multiple products like Symantec or Adobe). For safety's sake, make a backup of Registry keys [Hack #86] before deleting them.

- Before uninstalling the application, look through your hard disk to see where the program stores its files and folders. Then, after you run the uninstallation routine, look for those files and folders and delete them if they haven't been deleted. Often, you'll find them in *C:\Program Files\ <Publisher>\<Program Name>*.

- After uninstalling the program, make sure no parts of the program are still being run at startup. To do that, delete their entries from \HKEY_ LOCAL_MACHINE\SOFTWARE\Microsoft\Windows\CurrentVersion\Run and HKEY_CURRENT_USER\Software\Microsoft\Windows\CurrentVersion\Run.

- Create a restore point so that you can restore your system to the state it was in before you installed the program. Choose Control Panel → Performance and Maintenance → System Restore and follow the wizard for creating a restore point. If you're testing an application and aren't sure you're going to keep using it, create a restore point before you install it. Then, after you've installed the application and decided not to use it, revert to that restore point instead of using the uninstallation routine; it's more thorough.

- Use RegSpy [Hack #87]. This downloadable program lets you watch and track changes made to the Registry whenever a program installs and runs, and it lets you roll back changes the program made.

Remove Stubborn Uninstall Entries from Already Uninstalled Programs

Inexplicably, even after you've uninstalled some programs, their entries still remain listed in the Add or Remove Programs dialog box. As time goes on, it's easy for you to forget what programs you've uninstalled, so when you see their entries there you'll assume the programs are still on your hard disk, but when you try to uninstall them you'll receive an error message. There's an easy way to remove those entries. First, try to uninstall the program from the Add or Remove Programs dialog box. If it doesn't uninstall, run the Registry Editor and open \HKEY_LOCAL_MACHINE\SOFTWARE\Microsoft\Windows\ CurrentVersion\Uninstall. Look for the entry of the uninstalled program (it will be the program name) and delete it. In some instances, instead of the program name, you'll see an entry like this: {3075C5C3-0807-4924-AF8F-FF27052C12AE}. In that case, open the DispayName subkey in that entry; it should have the name of the program—in this instance, Norton Antivirus 2002. When you find the proper entry, delete it. For safety's sake, make a backup of Registry keys [Hack #86] before deleting them.

Remove Access to Certain Microsoft Programs

As part of a settlement in a federal antitrust case, Microsoft was forced to allow non-Microsoft programs to be the default applications for certain uses, such as email, web browsing, and digital entertainment. Users also had to be allowed to remove access to Microsoft programs that accomplished those tasks. That ruling came well after Windows XP was shipped, though, so some copies of XP don't allow you to do that. However, if you have a later version of XP, or if you have installed Windows XP Service Pack 1 (also called SP1) or Windows XP Service Pack 2 (also called SP2), your copy of the operating system has those capabilities.

> To find out if you have SP1 installed, right-click My Computer and look on the General tab. The words "Service Pack 1" will be there if you have SP1 installed.

To remove access to Microsoft programs, first find out if your system has these capabilities. Choose Start → Control Panel → Add or Remove Programs and see whether the Add or Remove Programs dialog box contains a button in the left pane titled Set Program Access and Default. If it does, you can remove access to Microsoft programs. Click that button. You'll find three choices: Microsoft Windows, Non-Microsoft, and Custom. Click the double-down arrow next to any choice to see more details.

If you choose Microsoft Windows, your default programs for web browsing, email, instant messaging, digital entertainment, and accessing Java applications will be Microsoft programs. If you choose Non-Microsoft, the defaults will be the non-Microsoft programs your computer manufacturer installed on your PC. If you choose Custom, you can pick and choose between Microsoft and non-Microsoft applications, as shown in Figure 10-1.

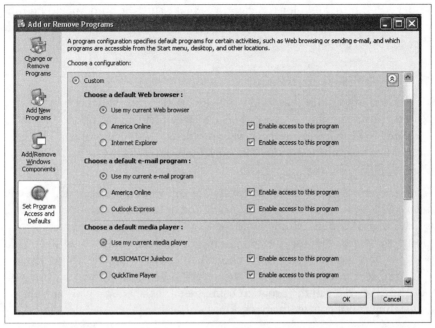

Figure 10-1. Choosing Microsoft or non-Microsoft applications for certain purposes

Keep in mind that "removing access" doesn't mean removing (deleting) the program. It means only the icon for the program will be removed. For example, if you remove access to Internet Explorer, it won't actually be deleted from your hard disk; you merely won't be able to see its icon. Also, be aware that not all email, instant messaging, digital entertainment, and web browsing programs will show up on the non-Microsoft or Custom lists, so you won't necessarily be able to use this screen to set them as your defaults.

All this means that the best use for the Set Program Access and Default dialog box is to remove the icons of some Microsoft programs; it doesn't offer a lot of functionality beyond that.

See Also

* "Remove "Uninstallable" XP Utilities" [Hack #15]

Force XP-Incompatible Applications to Run

Don't throw away your old programs that can't run under XP. Use these hacks to force them to work.

Some older applications, including old games and programs written specifically for an earlier version of Windows, might not run properly or run at all under XP. But there's a lot you can do to make sure they run, including running an automated Compatibility Wizard and using a little-known Microsoft tool to solve compatibility problems.

Use the Compatibility Wizard

If you find a program that won't run under XP, start with the easiest step. Run the Compatibility Wizard: choose Start → Help and Support → Fixing a Problem → "Application and software problems" → "Fix a problem" → "Getting older programs to run on XP," and then scroll down and click Program Compatibility Wizard.

You'll be prompted to choose the software you want to fix and then you will be asked a series of questions, including the operating system for which the software was written, or on which it last ran properly, and the screen resolutions recommended for the program. Figure 10-2 shows the wizard in action. Once you've made your choices, the wizard applies those settings and tries to run the program. If the settings work, the wizard will let you specify to always run the program using them. If they don't work, try different settings until you get them working properly.

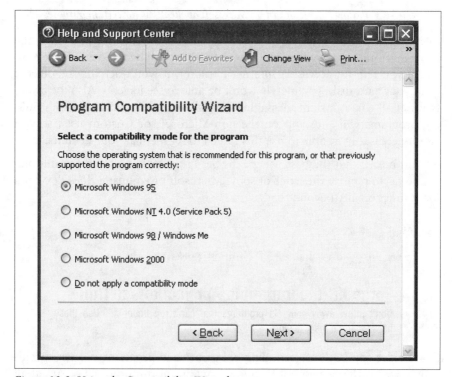

Figure 10-2. Using the Compatibility Wizard

Sometimes you'll find a program won't even install on your system. In those instances, run the Compatibility Wizard on the installation or setup program, which commonly goes by *Setup.exe* or a similar filename. Then, after it installs, see if it works properly. If it doesn't, run the wizard again, this time on the installed program.

If you're not a fan of wizards, there's another way to set the program's compatibility settings. Right-click the program's shortcut icon and choose Properties → Compatibility. Then you can manually configure compatibility settings, as shown in Figure 10-3. You can change the same settings as you can using the wizard. You might have to try several different settings before you find one that works.

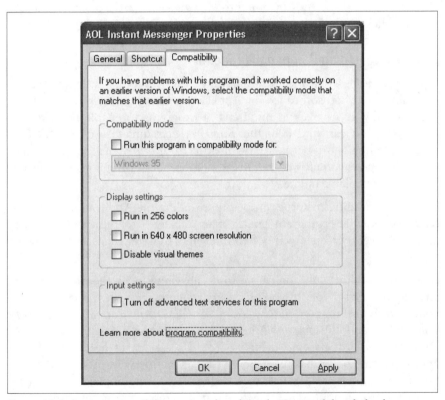

Figure 10-3. Setting compatibility settings directly in the Compatibility dialog box

At the bottom of the Compatibility dialog box shown in Figure 10-3, you'll notice a setting that lets you turn off "advanced text services." That setting is applicable if you use speech recognition and text services, so if you use them in the application that won't run, try turning them off for this application to see whether it helps. If the program doesn't use these services, don't bother using the setting.

If the Compatibility Wizard doesn't work, try these steps:

1. Check the software manufacturer's web site to see if an update, patch, or fix is available.

2. Use Windows Update to see if a fix is available, by choosing Start → Control Panel → Windows Update.

3. Update your sound card and video card drivers by checking the manufacturer sites and downloading new drivers.

4. If the problem program is a game that uses DirectX, upgrade to the newest version of DirectX by going to *http://www.microsoft.com/downloads/* and clicking the DirectX link or searching for DirectX.

Use the Application Compatibility Toolkit

If the wizard doesn't work, turn to a more powerful tool, a little-known free program from Microsoft called the Application Compatibility Toolkit. It will automatically apply fixes to hundreds of programs to enable them to run under XP. You can find it in the *\Support\Tools* directory of the XP CD, though a much better bet is to download it from *http://www.microsoft.com/ windows/appcompatibility/default.mspx* because newer versions are always being made available online.

Turn off your antivirus program before installing the Application Compatibility Toolkit. The program makes many changes to numerous Registry entries, and antivirus software often interprets those changes as a malicious script.

After you install it, you don't have to do anything to fix the programs; the analyzer does it for you. It won't fix every program, though. To see if it fixed yours, go to *C:\Program Files\Microsoft Windows Application Compatibility Toolkit\Applications\Compatibility Administrator*, run *Compatadmin.exe*, and go to *\System Database\Applications*. You'll see a list of hundreds of programs that the toolkit has fixed. Scroll to see whether your problem application is on the list and, if it is, to see what fixes were applied. Figure 10-4 shows the fixes it applied to the MusicMatch Jukebox music software.

See Also

- "Force Older Programs to Use XP Common Controls" [Hack #90]

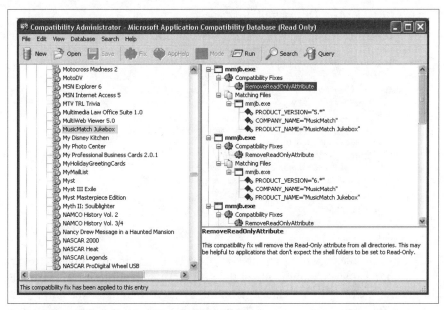

Figure 10-4. The Application Compatibility Toolkit

Force Older Programs to Use XP Common Controls

Older Windows programs look ancient and outdated in XP because they don't use the newer-style buttons and checkboxes. Here's how to make them use XP common controls.

When you run an older program in XP, the operating system applies an XP-type frame around it, with rounded titlebars. But the older program itself still uses its older-style interface. You can, however, force older programs to use XP-type common controls for things such as checkboxes and buttons. You'll have to create a manifest file (a specifically formatted XML file) and place it in the same directory as the older file.

Example 10-1 shows the code to put in your manifest file. For *Program Name*, enter the name of the program, and for *Description of Program*, enter a description for the program.

Example 10-1. Creating a manifest file

```
<?xml version="1.0" encoding="UTF-8" standalone="yes"?>
<assembly xmlns="urn:schemas-microsoft-com:asm.v1" manifestVersion="1.0">
<assemblyIdentity
    version="1.0.0.0"
    processorArchitecture="X86"
    name="Program Name"
```

Example 10-1. Creating a manifest file (continued)

```
    type="win32"
/>
<description>Description of Program</description>
<dependency>
    <dependentAssembly>
        <assemblyIdentity
            type="win32"
            name="Microsoft.Windows.Common-Controls"
            version="6.0.0.0"
            processorArchitecture="X86"
            publicKeyToken="6595b64144ccf1df"
            language="*"
        />
    </dependentAssembly>
</dependency>
</assembly>
```

To create the file, open Notepad, copy the text into it, and save it to the same folder as the executable file of the program you want to force to use XP common controls. Give it the same name as the program's executable file, but with an extension of *.manifest*. For example, if the program's executable file is named *oldprogram.exe*, give the manifest file the name *oldprogram. exe.manifest*.

See Also

- "Force XP-Incompatible Applications to Run" **[Hack #89]**

 Launch Applications with Command-Line
#91 Shortcuts
Launch applications quickly and customize what they do when they run, by using command-line shortcuts, parameters, and switches.

Windows is a graphical operating system, but all these pretty icons, menus, and clicking often get in the way of getting work done. That's particularly true when you want to launch applications.

I started computing in the days of DOS, when real men and women didn't use mice and icons (sometimes because it wasn't an option). So, I look for any chance I can get to use the command line, particularly when doing so saves me time and lets me take more control of my computer.

That's why I frequently launch applications using command-line shortcuts, along with parameters and switches. Parameters and switches let you customize the way programs launch. They're usually specific to each individual program, though some work on many or all programs.

An even bigger timesaver is to use the command line along with keyboard shortcuts. That way, you can press a key combination—such as Ctrl-Alt-W, for example—and launch Microsoft Word with a new document open, based on a specific template.

Create Keyboard Shortcuts for Running Applications

First you'll create a desktop shortcut to the application, and then you'll customize the shortcut so that it launches when you use a specific key combination. Right-click the desktop and choose New → Shortcut. Enter or browse to the filename of the application for which you want to create a shortcut Include its path and surround it with quotation marks, such as "C:\Program Files\Microsoft Office\Office10\WINWORD.EXE". Click Next; then, in the "Select a name for the shortcut" box, type the name of your new shortcut (such as Basic Word), and click Finish. Right-click the shortcut you just created and choose Properties. In the Shortcut tab, shown in Figure 10-5, put your cursor in the "Shortcut key" box and press the key combination you want to use to start the program. It has to be a combination of Ctrl-Alt, Shift-Alt, or Shift-Ctrl, plus a letter key, such as Ctrl-Alt-A, Shift-Alt-A, or Shift-Ctrl-A. In our instance, we're using Ctrl-Shift-W. Click OK. Now the program will launch whenever you press the shortcut key combination.

The Shortcut tab contains a variety of entries that let you customize how the program launches when you use the shortcut. The Run drop-down list lets you start the program minimized, maximized, or in a normal window. The "Start in" box lets you determine the start location for the application. You can even customize the ScreenTip that appears when you hover the mouse cursor over the shortcut. In the Comment box, type the text you want to appear as a ScreenTip. Figure 10-6 shows how such a customized ScreenTip looks when a mouse cursor hovers over it.

Customizing Shortcuts with Switches and Parameters

Launching applications with a keyboard shortcut is a timesaver, but there's still a lot you can do to customize those shortcuts. For example, you can set up a number of separate keyboard shortcuts for Word—for example, to launch Word with new documents based on a different template, or to open Word to specific, already-created documents.

For example, let's say you want to launch Word and have it automatically open a specific document, one called *chapter 9.doc* in the *C:\Hacks* directory. Type this (all on one line) in the Target box displayed in Figure 10-5:

```
"C:\Program Files\Microsoft Office\Office10\WINWORD.EXE" "C:\Hacks\chapter
9.doc"
```

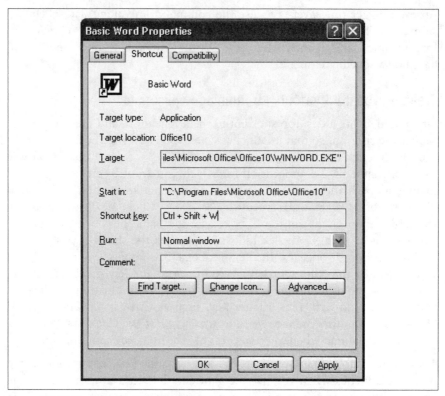

Figure 10-5. The Shortcut Properties dialog box

Figure 10-6. A customized ScreenTip

Doing this gives you much more control than double-clicking the document or creating a shortcut to the document because, in addition to launching individual files, you can use a variety of switches to customize how you launch those files. For example, let's say you want to launch Word without the splash screen. Use the /q switch, like this:

```
"C:\Program Files\Microsoft Office\Office10\WINWORD.EXE" /q
```

Then you can combine switches with opening individual files, like this:

```
"C:\Program Files\Microsoft Office\Office10\WINWORD.EXE" /q "C:\Hacks\
chapter 9.doc"
```

This command opens the file and bypasses the splash screen. Use keyboard shortcuts along with these switches and syntax to create as many customized versions of Office applications as you like. Tables 10-1, 10-2, and 10-3 list switches for Microsoft's Word, Excel, and PowerPoint, respectively.

Table 10-1. Switches for starting Word

Switch	What it does
/a	Stops add-ins and global templates, including the Normal template, from being loaded automatically. It also locks Word's settings so that they cannot be read or modified.
/l addinpath	Loads a specific Word add-in.
/m	Starts a new instance of Word without running AutoExec macros.
/m filen	Opens the file specified by number on the File menu's Most Recently Used list.
/m macroname	Runs a specific macro and prevents Word from running any AutoExec macros.
/n	Starts a new instance of Word without opening a document. Documents opened will not appear as choices in the Window menu of other Word instances.
/t templatename	Starts Word with a new document based on the specified template.
/w	Starts a new instance of Word with a blank document. Documents opened will not appear as choices in the Window menu of other Word instances.
/r	Opens Word, reregisters it in the Registry, and then quits. Use this switch if there have been problems with Word's settings and you want to reregister it. At times, certain Registry keys associated with Word can get corrupted. If you use this switch, you'll delete the corrupt Registry keys and re-create them from scratch. Then your problems should go away.
/q	Starts Word without the splash screen.

Table 10-2. Switches for starting Excel

Switch	What it does
/r workbook path/ file name	Opens the specified workbook as read-only.
/e	Opens Excel without a startup screen and without a new blank workbook.
/m	Opens Excel with a new workbook that contains a single macro sheet.
/p workbook path	Opens Excel and uses the specified path as the active path instead of the default path.
/o	Opens Excel and then reregisters it in the Registry. Use this switch if there have been problems with Excel's settings and you want to reregister it.

Table 10-2. Switches for starting Excel (continued)

Switch	What it does
/regserver	Opens Excel, reregisters it, and then quits.
/unregserver	Opens Excel, unregisters it, and then quits.

Table 10-3. Switches for starting PowerPoint

Switch	What it does
/s	Opens a presentation into the slide-show window.
/p	Prints the presentation.
/n template_name.pot	Creates a new presentation based on the specified template.

See Also

- "Control Windows Explorer with Command-Line Shortcuts" [Hack #22]

HACK #92   Open and Create Microsoft Documents Without Microsoft Office

When it comes to word processing and spreadsheets, it's an all-Microsoft world. But you don't have to pay hundreds of dollars for Office to create and read Microsoft files; instead you can download a free office suite.

For better or worse, the Windows world has settled on Word and Excel as the word processing and spreadsheet standards. But as anyone who has recently bought a new computer can tell you, buying an office suite that includes them can push up the cost of your computer by several hundred dollars.

If you want to play well with others, you need to be able to create and read Word and Excel files. That doesn't mean, however, that you need to buy Microsoft Office. In fact, you can download a free office suite that includes a Word-compatible word processor, an Excel-compatible spreadsheet, as well as image-editing and photo album software. It's called the 602Pro PC SUITE, and it is available from 602 Software (*http://www.software602.com*).

The word processor, 602Text, reads Word documents, including all formatting, and can format and save Word documents as well. The spreadsheet, 602Tab, reads and writes Excel files. You won't get a number of Office extras, such as being able to use macros, but at least one feature of the program is superior to Word. When you open or save a document, you're shown file thumbnails that have the first several lines of the document, as shown in Figure 10-7. Look closely, and you'll see a small magnifying glass in the lower right of each document. Click it, and you'll see even more of the text. It's a great way to preview information in files so that you know you'll be opening the right file.

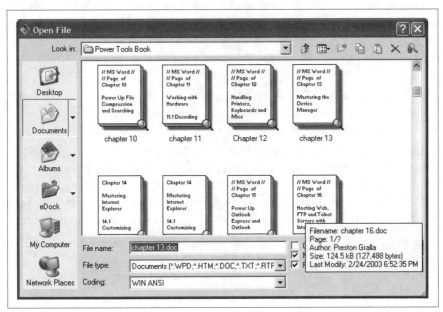

Figure 10-7. Opening a file with 602Pro PC SUITE

See Also

- The OpenOffice.org office suite (*http://www.openoffice.org*) is a free, open source software suite that includes a word processor, spreadsheet, drawing program, equation editor, and presentation software. It opens and saves Microsoft Office formats as well as many other formats. Versions are available for Windows, Macintosh, Linux, and Solaris.

HACK #93 Stop Hidden Fields in Word from Stealing Your Files and Information

Hidden fields in your Word documents can be used to peer into your PC and even grab your files. Here's how to prevent that from happening.

A little-known trick in Word can let malicious users steal your private information and can even allow someone to get access to the files on your PC. It does this by using Word Fields, which are used to insert self-updating information into Word documents, such as page numbers in a header or footer. Some fields, though, can be hidden, and because you can't see them, you can't tell what they're doing.

One of these hidden fields, IncludeText, is generally useful; it can insert Word documents or Excel spreadsheets into other Word documents. However, the field can also be used maliciously. For example, let's say someone sends you a document, you edit it, and then you send it back to the person who sent it to you. If it included a hidden IncludeText field with specific files and their locations on your hard disk, those files on your hard disk could be sent back to the document originator without your knowing it.

There are several ways to solve the problem. One is to install a Microsoft patch that fixes the vulnerability. For more information and to download it, go to *http://support.microsoft.com/default.aspx?scid=kb;en-us;329748*.

Another way to solve the problem is to download the free Hidden File Detector from *http://www.wordsite.com/downloads/hfd.htm*. It adds a new menu item, Detect Hidden Files, to Word's Tools menu. When you choose it from the menu, a dialog box alerts you to any documents that have been inserted into the file by a Word Field that could be functioning as spyware.

You can also try to solve the problem yourself by choosing Edit → Links to see if your document contains links to other files. (If none exists, the Links option will be grayed out.) If you find them, delete them, and the problem should be fixed.

H A C K
#94 Speed Up Your Hard Disk by Improving Defragging

One of the simplest ways to speed up your PC is by defragmenting your hard disk. Here's how to get the most out of XP's built-in defragmenter and a third-party program that should speed up your hard disk even more.

Perhaps the simplest way to speed up your PC is to use a disk defragmenter, which will help you open applications and files more quickly. As you use applications and files, they get spread out in fragments across your hard disk. The next time you use them, they take longer to open because your hard disk has to find each disparate fragment so that they can be assembled when you open the file. A disk defragmenter stores files and applications contiguous to one another so that they can be fetched much more quickly than if they were spread out across your whole disk.

XP includes a built-in defragmentation program (sometimes called a *defragger*), which you can run by choosing Control Panel → Performance and Maintenance → "Rearrange items on your hard disk to make programs run faster." But there are ways you can use it more effectively, and there are third-party programs that do a more effective job of defragmentation as well.

Defragment Boot Files

One of the biggest improvements of XP's defragger over previous Windows versions is that it can perform a *boot defragment*, placing all boot files contiguous to one another so that you boot faster. The boot defragment option is usually enabled by default, but there's a possibility that it could be disabled, or enabled improperly. You can make sure it's enabled, using a Registry hack. Run the Registry Editor **[Hack #83]** and go to HKEY_LOCAL_MACHINE\ SOFTWARE\Microsoft\Dfrg\BootOptimizeFunction. Find the Enable string. If the String value is set to N, change it to Y. If it is Y, leave it as it is, since that means boot defragmentation is enabled. Exit the Registry and reboot. The next time you defragment your disk, the boot files will be defragmented.

 You can also defragment the paging file, the hibernation file, and the Registry hives **[Hack #83]** using the freeware program PageDefrag (*http://www.sysinternals.com*).

Run the Disk Defragmenter from the Command Line

If you prefer the command line to the graphical interface, you can avoid maneuvering through menus and dialog screens to defragment your hard drive. (Using the command line also gives you greater control over the defragmentation process, as you'll see in this hack.) To defragment a hard drive, type defrag C: at a command prompt, where C is the hard drive you want to defragment. When you use the command line, you won't see a visual display of the defragmentation process, and you won't be able to pause it or cancel it.

defrag also works invisibly in the background to make sure your programs load more quickly. It's set up so that every three days, when your computer is otherwise idle, it moves program code to the outside of the disk to make programs load more quickly. You can force it to do that manually, without having to do a full defragment, by using the -b switch, like this:

```
defrag C: -b
```

It takes only a few minutes for defrag to do this, in contrast with a full defragmentation, which can easily take more than 20 minutes, depending on how fragmented your system is and the speed of your processor.

You can use several other command-line switches with the defrag command:

/A   Analyzes the drive you want to defragment and shows you a brief analysis report, summarizing the hard-disk size and total fragmentation. It only displays the report, however; it does not defragment the drive.

/V Analyzes the drive you want to defragment and shows you a comprehensive analysis report, detailing the size of the hard disk, the percentage of free and used space, total fragmentation, and total number of
fragments, among other details. It gives the analysis report, defragments the hard disk, and then gives an analysis of the hard disk after
defragmentation.

/F Forces the drive to be defragmented, even if there isn't a certain minimum amount of space. Normally, you can defragment the drive only if
your hard disk has at least 15% of its space free.

What to Do If the Disk Defragmenter Won't Defragment Your Drive

There will be times when the Disk Defragmenter won't defragment your
drive, or will defragment it only partially. It won't defragment your drive if
you don't have at least 15% of the drive's space free. To solve the problem,
as explained previously, type defrag C: /F at the command line, where C is
your hard drive.

There are also certain files and areas that the Disk Defragmenter won't
defragment: the Recycle Bin, the Windows page file, and *Bootsect.dos*,
Safeboot.fs, *Saveboot.rsv*, *Hiberfil.sys*, and *Memory.dmp*. There's not much
you can do about it, though it's a good idea to empty the Recycle Bin before
defragmenting.

Often, the Disk Defragmenter won't defragment every file on the first pass.
Your best bet here is to use brute force: run it again until it defragments the
files it missed the first time around. Also, keep in mind that the Disk Defragmenter won't defragment any files that are currently in use, so make sure to
close all programs; if some files won't defragment, it might be because
they're being used by an open program. Sometimes, programs might seem to
be shut down, but in fact might be running in a kind of phantom mode. For
example, Outlook sometimes stays running even after you've shut it down.
To make sure your programs are completely shut down before running the
Disk Defragmenter, run the Task Manager by pressing Ctrl-Alt-Del or right-
clicking the taskbar and choosing Task Manager. Check both the Applications and Processes tabs to see if any programs, like Word for Windows
(*Winword.exe*) or Outlook (*Outlook.exe*), are still running. These two programs sometimes continue running even after you've shut them down.

Get a Better Disk Defragmenter

For most purposes, XP's Disk Defragmenter works fine. But if you're a system administrator who needs to defragment multiple machines or defragment servers, you'll be better off with a better defragmenter. Even single

users of XP might want a better disk defragmenter for purposes such as easy scheduling of defragmenting and the ability to defragment files that XP's defragmenter can't handle. Two of the best XP defragmenters are available as try-before-you-buy software:

Diskeeper

> This defragmenter can automatically defragment a disk on bootup, allows you to remotely schedule boot-time defragmentation on multiple machines, will let system administrators create different defragmentation schedules for different groups of machines, will defragment disks that have little free disk space, and makes it easy to deploy on multiple machines. Get it at *http://www.execsoft.com*. It's free to download and try, but you'll have to pay if you decide to keep it. The version for home users costs $19.95. The Pro version, which contains more features, costs $49.50. License packs are available for multiple users.

PerfectDisk2000

> Like Diskeeper, this defragmenter allows administrators to schedule defragmentation of machines across a network, and it can defragment disks with little free hard-disk space. It can defragment files that XP's built-in defragmenter can't, such as the Windows page file. It also offers boot-time defragmentation. You can get it at *http://www.raxco.com*. It's free to download and try, but it is $44.95 per workstation should you decide to keep it. Figure 10-8 shows the options for using PerfectDisk2000.

Extend Your Screen Real Estate with Virtual Desktops

> Virtual desktops allow you to stretch your screen real estate well beyond its normal size, as well as to organize different views of your workspace.

At any point during the day, I might be writing software, listening to music, purchasing computer equipment, messing with my GPS and software, playing computer games with my son, or working with my editor. Sometimes, I'm doing all those things at once. It's a wonder I can keep all the windows organized. Fortunately, I don't have to do all the organizing myself.

Virtual Desktop Manager (VDM) gives me a way to organize the work I'm doing, using up to four switchable desktops. VDM is part of the unsupported PowerToys collection from Microsoft that includes Tweak UI [Hack #8].

Download VDM from *http://www.microsoft.com/windowsxp/pro/downloads/ powertoys.asp* and install it on your machine. Once you have installed VDM, you will not notice anything new. You have to activate its toolbar before you

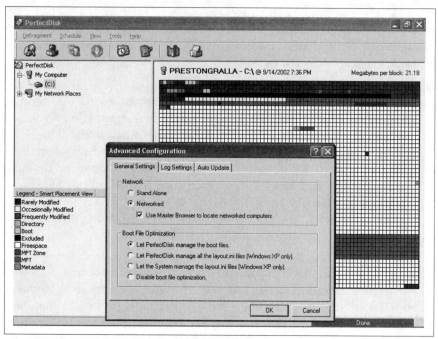

Figure 10-8. PerfectDisk2000 options

can begin using it. To activate VDM, right-click the taskbar at the bottom of the screen and select Toolbars → Desktop Manager, as shown in Figure 10-9.

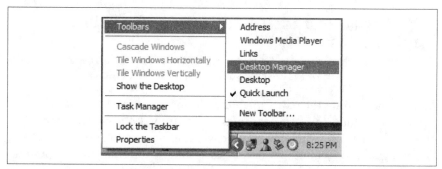

Figure 10-9. Activating the Virtual Desktop Manager

After you activate VDM, you will notice a new toolbar on the taskbar at the bottom of the screen, as shown in Figure 10-10. To switch between desktops, press one of the numbered blue buttons. At first, the desktops will appear the same because you haven't done anything in them to make them unique.

Figure 10-10. The Virtual Desktop Manager toolbar

Click button 1 and then launch your web browser. Next, click button 2 and then open your email program. Next, click button 3 and then open the My Computer icon. Now, click the green button with an icon of a window on it. Your screen should look something like Figure 10-11. Click one of the four images of the desktop to switch to that virtual desktop.

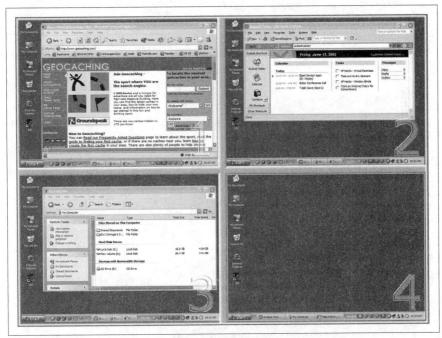

Figure 10-11. The Virtual Desktop Manager preview screen

Without changing a single option, VDM is a very useful addition to Windows XP. But if you don't twiddle with it, you can't really call yourself a hacker, now can you? If you right-click any of the buttons on the VDM toolbar, as shown in Figure 10-12, you will be able to configure VDM to suit your needs.

Your desktop has a background image that you can set as you wish. When you purchased your computer or installed Windows XP, the background image was a grassy hill with a blue sky. Since VDM provides you with four separate desktops, you can customize each with a different background

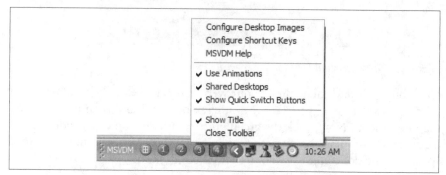

Figure 10-12. The Virtual Desktop Manager toolbar configuration menu

image. If you choose the Configure Desktop Images item from the toolbar's menu, you will see the dialog box shown in Figure 10-13.

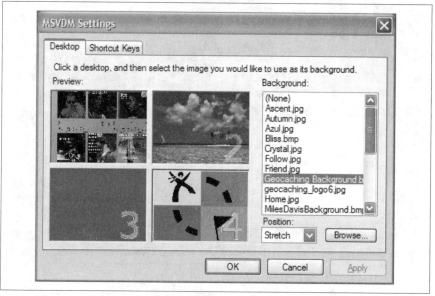

Figure 10-13. Virtual Desktop Manager background image settings

To change the background for one of the virtual desktops, specify which desktop area you want to change on the left side of the window. Then, locate a file from the list on the left. The list of images comes from both *C:\ WINDOWS\Web\Wallpaper* and *C:\Documents and Settings\<Your Name>\ My Documents\My Pictures.* If you want to use a picture not in the list, click the Browse button and locate the file. However, you might find that VDM changes your original background picture to a solid color when you first run it. Just change it back to your preferred background.

Look at Figure 10-13; notice that desktop 3 is shown in gray. This is how VDM informs you that you have no background image set for the desktop. When you switch to that desktop, the background will be whatever color you have selected in your display properties.

In addition to pressing the numbered buttons, you can use keyboard short-cuts to switch between the desktops. Hold down the Windows key (if your keyboard has one; if it doesn't, you can change the key assignments, as explained next) and the number keys 1 through 4 to switch to the appropriate desktop. To switch to the VDM preview screen, hold down the Windows key and press V. To change the key assignments that switch between the desktops, choose Configure Shortcut Keys from the toolbar menu and use the dialog box shown in Figure 10-14.

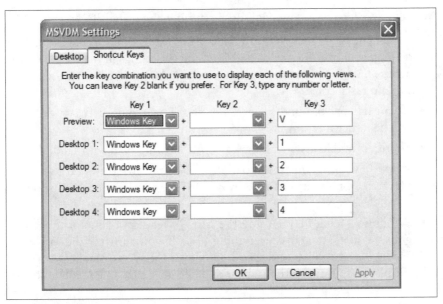

Figure 10-14. Virtual Desktop Manager shortcut key settings

 I'm not a big fan of animation on my computer when I'm trying to work. I don't like wasting CPU cycles and I don't like waiting for them to finish. (Also, it reminds me of the talking paperclip in Word.) So, I generally turn off all animation in the Windows desktop and in Explorer. If you want to speed up the switch between virtual desktops, uncheck the menu item named Use Animations.

Look at Figure 10-11 again. Notice that each separate desktop has taskbar buttons for every program that is running. VDM does this so that you can move running programs between the desktops. I prefer each desktop to have taskbar buttons for programs that run on that desktop. To do this, right-click VDM on the taskbar and uncheck the menu item named Shared Desktops.

If you would rather rely on keyboard shortcuts and reclaim space on the taskbar, right-click VDM and uncheck the Show Quick Switch Buttons menu item.

The least useful bit about VDM is the fact that it actually wastes valuable space to tell you it's there. If you uncheck the item named Show Title, the letters MSVDM will disappear from the toolbar.

You should keep the following things in mind when using VDM:

- If you choose a background image using the Settings dialog, the VDM settings will override the background image settings in the Display Properties dialog (your previous image won't be selected anymore; you'll have to reselect it).

- If you use background images, the act of switching between desktops will be noticeably slower.

- Shortcuts and icons on the desktop will show up on all virtual desktops.

- If you have programs that float above all other windows on the screen (such as a program with an Always On Top option), they will show up on all desktops.

- Windows Media Player using the MiniPlayer skin is one of those programs that float above everything else. If you turn on the Windows Media Player toolbar and then minimize the player, a smaller version of the player appears on the taskbar and becomes available to all desktops.

See Also

- Another popular product is the shareware application Cool Desk. It costs $24.95 and supports up to nine separate desktops. You can download Cool Desk at *http://www.shelltoys.com/virtual_desktop/index.html*.

- One of the more interesting desktop managers is Vern. Vern is free to download, but the author asks users who enjoy it to contribute. You can download Vern from *http://www.oneguycoding.com/vern/*.

—*Eric Cloninger*

Build a Better Backup Strategy

Don't be blindsided by disk crashes and other disasters. Here's how to have a backup ready at any time for any reason.

I used to use 3.5-inch disks for backup; to back up my hard drive using that method today would require approximately 98,000 disks. Granted, we don't use disks for major backup procedures anymore; nonetheless, a lot of the thinking that goes into a backup is still pretty ancient.

I don't believe any users actually set out on a given day to destroy a functional operating system, but you know as well as I do that it happens. A little tweak here, a Registry edit there, a power surge or perhaps a badly behaved application that trashes the computer. We've all been there and when it happens, I can almost guarantee you that if you listen closely you'll hear something approximating, "Darn. I meant to _____," where the blank is whatever backup task you have been putting off.

In addition to making yourself *do* the backup, there are a few steps I recommend to make your backup procedure easier, more convenient, and more effective.

Map Out a Backup Plan

I recommend separating the operating system and programs from the data when it's backed up. All three components—operating systems, programs, and data—have become huge over the years. In most cases, lumping them into a single, large backup is a waste of time, especially for home users.

Before you actually back up anything you need to ask yourself some questions:

How will the backup be saved? Many of today's computers come with devices that are suitable for backups; CD-R and CD-RW drives, tape drives, removable cartridge drives, and even a second hard drive can be used to store backups. With the exception of the second hard drive, any of those mentioned can be removed from the site where the system is located, and even the hard drive can be relocated by using specialty cradles that allow it to be plugged in and removed easily. There are a number of web-based hosting services that can be used for offsite storage for a monthly subscription fee. Business users normally back up to a company server, either local or remote, and the IS department takes over from that point.

The best system is one you think you'll actually use so that you'll have the backup.

Where will the backup be stored once it's created? If fire, flood, or theft should strike where the system is located, the backup should be available from another location to restore the system and datafiles. Unfortunately, safe storage of the backup can be hard to get on-site. If you don't use an off-site service, consider storing your backups in one of the small fireproof chests that can be purchased at most department or office supply stores.

What files should be backed up? At one time, it was accepted, if not almost reasonable, to back up everything on a system at one time. But the amount of data and the size of applications make that procedure very outdated. Here are three categories of data:

System files

> There is no need for the average user to back up operating system files. What *is* important is to protect the original media (i.e., the Windows XP CD and all your program installation discs). Windows XP comes with System Restore, which backs up all your system files automatically, or you can create a restore point whenever you prefer. System Restore is specifically designed to act in concert with the operating system to restore it in case of a system problem.

> If you don't like or trust System Restore, a number of programs are available that image the system and allow you to reinstall it in a fraction of the normal time. Ghost by Symantec is one of the popular choices (*http://www.symantec.com/ghost*).

Archive files

> These are files acquired through any number of methods, either downloaded or created by you, that don't change once they have been created. Image and audio files are good examples in this category. They are looked at and listened to for enjoyment, but as a rule they seldom, if ever, receive any modification once they have been added to your system. Don't back these up more than once.

Current datafiles

> More than anything else on your system, these are the files you most want backed up and protected on a regular basis. The list of included files will vary by user, but a few examples are text documents, spreadsheets, financial records, databases, email, Internet favorites, personal information managers (PIMs), web site projects, and any other type of data you create and work with or modify on a regular basis.

If the thought of losing one day's work makes the hair on the back of your neck stand upright, you'd better have a tightly structured backup plan and ensure that it's adhered to without fail. If you have a computer full of spam and Freecell stats, it doesn't make much difference when, or even if, you back up.

System Organization Aids the Backup Process

How you organize your system can make backup a relatively painless process. Structuring the system so that your datafiles are organized in one area facilitates pointing the backup program to one area instead of having to gather files from widespread locations. In Windows XP, the My Documents folder is an excellent choice for this purpose. Many programs default to saving created files in this location, including Office XP.

Many power users don't use My Documents because of its corny name; however, some of us have realized it's a nice shortcut to have (along with My Pictures); because the applications default to these locations, you have less chance of spreading your documents and photos around the computer trying to find your chosen folder. If you don't like the name, change it [Hack #12]. Or, if you'd rather use your own organization structure but want to designate one of your folders as "My Documents," you can do that, too [Hack #8].

Whatever location you choose, the important point is to use it for all the data you create and work with or modify on a regular basis that will be a part of the backup.

The Backup Utilities in Windows XP

While it isn't absolutely essential to have a utility specifically designed for backing up a computer system, it can make life easier. Both Windows XP Home and Professional come with what Microsoft calls the Backup and Restore Utility, better known as NTBackup. Unfortunately for XP Home users, Backup and Restore is not installed by default, nor is it as fully functional as the version installed by default in XP Professional. Supposedly, the reason it's not installed by default in XP Home is because XP Home does not support Automated System Recovery (ASR), which is a part of Backup and Restore. This in no way prevents you from making a full backup in Home Edition, but it does limit the recovery or restore options. Bottom line: if you have XP Professional, you're ready to go. If you have XP Home, follow these directions to install the Backup Utility manually:

1. Insert the Windows installation CD into your CD drive and navigate to *<CD Drive>:\VALUEADD\MSFT\NTBACKUP*, where *<CD Drive>* is replaced by *E:* or whatever letter represents your CD-ROM drive.

2. Double-click the *Ntbackup.msi* file to start the wizard that installs the Backup Utility.

3. When the wizard is complete, click Finish.

The "Restore" CD

A few years ago, I wouldn't even have had to add this sidebar, but a trend I heartily dislike has been gaining a foothold in the computer industry. That trend is the supplying of "restore CDs" by PC manufacturers. These useless little circles of plastic are used to restore a PC to factory specifications. "Factory specifications" means the CD basically wipes your system clean and reinstalls XP and, along with it, all the other garbage (commercial sweetheart deals) PC manufacturers use to pump up their coffers while depriving you of an unadulterated copy of a Windows XP installation CD. Unfortunately, if you fall into this group, you'll need to buy your own third-party backup program. Or, if you feel comfortable doing so, borrow a real Windows CD from a friend and install the Backup Utility on your system. The Backup Utility is something you should have received with your own copy of Windows to begin with. OK, kicking my soapbox back under the desk and moving on...

Here are a few things every hacker should know about NTBackup.

I want my CDs! This really should go under the "you've got to be kidding me" category, but NTBackup does not allow you to back up directly to a CD-R or CD-RW drive. Allegedly the best, most stable, and advanced operating system Microsoft has offered, XP, has no CD burner support in backup. The solution is to back up to an alternative drive and then copy it to CD. Many alternative backup programs are available that do support direct backups to CD-R and CD-RW. Microsoft says it's by design. I say it's from a lack of design. Considering how popular CD-Rs and CD-RWs have become as backup media—and how inexpensive they are—this lack of design presents a major problem for most people.

However, there is a way to store your backups on CDs (or DVDs, if you're in the early-adopter wave and already have a DVD burner). First, back up as you would normally, and then copy the resulting file to a CD-R or CD-RW. If you have to restore a backup from the CD-R or CD-RW, you'll be able to do that directly; you won't have to copy the file to another medium first.

One problem you'll run across is that your backup might be larger than the 650MB or 700MB that CDs hold. To solve the problem, create two or more backup sets, each smaller than 650MB or 700MB (depending on your CD's capacity). Separating data from programs or operating system files as suggested earlier will help you do this. Then copy each resulting set individually to a different CD.

Restoring a backup. When a backup is created the data is not saved in the same way you see it in the backup window where you select the files and folders. A backup is a single file that has to be broken apart during the restore process. To do so, it's necessary to use the same program that created the backup file to restore it to your system. Normally this is not a problem, except in one special circumstance. Restore will want to return your data to the location it occupied during the original backup. For example, if you backed up data from *D:* and no longer have a drive *D:* when you want to restore, the process will fail.

XP Home, NTBackup, and ASR. Windows XP Home Edition does not support ASR. I've been told this is why NTBackup is not installed by default in Home, but if that's the case, why include the item on the Home CD in the value-added directory? Whatever the reason, it's something you need to be aware of, in spite of the option for ASR that appears in NTBackup when installed on an XP Home machine. XP Professional users are good to go with ASR.

Get a Better Backup Program

XP's built-in backup program leaves a lot to be desired. But there are downloadable try-before-you-buy backup programs that offer you more features. Two of the best are Backup Plus and NTI Backup NOW! Deluxe:

Backup Plus
> One of the strengths of this program is its simplicity, particularly when restoring backups. Even though the program stores its backup file with a *.bac* extension, in fact, the backup files are *.zip* files. So, if you want to restore files or folders, you only need to rename the backup file so that it has a *.zip* extension and then open the file with an unzipping program, such as WinZip, the one built into Windows. Once you open the file, you can unzip it as you would any normal *.zip* file. The program also lets you schedule backups and, unlike XP's backup program, will back up to any kind of media, including CD-Rs and CR-RWs. Backup Plus is try-before-you-buy software. You can download it from *http://www. backupplus.net* and try it for free; it costs $39.95 if you decide to keep it.

NTI Backup NOW! Deluxe
> This is one of the more powerful and flexible backup programs you can find. It can back up to any media (including DVD-Rs), includes password protection for backup jobs, can span media and drives when

backing up, and lets you make a complete image of your hard disk so that you can restore your entire system. NTI Backup NOW! Deluxe is try-before-you-buy software. You can download it from *http://www.ntius. com* and try it for free; if you decide to keep it, you must pay $69.99.

—*Jim Foley and Preston Gralla*

HACK #97 Go Beyond Messaging with Windows Messenger

Share a common whiteboard, where you can collaborate on work in real time over the Internet, and get alerts delivered to your desktop with Microsoft's instant messaging tool.

Windows Messenger can do far more than merely let you chat with other people. Hidden inside it are powerful collaboration tools for working with others over the Internet, as well as the ability to get automated alerts delivered to your desktop.

> Don't confuse the instant messaging program Windows Messenger with the XP Messenger Service, which is used to send notifications over local area networks—for example, when a network administrator wants to notify network users that a server is about to go down. They're completely separate programs with different purposes. The XP Messenger Service has been used by spammers as a backdoor way of sending spam pop ups. To see how to turn the XP Messenger Service off so that you don't get spam, see "Kill Spyware and Web Bugs" [Hack #34].

Using .NET Alerts with Messenger

One of Windows Messenger's more useful features is its ability to deliver to you a variety of alerts called *.NET alerts*—messages, reports, or bulletins, such as weather reports, stock quotes, breaking news, and traffic reports. I'm a news junkie, and, where I live in New England, weather-watching is considered a contact sport. (If you don't believe me, try making your way through a February nor'easter with your body intact.) So, I use .NET alerts to stay on top of breaking events and to get the latest bad news about the weather. Here's how you can do it.

First, sign up for alerts by clicking the Alerts tab (the one that looks like a bell). If for some reason Messenger doesn't show you any tabs, choose Tools → Show Tabs → Microsoft .NET Alerts. You'll be prompted to sign up for an Alert provider, as shown in Figure 10-15.

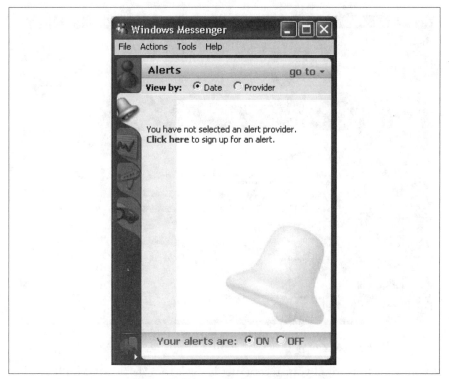

Figure 10-15. Signing up for .NET alerts

Next, you'll be sent to a web page where you can choose from a variety of alerts. Choose the alert you want, and fill out the form. The form for each alert is different and requires different information and different steps. In my instance, I signed up for MSNBC News to get its breaking news, and Weather.com alerts for the weather. I'm an eBay fan, so I signed up for alerts that will track auctions I'm interested in. And, like any long-suffering (but recently rewarded) Bostonian, I'm a Red Sox fan, so I also sign up for ESPN.com.

When you're done adding alerts, use the navigation on the web page to go to your My Alerts page, shown in Figure 10-16. From here you can edit, manage, add, and delete alerts.

Alerts will now be delivered to you on the schedule you chose. They'll appear as a small window near the Notification area, as shown in Figure 10-17. As you can see, it's another lovely day in Cambridge, with a high reaching all the way up to a stratospheric reading of 30 degrees. To read the full alert, click it and you'll be sent to a web page with the full alert.

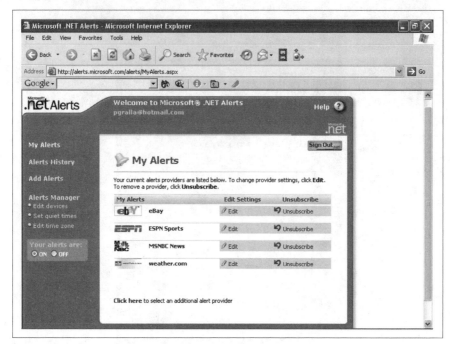

Figure 10-16. Managing all your alerts from your My Alerts page

If you want to read all your recent alerts, click the Alerts tab. You'll be able to view them by date or alert provider.

Collaborate Long-Distance with the Whiteboard

Chat windows are fine for simple communication, but when you're working long-distance with others, you often need more collaboration than that. In particular, you might want to share drawings, images, and text. You can do that using the *whiteboard*: a tool that lets you collaborate in real time over the Internet or a network with other Windows Messenger users. It's a drawing program, similar to Microsoft Paint, which allows you to share drawings, diagrams, images, and text. The same whiteboard appears on the systems of both participants, and each person can draw, annotate, and mark up the whiteboard in any way they want. The other participant sees the markup, in real time, and can in turn mark it up as well.

To start a whiteboard with someone, double-click the person's contact name and click the Start Whiteboard link on the right side of the Messenger conversation screen. An invitation goes out to the contact, and, if he agrees, a small Sharing Session window appears, as shown in Figure 10-18.

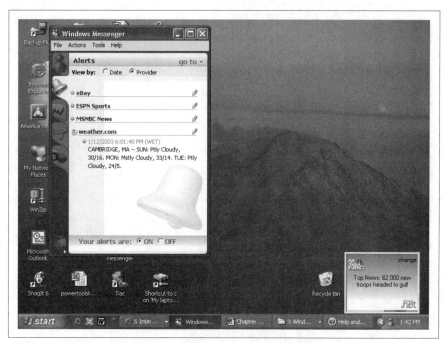

Figure 10-17. Alerts appearing as small windows near the Notification area

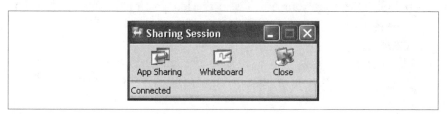

Figure 10-18. Launching a whiteboard session

Click the Whiteboard button, and the whiteboard appears. Now both of you can use the markup tools. They're largely self-explanatory and work like Windows Paint or similar graphics programs. You can see the whiteboard in action in Figure 10-19. Make sure, though, to use the remote pointer, a small hand you can drag around the screen that helps you better highlight what you're currently working on together. If you look closely at Figure 10-19, toward the middle of the screen, you can see it.

The buttons along the lower right of the screen let you create new pages and navigate among those pages. When you create a new page and navigate among pages, the other participant comes along with you to those pages.

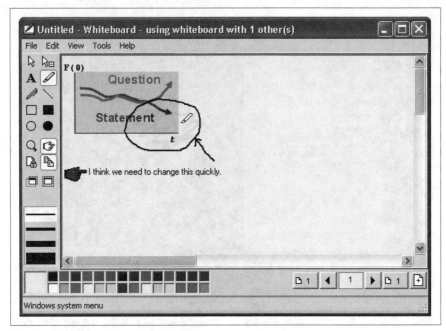

Figure 10-19. The whiteboard in action

Additionally, there are four buttons in the left part of the whiteboard that serve special purposes:

Lock Contents
When you click this button, it locks the whiteboard and prevents anyone else from making changes to it. To unlock the contents, click the button again.

Unsynchronize
When you click this button, you can jump to another page or create another page, and you'll do that privately; for the purposes of creating and navigating among pages, you're not synchronized with the other participant. When you click the button again, other participants' whiteboards will switch to the page you're viewing.

Select Window
Click this button, and then the next window you click anywhere in XP or any application will automatically be pasted into the whiteboard.

Select Area
Click this button, and you'll be able to select an area anywhere in XP or an XP application and paste it into the whiteboard.

When you're done using the whiteboard, click the Close button in the Sharing Session window. You'll be given the option of saving the whiteboard. If you save it, it will be saved in its own proprietary format (as a *.nmw* file). To view that whiteboard again, double-click it in Windows Explorer.

Share Applications with Messenger

The whiteboard is useful for basic collaboration, but an even more powerful tool is Messenger's application sharing. It allows two people to work in the same application on the same document. Whatever is on your screen appears on the other person's screen, and the two of you can work on the document together. I've found it to be ideal for collaborating on spreadsheets, it's easy to share "what-if" scenarios this way.

To start a whiteboard with someone, double-click the contact name and click the Start Whiteboard link on the right side of the Messenger conversation screen. An invitation goes out to the contact, and, if he agrees, a small Sharing Session window appears, as shown previously in Figure 10-18. Once he agrees, click App Sharing, and you'll be able to choose which file and application to share, as shown in Figure 10-20. You can share only programs and files that are already open on your PC.

Click one or more programs and click Share; the applications open in a window on the other person's computer. You have full control over the application; they can only watch what you do. In that sense, it's not full collaboration. If you want the other person to also be able to control the document, click the Allow Control button; the other person will be able to work on the application and document after he requests your permission. Only one person at a time can control the document; you can pass control over it back and forth.

HACK #98 Universal Messaging: Trillian Unites AIM, MSN, Yahoo!, and ICQ

It's the Esperanto of the instant messaging world; Trillian lets you communicate with all the major messaging programs.

I live, therefore I message. That's the credo of not just teenagers everywhere, but also people like me. I use instant messaging to keep in touch with editors, friends, and other authors, as well as readers of my books. And I frequently use it along with conference calls; while the larger group is speaking over the phone, I instant-message others in the phone conference to get background information and make occasionally less-than-flattering remarks about speakers who revel in the sounds of their own voices.

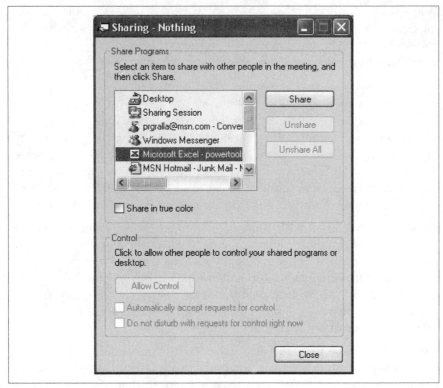

Figure 10-20. Choosing an application or applications to share

But as all instant-message users know, there's a big drawback to instant messaging: the major instant messenger programs, including Windows Messenger, can't communicate with one another. That's a bit like being able to make phone calls only to people who use the same brand of telephone as yours. Given the economics and ego that drive the instant messaging industry, this shows no sign of changing any time soon.

However, there's a great workaround, and it's free. The universal instant messaging program Trillian will let you communicate with users of ICQ, Windows Messenger, Yahoo! Messenger, and AOL Instant Messenger as well as the old Internet chat standby, IRC. You don't need to install any of those programs; just run Trillian (*http://www.ceruleanstudios.com*), shown in Figure 10-21.

After you install Trillian, enter the usernames and passwords from your other instant messengers. When you do that, Trillian automatically uses those contact lists, so you don't need to reenter them. To enter a new contact from inside Trillian, choose the Add Contact button, tell Trillian which

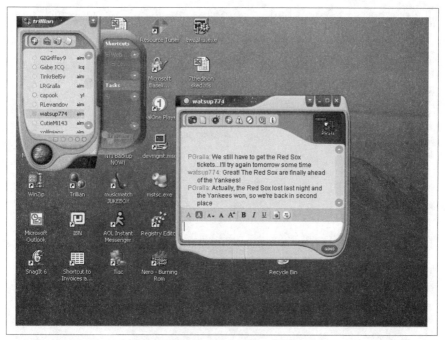

Figure 10-21. Universal instant messaging with Trillian

program your contact uses, and then fill in the contact information. Because instant messaging programs store your contacts on their servers, rather than locally on your PC, when you add contacts like this these new contacts will be available not only in Trillian, but also when you use your instant messaging program.

If you have accounts on more than one instant messaging program, Trillian signs you into all of them when you log in, so you get a single sign-in but you're available everywhere.

Trillian lets you use only some of the features of each individual instant messenger program. For example, you'll be able to send files as you can with instant messengers. But you can't, for example, use the Windows Messenger whiteboard or application sharing.

One problem with instant messaging with any program is the way it leaves you open to the world: anyone who wants to contact you can do so, including increasingly aggressive messaging spammers. Each individual program gives you controls over who can contact you and how you want to be contacted, and Trillian also lets you customize your privacy for each program. Right-click the big Trillian icon near the bottom of the Trillian screen and choose Preferences. Then, scroll to the bottom of the list to where it says

Chatting Services. You'll find ways to customize your privacy, which differ according to the service's capabilities, as shown in Figure 10-22.

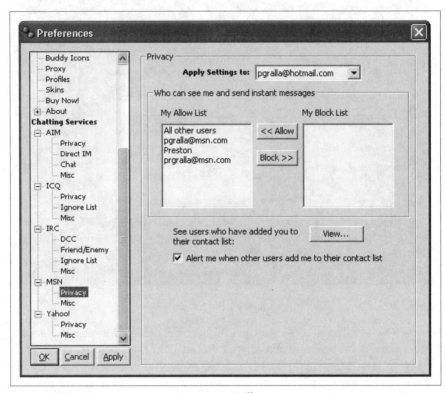

Figure 10-22. Customizing privacy options in Trillian

Trillian is skinnable, so you can easily change its appearance. To choose a new skin, select Skins in the Preferences screen shown in Figure 10-22, and choose either Launch Skin Chooser to choose from any skins already on your system, or Get More Skins to choose from skins online.

Trillian is one of the few programs that take advantage of XP's transparency capabilities. To make Trillian transparent, right-click anywhere in the program and choose Advanced Options → Transparency. Then you can choose a transparency of anywhere from 10% to 90%, where 10% is the least transparent and 90% is the most transparent. I suggest using 10%; any more than that and it becomes very difficult to see the program or chat with it.

There are two versions: the basic Trillian one is free, and the other, called Trillian Pro, costs $25. The Pro version includes a plug-in system that allows third-party developers to create plug-ins you can download for free. For example, there are plug-ins for delivering the weather and news, checking your POP3 email accounts, integrating with WinAmp MP3 software, and more. The Pro version has other features as well, such as the ability to video-conference using the Yahoo! portion of Trillian.

See Also

- Gaim (*http://gaim.sourceforge.net*) is another universal instant messenger. Earlier versions tended to crash unexpectedly on XP, but more recent versions are more stable. It's not as handsome-looking as Trillian, and it doesn't take advantage of as many of the built-in features of each instant messenger in the same way Trillian does. But it's open source and runs on many other platforms, not just on Windows.

CHAPTER ELEVEN

Graphics and Multimedia
Hacks 99–107

XP is Microsoft's first attempt to truly integrate multimedia hardware and graphics-playing abilities. In previous versions of Windows, things such as movie making, music recording, CD burning, and graphics seemed an afterthought rather than a core part of the operating system.

But with XP, that changed. It's not only that Microsoft dressed up the operating system to make it look better; XP also now offers Windows Media Player, a fully featured piece of music and entertainment software, and Windows Movie Maker, which lets you create home movies and videos.

In this chapter, you'll find hacks for improving your created movies, burning CDs more easily, importing lyrics into iTunes and the iPod, converting graphics among formats, and more.

HACK #99   Image Conversion in a Pinch

When you need to convert images from one format to another or shrink the size of existing images, try these two graphics tools.

I frequently have to convert graphics from one format to another. For example, I might need to convert a high-quality, very large bitmap TIFF file to a much smaller GIF or JPEG for posting to the Web. Sometimes, I need to shrink the size of a file, while keeping the same format—for example, when sending a picture via email to relatives or friends. When I'm creating my own icons [Hack #19], I need to convert graphics to the *.ico* format. Also, I sometimes work with an artist who needs a file in a particular format.

XP's built-in Paint program can't really do the trick. It can convert only a handful of graphics formats (for example, it can't handle *.pcx* or *.ico* format), and it won't let you customize the graphic; for example, you can't alter the compression of *.jpg* files to make them smaller. Also, it can't do batch conversions; to convert a file you have to open it and then save it in a different format.

For the kind of image conversion I do, I don't need a full-blown graphics program like Photoshop that carries a full-blown price tag of up to $600 (Photoshop Elements is an alternative, but that's not free either). Instead, I turn to the freeware and shareware programs detailed in the rest of this hack.

IrfanView

For most image-conversion chores, I turn to the free program IrfanView (*http://www.irfanview.com*), which is named after its creator, Irfan Skiljan. It lets you convert images individually or in batches, handles a wide variety of formats, and gives you a great deal of control over the conversion. For example, when converting to a JPEG, you can set the image quality, whether to save as color or grayscale, and whether to save as a *progressive graphic*—one that gradually paints on the screen as it downloads over the Web.

To do a batch conversion, after you run the program choose File → Batch Conversion, browse to the directory that has the files you want to convert, and select them. Choose the output format and any options you want to apply to the files. For example, for a certain project I needed to convert a group of large graphics in TIFF format to JPEG format, and the resulting files had to be very small, in grayscale, and in progressive format. Figure 11-1 shows the options I chose in IrfanView.

If you need to convert only an individual file, call up the file, save it in whatever format you want, and use options like those shown in Figure 11-1.

IrfanView does much more than image conversion. I use it as my all-purpose file viewer, for example. It also works with scanners to bring images into your PC, and it includes basic image-editing tools.

Image Converter .EXE

One thing IrfanView can't do is display before-and-after pictures of the graphic you're converting. For example, you can't preview what the converted picture will look like after it is converted. This can make image conversion a hit-or-miss affair: first you'll have to choose your conversion options, then convert the image, and then finally look at the output. If you're not happy with the results, you have to start back at the beginning, choose different options, and hope this time it works.

Image Converter .EXE (*http://www.stintercorp.com/genx/imageconverter.php*) shows you a side-by-side comparison of the before-and-after images, before

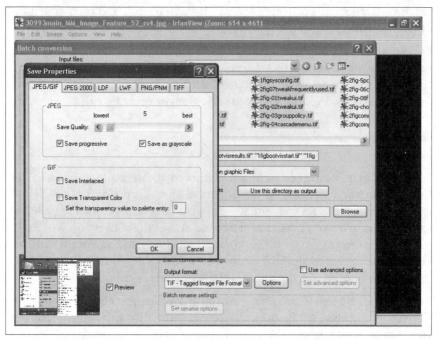

Figure 11-1. Converting a batch of files with IrfanView

you do the actual conversion. It also shows you the size of each image. That way, before you do the conversion, you can keep tweaking it until you have the size and quality you want. Figure 11-2 shows an example of shrinking a JPEG file while still trying to retain as much detail and quality as possible. The image on the left is the original image and is 242KB. The one on the right is only 36KB, but there is very little difference in the quality of the two, so I chose to save the one on the right.

The program does batch conversions, and it lets you convert files one at a time. It also lets you edit and add a wide variety of special effects when you convert, such as changing the color depth and contrast, adding a motion blur, posterizing the image, and more. The program is shareware and free to try, but you're expected to pay $35 if you decide to keep it.

See Also

- Paint Shop Pro (*http://www.paintshoppro.com*) is an excellent all-around graphics program that also does image conversion, including batch image conversion. It's shareware and free to try, but it has a registration fee of $99.

Figure 11-2. A side-by-side comparison of image quality and size

- The Quintessential Player, available for free from *http://www.quinnware. com*, does a very good job of converting music from one digital format to another. For details, see "Use Ogg Vorbis for Digital Music" **[Hack #104]**.

HACK
100
Problem-Free CD Burning

XP lets you easily record digital music to your PC and burn music CDs. Here's how to make sure your digital music doesn't skip, pop, crackle, or hiss, as well as other advice on CD burning.

Windows Media Player lets you burn CDs, as well as *rip* digital music from CDs and put them on your hard disk; but, as anyone who has ever burned and ripped music knows, the process is never problem-free. When you rip music, you might find that your digital music files skip and pop. And when you burn CDs, you might find that those CDs skip and have similar problems as well.

I've had many problems like that myself, particularly when copying opera CDs, which, as you'll see later in this hack, suffer from a nagging problem that causes most copied CDs to skip at least several times per CD.

What to Do If Your Digital Music Files Skip and Pop

When you rip music from CDs or old LPs, you might find that the digital music you rip to your PC skips and pops. There can be many causes for skipping and popping, so this section provides a number of ways to fix a variety of problems.

Cleaning up .wav files. If you're recording from old LPs, the problem most likely isn't with your computer. You're probably recording the music faithfully, but the vinyl on the LP has been damaged, so the resulting digital music suffers from skips and pops. You can solve the problem by cleaning up the skips and pops using downloadable software.

Both WAVclean (*http://www.excla.com/WAVclean/English*) and Wave Corrector (*http://www.wavecor.co.uk*) will eliminate pops, skips, crackles, hisses, and similar noises from music you record from old LPs. Both programs require a several-step process.

First, record the digital music using Windows Media Player or similar ripping software. You'll have to record in *.wav* format because that's the only format these programs handle. Next, clean up the *.wav* files with one of the programs. Which one you use depends on whether you want to automate the cleanup or take a hands-on approach, and on how bad the problems are that you want to correct. WAVclean is the more automated of the two; load the *.wav* file, select Scrub, and choose from basic settings, and it eliminates hisses and crackles. It won't, however, clean up deeper scratches, so it's best for recordings that suffer from just hissing and crackling.

With Wave Corrector, on the other hand, you see an actual oscilloscope view of the music files, with pops and similar problems highlighted in blue. You can either have the program make the edits to the file itself, or preview the edits and do the correcting yourself. Wave Corrector also includes a recording feature so that you don't have to use Media Player or other ripping software, such as Musicmatch Jukebox (*http://www.musicmatch.com*) or Quintessential Player (*http://www.quinnware.com*).

Once you've cleaned up the music, you can convert it to *.mp3*, *.wma*, or *.ogg* digital music to save on your hard disk using Musicmatch Jukebox or Quintessential Player, or you can burn directly from a *.wav* file to a CD using Windows Media Player, Musicmatch Jukebox, or similar software.

Both programs are shareware and free to try, but you are expected to pay if you continue using them. WAVclean costs $30 to register, and Wave Corrector costs $45.

Other advice for reducing skips and pops. If you've recorded the digital music from a CD rather than an LP, the problem might be dirt and grime on the original CD, and physically cleaning it might solve the problem. Wipe the bottom of the CD clean. The bottom of the CD might be scratched, and that can cause problems as well. In that case, you can try some of the CD-cleaning devices sold at music stores and computer stores.

> Don't let your friends and family stomp around during recording! With enough movement, CD players can skip just like turntables, for those of you who remember such antiques.

Additionally, if the ripping software you're using allows it, try slowing down the speed with which you rip your music, or ripping it at a lower bit rate.

> Windows Media Player doesn't let you adjust the speed with which you rip music, but it does let you alter the music's bit rate. Musicmatch Jukebox lets you adjust the ripping speed as well as the bit rate.

Finally, if you have a very old CD drive, the drive itself might be a problem. With some older, slower drives, when you rip music you'll frequently get skips. If that's your problem, the only solution will be to buy a newer drive.

What to Do If Your Burned Music CDs Skip

On occasion, your source and the digital music files will be free of skips, but when you burn a CD, the resulting CD skips. Sometimes, if you slow down the speed that you burn to a CD, you'll solve the problem. Most burning software will let you adjust your burning speed. In Windows Media Player, choose Tools → Options → Devices and highlight your CD drive. Then, click Properties and choose the Recording tab, as shown in Figure 11-3. From the "Select a write speed" drop-down box, choose a slower speed than Fastest. Also, close all other programs when you're burning a CD so that all your CPU, RAM, and system resources are devoted to CD burning.

If that doesn't solve the problem, try using analog rather than digital CD writing. Choose Tools → Options → Devices, highlight the CD drive you want to use analog playback, click Properties, and go to the Audio tab. From the Copy section, choose Analog. If that still doesn't work, go back to the same tab and choose "Use error correction." This will slow down the CD burning process even further, but it might solve the problem.

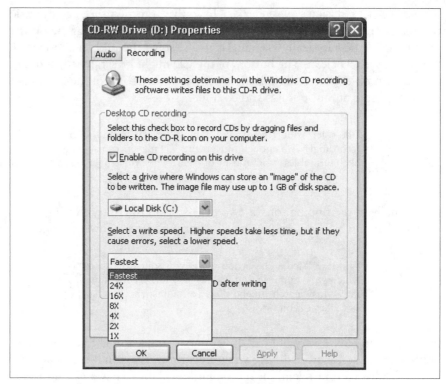

Figure 11-3. Slowing down CD burning in Windows Media Player

What to Do If Long Selections Are Interrupted by Skips

On opera CDs, or any CD with particularly lengthy pieces, a single aria or other musical selection is sometimes spread out over two or more contiguous tracks. When a CD player plays the CD, the aria sounds as if it were one track; the music flows smoothly, without interruption. However, Windows Media Player and similar burning software, such as Musicmatch Jukebox, automatically add pauses between tracks when you burn to a CD, so when you rip music from the opera CD and then burn it, the aria will be interrupted.

Some software lets you eliminate the pause between tracks when you burn to a CD. But then it eliminates *all* pauses, so the entire opera plays as if it were one long, single track, with no pauses, and you can't listen to it.

What's a Cecilia Bartoli or Renée Fleming fan to do?

You can solve the problem by using a program that makes an exact duplicate of an entire CD, instead of copying individual files. Both Exact Audio

Copy (*http://www.exactaudiocopy.de*) and Nero Burning ROM (*http://www. nero.com*) will do that. They'll make images of the CD and then let you use those images to burn a CD. I've found that opera CDs burned with them generally don't have the unnatural pauses. Exact Audio Copy is free, while Nero Burning ROM is shareware and free to try, but $69 if you keep using it.

Music from the Library

If you're looking to build up a digital music or CD collection, the Internet isn't the only place to turn. Another excellent place is the public library. Many libraries have excellent CD collections, particularly if you're interested in classical music, opera, or jazz. While the legalities of the issue are questionable at best, technically you can rip music from your library's CD collection, and burn CD collections from the ripped music as well. Many libraries allow you to search the catalog and make requests via the Internet, so you can make requests from home and be notified via email when the CDs are in. In Cambridge, Mass., where I live, I regularly make requests this way, and the library is part of a regional library network, so I have access to the entire library network's music collection. I frequently refer to the *Penguin Guide to Compact Discs* to find the best recording of a particular opera, request the CD, and then add it to my digital music collection.

See Also

- "Use Ogg Vorbis for Digital Music" [Hack #104]
- "Hack Windows Media Player with TweakMP" [Hack #105]

Save Streaming Music to Your PC
Build up a digital music collection by saving files in MP3 format when you listen to Internet radio stations.

When I'm at my PC, I spend a fair amount of time listing to streaming Internet radio stations, such as that which you can find at *http://www.shoutcast. com*, *http://www.live365.com*, or the many radio stations available directly from Windows Media Player and Musicmatch Jukebox.

> To listen to radio stations with Windows Media Player, first launch it by choosing Start → All Programs → Accessories → Entertainment → Windows Media Player, and then click the Radio Tuner button.

Often, I'll want to listen to a particular song again after hearing it—for example, a pavan by the English Renaissance composer John Dowling that I don't have on my CD collection. But because radio stations stream music to your PC, that music apparently can't be called back up and listened to again. Same deal with sample clips on Amazon.com and other sellers of digital music—once you've listened to the clip, you can't save it like other files.

However, there is a way to save streaming music or any streaming audio to your PC as a digital music file. Super Mp3 Recorder (*http://www. supermp3recorder.com*) lets you capture streaming music in MP3, Ogg, and WAV formats. It's shareware and free to try, but if you continue to use it, you're expected to pay $19.95, or $29.95 for the Professional version, which lets you do sound editing and automatically start recording at preset times.

To record streaming music, install and run the program, then choose Option, which will bring up the screen shown in Figure 11-4. This screen lets you choose which format to record your music. Unless you're planning to edit the sound file, choose MP3 as your recording format because WAV produces files that are extremely large.

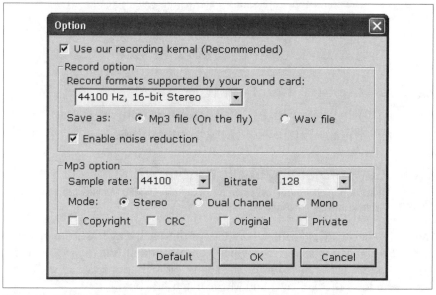

Figure 11-4. Choosing your file format and sound quality before recording

Click OK and return to Super Mp3 Recorder's main screen. Now click Volume Control. This lets you not only set the volume control, but also choose from which input you want to record. The program can record from a CD player, microphone, auxiliary input, and several other sources. By default, it's enabled to record only from a CD, so you have to choose the Wave Out option if you're recording from an audio stream.

By default, the recorded music files are stored in the *C:\Program Files\Super Mp3 Recorder Professional* folder. To change the location, click the Browse button and choose a new folder.

Now you're ready to record. Listen to your radio station (or any other streaming input) and, when you want to record, click the Start Recording button. The program will tell you it has started recording, show you how long you've been recording, and display information about your recording format, as shown in Figure 11-5.

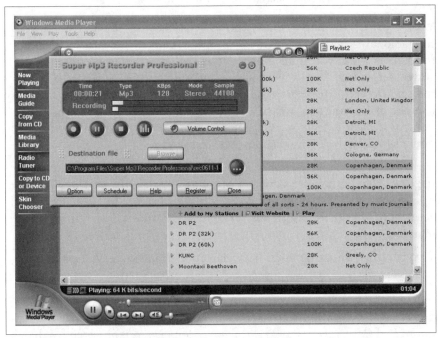

Figure 11-5. Recording an Internet radio station and saving to an MP3 file

The program's controls work like a CD player's, so you can pause and stop recording. When you've finished recording, go to the location where you've chosen to save your files, and the music file will be there, ready to play. The file will have an odd name, such as *rec0611-143130.mp3*. If you want it to have a more understandable filename, before you start recording give it a filename of your choosing in the "Destination file" box, shown in Figure 11-5.

See Also

- RipCast Streaming Audio Ripper is a similar program, but is designed to work with SHOUTcast servers that deliver streaming MP3 files, so it won't work for all streaming audio formats. It's shareware and free to try, but you're expected to pay $9.98 if you continue to use it. It's available from Internet download sites and from *http://www.xoteck.com/ripcast*.

Import Lyrics into iTunes and iPod

102

For all you karaoke-obsessed individuals, there are a number of ways to incorporate song lyrics into an iPod and iTunes workflow.

Whenever "It's the End of the World (As We Know It)" by R.E.M. comes on the radio, are you and your friends prone to getting into near-violent arguments over what you think Michael Stipe is singing? Do you find yourself correcting your girlfriend when she is (incorrectly) singing along to songs in the car? Do you love to get drunk and serenade countless strangers at every karaoke event you trip across? If you answered yes to any of these questions, this hack is for you. I'm going to walk you through a few available options to bring lyrics into iTunes and your iPod.

Sure, you could launch Firefox or Internet Explorer and manually look up the lyrics to your favorite songs on Absolute Lyric (*http://www.absolutelyric.com*) or a similar site, but then again, it is the 21st century. It's time to start acting more like The Jetsons and less like The Flintstones; it's time to automate.

Two good lyric-hunting options available to Windows users are Canto Pod and EvilLyrics.

Canto Pod

Canto Pod (*http://www.staylazy.net/canto*; donateware), powered by Sharedlyrics.net, is a lyric-searching program for all flavors of Windows. On first launch of Canto Pod, you will need to register for a free account with Sharedlyrics.net. After registering, you will be taken to a preferences pane where you select your iPod and enter your login name and password. After logging in, click Save, and you will be taken to the main Canto Pod page shown in Figure 11-6.

Once Canto Pod finds lyrics to your song in the Sharedlyrics.net database, you simply double-click the song you want, and Canto Pod uploads the lyrics to your iPod as a Contacts file. As an added bonus, it works with any

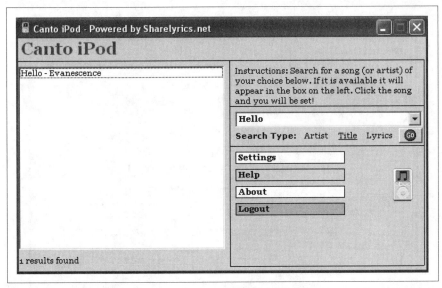

Figure 11-6. Canto Pod's main interface, searching for "Hello"

generation of iPod. Unfortunately, however, at this time the Sharedlyrics.net database seems to be a bit sparse.

EvilLyrics

EvilLyrics (*http://www.evillabs.sk/evillyrics/index.php*; donateware), a Windows program that works with a variety of players, including iTunes, is probably the most comprehensive and best working of all the lyric-oriented programs I've seen. To use it, download and install the program. Make sure you check the box to install the iTunes plug-in during setup, as shown in Figure 11-7.

Immediately after installing the program, you are going to want to update the karaoke index by navigating to the preferences pane and selecting the Advanced tab shown in Figure 11-8. Click the "Update index" button and wait for a notice that the index has been updated. Click Apply and then OK to close the Preferences dialog box.

The interface is simple. You can either type in a search or simply start playing a song in your player of choice while EvilLyrics is open; it will automatically start searching for matches to the currently playing song. After conducting a search, as shown in Figure 11-9, you can launch the results in your web browser of choice to see if a timed karaoke version of the file is available and to see a rating of its timing by other users.

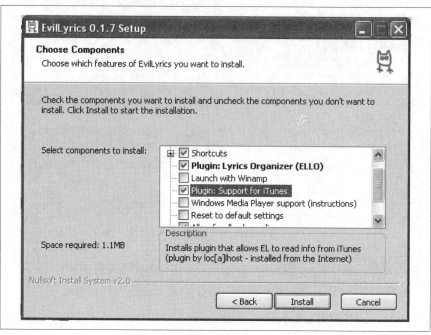

Figure 11-7. Checking the Plugin: Support for iTunes option when installing EvilLyrics

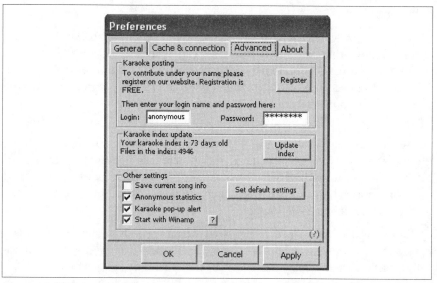

Figure 11-8. Updating the Karaoke Index on the Advanced preferences tab

Figure 11-9. EvilLyrics's main interface, after searching for "seven nation army"

From the web page, you simply click Import into EvilLyrics to download the karaoke file. If you click the in-browser option, the information for the current search shows up in your browser, as shown in Figure 11-10.

Once the file loads in EvilLyrics, click the magnifying glass to launch a little window with the lyrics. If you click this button at the beginning of the song, the lyrics should scroll along line by line, nicely in sync with the tune. Call all your friends over and throw a karaoke dinner party!

Hacking the Hack

Remember that if you have a third-generation iPod or later, you can simply save the lyrics to your favorite songs as plain-text files in your iPod's *Notes* folder for portable reading. Consider including links to the song files on your iPod so that you can pull up a song's lyrics on the iPod and click the

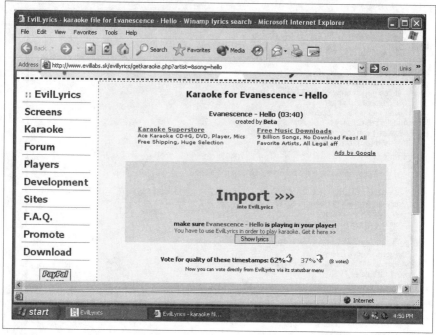

Figure 11-10. Downloading the karaoke file

link to begin playing that song as you read along. To find out how to create this type of link in your notes, see *iPod and iTunes Hacks* by Hadley Stern (O'Reilly).

—*C. K. Sample III*

Convert from Apple iTunes Format

103

Apple iTunes doesn't allow you to freely copy your music to devices other than your iPod. This hack shows you how to strip iTunes digital rights management so that you can use your files however you'd like.

I love my iPod and the iTunes Music Store is truly "the killer app." I love the convenience of being able to buy "that one song" that I remember from 1978 without having to buy an entire album.

The iTunes software itself is a mixed bag. It's slow starting up and it uses a lot of memory compared to other music players. I'd like to be able to listen to music I've purchased without having to run the iTunes program. I would also like to be able to listen to the songs I bought from the iTunes Music Store on something other than my iPod. This part of the hack will show you how to strip the digital rights management (DRM) features from your purchased music so that you can choose the time and place you listen to your music.

This hack will discuss technical aspects of doing this. I won't discuss the legal or ethical issues related to digital music because I'm a simple country engineer, not a lawyer. I might not have legal training, but I'm a pretty fair judge of what is right and what isn't. The tools I am about to describe might be able to be used by some to step over the line from fair use to something that is not legal. Just remember, just because you can do something, it doesn't mean you should.

The software used in this hack is called iOpener, and it can be found at *http://hymn-project.org/download.php*. If that site disappears, you might need to rely on Google or another search engine to find it. Download the binary version of the program, not the source files. The filename will be something like *iOpener-0.2-setup.zip*.

Before you perform this hack, you need to take a few precautions. I've read reports on the Internet where some users claim iOpener rendered their original files unplayable. I'm skeptical because I've used it without any problems, but it's better to be safe than sorry. The first thing you need to do is copy your iTunes music to a safe location. Most likely, your iTunes music is in a folder called *My Documents\My Music\iTunes\iTunes Music*.

Once you've made copies of your audio files, install iOpener on a machine that is already authorized to play protected iTunes content. Start the iOpener program and have your iTunes username and password ready. iOpener works by looking at all the files in your *iTunes Library* and *Purchased Music* folders. If protected iTunes files are in there, it will use your username and password to unlock them. It will not work for music that was purchased using a different account name. Once iOpener has found and converted the music files, it won't try to convert them again. iOpener also converts whenever you add new files to the *iTunes Library* and *Purchased Music* folders. This can make iTunes very slow, especially the first time you launch it, so be prepared for a long wait if you have a lot of music in these folders.

You can manually start the conversion process by clicking the iOpener icon in the taskbar and choosing Show iOpener. You will see the screen shown in Figure 11-11. In the main screen, you click the button labeled iOpen! and the program will start doing its job. The Prefs button allows you to tell iOpener to back up your music prior to converting (recommended) and whether to convert music every time you add files (it's up to you). That's the program in its entirety. It isn't flashy and it doesn't have sexy features, but it does do this one thing, and it does it well.

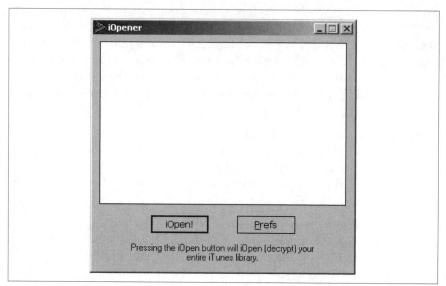

Figure 11-11. The iOpener main screen

After iOpener converts the files, you can look around in your iTunes music folders. Notice that you now have two copies of every song. One of the files has a *.m4p* file extension and the other has a *.m4a* file extension. The *.m4p* file is a DRM-protected iTunes file and the *.m4a* file is an unprotected AAC audio file.

Your iTunes Music Store login name and account information are stored within the unprotected AAC file. All you've done to this point is remove the playback restrictions from the file. In fact, the author of iOpener did this deliberately and I agree with his reasoning. Play it smart and don't use this power for evil.

At this point you have unprotected AAC files. But there's not much you can do with them, so you need to convert them to another format such as MP3 or Ogg Vorbis [Hack #104] that can be used by a variety of devices.

A good choice for conversion is the Quintessential Player, available for free from *http://www.quinnware.com*. For details on how to install and use it, see "Use Ogg Vorbis for Digital Music" [Hack #104]. You'll need an input plug-in to read the AAC format. Go to the Quinnware web site and look for the MP4 plug-in. Download the plug-in and run the installer on your computer.

Start the Quintessential Player after you've installed the M4P plug-in. Load the unprotected iTunes files into the Playlist Editor using the Add or + button or by dragging and dropping files from Windows Explorer. Remember, you want the files with the *.m4a* extension, not files with a *.m4p* extension. Right-click any of the files in the playlist and choose Convert → Convert All Files → Ogg Vorbis if you're going to convert the files to Ogg Vorbis, or choose another format to which you want to convert them. The software will now go about converting the files.

When the conversion is complete, the converted files will be in the output directory that you specified in the Ogg Vorbis encoder settings [Hack #104]. You'll be able to use the files in any way you want.

> For this hack to work, your machine must have already been authorized by iTunes to play protected files. That means you have to play at least one iTunes Music Store file using iTunes before attempting this hack. Also, some files might not convert cleanly in Quintessential. You might have to use the command-line tool hymn (*http://hymn-project.org*; free) to do the conversion and then open the hymn-converted file in Quintessential.
>
> Finally, iOpener does not work on audio books purchased at iTMS. The file is no different from audio files, it just has a different file extension. So, convert them with hymn.

See Also

- "Use Ogg Vorbis for Digital Music" [Hack #104]
- "Import Lyrics into iTunes and iPod" [Hack #102]

—Eric Cloninger

Use Ogg Vorbis for Digital Music

Ogg Vorbis is the most compact digital music format, with the highest quality at the lowest file size. You can rip and burn with Ogg Vorbis, convert existing music files to Ogg Vorbis, and convert Ogg Vorbis to other file formats.

The best format for digital music is one you might never have heard of— *Ogg Vorbis*. Its sound quality is much better than the MP3 or Windows Media formats: it's much better than MP3 when it comes to compressing the audio, and it rivals the AAC format for sound quality. Additionally, software and hardware manufacturers are free to use Ogg Vorbis in their products as they see fit without licenses or royalties. It also means you can use it as well. Other popular formats, even MP3, are burdened by patents or terms of use that can prevent their use or adoption.

Ogg refers to the format of the file that contains the information. *Vorbis* refers to the method used to encode the audio. Ogg is a format that can handle many different types of media, not just audio. Video, spoken word, and streaming data uses exist for the Ogg format, and all of them go by different names. Generally speaking, though, when people refer to Ogg, they really mean Ogg Vorbis.

In this hack, you'll learn how to create Ogg Vorbis files from your CDs and how to convert existing music files to Ogg. Then, we'll discuss some of your playback options for Ogg Vorbis audio files.

Ripping CD Audio to Ogg Vorbis

The group that designed the Vorbis encoder also wrote software to do the encoding. This encoder has been incorporated into quite a few pieces of software that will rip CDs and encode the music to Ogg Vorbis, including Winamp (*http://www.winamp.com*), dMC CD Audio Input (*http://www.dbpoweramp.com*), and the Quintessential Player (*http://www.quinnware.com*).

I'll focus on the Quintessential Player (a.k.a. QCD) because it gave me the features I wanted at the right price (free). Download the installer for QCD from the Quinnware web site at *http://www.quinnware.com*. There is usually a download link on the main page. You will also need to visit the *plugin* gallery, find the QCD plug-in that supports Ogg Vorbis, and download it to your PC. First install QCD, and then install the QCD Ogg Vorbis plug-in. It might be necessary to reboot your computer after installation.

When you run the program, it looks like Figure 11-12. QCD is meant to be in front when you need it and be out of the way when you don't need it. Therefore, it doesn't have the usual "menu bar and square border" look that other programs do. The small button in the upper left brings up the menus. You can also right-click most anywhere in the player and bring up the menus.

With QCD running, click the menu button in the top left or right-click in the main player area. Look for the menu item called Preferences or press Ctrl-P. In the list of options on the left side, search for the item called Encode Format and click it. You should see the screen shown in Figure 11-13. Choose Ogg Vorbis from the list of choices. (If you do not see that choice, you did not install the Ogg Vorbis plug-in correctly.)

Figure 11-12. The Quintessential Player

Your choices with Ogg Vorbis encoding are variable bit rate (VBR) encoding and constant bit rate (CBR) encoding. Your best choice is a VBR setting of 5, which will have very good playback quality: better than 160Kbps CBR in MP3 and with about the same file size.

After you've chosen the encoding format and settings, choose Output Files, which is directly beneath Encode Format. This screen allows you to customize where you want your ripped files to be stored and how you want the files named. Make your choices, and you're ready to start ripping.

Insert an audio CD into your CD player. Dismiss any screens that might appear as a result of having the "autorun" feature enabled; you want to be inside QCD and you don't want any other programs interfering. In QCD, find the button labeled Add or + in the playlist editor and choose the audio CD you wish to import into QCD.

Once you've loaded the audio tracks into QCD, you can begin the encoding process. Right-click inside the playlist editor on one of the track names, as shown in Figure 11-14.

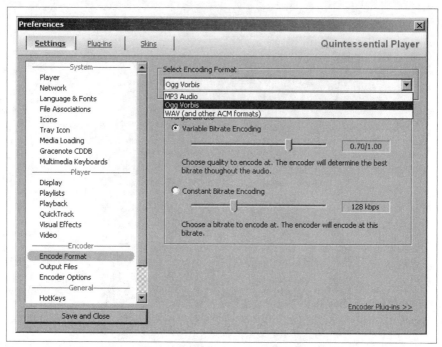

Figure 11-13. The QCD Encode Format Settings screen

Choose the Convert menu item, then choose the Convert All To menu item, and finally choose the Ogg Vorbis menu item. This should start the ripping and encoding process. At this point, you should step back from your computer and let it do its job without having to compete with you doing other tasks. It shouldn't take more than 15 minutes to rip and encode a 74-minute audio CD, and you'll have all the files in the Ogg Vorbis format when you're done.

Converting Existing Audio Files to Ogg Vorbis

Imagine taking a photograph of someone with a Polaroid™ camera or a cell phone camera. Place that picture on top of a table and then take a photograph of that picture. Do you think the copied photograph will look very flattering? Would you want that copied photograph to be your only memento of your grandparents? Probably not. You would not want to lose any of the picture quality any more than you would want to lose music quality in your audio files.

MP3 and Ogg Vorbis are both *lossy* formats. That means they both discard some of the audio signal to make the encoding as efficient as possible. The

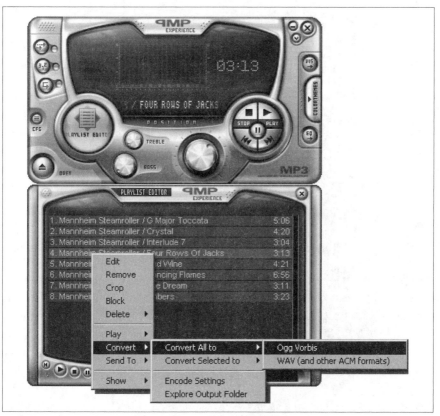

Figure 11-14. Converting audio tracks to Ogg Vorbis using QCD

part of the audio signal that is discarded is the stuff most of us can't hear very well or don't care to hear. Then again, maybe it is something you want to hear. When you convert files from one lossy format to another, you are compounding the loss of audio information in the first format when you encode the second time. It's no different from taking a photograph of a photograph.

Having said that, sometimes it's not possible to start with the original recording or the film negative. I wanted to point out that converting lossy formats leads to degraded sound quality. If you are comfortable with that, so am I.

Converting MP3 files to Ogg Vorbis is a snap using the Quintessential Player. Load existing media files into the Playlist Editor using the Add or + button or by dragging files from Windows Explorer. Figure 11-15 shows a number of MP3 audio files queued up in QCD. Right-click any of these files and choose Convert → Convert All Files → Ogg Vorbis just like you did earlier. This time, instead of ripping from the audio CD, you are converting from MP3 to Ogg Vorbis.

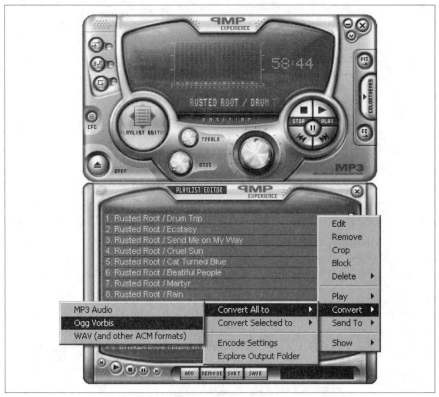

Figure 11-15. Converting MP3 audio files to Ogg Vorbis using QCD

Converting from MP3 to Ogg Vorbis takes about half as long as it takes to rip an audio CD to Ogg Vorbis. When the conversion is complete, the converted files will probably be in the same folder as the MP3 files, unless you changed the output directory in the Ogg Vorbis encoder settings.

Playback Choices for Ogg Vorbis

The Quintessential Player is one of many PC-based players. When choosing a player, it's entirely up to you to decide what features you want, and there are so many that it's not possible to review them all here. Instead, Table 11-1 lists some of the more popular players and their web sites. I'll let you decide.

Table 11-1. Ogg Vorbis players

Program	Cost	Web site	Additional software required for Ogg Vorbis playback?
Quintessential Player	Free (send the author a postcard if you like it)	*http://www. quinnware.com*	No
WinAmp	Free for the *Lite* version $14.95 for the *Pro* version	*http://www.winamp. com*	No
Windows Media Player 9 and 10	Free (bundled with Windows XP)	*http://www. windowsmedia.com*	Yes; download and install from *http:// www.illiminable. com/ogg/*
iTunes	Free	*http://www.itunes. com*	Yes; download and install from *http:// qtcomponents. sourceforge.net/*
dbPowerAmp	Free	*http://www. dbpoweramp.com*	No

In addition to using your PC, you can also use your Palm Powered or PocketPC device to play Ogg Vorbis audio. Flash- and hard drive-based players are also available. Kenwood produces a home theater receiver that supports Ogg Vorbis. Device manufacturers aren't lining up too quickly to support the format, but it is a steady improvement. The company that owns the patent on MP3 started enforcing its rights and because of that, manufacturers are increasingly adopting Ogg Vorbis. I'm hoping we will see more of this trend in the future.

For your Palm Powered handheld, there are two players: AeroPlayer by Aerodrome Software and Pocket Tunes by NormSoft. I have used both of these products with Ogg Vorbis files and they both work great. AeroPlayer and PocketTunes each cost $14.95 and can be downloaded from *http:// www.palmgear.com*. Pocket PC users have a variety of choices available at *http://www.pocketgear.com*. MortPlayer is a freeware playback option that gets good reviews, and Pocket Player is a highly rated commercial package that costs $19.95.

If you want a dedicated music player, you have a good selection to choose from. As of this writing, the Apple iPod does not support Ogg Vorbis and I wouldn't hold my breath waiting for it. The iRiver 700 and 800 series Flash players support Ogg Vorbis, as do their hard drive-based players. Go to *http://*

www.iRiverAmerica.com for details. The Rio Karma is another hard drive-based player that supports Ogg Vorbis (*http://www.rioaudio.com*).

Ogg Vorbis is a promising piece of technology that has a bright future. Open standards and quality software choices make it a great choice for manufacturers and software developers. Exceptional acoustic properties and compression ratios should help as well. If hardware manufacturers will adopt it, it might someday unseat MP3 as the format of choice.

See Also

- For more information about Ogg Vorbis, including technical details, go to *http://www.xiph.org* and its affiliated web sites.

—Eric Cloninger

H A C K
105 Hack Windows Media Player with TweakMP
Windows Media Player isn't the most convenient media player, CD ripper, or CD burner around. But the TweakMP PowerToy gives it extra features and convenience.

Not everyone is a fan of Windows Media Player. It can be confusing and awkward to use, and lacks some basic, useful features. A free, simple utility from Microsoft, the TweakMP PowerToy, can solve those problems. Anyone who uses Windows Media Player should download and use it.

> Microsoft says the TweakMP PowerToy is "unsupported," which means the company won't answer technical support questions if you run into trouble using it. On the other hand, when was the last time Microsoft answered any of your technical support questions, including ones for all its supported products, such as Windows XP and Microsoft Office?

First, head to the basic information page about the TweakMP PowerToy, at *http://www.microsoft.com/windows/windowsmedia/9series/player/plugins/tweakmp/readme.aspx*.

When you get there, you might see it's a version behind Windows Media Player itself. As of this writing, Windows Media Player is up to Version 10, but TweakMP says it's written for Version 9. That doesn't matter; TweakMP Version 9 works fine with Windows Media Player Version 10. And by the time you read this, TweakMP might have been updated.

Scroll down the page to "Installing the plug-in," click the link that leads to the download page, and then scroll down the download page until you see

---

TweakMP PowerToy Plug-in for Windows Media Player. Click to download the file, and then double-click the downloaded file to install it.

Once it's downloaded, fire up Windows Media Player and choose Tools → Plug-ins → TweakMP to run the utility. A screen like that pictured in Figure 11-16 will appear.

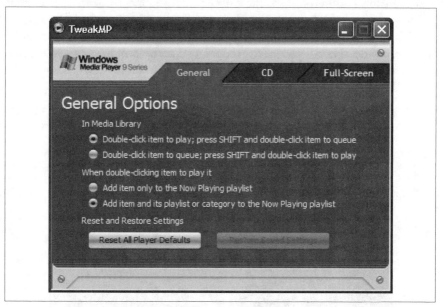

Figure 11-16. The TweakMP PowerToy

Each tab controls a different set of features. The General tab controls overall operation of Windows Media Player; the CD tab controls how you can rip and burn CDs; and the Full-Screen tab controls how Windows Media Player works in full-screen mode. Here's what you need to know about what each tab does.

General

This tab lets you control how to play files, and add them to a queue to be put on a playlist. You have the choice of playing the item (double-click) or adding it to a playlist (Shift–double-click). And you can choose what should happen when you play a file. Should it be added to the Now Playing playlist, or do you want to add the item *and* its entire category or playlist to the Now Playing playlist? The General tab is shown in Figure 11-16.

CD

This is probably the TweakMP PowerToy's most useful tab, and it has the single feature that makes the download worth it: it automatically levels the volume of files when you burn a CD. Typically, if you burn a CD from files you've gathered from different sources or ripped from different CDs, the volume on each is different. So, the burned CD might have some tracks that play too softly and others that play too loudly. But the TweakMP PowerToy will automatically level all the tracks so that they play at the same relative volume. To do this, all you need to do is check the box next to "Automatically level the volume of files when copying to an audio CD," as shown in Figure 11-17.

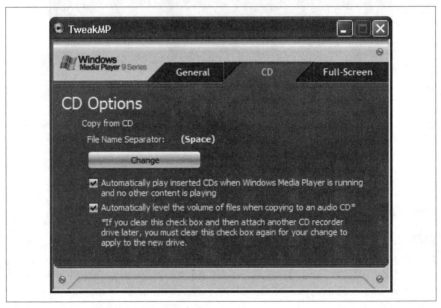

Figure 11-17. The CD tab of TweakMP

Another useful feature is the ability to change the separator used between the filename details (such as the title of the song and its artist) when you rip files from a CD. By default, a space is put between them. But this tab will let you use another character or set of characters up to five characters long instead. (You can't use \, /, :, *, ?, <, >, or |.) Just click the Change button, type the character or characters in the "File name separator" box, and click OK.

This tab also lets you control whether Windows Media Player will automatically play a CD when you insert it into the drive.

Full-Screen

The Full-Screen tab, shown in Figure 11-18, lets you control Windows Media Player's full-screen mode.

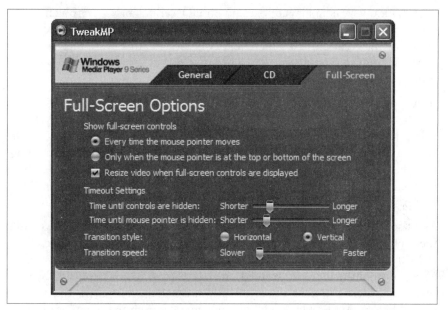

Figure 11-18. The Full-Screen tab

Windows Media Player's full-screen mode operates when it is maximized, and this tab controls its behavior. So, this tab controls whether the full-screen controls should appear whenever the mouse cursor moves, or only when it's at the top or bottom of the screen, and whether the video portion of the screen should be resized when the full-screen controls are displayed. You can also control the time it takes before the controls hide when there is no mouse movement, and the time it takes to hide the mouse pointer when there is no mouse movement. You can also control transitions when the controls fade in and out.

See Also

- "Problem-Free CD Burning" [Hack #100]
- "Save Streaming Music to Your PC" [Hack #101]
- "Fix Windows Media Player's Privacy Problems" [Hack #106]

Fix Windows Media Player's Privacy Problems

106 Lurking beneath Windows Media Player's slick exterior are potential invasions of your privacy. Here's how to fix them.

XP's Windows Media Player poses potentially serious privacy problems that, theoretically, could allow Microsoft to track what DVDs you play and could allow for the creation of a supercookie on your PC that would let web sites exchange information about you. There are things you can do, however, to protect your privacy when you use Windows Media Player.

If you use Windows Media Player to play DVD movies, whenever a new DVD is played Media Player contacts a Microsoft server and gets the DVD's title and chapter information. The server, in turn, identifies your specific version of Media Player, uses a cookie to identify the DVD you're watching, and then records information about the DVDs you watch onto a database on your hard disk in *C:\Documents and Settings\All Users\Application Data\ Microsoft\Media Index.*

Microsoft claims the cookie used is an anonymous one that can't personally identify you. The company also says it does not keep track of what DVDs individuals watch, and that the database created on your PC is never accessed from the Internet. Instead, the company says, it's used only by your own computer; the next time you put a DVD in your drive that you've played before, Media Player will get information from that database instead of getting it from a Microsoft web server.

Still, Microsoft has had its share of problems with privacy before, so you might or might not trust the company to keep the information private. There are two solutions to the problem. You can change your cookie controls to the highest level **[Hack #35]** so that your PC will reject all cookies. That carries with it its own set of problems, however, because then you won't be able to use customization and other features of many web sites. A better solution is to open Media Player and choose File → Work Offline. That way, Media Player won't contact a Microsoft server.

As for the so-called *supercookie* Windows Media Player creates, it's a unique ID number in the form of a 128-bit GUID assigned to your player and stored in the Registry. You can find it in HKEY_CURRENT_USER\Software\ Microsoft\WindowsMedia\WMSDK\General\UniqueID. This ID number can be retrieved by any web site through the use of JavaScript. The ID number is called a *supercookie* because it can be retrieved by *any* web site. Normally, web sites can retrieve only cookies they create and put on your PC, so it becomes difficult for web sites to share information about you. However, this supercookie can be retrieved by any site to track you, and web sites can share this information with each other, allowing them to create a sophisticated profile about your Internet usage. Additionally, cookie blockers can't block its use.

There's an easy way to fix the problem and protect your privacy, though. From Windows Media Player, choose Tools → Options → Player. In the "Internet settings" section, uncheck the box next to "Allow Internet sites to uniquely identify your Player." That's all it takes; the problem will be fixed.

If you download and install Windows Media Player, you can stop these privacy problems before they begin if you pay attention to the installation questions. During the installation, look for the screen asking you for your privacy preferences, as shown in Figure 11-19.

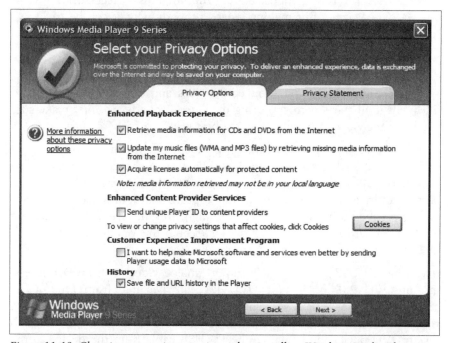

Figure 11-19. Choosing your privacy options when installing Windows Media Player

The Enhanced Content Provider and Customer Experience Improvement Program options are the ones that can be problematic. When you check boxes in those areas, Windows Media Player will report on your music and movie use to Microsoft and will also put the supercookie on your PC. So, if privacy is a concern of yours, just say no.

See Also

- For more information about Windows Media Player privacy issues, read articles about it by privacy expert Richard Smith at *http://www. computerbytesman.com/privacy/supercookie.htm* and *http://www. computerbytesman.com/privacy/wmp8dvd.htm*.

HACK 107 Make Videos with Windows Movie Maker

You can make better home movies and other videos with XP's built-in video maker.

XP is Microsoft's most media-aware operating system and it comes with Windows Movie Maker, built-in software for making and editing videos and home movies. (To run it, choose Start → All Programs → Accessories → Windows Movie Maker.) But making videos properly with it can be tricky, so check out these tips on how to make better home movies and videos.

Capture the Video Properly

Windows Movie Maker lets you edit movies and add special effects and titles, but it all starts with capturing the video properly. So, first make sure you bring the video into your PC in the best way.

If you have an analog video camera or videotape, you need some way of turning those analog signals into digital data. You can do this via a video capture board, or by using a device you can attach to your FireWire or USB port. If you're going the route of a video capture board, make sure the board has XP-certified drivers; otherwise, you might run into trouble. To find out whether a board has XP-certified drivers, search the Windows Compatibility List at *http://www.microsoft.com/windows/catalog*.

If you have a USB port, you can import analog video with DVD Express, Instant DVD 2.0, or Instant DVD+DV, all available from *http://www. adstech.com*. They're hardware/software combinations; to get the video into your PC, connect the analog video device to the USB Instant Video or USB InstantDVD device, and then connect a USB cable from the device to the USB port on your PC. (A similar product, called the Dazzle Digital Video Creator, will do the same thing. For details, go to *http://www.dazzle.com*.)

Check your system documentation to see what type of USB port you have. If you have a USB 1.1 port, you won't be able to import high-quality video, and you'd be better off installing a video capture card. USB 2.0 will work fine, though.

If you have a FireWire-enabled PC, you're also in luck because its high-speed capacity is also suitable for importing video. You'll have to buy extra hardware, called SCM Microsystems Dazzle Hollywood DV-Bridge. Plug your RCA cable or S-Video cable into Hollywood DV-Bridge, and then plug a FireWire cable from Hollywood DV-Bridge into your FireWire port, and you'll be able to send video to your PC. It's available at online stores such as *http://www.buy.com*.

Once you've set up the hardware and your camera, recording the video is easy. Open Windows Movie Maker, choose File → Record, start the camera or video, and click Record.

Capturing Video with a Digital Video Camera

If you have a digital video camera or webcam, you shouldn't need any extra hardware to capture video from it, as long as you have a FireWire port on your PC. These devices generally include built-in FireWire ports (the cameras might call the port an IEEE-1394 port or an i.Link port). If you don't have a FireWire port on your PC, you can install a FireWire port card. These generally cost much less than $100. Make sure the card is Open Host Controller Interface (OHCI)–compliant.

When you plug your digital camera into a FireWire port and turn it on, Windows will ask you what you want to do with the camera. Tell it you want to Record in Movie Maker, and it will launch Movie Maker to the Record dialog box with a video showing in the preview window.

Best Settings for Recording Video

Before you start recording, you'll see a preview of your movie in the Record dialog box, shown in Figure 11-20. This is your chance to change your video settings, and choosing the proper setting is perhaps the most important step in creating your video.

Look at the Setting drop-down box in Figure 11-20. This box lets you choose the quality of the video you're creating, which is the most important setting. What you choose for this setting will depend on the input source; digital video cameras, for example, let you record at a higher quality than analog video cameras, so they will give you a wider range of options. Movie Maker comes with a number of preset profiles, including three basic ones: High, Medium, and Low quality. When you choose your profile, Movie Maker tells you how many hours and minutes of recording time you have, based on your disk space and the disk requirements of the profile. For example, you might have 193 hours of recording time based on the High setting, but 1,630 hours based on the Low setting.

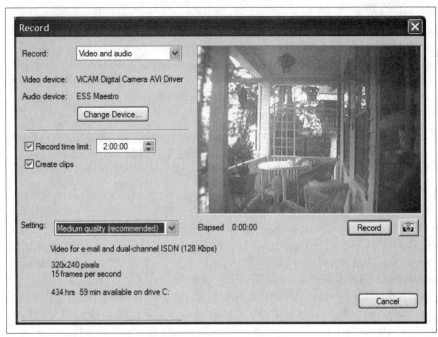

Figure 11-20. Options for recording video in Windows Movie Maker

Those three profiles aren't your only choices, though. You can choose from a much wider variety of profiles (as a general rule, I suggest doing that), based on what you plan to do with the eventual video. Do you plan to post the video on the Web? Just play it back at home? Run it on a personal digital assistant? These other profiles are designed for specific purposes like those.

To select the profile, choose Other in the Setting drop-down list. Underneath it, a new drop-down list appears, shown in Figure 11-21, with a range of profiles from which you can choose. They're prebuilt for specific uses— for example, recording video to post on the Web, for color PDA devices, and for broadband NTSC (National Television System Committee), which is standard TV.

Whenever you choose a profile, you'll see underneath it the frame size of the video and the frames per second. If you choose a profile from Other, you'll also see the video bit rate. Here's what the settings mean:

Video display size
    The size of the video, in pixels—for example, 740×480, or 320×240.

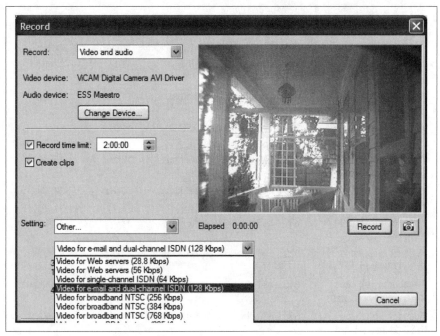

Figure 11-21. Choosing from additional preset profiles

Frames per second
> The number of frames captured per second. For smooth video, you need 30 frames per second, which is the "high-quality" setting. The medium- and low-quality settings record at 15 frames per second.

Video bit rate
> The bit rate of the recorded video—the higher the bit rate, the greater the quality.

Audio bit rate and properties
> These settings aren't shown in the Windows Movie settings, but they vary according to which profile you choose. Audio properties are measured in kilohertz (kHz)—the higher the number, the greater the quality. Audio bit rate measures the bit rate—again, the higher the bit rate, the greater the quality.

To help you make the best choice among profiles, Table 11-2 shows the settings for all the Movie Maker profiles.

Table 11-2. Settings for Movie Maker profiles

Profile name	Video display size	Video bit rate	Audio properties	Audio bit rate
Video for web servers (28.8Kbps)	160 × 120 pixels	20Kbps	8kHz	8Kbps
Video for web servers (56Kbps)	176 × 144 pixels	30Kbps	11kHz	10Kbps
Video for single-channel ISDN (64Kbps)	240 × 176 pixels	50Kbps	11kHz	10Kbps
Video for email and dual-channel ISDN (128Kbps)	320 × 240 pixels	100Kbps	16kHz	16Kbps
Video for broadband NTSC (256Kbps)	320 × 240 pixels	225Kbps	32kHz	32Kbps
Video for broadband NTSC (384Kbps)	320 × 240 pixels	350Kbps	32kHz	32Kbps
Video for broadband NTSC (768Kbps)	320 × 240 pixels	700Kbps	44kHz	64Kbps
Video for broadband NTSC (1500Kbps total)	640 × 480 pixels	1,368Kbps	44kHz	128Kbps
Video for broadband NTSC (2Mbps total)	640 × 480 pixels	1,868Kbps	44kHz	128Kbps
Video for broadband film content (768Kbps)	640 × 480 pixels	568Kbps	44kHz	128Kbps
Video for broadband film content (1500Kbps total)	640 × 480 pixels	1,368Kbps	44kHz	128Kbps
Video for color PDA devices (150Kbps)	208 × 160 pixels	111Kbps	22kHz	32Kbps
Video for color PDA devices (225Kbps)	208 × 160 pixels	186Kbps	22kHz	32Kbps
DV-AVI (25Mbps)	720 × 480 pixels (NTSC); 720 × 525 pixels (PAL)	1,411Kbps	48kHz	16Kbps

Tips for Making Your Own DVDs

If you use Movie Maker to make or copy your own videos and burn them to DVDs, consider these tips:

- The USB 1.0 standard is not fast enough to connect a camera or other video input to your PC. Its throughput of 11Mbps isn't fast enough for capturing high-quality video, which is 30 frames per second with 24-bit color at a resolution of 640×480, and requires speeds of at least 210Mbps. USB 2.0, which has a speed of 480Mbps, and FireWire, which has a speed of 400Mbps, will work, however.

- Make sure you have a substantial amount of free hard-disk space if you're going to burn your videos to DVDs. The video will be cached onto your hard disk before it's burned to DVDs, so you'll typically need several free gigabytes.

- Defragment your hard drive [Hack #94] before creating and burning DVDs for best performance. If you have a second hard drive, use that for DVD creation rather than your primary hard drive. Regardless of the speed of your CPU, turn off any background applications that are running when you import video and create your DVD.

- If you're burning high-quality video to a DVD, figure that you'll be able to fit about an hour's worth on a single DVD. At a lower quality (lower bit rate), you can fit up to about two hours on a DVD. Keep in mind, though, that if you write at the lower bit rate, the DVD might not be able to be played on a set-top DVD player, though it will work on your PC's DVD player.

- There's no single accepted standard for DVD burning, so not all DVD disks that you burn will work on all set-top DVD players. Generally, most set-top DVD players will play DVD-R discs, but all of them might not play DVD-RW or DVD+RW disks. Manufacturer information can't always be trusted, but check the companies'web sites for the latest details.

- After you've created your video and you're ready to burn it to a DVD, set aside plenty of time. It can take up to two hours to burn a one-hour DVD, depending on your CPU and drive speed.

See Also

- If you want features beyond those offered by Windows Movie Maker, try a variety of software from Ulead Software, including Ulead Video-Studio, Ulead DVD Movie Factory, and Ulead DVD Workshop. They go far beyond basic video-editing tools, and they let you use transitions and add special effects and menus. The software also includes backgrounds, preset layouts, and music you can add to your videos. In addition, they will burn to DVD, VCD, and SVCD and can save files in a variety of video formats. They're shareware and available to try for free, but you're expected to pay if you keep using them. For details, go to *http://www.ulead.com*.

CHAPTER TWELVE

System Performance
Hacks 108–114

XP provides you with a variety of ways to hack your system to juice up its performance. Built-in tools, like the Performance Console, can monitor dozens of performance metrics and then take automated actions when those metrics fall below a certain level. You can make better use of your existing RAM by using a variety of different hacks, and the Registry offers many ways to speed up system performance as well.

In this chapter, we'll cover all those ways, as well as others, to help you make sure XP runs as efficiently as possible. You'll also see how you can fix a variety of problems that can bedevil your system if you upgrade to SP2.

HACK 108 Track System Performance with the Performance Console

Before you can hack away at things to speed up your computer, you should know how to monitor system performance in the first place. As a power user, you'll like knowing what's causing those slowdowns and blips in performance. The Performance Console is a great hacker's tool for monitoring and tracking resources of all kinds.

Computers get faster every year, but somehow we sometimes still end up waiting around for them to finish a task.

To figure out what's slowing down your computer and to get to the root of the problem, use the Performance Console (perfmon) to track and graph the activities of Windows XP and its components. First, I'll show you how to set up a log, and then I'll give you some ways to put the console logs to good use.

Setting Up Your Logs

Choose Start → Run and type perfmon. You'll see the Microsoft Management Console (MMC) with the Performance titlebar. In the left pane, click

Reducing Visual Effects

Windows XP's visual effects—such as fading and sliding menus, background images for folders, and drop shadows for icon labels—make it the snazziest-looking operating system Microsoft has produced so far. But all those effects can take their toll on system performance, especially if you have an older computer.

XP gives you the option of balancing these visual effects against system performance. You can go full-bore and use all the visual effects, you can turn all of them off, you can have your system decide which to use, or you can pick and choose which effects to turn on and off. Right-click My Computer and choose Properties → Advanced → Settings (under the Performance section). To turn off all visual effects, choose "Adjust for best performance." To use all visual effects, choose "Adjust for best appearance." To turn individual effects on and off, choose Custom, then check the effects you want to use and uncheck the ones you don't. Experiment to see how they affect system performance.

System Monitor to see a graph of your current system performance, including your processor, memory, and disk. You can use the toolbar buttons to configure the graph data and format. This graph is useful for seeing what's going on now, but it's useless for looking at the long-term picture.

To create log files of your system's performance, click Performance Logs and Alerts in the left pane of the MMC. You can create counter logs (with the values of performance indicators, measured on a regular basis), trace logs (with the values of performance indicators when something happens, such as a program crash), and alerts (an action for Windows to take when a counter hits a specified value). Log files stored in text format contain one line per observation, with values separated by either commas or tabs, and are usually stored in the *C:\Perflogs* folder. You can import these log files into a spreadsheet or database for analysis, reporting, and graphing. SQL and binary (nontext) log file formats are also available. (See article Q296222 in the Microsoft Knowledgebase for how to log data directly to an SQL database.)

Create a counter log by right-clicking Counter Logs in the left pane and choosing New Log Settings from the shortcut menu. Give the new log a name and press OK. Specify the statistics you want to log by clicking Add Counters on the General tab of the Properties sheet for the log (see Figure 12-1). A nice feature of this utility is that you can choose whether to monitor the local computer or another computer on your LAN. Don't add more than a few counters, or your log file will grow quickly and be confusing to analyze. To select a counter, first select the performance object (that is, the part of the computer system you want to monitor, such as memory or disks), and then choose counters from the list.

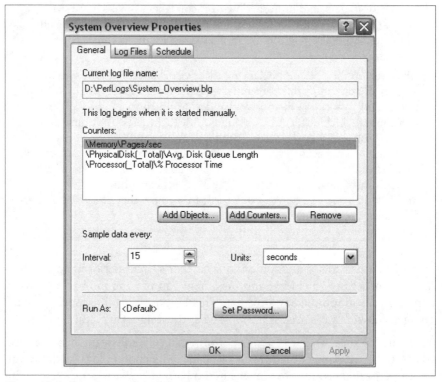

Figure 12-1. Creating or editing a performance log

Set the interval to the frequency at which you'd like to sample the data. Don't choose too frequent an interval, or your log file will take over your entire hard disk (start with once a minute). On the Log Files tab, specify the file type, name, and location. If you plan to import this file into a spreadsheet or database program, choose Text File (comma-delimited) for the type. On the Schedule tab, specify when the log start and stops—manually, or automatically on a schedule.

> The Performance console itself can slow down your computer considerably. Run it only when you need it, and don't set the logging interval to be too short. Set logs to stop after a day or two; otherwise, they'll run until your hard disk fills up.

What to Watch

These counters are often worth logging:

\Memory\Pages/sec
> Number of pages read from disk or written to disk when Windows runs out of memory. Swapping information to and from the disk can slow down your system significantly. Consider adding more memory.

\PhysicalDisk\Avg. Disk Queue Length
> Number of read and write requests that are waiting for the disk to respond. High numbers indicate that a faster disk drive would speed up performance.

\PhysicalDisk\% Disk Time
> Percentage of the time the disk was busy. This is another indicator of a slow or overloaded disk.

\Processor\% Processor Time
> Percentage of the time the processor was busy with all types of processes. This counter can tell you whether delays are caused by an overloaded CPU.

Viewing Performance Logs

With the System Monitor in the MMC, you can view a log as a graph. Click System Monitor in the left pane of the MMC window and click the View Log Data icon on its toolbar. Add the log file to the list. When you are looking at the graph, click the Properties button on the toolbar to change how the graph looks.

To look at the contents of a comma-separated (*.cvs*) log file in Excel or your default spreadsheet program, double-click the filename in Windows Explorer. Excel might complain that the file is still open (since the Performance Console is still appending information to it); click Notify to see what's in the file so far. In Excel, you can analyze, graph, and print the counters.

Performance Alerts

Create an alert to let you know when a counter exceeds a specified value. For example, the Performance Console can let you know when the idle processor time drops lower than 10%. Right-click Alerts in the left pane of the MMC window and choose New Alert Settings to create a new alert. Add one or more counters, and specify the limit (upper or lower) beyond which Windows should take action. On the Action tab, specify what Windows does when the alert occurs: specifically, you can have it add a note to an event log or run a program.

—*Margaret Levine Young*

H A C K   Get the Most Out of Your RAM
109
The best way to improve system performance is to make better use of your RAM. Here are several hacks to show you how to try this before you buy more.

No matter how much memory you have, you could always use more. Installing more RAM is generally the quickest way to better XP performance.

But you can also speed up XP by making better use of the RAM you already have. In this hack, we'll look at how you can speed up your system performance by using your RAM more effectively.

Make Better Use of Your Memory with the Task Manager

If your system doesn't have enough RAM, or if it uses what it has improperly, your system slows down. That's because in those circumstances it moves data and programs to a paging file on your hard disk, and your hard disk is slower than RAM. A certain amount of this is normal, but if you use a paging file too often, or if even your paging file can't handle the memory load, you'll run into system slowdowns and problems.

The Task Manager's Performance tab, shown in Figure 12-2, provides the best way to monitor memory use. To run the Task Manager, press Ctrl-Alt-Del, then click the Performance tab. With it, you can interpret the information and make better use of your memory.

The most important parts of the screen shown in Figure 12-2 are the charts that report on paging file use and the tabular material below it that gives a more detailed view of your current use of memory.

The charts relating to the Page File are self-explanatory: they show current usage, as well as usage over time. If you see Page File use is frequently high, it means either your system isn't making the most efficient use of RAM, or you need more RAM. In that case, follow the advice later in this hack for how to make better use of RAM.

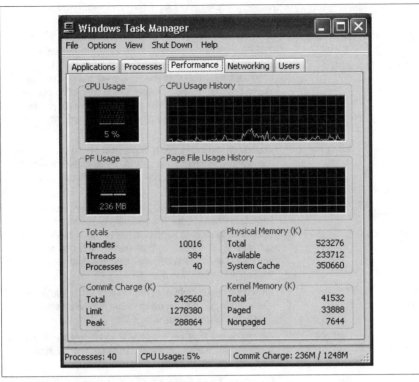

Figure 12-2. The Task Manager's Performance tab

The data below the Page File chart can be almost impossible to decipher. Table 12-1 details what the data means, and makes recommendations on how to use that information to make better use of RAM.

Table 12-1. Understanding Performance tab memory reporting

Category	Subcategory	What the data means
Totals	Handles	Lets a program use system resources such as registry keys, fonts, and bitmaps. Sometimes, poorly written programs don't close down their handles when the program closes, leading to memory loss. As a practical matter, you won't need to monitor this number.
	Threads	A discreet portion of a program executing a single task independently of other parts of a program. Again, as a practical matter, you won't need to monitor this number.
	Processes	Reports on the number of programs and services (processes) currently running on your system. Monitor this to see whether you have too many programs and services running on your PC. To shut down unnecessary services, see "Halt Startup Programs and Services" [Hack #4].

Table 12-1. *Understanding Performance tab memory reporting (continued)*

Category	Subcategory	What the data means
Commit Charge (K)	Total	The total amount of physical memory (RAM) and virtual memory (page file) currently in use, in kilobytes. The more programs, files, and data you have open, the greater your commit charge will be. The greater the commit charge, the more demands will be put on your system. To reduce the commit charge, close programs and files, especially large files.
	Limit	Reports on the total amount of physical and virtual memory, measured in kilobytes, that is currently available for your PC. To increase the limit, you can increase the Page File size or add RAM to your system.
	Peak	Reports on the highest total amount of memory, measured in kilobytes, that has been in use during your current session. Check this value each session to see whether the Peak value is frequently at or near the Limit value. If it is, you need to increase your memory, by either adding RAM or increasing your Page File size.
Physical Memory (K)	Total	Displays the total amount of RAM in your PC, in kilobytes. This number can be confusing; to find out the amount of RAM in megabytes, divide it by 1,024.
	Available	Reports on the total amount of RAM, in kilobytes, currently available. When available RAM is used up, your system begins to use its Page File.
	System Cache	Reports on the total amount of RAM, in kilobytes, that is being used for the most recently accessed data and programs. Programs and data can be in the system cache even after they have been closed down; the PC looks to the system cache first when opening a program or file, since it can be opened from the cache faster than from the hard disk.
Kernel Memory (K)	Total	The total amount of memory, in kilobytes, in use by the primary components of the XP kernel. The kernel comprises the core programs and files that make up the operating system.
	Paged	The total amount of memory in a Page File, in kilobytes, used by the primary components of XP.
	Nonpaged	The total amount of RAM, in kilobytes, used by the primary components of XP.

Here's how to use the information on the tab to make better use of RAM:

- If the Total Commit Charge exceeds the Total Physical Memory, you probably need more RAM. When the Commit Charge is regularly higher than the Physical Memory available, it means you have to regularly use a Page File, which slows down your system. Buy more RAM; it's inexpensive and will boost system performance.

- Before running a memory-intensive application, use the Processes Tab to identify memory-hogging applications, and close them down. The Processes tab of the Task Manager lists every process and program in use and shows the total amount of memory each uses. Click twice on the Mem Usage heading on the tab to reorder the list of programs and processes so that those requiring the most memory show up at the top. Close programs you don't really need before running a memory-intensive application.

- If the Peak Commit Charge is frequently at or near the Limit Commit Charge, you need to increase your memory. When this occurs, it means your PC is frequently out of memory or close to being out of memory. Either add RAM or increase your Page File size.

 For more advice on how to use the Task Manager to speed up your system, see "Speed Up System Performance with the Task Manager" [Hack #112].

General Advice for Making Better Use of RAM

So, you've learned how to use the Task Manager. Here are some additional tips for making better use of your existing RAM:

Remove DLLs from cache memory. If you notice your system running slowly after XP has been running for some time, or if your RAM seems to be getting low for some reason, the culprit might be left-behind DLLs from programs that are no longer running, but that XP still keeps in memory. Sometimes XP keeps DLLs in cache memory even when the program that required them is no longer running, and this cuts down on the memory available to other applications.

You can use a simple Registry hack to have XP automatically remove from cache memory DLLs that are no longer needed by programs. Run the Registry Editor [Hack #83] and go to HKEY_LOCAL_MACHINE\SOFTWARE\ Microsoft\Windows\CurrentVersion\Explorer. Create a new DWORD value named AlwaysUnloadDll, and give it a data value of 1. Exit the Registry and reboot for the new setting to take effect. Note that this setting might cause problems with some programs. Some Windows programs—especially older and 16-bit programs—can issue error messages with this setting in effect; so if that starts happening, delete the new key or give it a value of 0.

Reduce the number of colors. Using 32-bit color takes up a great deal more memory than 16-bit color, and it puts a greater strain on your processor. If you primarily use business applications such as word processors and spreadsheets, you most likely won't notice a different between 16-bit and 32-bit color, so going with 16-bit color is a good bet. To change your color depth, right-click the desktop, choose Properties → Settings, and in the Color Quality box choose 16 bit.

Avoid DOS applications. DOS applications don't allow XP to manage memory properly, and they hold on to the memory they use, not allowing it to be swapped out for use for other programs or processes. If you use any DOS applications, replace them with Windows versions.

Reduce the icons on your desktop. Every icon on your desktop uses memory. Delete icons you don't use regularly by running the Clean Desktop Wizard. Right-click the desktop and choose Properties → Desktop → Customize Desktop → Clean Desktop Now. A wizard will step you through the process of deleting unused icons. If you want the wizard to run every 60 days, check "Run Desktop Wizard every 60 days."

Reduce the applications and services running in the background. You might have many programs and services running in the background, without realizing it. Look at your Notification area, and see if there are any programs running that you don't require. Shut them down, and make sure they don't load at startup. Also, XP frequently starts services on startup that you might not need [Hack #4]. For example, if you don't use a wireless network card, you don't need the Wireless Zero Configuration service.

See Also

- "Speed Up System Performance with the Task Manager" [Hack #112]

HACK 110   More Power: Registry Hacks to Speed Up XP

Put your Registry-hacking knowledge to good use: hack your way to running Windows XP at top speed.

Creating and marketing tuning and customization utilities for the Windows XP operating system is quickly becoming big business. A Google search will turn up hundreds of sites and programs dedicated to tweaking Windows XP. But no matter what type of interface is developed to make system tweaking easier and safer for the average user, the end result is that the changes are reflected in XP by modifying the Registry. For some people, commercial tweaking utilities might be the method of choice, but with a few precautions and safeguards it's possible to enhance system performance using only those tools supplied with Windows XP.

As you learned in Chapter 7, you can use the Registry Editor [Hack #83] to edit the Registry. Make sure you take the precautions outlined in that chapter and back up your Registry [Hack #86], no matter how comfortable you are editing the thing.

No single tweak is going to take an ancient PC and turn it into a gamer's dream machine. It's even unlikely that a number of tweaks will achieve substantial performance gains, but every little bit does help. As long as you keep your expectations realistic, you'll learn something about the Registry and hopefully see a performance increase in the process.

Menu Speed

When XP first appeared, there was a lot of conversation about the new interface, both good and bad. In spite of the initial complaints, most users stick with the default settings rather than reverting to the Classic interface found in previous Windows versions. But you might want to change the delay you notice when you click the Start menu. I see no reason for there to be any delay when I click the Start menu. Effects are pretty, but I wouldn't click it if I didn't have business inside, so let's get it open and get moving. The default speed can be adjusted with a quick Registry hack.

Go to the Registry key `HKEY_CURRENT_USER\Control Panel\Desktop\MenuShowDelay`. The default value is 400. Set it to 0 to remove the delay completely, but if you do that it will be nearly impossible to move the mouse fast enough not to activate All Programs if you mouse over it en route to your final selection. Pick a number that suits your style, make the change, and then test it until you find a good compromise between speed and usability.

Place Windows Kernel into RAM

It's a given that anything that runs in RAM will be faster than an item that has to access the hard drive and virtual memory. Rather than have the kernel that is the foundation of XP using the slower Paging Executive functions, use this hack to create and set the `DisablePagingExecutive` DWORD to a value of 1.

> Perform this hack *only* if the system has 256MB or more of installed RAM!

Edit the Registry key `HKEY_LOCAL_MACHINE\SYSTEM\CurrentControlSet\Control\Session Manager\Memory Management\DisablePagingExecutive` to 1 to disable paging and have the kernel run in RAM (set the value to 0 to undo this hack). Exit the Registry and reboot.

Alter Prefetch Parameters

Prefetching (the reading of system boot files into a cache for faster loading) is a commonly overlooked component that can have a significant impact on system boot time. This tweak allows you to select which components will make use of the prefetch parameters. To see which files are gathered using each setting, clear the prefetch cache located at *C:\Windows\Prefetch* and then enable one of the settings listed in this hack. Clear the cache and repeat for each setting.

Set the Registry key HKEY_LOCAL_MACHINE\SYSTEM\CurrentControlSet\Control\ Session Manager\Memory Management\PrefetchParameters\EnablePrefetcher to 0 to disable prefetching, 1 to prefetch application launch files, 2 to prefetch boot files, or 3 to prefetch as many files as possible.

Disable 8.3 Name Creation in NTFS

Files that use the 8.3 naming convention can degrade NTFS drive performance. Unless you have a good reason for keeping the 8.3 naming convention intact (such as if you're using 16-bit programs), a performance gain can be achieved by disabling it.

Set the Registry DWORD key HKEY_LOCAL_MACHINE\SYSTEM\CurrentControlSet\ Control\FileSystem\NtfsDisable8dot3NameCreation to 1. Exit the Registry and reboot.

—*Jim Foley*

H A C K   Repair and Recover with the Recovery
111   Console

If Windows won't start, use the DOS-like Recovery Console to make repairs.

The Recovery Console is one of the last-ditch tools you can use if your Windows installation doesn't start up at all. Before you resort to the Recovery Console, if Windows starts up make sure you've already tried System Restore (especially if you've recently changed your hardware).

> To run System Restore, choose Control Panel → Performance and Maintenance → System Restore.

If it won't start, try running the Windows XP Setup Wizard from the installation CD and choosing its Repair option, or try starting Windows in Safe Mode.

If none of these easier paths works, you're stuck using the DOS-like Recovery Console to figure out what's wrong with Windows, your system or boot partition, or your disk's master boot record (MBR). You can use its DOS-like commands to look at the files and folders that make up Windows, and possibly to repair them. You can also repair the master boot record and boot sector.

> You can configure the Recovery Console not to require the administrator password on login. In the Registry Editor [Hack #83], set the value of the HKEY_LOCAL_MACHINE\SOFTWARE\ Microsoft\WindowsNT\CurrentVersion\Setup\RecoveryConsole\ SecurityLevel key to 1.

Starting the Recovery Console

To start the Recovery Console, boot your computer from the Windows XP installation CD and follow the prompts. When it asks which Windows installation you want, type the number of the installation (1, if Windows XP is the only operating system installed) and press Enter. Type the password for the Administrator account. When the Recovery Console is running, you see the prompt D:\WINDOWS>, which tells you the name of the current folder (directory).

> If you plan to use the Recovery Console often, add it to your boot menu (the menu that appears if you have a multiboot system). You must be logged in as an administrator. Choose Start → Run and type the command d:\i386\winnt32.exe /cmdcons (replace *d:* with your CD drive's letter if it's not D). The Recovery Console occupies about 7MB of disk space and stores its program files in *Comdcons* on your system drive.

Now you can type commands and press Enter, just like in the good old days of DOS! However, not all DOS commands work (see the "Hacking the Hack" section at the end of this hack), and you can't examine files in all folders. You are restricted to the Windows program folder (*C:\Windows* on most systems), its subfolders, the root folder of the Windows partition (*C:* on most systems), removable drives (including disk, zip, and CD drives— but these are read-only), and the *Cmdcons* folder (which contains the Recovery Console program itself, if you have added it to your boot menu).

If you know DOS, the Recovery Console's commands look familiar, though only a few are available and some work differently. To see a list of all the available commands, type help and press Enter. To find out how a specific command works, type the command, followed by a space and /? (for example, expand /?). When you are done using the Recovery Console, type exit and press Enter to reboot your computer.

Looking Around

Use these commands to examine your system:

cd *folder*
> Changes the current folder to the folder you name. In the folder name, two dots (..) represent the parent folder of the current folder. To move to a different drive, type its drive letter and a colon and press Enter.

dir *folder* *or* dir *filename*
> Lists the contents of the folder, including files and subfolders. For the filename, you can use * as a wildcard character (for example, dir *.dll). You see the last modification date and time, attributes, size (in bytes), and filename. The attributes are represented by letters: d (directory or folder), h (hidden), s (system), e (encrypted), r (read-only), a (changed since last backup), and c (compressed).

map
> Lists the drive letters with their file format (FAT32 or NTFS), size, and pathname.

type *filename*
> Displays the contents of the file as text. For executable, graphic, and other nontext files, you see garbage.

If a filename or pathname includes spaces, enclose it in double quotes.

Fixing the MBR, Boot Sector, or Boot Menu

If your system can't find a partition from which to boot, try fixing the MBR. Type fixmbr to rewrite the MBR on the boot partition (the drive or partition from which the computer starts up).

If the system finds the boot partition but the Windows boot sector is fouled up on the Windows partition (the drive or partition where Windows is installed), rewrite the Windows boot sector by typing fixboot. To specify which drive is the Windows partition, you can add the drive letter (e.g., fixboot c:).

Windows XP includes a boot menu that allows you to choose which operating system to start up. (It doesn't appear if your system has only one operating system.) To fix the boot menu, use the bootscan command. Type bootcfg /scan to look at all your partitions and drives and scan for Windows installations. Type bootcfg /list to list the entries in *boot.ini* (the file that contains your boot menu entries).

Fixing Windows

If something is wrong with your Windows installation, use these commands to modify or replace the problematic files:

attrib *filename flag*
> Changes the attribute of a file (*filename*). The *flag* is + (adds, or turns on) or - (removes, or turns off), followed by r (read-only), s (system), or h (hidden).

chkdsk *drive*
> Checks and repairs files and folders on *drive*. Add the /p switch to check the drive even if no problems are marked.

copy *sourcepath1 sourcepath2*
> Copies the file from *sourcepath1* and names the new file *sourcepath2*. The asterisk wildcard (*) doesn't work, so you can copy only one file at a time.

diskpart
> Lets you add or delete partitions, though you can't resize or move them. (For that, you need a program like PartitionMagic; go to *http://www.partitionmagic.com*.)

expand *pathname*
> Decompresses files from a *.cab* file and puts the result in the current folder. If the *.cab* file contains more than one file, add /f:* to extract all the files. Or add /f:* /d to list all the files in the *.cab*, and then use the expand *pathname* /f:*filename* command to extract just the one you want.

Hacking the Hack

By default, the Recovery Console doesn't allow you to use wildcards, copy files from local drives to removable media, or use the cd command to list files in subfolders in all folders on all local disks. It also issues a warning message every time you copy files that overwrite existing files.

However, if you have XP Professional Edition, you can change that behavior using the Group Policy Editor. At a command prompt, type gpedit.msc to run the Group Policy Editor. Go to Local Computer Policy\Computer

Configuration\Windows   Settings\Security   Settings\Local   Policies\
Security Options. In the list of policies on the right, double-click "Recover console: Allow floppy copy and access to all drives and all folders." Select the Enabled option and click OK.

Doing this won't actually make the changes; at this point, you'll have to use the Recovery Console itself to do that. Open the Recovery Console and use the following commands to customize its behavior:

set allowwildcards = true
> This command lets you use the * and ? wildcards with the Recovery Console commands.

set allowallpaths = true
> This command lets you use the cd command to list all files and subfolders on all folders on all local disks.

set allowremovablemedia = true
> This command lets you copy files from local drives to removable media.

set nocopyprompt = true
> This command lets you copy files that overwrite existing files without getting a warning prompt.

—Margaret Levine Young

HACK
112   Speed Up System Performance with the Task Manager

This humble tool does more than show you what applications are running; it can help you juice up your PC's performance as well.

Most XP users know the Task Manager will show them all programs and processes running on their system and that it will let them shut down any they don't want to run any longer. But it can do much more than that; it can also help fine-tune system performance.

> The Task Manager can also help you get the most out of your existing RAM. For details, see "Get the Most Out of Your RAM" [Hack #109].

There are three common ways to run the Task Manager:

- Press Ctrl-Alt-Del
- Press Ctrl-Shift-Esc
- Right-click the taskbar and choose Task Manager

The Task Manager, shown in Figure 12-3, has five tabs, but you'll use the Applications, Processes, and Performance tabs to help improve system performance. At the bottom of each tab, you'll find a quick summary of the current state of your system, including current CPU use, the number of processes running, and how much memory is dedicated to your system.

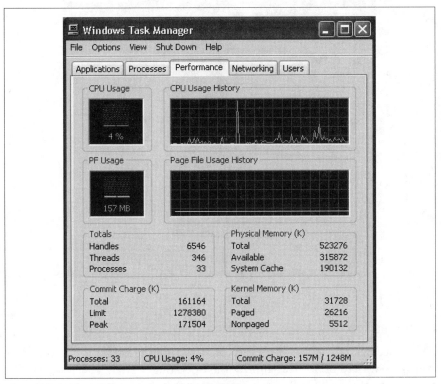

Figure 12-3. The Performance tab of the Task Manager

Before you can learn how to use these tabs to improve performance, you'll need some background about each tab.

Applications Tab

The Applications tab displays a list of every application currently running on your PC, such as Word, Excel, and any other application. It also reports on the status of each application—primarily, whether the application is running, or not responding to input.

When you right-click an application, a menu of choices lets you manage the application in several ways; you can switch to it, move it to the front, minimize it, maximize it, or close it, as shown in Figure 12-4.

Figure 12-4. The Task Manager's Applications tab

Processes Tab

The Processes tab reports on every process running on your computer, as well as a variety of services run by the operating system. It reports on the percentage of the CPU that each process uses, as well as how much memory each process uses.

When you right-click any process, you get a menu of choices that allow you to manage the process in a variety of ways, including closing that process as well as any related processes, as shown in Figure 12-5.

Performance Tab

The Performance tab shows a variety of performance measurements, including total CPU use, CPU usage history, page file usage history, memory used, and other statistics, as shown in Figure 12-6. You'll use this tab more than any other when tracking system performance and unstopping bottlenecks.

Figure 12-5. The Task Manager's Processes tab

The Performance tab has tabular material and four graphs that detail your computer's current performance. The graphs are straightforward and easy to understand:

CPU Usage
Shows you the percentage of your CPU that your PC is currently using

CPU Usage History
Shows usage over time

PF Usage
Shows you how much of your page file you're currently using

Page File Usage History
Shows usage over time

Task Manager updates its data every two seconds, and each vertical line on the graphs represents a two-second interval. To change the update time, from the Task Manager choose View → Update Speed and select High or Low. When you select High, updates take place twice a second. When you

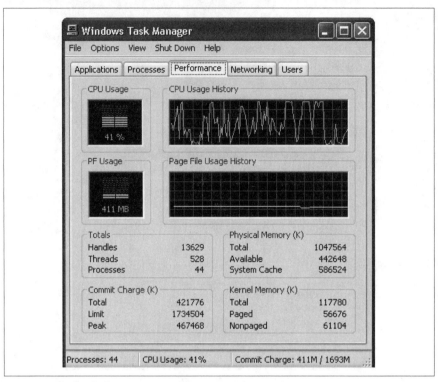

Figure 12-6. The Task Manager's Performance tab

select Low, updates take place once every four seconds. To stop updating altogether, select Paused. To do an immediate update, press F5.

Monitor CPU Use

Today's microprocessors (1GHz or higher) can handle most tasks easily, but CPU-intensive software or tasks such as computer-aided design (CAD) programs, CD burning, and games can slow down a system significantly. You can use the Task Manager to monitor your CPU use and, based on what you find, take steps to help your system run faster.

You'll monitor your CPU usage by using the Processes and Performance tabs of the Task Manager. You'll check two things: total CPU load and how much of the CPU any individual process or program uses.

Finding out how much of the CPU individual programs and processes use. A common cause of CPU slowdown is that one or more programs or processes take up too much of the CPU's attention. You can check the percentage of the CPU that any individual program uses. Once you determine that, close the application; your system will get a quick performance boost. If you need to run that application, close any other applications that take up too much CPU attention.

From the Task Manager's Processes tab, double-click the CPU heading. It will reorder the listing of processes and programs in descending order, listing those that use the most CPU time at the top. Note that, frequently, the top listing will be titled System Idle Process, which reports on the percentage of your CPU that is idle. Look for any programs or processes that use a considerable amount of your CPU. If you find any, close them before starting any other CPU-intensive applications, such as CAD programs and CD-burning software.

Tracking CPU usage in real time. If your CPU regularly uses a high percentage of its capacity, it means there's a bottleneck. You should upgrade the CPU, buy a new computer, or run fewer programs. But how can you know whether your CPU has a bottleneck? Check your CPU use. Run Task Manager and choose Options → Hide When Minimized. Now, whenever you minimize the Task Manager, it will sit in the system tray area of the taskbar.

Now, minimize the Task Manager. It will display as a small bar graph in the system tray that lights up green as you use your CPU. To see your current CPU usage, hold your mouse cursor over the Task Manager's icon in the system tray. Try running different combinations of programs and monitor your CPU use with each combination. If you find your CPU is overburdened on a regular basis, it's time for an upgraded CPU or a new computer.

Give Program and Processes More of Your CPU's Attention

XP gives a *base priority* to every program and process running on your PC; the base priority determines the relative amount of CPU power the program or process gets, compared to other programs. Here are the priorities XP assigns:

- Low
- BelowNormal
- Normal
- AboveNormal
- High
- RealTime

Most programs and processes are assigned a Normal priority. But you might want to give a program like a CAD or graphics program more of your CPU's attention. That way, the program will get the CPU power it needs and will therefore run more smoothly and quickly. If there are programs or processes that normally run in the background or rarely need your CPU, you can give them less of your CPU's attention.

You can use the Task Manager to change the priorities assigned to any process or program. The priorities of Low, BelowNormal, Normal, AboveNormal, and High are self-explanatory, but you might not quite understand RealTime. RealTime devotes an exceedingly high number of CPU cycles to the given task—so much so that even the Task Manager might not be able to interrupt any program or process assigned that priority. So, you shouldn't assign a RealTime priority to any program or task, unless it will be the sole program or task running on the PC. Of course, if it's the only program or task running, you really don't need to give it a high priority because it already has your CPU's complete attention.

To change the priority of a running program or process from the Processes tab, right-click the program or process whose priority you want to change, highlight Set Priority, and choose the priority for the program, as shown in Figure 12-7.

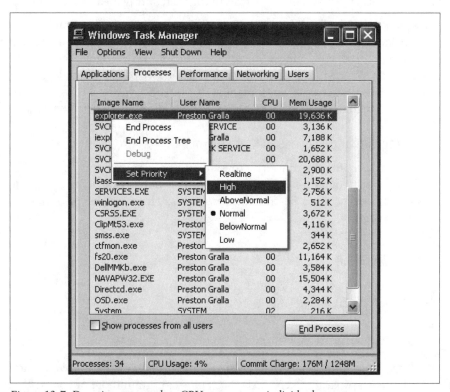

Figure 12-7. Devoting more or less CPU power to an individual program or process

Be careful when using this feature because it can have unintended conse-
quences and lead to system instability. If you find it causes problems, stop
using it.

Keep in mind that when you assign a new priority to a process or program, that new priority sticks only as long as the
program or process is running. Once the program or process
ends and you restart it, it defaults to the priority assigned to
it by XP.

Hack Your Way to a Cleaner Hard Disk

Cut through the clutter, clean up your hard disk, and reclaim space you never
knew you had with these hacks, techniques, and downloads.

No matter how much hard-disk space you have, it's just never enough. Your
hard disk is littered with old files you no longer need, temporary files, cache
files, and more clutter than an old attic. Here's how to hack your way to a
cleaner hard disk.

Create Separate Hard-Disk Cleanup Profiles

XP's Disk Cleanup tool (Control Panel → Performance and Maintenance →
"Free up space on your hard disk") is a quick-and-dirty way to clean your
hard disk of unnecessary files. It calculates how much hard-disk space you
can save by deleting a variety of different file types and caches or compressing and archiving old files you rarely use (see Figure 12-8).

But enabling and disabling all its various options each time can be time-consuming. And simply using the settings from the last run might not quite suit
your fancy. Sometimes you might want only certain files deleted and others
kept around a little longer. For example, your temporary Internet files speed
up your browsing experience by keeping on hand the graphics files associated with sites you frequently or have recently visited.

To solve this problem, you can create separate disk-cleanup profiles; that
way, whenever you want your hard disk cleaned in a certain way, you can
run just that one profile. For another set of cleanup options, just use a different profile.

While these profiles aren't available via the GUI, you can get at them under
the covers by using the command-line version of the Disk Cleanup tool:
cleanmgr.exe. First, you need to create a new disk-cleanup profile. Type
cleanmgr /Saveset:*n*, where *n* is any number between 1 and 65535. The Disk

Figure 12-8. The Disk Cleanup tool reporting how much hard-disk space it can free up

Cleanup Settings dialog will appear, as shown in Figure 12-9, allowing you to select which items you would like to be cleaned using this profile.

While at first blush it might appear you've reached the same dialog you reached using the GUI version of Disk Cleanup, take a closer look. You'll notice you're offered more cleanup options. You're able to automatically remove debug dump files, setup log files, catalog files for the Content Indexer, temporary setup files, old *Chkdsk* files, and various other items the GUI version doesn't offer to clean for you.

> If you're creating a profile to clean a drive other than the one containing Windows, most of these options won't be enabled. You'll be able to automatically clean only the Recycle Bin and catalog files for the Content Indexer.

Make your selections and click OK to create your cleanup profile. To run this profile at any time, type cleanmgr /Saverun:*n*, where *n* is the number of the profile you've just created.

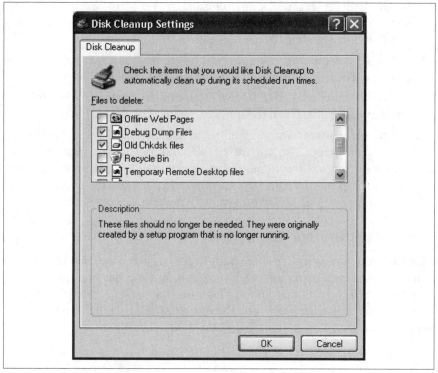

Figure 12-9. The Disk Cleanup Settings screen

When using Disk Cleanup, from either the command line or the Windows GUI, be careful when letting it delete downloaded program files. These are often ActiveX programs and Java add-ins that are frequently useful, so let it delete them only if you know you don't use them.

Clean Your Hard Disk Without Disk Cleanup

Frequently, cleaning your hard disk manually is more effective than using Disk Cleanup. Disk Cleanup won't find all the files you want to delete, and it might also delete files you'd prefer to keep. For example, Disk Cleanup won't delete all the files in your *TEMP* directory, even though it says it will. Also, it doesn't touch files that are less than one week old.

A manual cleaning should include the following steps:

1. Empty the Recycle Bin.
2. Search for all files that end in *.bak* and *.tmp* and that start with ~ (use the wildcard * when you search—for example, *.tmp, *.bak, and ~*.*).

Delete them all, except for any files that are dated the current or previous day. You might find some files can't be deleted because they are in use. Don't worry about it; just leave them.

3. Delete your temporary Internet files by running Internet Explorer and choosing Tools → Internet Options → General → Delete Files.

4. Delete files in your \TEMP folders. There might be two of these folders: one named C:\TEMP and the other named C:\Windows\TEMP.

5. Delete old system restore points, which can take up a substantial amount of space. You can delete all your old system restore points except the most current one, so before doing this, make sure you don't need any old points. Run Disk Cleanup, then choose the More Options tab and click the Clean Up button in the System Restore section.

Download a Better Disk-Cleanup Tool

Disk Cleanup works fine for a free built-in tool. But you can download tools that can do an even better job; such tools can find and delete duplicate files, delete *orphan* shortcuts that link to programs that no longer exist, and similar functions. There are many out there; two of the best are CleanUp! and System Mechanic.

CleanUp! (*http://www.emesoft.se*; $18, trial version available) expands on XP's Disk Cleanup tool by finding and deleting shortcuts and favorites that are no longer valid, giving you a list of Registry entries that point to files no longer on your hard disk, and letting you examine and delete Internet Explorer AutoComplete entries.

System Mechanic (*http:/www.iolo.com*; $59.95, trial version available) is far more than a disk-cleanup tool. In addition to normal cleanup tasks, it finds and deletes obsolete and junk files that are left behind by uninstalled programs, finds and deletes duplicate files, finds and fixes broken shortcuts, cleans out the Registry, lets you fine-tune Windows settings, provides privacy protection, and more. In all, it offers a suite of 15 utilities.

HACK 114 Fix SP2 Upgrade Woes

The Windows XP Service Pack 2 (SP2) is a boon for those looking for better security and wireless access. But it can also block automatic updates, kill applications, and worse. Here's what you can do to solve these problems.

SP2 is a must-have, if only for its new security features. But it's far from perfect. It's caused all kinds of problems on many people's systems, and yours might be one of them. You might find out you can't use the Microsoft Automatic Updates site, the Windows Firewall won't let some of your applications run, and your firewall or antivirus software doesn't appear to work after you install SP2. In this hack, you'll learn what you can do to fix those problems, and as a last resort, if you can't fix them, how to uninstall SP2.

Solve Windows Update Problems

One excellent way to keep Windows up-to-date is to visit the Windows Update site (*http://v5.windowsupdate.microsoft.com*). But some people have found that when they visit Windows Update after installing SP2, or click a link on the page, they get the error message: HTTP Error 500 - Internal Server Error, Error 0x8ddd0010. As always with the Web, the page doesn't offer help about what went wrong or how to fix it.

If the page does load, you might run into another problem: when you click the "View installation history" link, or when you click the Details link, you get only a blank page. You might also be told that a pop up has been blocked.

The problem is that Internet Explorer's pop-up blocker, installed by SP2, is blocking pop ups that you need to use the site. To fix the problem, you need to tell SP2 to allow pop ups from the Microsoft Update site.

To do this in Internet Explorer, choose Tools → Pop-up Blocker → Pop-up Blocker Settings. In the box next to "Address of web site to allow," type http://v5.windowsupdate.microsoft.com, and click Add, as shown in Figure 12-10.

Click Close. From now on, pop ups won't be blocked at the site, so it should work. If blocking pop ups cause problems at other sites, repeat these steps, and type in the appropriate URLs.

> For more information on using SP2's pop-up blocker, see "Stop Pop Ups with SP2—and Without It" **[Hack #33]**.

Fix Problems with the Windows Firewall

Perhaps the biggest security addition in SP2 is that the Windows Firewall **[Hack #77]** (formerly called the Internet Connection Firewall, or ICF) is turned on. The firewall provides basic security, although it's not nearly as effective as other firewalls, such as ZoneAlarm **[Hack #78]**.

But the Windows Firewall can cause a number of problems with your system. Here's what you need to do to fix them.

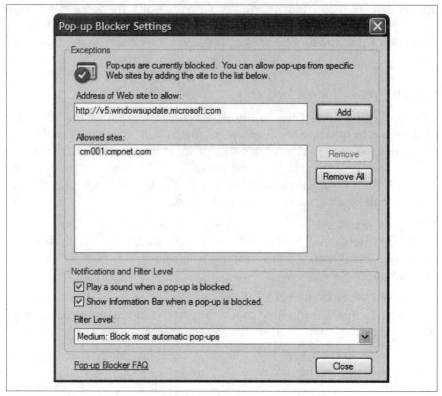

Figure 12-10. Telling Internet Explorer to allow pop ups from Windows Update

Can't configure the firewall. XP gives you control over how you use the Windows Firewall—for example, by allowing certain programs and services through, and even just by turning it on and off.

You configure it by clicking the Security Center icon in the system tray and then, when the Security Center appears, clicking the Windows Firewall icon at the bottom of the screen. The Windows Firewall dialog box appears, as shown in Figure 12-11.

> If there is no Security Center icon in your system tray, you can get to the Security Center by choosing Security Center from the Control panel, and then clicking the Windows Firewall icon at the bottom of the screen.

But you might find when you click one of the tabs that some or all of the options are grayed-out, so you can't configure it. What gives?

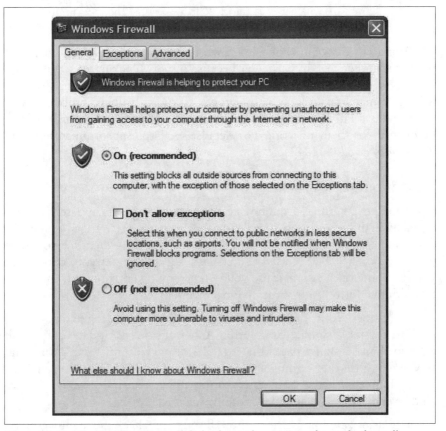

Figure 12-11. The Windows Firewall dialog box, where you configure the firewall

The problem is that you're not logged on using an administrator account. Log off, then log back on with an administrator account, and you'll be set.

Windows Firewall blocks programs or services. You've just installed SP2, and you're ready to chat with a friend, telling about your experiences. So, you fire up AOL Instant Messenger, but no one can send you messages. What's wrong?

Actually, nothing is wrong. The Windows Firewall is doing its job. It blocks incoming connections that you haven't initiated, so it's blocking AOL Instant Messenger messages from getting through.

To solve the problem, you need to add AOL Instant Messenger as an exception; in essence, you tell the firewall to let it through. Other programs might require that you open certain ports in the Windows Firewall. For details on how to allow exceptions and open ports, see "Punch an Escape Hole

Through Your Firewall" **[Hack #80]** and "Close Down Open Ports and Block Protocols" **[Hack #81]**.

The Windows Firewall has been known to cause problems with dozens of programs and games, in particular because of port blocking. It's not always obvious what ports you need to open to allow these applications to work. Microsoft maintains a long list of programs known to have problems with the Windows Firewall, and includes information about what ports need to be opened for them to work. For details, see *http://support.microsoft.com/ default.aspx?kbid=842242*.

Fix Antivirus Alert Problems

For many people, the most annoying thing about SP2 is its apparent incompatibility with Norton Anti-Virus and other antivirus software and firewalls. Even though you have Norton Anti-Virus turned on, whenever you start your computer SP2's Security Center flashes a warning at you, telling you your computer is at risk because you're not running antivirus software. You might think Norton Anti-Virus no longer works.

In fact, it does work; the problem is that SP2 doesn't recognize it's there. Luckily, the fix is simple: run Norton Anti-Virus's Live Update, and it will download and install a patch that lets SP2 recognize Anti-Virus is running, so you won't get the warning anymore. To run Live Update in Norton Anti-Virus, double-click the Anti-Virus icon in the system tray, then click Live Update and follow the directions for updating.

If you're using other antivirus or firewall software, check the manufacturer's web site to see if patches are available to fix the problem. If none is available, you can tell the SP2 Security Center to stop flashing alerts at you. From the Control Panel, choose Security Center. Click "Change the way Security Center alerts me" in the Resources section on the lefthand part of the screen. Clear the checkboxes in the Alert Settings dialog marked Firewall and Virus Protection, as shown in Figure 12-12.

Click OK. SP2 will stop hounding you from now on.

Uninstall SP2

As a last resort, you can always uninstall SP2. You can do this just like you would any other piece of software using the Add or Remove Programs tool in the Control Panel. From the Control Panel, choose Add or Remove Programs. Scroll down until you see the Windows XP Service Pack 2 entry. Highlight it, as shown in Figure 12-13. Click Remove, and it will be removed from your system.

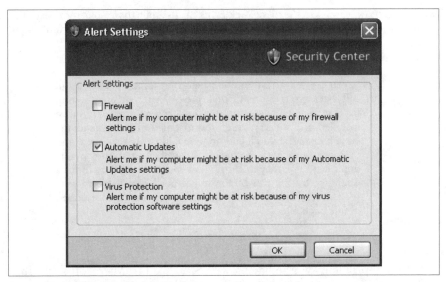

Figure 12-12. Turning off security alerts

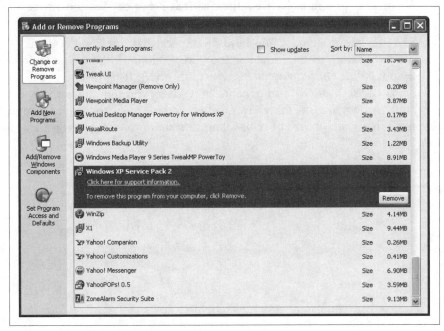

Figure 12-13. The quick and easy way to remove SP2

However, there's a chance SP2 won't show up on the Add or Remove Programs screen. Don't fret—you can still uninstall it. Microsoft includes a hidden wizard you can use to get rid of SP2. From the command line or Run box, type c:\windows\$NtServicePackUninstall$\spuninst\spuninst.exe and press Enter. The Windows XP Service Pack 2 Removal Wizard will start. Click Next and follow the on-screen instructions for removing SP2.

> If you created a restore point before installing SP2, you can roll back your system to a pre-SP2 state using System Restore. But there's a very serious "gotcha" here. If you've installed any software after you installed SP2, or made any system changes, you'll end up uninstalling that software and undoing those system changes as well. And restore points don't last long; they might stay on your system for as little as a few weeks. So, this option might not be available to you. It's a much better idea to uninstall SP2 in the ways described in this hack.

See Also

- For any problems you're having with SP2, head to Microsoft's SP2 support site at *http://support.microsoft.com/windowsxpsp2*.
- A variety of programs have conflicts with SP2. For details, and advice on how to solve them, go to *http://support.microsoft.com/kb/884130*.
- SP2 uses more memory and hard-disk space than previous versions of XP. If you want to slim down SP2, or any version of XP, for that matter, try out XPlite (*http://www.litepc.com/xplite.html*). It will let you remove up to 120 separate XP components, and so lets you slim down the operating system considerably. Even after you remove the components, you'll have the option of reinstalling. It's shareware; registration fee is $40.
- "Stop Pop Ups with SP2—and Without It" [Hack #33]
- "Protect Your Computer with the New Windows Firewall" [Hack #77]
- "ZoneAlarm: The World's Best Free Firewall" [Hack #78]
- "Punch an Escape Hole Through Your Firewall" [Hack #80]
- "Close Down Open Ports and Block Protocols" [Hack #81]

CHAPTER THIRTEEN

Hardware
Hacks 115–120

You probably notice your hardware only when it causes problems. When everything goes according to plan, it's invisible, which is the way we like it.

You can tweak your hardware in a variety of ways to make it run better, and you can use XP's built-in utilities to troubleshoot any problems. In this chapter, we'll look at hacks to help you troubleshoot hardware problems, remap your keyboard, make laptop and LCD screens more readable, and set up a cheap network by connecting two PCs.

HACK 115 Troubleshoot Hardware by Decoding Device Manager Error Messages

The Device Manager is a great hardware troubleshooting tool, but you'll need this hack to make sense of the error messages it relays to you. Here's how to decode the cryptic messages and how to use the messages to solve hardware woes.

If you install and uninstall enough hardware on your system, error messages and system conflicts are a way of life. XP does a far better job than previous versions of Windows at keeping conflicts to a minimum, but on occasion they still pop up.

The first step in resolving these problems is to use XP's built-in Hardware Troubleshooters. Choose Start → Help and Support → Hardware → "Fixing a hardware problem," and under "Fix a problem" click Hardware Troubleshooter. It's a wizard-style interface, so follow the prompts.

But that won't always solve the conflict. Luckily, XP includes a built-in way to resolve system conflicts by hand: using the Device Manager, XP's best all-around hardware-troubleshooting tool. Run it by typing devmgmt.msc at a command prompt or in the Run box. You'll see a list of all the devices installed on your system, as shown in Figure 13-1.

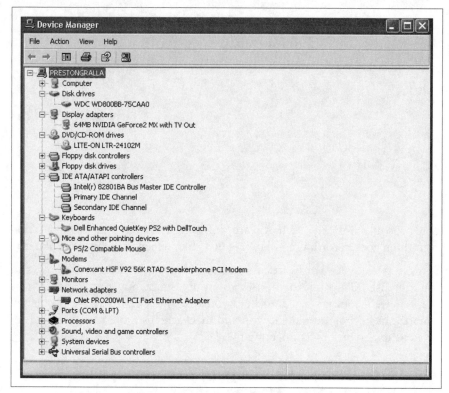

Figure 13-1. The Device Manager displaying all the devices installed on your system

To find information about any device, right-click it and choose Properties. The device's multi-tabbed Properties dialog box appears, as shown in Figure 13-2. You'll be able to get comprehensive information about the device from here. You can also troubleshoot by clicking the Troubleshoot button.

When you open the Device Manager to the view shown in Figure 13-1, an icon will be displayed next to any device involved in a system conflict. A yellow exclamation point means the device has a problem or conflict of some sort. A red "X" means the device is disabled. A blue "i" (which stands for information) means the device's resource configuration has been altered via the Device Manager.

> The blue "i" icon shows up only when you choose one of two views: "Resource by type" or "Resource by connection." To switch to those views, use the View menu.

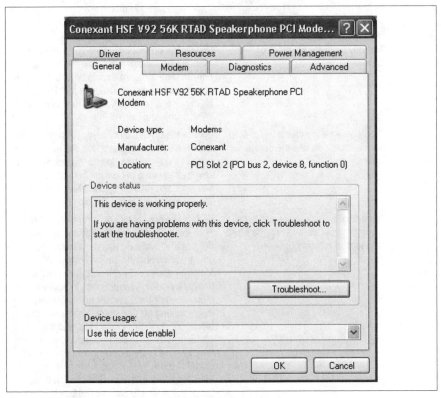

Figure 13-2. The Device Manager's General tab

Only the yellow and red icons mean there's a problem of some sort. To find out more details about the problem, double-click the device that has an icon next to it, and an error message and error code will appear in the "Device status" section of the General tab shown in Figure 13-2. Those error messages are supposed to help you solve the hardware problem. Unfortunately, though, they're cryptic at best, and, as a general rule, you won't be any closer to resolving the problem after you read them.

However, armed with the right knowledge, you can resolve the problems based on the error message you see. The advice in Table 13-1 (adapted from Microsoft Knowledgebase Article 125174) tells you how to use the Device Manager to solve the problem.

Table 13-1. Device Manager error codes, messages, and potential solutions

Code	Error message	Recommended solution
1	This device is not configured correctly.	Update the drivers by choosing Update Driver from the Driver tab, and follow the instructions in the Hardware Update Wizard. You can also try removing the device in the Device Manager and running the Add New Hardware Wizard from the Control Panel.
2	The <type> device loader(s) for this device could not load the device driver.	Update the drivers by choosing Update Driver from the Driver tab, and follow the instructions in the Hardware Update Wizard. You can also try removing the device in the Device Manager and running the Add New Hardware Wizard from the Control Panel.
3	The driver for this device might be corrupt or your system may be running low on memory or other resources.	Update the drivers by choosing Update Driver from the Driver tab, and follow the instructions in the Hardware Update Wizard. You can also try removing the device in the Device Manager and running the Add New Hardware Wizard from the Control Panel. In addition, check memory and system resources by right-clicking My Computer, choosing Properties and then the Advanced tab, and then clicking Settings under Performance to see whether that is the problem. You might have to install more RAM to solve the problem. Also, try clicking Troubleshoot on the General tab of the device to run the Troubleshooting Wizard.
4	This device is not working properly because one of its drivers may be bad, or your Registry may be bad.	Update the drivers by choosing Update Driver from the Driver tab, and follow the instructions in the Hardware Update Wizard. You can also try removing the device in the Device Manager and running the Add New Hardware Wizard from the Control Panel. If neither of these resolves the problem, get a new *.inf* driver file from the hardware manufacturer.
5	The driver for this device requested a resource that Windows does not know how to handle.	Update the drivers by choosing Update Driver from the Driver tab, and follow the instructions in the Hardware Update Wizard. You can also try removing the device in the Device Manager and running the Add New Hardware Wizard from the Control Panel.
6	Another device is using the resources this device needs.	Click Troubleshoot on the General tab to run the Hardware Troubleshooter.
7	The drivers for this device need to be reinstalled.	Click Reinstall Driver.

Table 13-1. Device Manager error codes, messages, and potential solutions (continued)

Code	Error message	Recommended solution
8	Code 8 has many error messages associated with it.	Click Update Driver. You can also try removing the device in the Device Manager and running the Add New Hardware Wizard from the Control Panel.
9	Code 9 has several error messages associated with it.	Try removing the device in the Device Manager and running the Add New Hardware Wizard from the Control Panel. If that doesn't work, contact the manufacturer for the correct registry settings or updated drivers. You might also need to update your system's BIOS.
10	This device either is not present, is not working properly, or does not have all the drivers installed. This code may also have a manufacturer-specific error message associated with it, depending on the device.	Make sure the device is physically connected to the computer properly. If that doesn't work, update the driver from the Driver tab.
11	Windows stopped responding while attempting to start this device and therefore will never attempt to start this device again.	Contact the hardware manufacturer for updated drivers.
12	This device cannot find enough free `<type>` resources that it can use. Note: `<type>` is a resource type, such as IRQ, DMA, Memory, or I/O.	Click Hardware Troubleshooter and run the Troubleshooting Wizard.
13	This device either is not present, is not working properly, or does not have all the drivers installed.	Click Detect Hardware. You can also try removing the device in the Device Manager and running the Add New Hardware Wizard from the Control Panel.
14	This device cannot work properly until you restart your computer.	Restart your computer.
15	This device is causing a resource conflict.	Click Troubleshoot on the General tab of the device, and run the Troubleshooting Wizard.
16	Windows cannot identify all the resources this device uses.	Click the Resources tab and manually enter the settings as detailed in the manufacturer's documentation.
17	The driver information file `<name>` is telling this child device to use a resource that the parent device does not have or recognize. Note: `<name>` is the *.inf* file for the device.	Click Update Driver. You can also try removing the device in the Device Manager, and running the Add New Hardware Wizard from the Control Panel.
18	Reinstall the drivers for this device.	Click Reinstall Driver.
19	Your Registry may be bad.	Click Check Registry.

Table 13-1. Device Manager error codes, messages, and potential solutions (continued)

Code	Error message	Recommended solution
20	Windows could not load one of the drivers for this device.	Click Update Driver.
21	Windows is removing this device.	Wait several seconds and then refresh the Device Manager view. If the device appears, restart your computer.
22	This device is disabled.	Click Enable Device.
22	This device is not started.	Click Start Device.
23	Several error messages may appear with Code 23.	Click Properties or Update Driver, depending on which button appears.
24	This device is not present, is not working properly, or does not have all its drivers installed.	Click Detect Hardware or Update Drivers, depending on which button appears.
25	Windows is in the process of setting up this device.	Restart your computer.
26	Windows is in the process of setting up this device.	Restart your computer.
27	Windows can't specify the resources for this device.	Remove the device in the Device Manager, and run the Add New Hardware Wizard from the Control Panel. If the device still does not work, get updated drivers or other assistance from the manufacturer.
28	The drivers for this device are not installed.	Click Reinstall Driver. You can also remove the device in the Device Manager and run the Add New Hardware Wizard from the Control Panel. If the device still does not work, get updated drivers from the manufacturer.
29	This device is disabled because the firmware for the device did not give it the required resources.	Check the device's documentation on how to enable its BIOS. If that doesn't work, enable the device in your computer's CMOS settings.
30	This device is using an Interrupt Request (IRQ) resource that is in use by another device and cannot be shared. You must change the conflicting setting or remove the real-mode driver causing the conflict.	Check the Device Manager to see if another device is using the same IRQ and disable it. If you can't find another device using the IRQ, look for drivers loaded in a *Config.sys* or *Autoexec.bat* file, and disable them.
31	This device is not working properly because Windows cannot load the drivers required for this device.	Click Properties. If that doesn't work, remove the device in the Device Manager, and run the Add New Hardware Wizard from the Control Panel. If the device still does not work, get updated drivers or other assistance from the manufacturer.

Table 13-1. Device Manager error codes, messages, and potential solutions (continued)

Code	Error message	Recommended solution
32	Windows cannot install the drivers for this device because it cannot access the drive or network location that has the setup files on it.	Restart the computer.
33	Windows cannot determine which resources are required for this device.	Contact the hardware manufacturer and configure or replace the device. Also try starting the Troubleshooting Wizard by clicking Troubleshoot on the General tab.
34	Windows cannot determine the settings for this device. Consult the documentation that came with this device and use the Resources tab to set the configuration.	Change the hardware settings by following the manufacturer's instructions and then using the Resources tab to configure the device. Also try starting the Troubleshooting Wizard by clicking Troubleshoot on the General tab.
35	Your computer's system firmware does not include enough information to configure and use this device properly. To use this device, contact your computer manufacturer to obtain a firmware or BIOS update.	Run the Troubleshooting Wizard by clicking Troubleshoot on the General tab. If that does not work, get a new or updated BIOS from your computer manufacturer.
36	This device is requesting a PCI interrupt but is configured for an ISA interrupt (or vice versa). Please use the computer's system setup program to reconfigure the interrupt for this device.	Check your computer's documentation for how to reconfigure the IRQ settings in the BIOS. Also, try starting the Troubleshooting Wizard by clicking Troubleshoot on the General tab.
37	Windows cannot initialize the device driver for this hardware.	Uninstall and then reinstall the driver. Also, try starting the Troubleshooting Wizard by clicking Troubleshoot on the General tab.
38	Windows cannot load the device driver for this hardware because a previous instance of the device driver is still in memory.	Restart the computer. Also, try starting the Troubleshooting Wizard by clicking Troubleshoot on the General tab.
39	Windows cannot load the device driver for this hardware. The driver may be corrupt or missing.	Uninstall and then reinstall the driver. Also, try starting the Troubleshooting Wizard by clicking Troubleshoot on the General tab.
40	Windows cannot access this hardware because its service key information in the registry is missing or recorded incorrectly.	Uninstall and then reinstall the driver. Also, try starting the Troubleshooting Wizard by clicking Troubleshoot on the General tab.

Table 13-1. Device Manager error codes, messages, and potential solutions (continued)

Code	Error message	Recommended solution
41	Windows successfully loaded the device driver for this hardware but cannot find the hardware device.	Uninstall and then reinstall the driver. Also, try starting the Troubleshooting Wizard by clicking Troubleshoot on the General tab. If the device is non-Plug and Play, you might need to run the Add Hardware Wizard. To do that, from the Control Panel choose Performance and Maintenance → System → Hardware → Add Hardware Wizard.
42	Windows cannot load the device driver for this hardware because there is a duplicate device already running in the system.	Restart the computer. Also, try starting the Troubleshooting Wizard by clicking Troubleshoot on the General tab.
43	Windows has stopped this device because it has reported problems.	Check the hardware documentation. Also, try starting the Troubleshooting Wizard by clicking Troubleshoot on the General tab.
44	An application or service has shut down this hardware device.	Restart the computer. Also, try starting the Troubleshooting Wizard by clicking Troubleshoot on the General tab.
45	Currently, this hardware device is not connected to the computer.	Reconnect the device to the computer.
46	Windows cannot gain access to this hardware device because the operating system is in the process of shutting down.	No fix should be necessary; the device should work properly when you start your computer.
47	Windows cannot use this hardware device because it has been prepared for "safe removal" but it has not been removed from the computer.	Unplug the device from your computer and then plug it in again.
48	The software for this device has been blocked from starting because it is known to have problems with Windows. Contact the hardware vendor for a new driver.	Get and install a new or updated driver from the hardware manufacturer.
49	Windows cannot start new hardware devices because the system hive is too large (exceeds the Registry Size Limit).	Uninstall any devices you are no longer using. To see devices that are using drivers, but are no longer attached to your computer, see "Uncover Hidden Hardware with the Device Manager" [Hack #116].

See Also

- "Uncover Hidden Hardware with the Device Manager" [Hack #116]

Uncover Hidden Hardware with the Device Manager

Hardware ghosts and other hidden devices can cause system conflicts, and the Device Manager won't report on them. This hack forces the Device Manager to uncover all your hidden hardware so that you can resolve any conflicts.

One of the strangest hardware problems you'll encounter in XP are hidden and ghosted hardware devices that are invisible to you but that can cause system conflicts. You won't be able to see them in the Device Manager [Hack #115] When you use that troubleshooting tool, you won't be able to uncover any problems they might be causing.

The Device Manager hides several types of these devices. Non–Plug and Play printers, drivers, and similar devices don't show up. Most newer devices are Plug and Play, so you'll most likely encounter this problem only if you have old hardware attached to your PC. (Plug and Play devices are automatically recognized and installed in XP.) In this instance, the device is physically present on your PC, but the Device Manager doesn't show you it's there.

Then there are the so-called *nonpresent* or *ghosted* devices—devices you've removed from your system without doing an uninstall, or whose uninstallation did not work properly. These devices aren't physically present in your system, but XP treats them as if they were and devotes system resources to them. For example, if you physically remove an old network card without doing an uninstall, it might cause IP and other kinds of conflicts because XP treats it as if it were still in your system.

The Device Manager also might not give you details about USB devices that you use only temporarily and that you frequently attach and remove—for example, MP3 players that you attach to your PC only when you want to add or delete MP3 files from them. Even when these devices aren't present in your system, XP devotes resources to them. If you replace one USB device with another of the same model, it's best to go through the uninstall process rather than just swap them.

And then there are devices you might have moved from one slot to another. XP might believe they are actually present in two slots, so it devotes resources for both slots to them.

Displaying these hidden devices can help with troubleshooting. For example, a hidden device could possibly conflict with a nonhidden device. And sometimes you might want to uninstall hidden devices—for example, when you've moved a non–Plug and Play network card from one slot to another and want to uninstall it from one slot.

But to do this kind of troubleshooting you'll need to force the Device Manager to display information about the devices; otherwise, you won't know how to solve the problem.

Forcing the Device Manager to display non–Plug and Play printers, drivers, and similar devices is a simple matter. Run the Device Manager by typing devmgmt.msc at a command prompt and pressing Enter, and then choosing View → Display Hidden Devices.

Displaying ghosted or nonpresent devices takes a little more work. You'll set a systemwide environment variable that forces the Device Manager to display them. First, right-click My Computer and choose Properties → Advanced → Environment Variables. The Environment Variable dialog box opens. This dialog box lets you set system variables for the entire system or for individual users. Environment variables control a variety of XP features, such as the location of your *Windows* directory and *TEMP* directories and the filename and location of the command processor that will launch when you run the command prompt.

The Environment Variables dialog box contains two sections: "User variables" and "System variables." To apply the variable to a single user, use the "User variables" dialog box; to apply the variable to all users, use the "System variables" dialog box. In this case, you'll want to create the variable systemwide, so click New in the "System variables" section. The New System Variable dialog box appears. For "Variable name," type devmgr_show_ nonpresent_devices. Once you've created the name, you need to give it a value. To turn the setting on, type 1 in the "Variable value" box. You can see the box filled out properly in Figure 13-3. Click OK and then OK again.

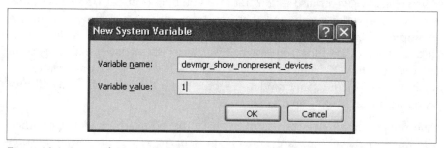

Figure 13-3. Setting the Device Manager to always show ghosted devices

So, now you've set the system variable properly, but the Device Manager won't display ghosted devices yet. First you have to tell it to display them. Run the Device Manager by typing devmgmt.msc at a command prompt or in the Run box and pressing Enter. Then, choose View → Display Hidden

Devices and the ghosted devices will appear, as shown in Figure 13-4. You should see quite a few devices now, including a lengthy list of non–Plug and Play drivers. Typically, devices that are not currently present on your PC will be shown as gray, rather than the black that connotes present devices. You might also see some devices listed more than once, as shown in Figure 13-4.

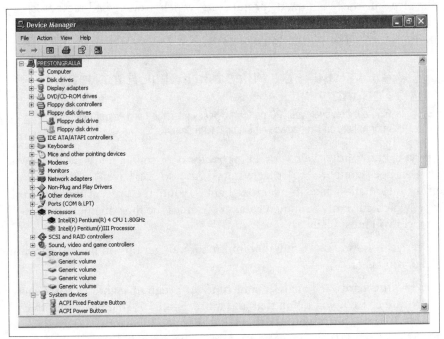

Figure 13-4. Displaying ghosted devices in the Device Manager

Now, use the Device Manager to troubleshoot any of those ghosted devices, as detailed in "Troubleshoot Hardware by Decoding Device Manager Error Messages" [Hack #115]. If you find any ghosted devices that you will no longer use on your PC, uninstall them from the Device Manager by right-clicking the device and choosing Uninstall.

Hacking the Hack

If you want to use the Device Manger only on occasion to show ghosted devices and you don't want to add another environment variable to your system, you can add the variable on an instance-by-instance basis—for example, for a single time that you run the Device Manager. At the command prompt, type set devmgr_show_nonpresent_devices=1 and press Enter. You won't get a prompt in response; the command prompt will stay blank.

At the same instance of the command prompt, type start devmgmt.msc and press Enter. The Device Manager will launch in a separate window. Now, enable the Device Manager to show ghosted devices in the same way you did previously in this hack.

Keep in mind that you have to run the Device Manager from the same instance of the command prompt in which you typed devmgr_show_nonpresent_devices=1. If you run the Device Manager outside the command prompt, it won't display ghosted devices.

HACK 117 Check Your PC's Pulse and Tweak It for Better Performance

Find out how well your PC performs, peer under the hood to get diagnostic information, and get advice on tuning it with Sandra.

Do you know how well your PC is *really* performing? How well do you think it does compared to other systems? And do you have any idea of nitty-gritty information like its memory bank layout, the current video refresh rate, which currently running process consumes the most memory, or which services you most likely can safely disable [Hack #4]?

Better yet—how about using that information to get tips on how to get your PC to run faster?

My favorite hardware analysis and tune-up program, Sandra (*http://www.sisoftware.co.uk/*), will do all that and more. Sandra is shareware and free to try for 30 days, but if you use it beyond that you'll have to buy Sandra Pro for $29. Sandra Pro also gives you access to about a half dozen analysis modules that Sandra doesn't have, such as modules about your network or fonts.

When you first run Sandra, you might be overwhelmed because you'll see several dozen icons, each of which runs a different diagnostic and benchmark test when double-clicked. For example, run the Memory Bandwidth Benchmark and Sandra returns results similar to the results shown in Figure 13-5, which measure the performance of one of my PCs. As you can see, it measures the speed of your memory and compares it to other memory chipsets. It also shows you the layout of your motherboard's memory bank, including the exact memory configuration in each bank. This is important when you want to add memory. Figure 13-5 shows me that I have two memory banks, each of which has a 128MB memory chip in it. That means if I want to upgrade I'm going to have to take out one of those chips and essentially throw it away.

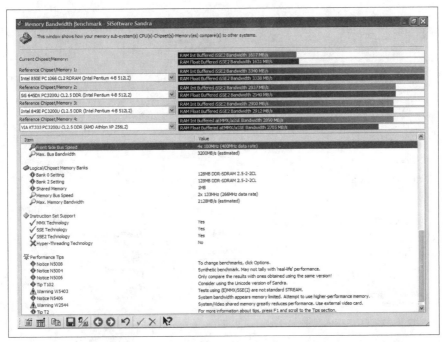

Figure 13-5. A memory bandwidth test and diagnostic for my PC

Sandra doesn't just give you diagnostics; it also offers recommendations on how you can fine-tune your PC. In this instance, it notes that my main system and my video system share memory, which reduces performance, and it suggests I install a video card with its own memory as a way to improve performance.

The fastest way to get an overview of your system—as well as to get comprehensive advice on fine-tuning every part of your system, not just one subsystem—is to run the Performance Tune-Up Wizard. It analyzes your entire system and offers tips on tuning up each subcomponent, as shown in Figure 13-6. For my PC, it offered about a dozen tips, including which background services I might want to disable, and ways to make my video system perform faster, among other advice.

See Also

- Fresh Diagnose (*http://www.freshdevices.com*) is a freeware diagnostic tool that gives you comprehensive information about your system.

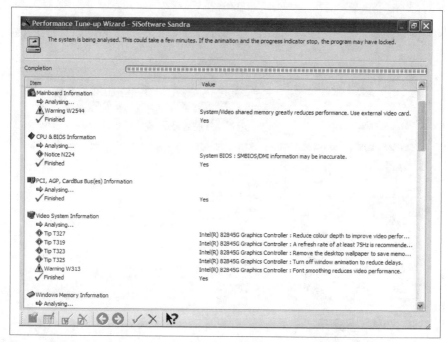

Figure 13-6. Sandra's systemwide tips for fine-tuning your PC's performance

HACK 118 Remap Your Keyboard

Create your own personalized, ultimate keyboard by remapping its keys to the way you want them to work.

Personal keyboard preferences are idiosyncratic; even a minor matter such as where the Alt or Ctrl keys should be located can inspire fevered debate. So, if you have personal preferences about where keys should be located, you can remap your keyboard to your own tastes using the TradeKeys utility from *PC Magazine*. It lets you map any key to any other key, including extended keys such as Right-Ctrl, Right-Alt, and the Windows logo key.

I find the utility particularly useful when I use one of my two laptops. Laptop keyboards are notoriously nonstandard, and I find the layout of my Dell Inspiron particularly maddening. Take the Windows key, for example. Instead of being located on the lower-left part of the keyboard, where Nature intended it to be, it's hidden away on the upper right. Similarly, the Menu key, instead of being on the lower-right where all good Menu keys should be found, is tucked away up on the right. So, I use TradeKeys to remap my Left-Alt key to be a Windows key and my Right-Ctrl key to be a Menu key. True, it leaves me with only one Alt key and one Ctrl key, but that's a small price to pay to get the Windows and Menu keys in their proper places.

Remapping the keys is simple, as shown in Figure 13-7. After you run the program, choose the key you want to change from the "Map from" area, and then choose the key you want it mapped to from the "Map to" area. For example, to remap my Left-Alt key to be a Windows key, I chose Left-Alt in "Map from" and Left-Window in "Map to." Then, I clicked "Map." Keep on mapping keys in this way until you're satisfied with your new keyboard; then choose Save. The new mapping will not take effect until you log off and then log back on. On some systems, you'll have to reboot.

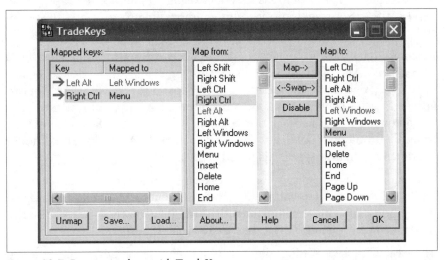

Figure 13-7. Remapping keys with TradeKeys

You can also create different keyboard layouts and use each depending on how you're using your computer. Some simple games, for example, use letter keys to control motions and actions. If you prefer using other keys, such as the larger Ctrl and Alt keys, for those motions and actions, you can create one keyboard layout for that game and another layout for your normal use. To create a new keyboard layout, first map it, then choose Save. Give it a descriptive name. Create multiple keyboard layouts that way. Then, when you want to use one, call up TradeKeys, choose Load, and choose the layout you want.

TradeKeys is free, but only if you pay an annual fee for access to *PC Magazine* utilities. You'll have to pay $19.97 for a year, or $14.97 for a year if you're a *PC Magazine* subscriber. Go to *http://www.pcmag.com* and click Downloads to download it and other "free" utilities.

HACK 119 Use ClearType for Better Laptop and LCD Resolution

Stop squinting at your laptop or LCD screen. Make any laptop or LCD screen easy to read.

Many people who use laptops complain that text is particularly difficult to read on LCD screens. Making matters worse is that many laptops are designed to work at very high resolutions (for example, 1400×1050 pixels), and at those resolutions the small type is particularly problematic on an LCD. The problem gets increasingly worse because laptop screens keep getting larger and their resolutions keep increasing. On my 15-inch laptop with 1400×1050-pixel resolution, it's almost impossible to read text. Desktop-style LCD screens also have the same problems.

A simple hack will make text easier to read on both laptops and LCD screens: use Microsoft's ClearType technology, built into XP. To enable ClearType, right-click the desktop and choose Properties. Select Appearance → Effects. The Effects dialog box appears. Check the box next to "Use the following method to smooth edges of screen fonts." Select ClearType from the drop-down box, click OK, and then click OK again. You'll notice the difference in how type is displayed.

You can use ClearType on a normal desktop PC monitor as well as on a laptop, but I don't recommend it. On a normal monitor, it makes text appear blurry, and people have complained that using it gives them headaches. I've tried it and can vouch for that—headaches quickly ensue.

The basic ClearType settings don't work equally well on all systems, but you can download and use the free Microsoft PowerToy called the ClearType Tuning Control to fine-tune how ClearType looks on your system. Download and install it from *http://www.microsoft.com/typography/ClearTypePowerToy.mspx*. After it's installed, when the first screen appears make sure the Turn on ClearType box is checked, and then click Start Wizard.

You'll come to a page with two different samples of text. Click the one that looks best on your system, and then click Next. You'll come to a page that displays a block of text in six different ways. Click the text that looks best and then click Finish. You'll come to a final page that displays text in four different fonts. If you're satisfied with the way the text looks, click Finish; you're done. If you want to try a different setting, click Back, and you'll come to the page that displays a block of text in six different ways. Choose a different text block, click Next, and if you're satisfied, click Finish. Otherwise, keep going back to the page with six blocks of text until you choose one that's best for your system.

From now on, if you want to fine-tune ClearType again, choose Control Panel → Appearance and Themes → ClearType Tuning, and the ClearType Tuning Control will run.

> Some users think ClearType looks better on some LCD screens than others. If you're creating screenshots for printing, you might try turning it off, since the effect doesn't always work as well on paper.

Hacking the Hack

When you enable ClearType, it's available only after you log on. So, the fonts displayed before logon won't benefit from ClearType. You can, however, use a Registry hack to enable Clear Type fonts even before logon. Run the Registry Editor [Hack #83] and go to HKEY_USERS\.DEFAULT\Control Panel\ Desktop. Open the FontSmoothingType entry and change its value to 2. (The default is 1, which means font smoothing is enabled, but ClearType isn't. A value of 0 turns off both font smoothing and ClearType.) Exit the Registry Editor and reboot.

Networking on the Cheap: Set Up a Direct Cable Connection

HACK
120

You don't need a full-fledged network to connect two PCs using XP. Here's how to create a fast, cheap connection that's great for sharing files and other network needs.

If you are reading this book, which is (as you know) called *Windows XP Hacks*, you probably get questions and pleas for help from your friends and family all the time (or you will, now that you've read the book!). You're the "computer guy" (women can be computer guys, too, my female editor tells me) and you have the ability to "make it better." If that's a fair assessment of your situation, let's go through a scenario that happens to us hacker types quite often.

It's 8:00 on a Sunday evening, and the phone rings. Your neighbor is panicking because his computer is acting crazy and he just finished working on a huge PowerPoint presentation for work the next day. You grab your trusty laptop and your bag of computer parts and go next door.

You sit down at the computer and play with it a bit. Sure enough, it's got problems. The CD burner doesn't work, and the floppy drive is shredding disks. How's he going to transfer his file to his work machine? He doesn't have a dial-up account or Internet access, so you can't upload his file somewhere and download it to your computer—or perhaps it's just too big for his 28.8bps modem to send.

Lucky for you (and for him), he's running Windows XP and so are you. Since you've read this book, you have exactly what you need on hand to save the day. You transfer his files to your laptop, burn a CD of the contents, and yet again save the day. He offers you money, but you refuse because you'll keep him in mind the next time you need to move your piano.

Remember the Boy Scout Creed: "Be Prepared"

Before you can be the hero in this story, you need to have the proper tools. You might not have all the parts you need on hand, but you can get them with a quick trip to your computer store. You could use three different cables: a null serial cable, a parallel data cable, or a null Ethernet cable. All three cables are shown in Figure 13-8.

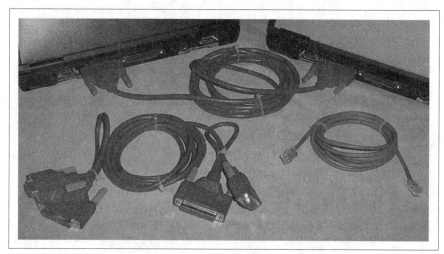

Figure 13-8. Null serial cable with DB-9 and DB-25 connectors (left), null Ethernet cable (right), and parallel data cable (back)

A *null serial cable* is the most universal cable; nearly every computer manufactured in the last 10 years has a serial port. The disadvantage is that serial transfer speeds are slower than parallel or Ethernet speed.

A null serial cable is *not* a serial modem cable; they look the same, but the connections are different. For this purpose, you want a cable that has female connectors on both ends. Serial cables can have two different connectors on the ends: DB-9 and DB-25. The DB-25 is an older connector that has 25 pins. If a computer has a DB-25 connector, it is probably too old to run Windows XP. I own a serial cable that has a DB-9 and a DB-25 connector on each end but I haven't used the DB-25 connector for years. If you want to carry a serial cable, it is probably safe to buy one that only has DB-9 connectors.

> If you have cable and some connectors lying around your office, you can make a null serial cable by connecting the same numbered pins on each connector, starting from the upper left, except for pins 2 and 3. Those pins are crossed so that pin 2 on one connector goes to pin 3 on the other, and vice versa.

A *parallel data cable* allows for faster data transfers than a serial cable. A parallel data cable is not the same as a parallel printer cable! What you are looking for has a *male* DB-25 connector on each end. It is often called a *LapLink* cable or an *FX* cable. LapLink and FX were commercial products that performed this function in the past. Since Windows XP has the functionality built in, all you need is the cable.

A *null Ethernet cable* is your best bet in terms of speed and ease of use. The advantages are that it works with all modern Windows operating systems and will be the fastest connection you can get. The disadvantages are that older computers might not have an Ethernet card or might not have TCP/IP installed. You can purchase a null Ethernet card at most computer stores for a few dollars.

> You can build a null Ethernet cable if you have an RJ45 crimper and RJ45 modular plugs by connecting the following pins with CAT-5 UTP cable: 1-3, 2-6, 3-1, and 6-2. The other pins are not necessary.

You can purchase the null serial cable and the null Ethernet cable for $3 or $4 each from almost any computer store. The parallel data cable is a little more difficult to find, but it's still a good choice. No matter which one you choose, you will be limited to connecting only two computers.

Cheap Networking with a Serial or Parallel Cable

Connect the computers using the serial or parallel cable. Make certain you are connecting the same type of ports. Turn both computers on and log in so that both computers are waiting for you.

Decide which computer will be the host and which will be the guest. The host computer will be the one that supports the incoming connection. The guest will be the one accessing the remote computer.

On the host computer, open the Network Connections control panel. Click the link labeled "Create a new connection." Click the Next button to get to the screen titled Network Connection Type. Choose the radio button labeled "Set up an advanced connection" and click Next. On the next screen, choose the radio button labeled "Connect directly to another computer" and click Next. When asked Host or Guest, choose Host and press Next. You will be asked what device you wish to use to make the connection. If you are using a parallel cable, choose Direct Parallel; if you are using a null serial cable, choose the appropriate Communications Port (the one to which you connected your null serial cable—it should be labeled on your PC, but if not, check the documentation) and press Next. Then you will be presented with the dialog box shown in Figure 13-9.

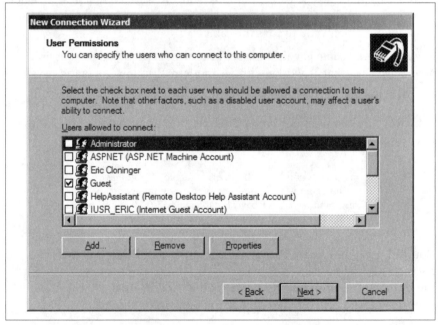

Figure 13-9. Host User Permissions screen

This dialog box asks you which users will have access to the host computer. If you are unsure about the computer's security, you should choose an appropriate user. If you know the guest computer does not present a security risk, just choose the Guest account and press Next. Now the computer has a network connection called Incoming Connections.

You need to know the network name of the host computer. If you do not know it, on the host computer right-click My Computer → Properties → Computer Name. The network name is the name next to the words Full Computer Name.

Now it's time to configure the guest computer. Again, go to the Network Connections control panel applet and click the "Create a new connection" link. Select "Set up an advanced connection," click Next, choose "Connect directly to another computer," and click Next. This time, when given a choice of Host or Guest, choose the Guest radio button and press the Next button. When asked for the connection name, type the network name of the host computer. If all goes well, you should see the dialog box shown in Figure 13-10. If you do, click the Finish button to close the dialog box.

Figure 13-10. The New Connection Wizard

At this point, you have a physical and logical connection between the two computers. Activate the connection by double-clicking its icon on the desktop or in the Network Connections control panel of the guest computer. When the computers recognize each other, you will be asked for the username and password. If you provided guest access on the host computer, you do not need to enter anything; just click the Connect button. If the connection is made, Windows XP will pop up a notification on the taskbar, as shown in Figure 13-11.

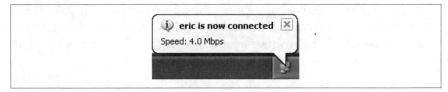

Figure 13-11. New connection notification

At this point, you have a network connection. You can use your Network Neighborhood window to browse or search for the host computer. Shared folders will work the same as if you were on an Ethernet network. If your folders and printers do not have permission for the user on the host computer, they will not have the ability to share files or print.

Keep in mind that this method is a one-way connection. One computer is specifically the host and the other is the guest. Those roles cannot be reversed without creating another connection. If you would like to be able to access the computers without designating one as the host, you will need to use an Ethernet connection.

Cheap Networking with an Ethernet Cable

If you need to connect two computers and you want a fast connection, you need nothing more than the null Ethernet cable described earlier. Both computers need an Ethernet card with correct drivers and the TCP/IP protocol installed. An advantage of the Ethernet option is that it works on all versions of Windows, as well as other brands of computers.

If your computer does not have an Ethernet card, you can purchase one for $30 or so. For most home applications, a 10BaseT Ethernet card is sufficient, though a 10/100 card is not much more expensive and can send 10 times as much data. There are also cards called *Gigabit* Ethernet, but they are considerably more expensive and very few manufacturers include this type of equipment in their consumer-grade equipment. My favorite Ethernet card is the 3Com 3C905BTX. It's reasonably priced and every operating system knows how to deal with it. The DLink DFE530TX and the SMC 1244TX are also widely recognized and can be found for less than $25. Installing an Ethernet card with the manufacturer's instructions in hand is not difficult, but if you aren't comfortable working with the hardware inside your computer, you should let a technician do the job.

Connect the two computers using the null Ethernet cable. If the drivers are installed on both computers correctly, a green or orange light will appear near the point where you plugged in the cable on each computer. These link lights indicate that a physical connection is present between the two computers and that the two Ethernet cards recognize each other. If you do not see the lights, it means the drivers are not installed correctly, the cable is not wired correctly, or the card does not have a link light. The most likely cause is that the drivers are not installed, but I find that about 1 cable in 10 that I purchase is wired incorrectly.

Once you have a physical link established between the two computers, it's time to make the TCP/IP protocol work. Go to the *Control Panel* folder and open the Network Connections section. (Under Windows 98 and Windows Me, this control panel is called Network.) Search for your connection in its list and double-click it. Then, open the item named Internet Protocol (TCP/IP). (Under Windows 98 and Windows Me, every card and every protocol are listed in the same dialog.) Search for the one that says TCP/IP and has the name of your Ethernet card next to it.

There are many ways to configure a local area network, but the quickest and easiest way to connect two computers using a null Ethernet cable is to set the values, as listed in Table 13-2.

Table 13-2. Suggested TCP/IP settings for null Ethernet connection

	Computer 1	Computer 2
IP Address	192.168.1.2	192.168.1.3
Subnet Mask	255.255.255.0	255.255.255.0
Gateway	192.168.1.1	192.168.1.1
Preferred DNS Server	Leave blank	Leave blank
Alternate DNS Server	Leave blank	Leave blank

At this point, the two computers will act is if they were on a larger network with routers and other equipment. You will not be able to access the Internet, but you will be able to share files and printers. The same restrictions apply here that apply to the other cabling options; the usernames on one computer must have appropriate permissions to access files and printers on the other computer.

If you plan to keep your cheap network connected all the time, use the Ethernet option. Ethernet has the advantage of being the fastest of the three cabling methods shown in this hack, and it is widely accepted as the high-speed networking choice. If you choose to add another computer at a later date or get broadband Internet access, the Ethernet option will be the easiest to adapt to the new network configuration.

—*Eric Cloninger*

Index

We'd like to hear your suggestions for improving our indexes. Send email to *index@oreilly.com*.

F

Colophon

Our look is the result of reader comments, our own experimentation, and feedback from distribution channels. Distinctive covers complement our distinctive approach to technical topics, breathing personality and life into potentially dry subjects.

The tool on the cover of *Windows XP Hacks*, Second Edition, is an antique fan. Fans have been used to provide relief from the heat since the late 1880s. Antique fans that pre-date 1900 are quite rare and are highly sought after by collectors.

Emily Quill was the production editor, and Audrey Doyle was the copyeditor for *Windows XP Hacks*, Second Edition. Katherine T. Pinard did the proofread. Jamie Peppard and Darren Kelly provided quality control. Peter Ryan, Keith Fahlgren, and Lydia Onofrei provided production assistance. Reg Aubry wrote the index.

Hanna Dyer designed the cover of this book, based on a series design by Edie Freedman. The cover image is a photograph taken from the PhotoSpin Power Photos Nostalgia CD, Volume 9, Disk 2. Emma Colby produced the cover layout with InDesign CS using Adobe's Helvetica Neue and ITC Garamond fonts.

David Futato designed the interior layout. This book was converted by Joe Wizda to FrameMaker 5.5.6 with a format conversion tool created by Erik Ray, Jason McIntosh, Neil Walls, and Mike Sierra that uses Perl and XML technologies. The text font is Linotype Birka; the heading font is Adobe Helvetica Neue Condensed; and the code font is LucasFont's TheSans Mono Condensed. The illustrations that appear in the book were produced by Robert Romano and Jessamyn Read using Macromedia FreeHand 9 and Adobe Photoshop 6.

Buy *Windows XP Hacks, 2nd Edition* and access the digital edition

FREE on Safari for 45 days.

Go to **www.oreilly.com/go/safarienabled**
and type in coupon code **KYGL-DLFI-J2I8-84IE-FXJ8**

Better than e-books

Search

over 2000 top
tech books

Download

whole chapters

Cut and Paste

code examples

Find

answers fast

Read books from cover
to cover. Or, simply click
to the page you need.

**Search Safari! The premier electronic reference
library for programmers and IT professionals**

Part# 40421

Related Titles Available from O'Reilly

Hacks

Amazon Hacks

BSD Hacks

Digital Photography Hacks

eBay Hacks

Excel hacks

Flash Hacks

Gaming Hacks

Google Hacks

Harware Hacking Projects for Geeks

Home Theater Hacks

iPod & iTunes Hacks

Knoppix Hacks

Linux Desktop Hacks

Linux Server Hacks

Mac OS X Hacks

Mac OS X Panther Hacks

Network Security Hacks

PayPal Hacks

PDF Hacks

PC Hacks

Smart Home Hacks

Spidering Hacks

TiVo Hacks

Windows Server Hacks

Wireless Hacks

Word Hacks

O'REILLY®

Our books are available at most retail and online bookstores.
To order direct: 1-800-998-9938 • *order@oreilly.com* • *www.oreilly.com*
Online editions of most O'Reilly titles are available by subscription at *safari.oreilly.com*

Keep in touch with O'Reilly

1. Download examples from our books

To find example files for a book, go to:

www.oreilly.com/catalog

select the book, and follow the "Examples" link.

2. Register your O'Reilly books

Register your book at *register.oreilly.com*

Why register your books? Once you've registered your O'Reilly books you can:

- Win O'Reilly books, T-shirts or discount coupons in our monthly drawing.
- Get special offers available only to registered O'Reilly customers.
- Get catalogs announcing new books (US and UK only).
- Get email notification of new editions of the O'Reilly books you own.

3. Join our email lists

Sign up to get topic-specific email announcements of new books and conferences, special offers, and O'Reilly Network technology newsletters at:

elists.oreilly.com

It's easy to customize your free elists subscription so you'll get exactly the O'Reilly news you want.

4. Get the latest news, tips, and tools

http://www.oreilly.com

- "Top 100 Sites on the Web"—PC Magazine
- CIO Magazine's Web Business 50 Awards

Our web site contains a library of comprehensive product information (including book excerpts and tables of contents), downloadable software, background articles, interviews with technology leaders, links to relevant sites, book cover art, and more.

5. Work for O'Reilly

Check out our web site for current employment opportunities:

jobs.oreilly.com

6. Contact us

O'Reilly & Associates
1005 Gravenstein Hwy North
Sebastopol, CA 95472 USA

TEL: 707-827-7000 or 800-998-9938
         (6am to 5pm PST)

FAX: 707-829-0104

order@oreilly.com
For answers to problems regarding your order or our products.
To place a book order online, visit:

www.oreilly.com/order_new

catalog@oreilly.com
To request a copy of our latest catalog.

booktech@oreilly.com
For book content technical questions or corrections.

corporate@oreilly.com
For educational, library, government, and corporate sales.

proposals@oreilly.com
To submit new book proposals to our editors and product managers.

international@oreilly.com
For information about our international distributors or translation queries. For a list of our distributors outside of North America check out:

international.oreilly.com/distributors.html

adoption@oreilly.com
For information about academic use of O'Reilly books, visit:

academic.oreilly.com

O'REILLY®

Our books are available at most retail and online bookstores.
To order direct: 1-800-998-9938 • *order@oreilly.com* • *www.oreilly.com*
Online editions of most O'Reilly titles are available by subscription at *safari.oreilly.com*